Tourism Today:
a geographical analysis

Douglas Pearce
University of Canterbury
Christchurch
New Zealand

Longman
Scientific &
Technical

Copublished in the United States with
John Wiley & Sons, Inc., New York

Longman Scientific & Technical,
Longman Group, UK Limited,
Longman House, Burnt Mill, Harlow,
Essex CM20 2JE, England
and Associated companies throughout the world.

Copublished in the United States with
John Wiley & Sons, Inc., 605 Third Avenue,
New York, NY10158

First published 1987

British Library Cataloguing in Publication Data
Pearce, Douglas G.
    Tourism today: a geographical analysis.
    1. Tourist trade
    I. Title
    338.4'791   G155.A1

ISBN 0-582-30145-9

**Library of Congress Cataloging-in-Publication
Data**
Pearce, Douglas G., 1949–
    Tourism today.

    Bibliography: p.
    Includes index.
    1. Tourist trade. I. Title.
G155.A1P359 1986   380.1'459104   85-24228
ISBN 0-470-20682-9 (USA only)

Set in Linotron 202 9/10 pt Palatino
Produced by Longman Group (FE) Limited
Printed in Hong Kong

For Chantal

Contents

List of Figures

List of Tables

List of Plates

Acknowledgements

Much of the field-work, data collection and library research on which this book is based was undertaken during a period of eight months' overseas study leave from the University of Canterbury in 1982. I am grateful to the University Council for granting this leave and for providing travel assistance. Research in France at this time was also supported by a Bourse d'Etudes Supérieures from the French Ministry of Foreign Affairs. I would like to thank the many individuals of the various universities, libraries, national tourist organizations and other agencies whom I contacted in 1982 and subsequently for their assistance and for providing access to a wide range of material. In particular, I wish to acknowledge the assistance of Monsieur René Baretje and his staff in making available the bountiful resources of the Centre des Hautes Etudes Touristiques, Aix-en-Provence. The hospitality of old friends not only made field-work in distant places enjoyable but also enabled a lot to be achieved in a comparatively short time; many thanks to Myrna, Philippe and Alice, Hélène, Agnès, Jean-Marie and Veerle, Eva, Wayne and Diane. Special mention must be made here of Madame Biart for her hospitality and welcome base in Brussels. Help with the compilation and analysis of data has been given by Grant Birmingham, Kathy Clark, Karen Eder, Fujo Kano and Suzanne Waters with financial support being provided by several grants from the University of Canterbury's Research Assistants' Fund. For their frank criticisms and valuable advice I would like to thank Bob Mings, who cheerfully reviewed the first draft of the entire manuscript; Doug Johnston, who read many of the early chapters and gave welcome technical advice; and Dick Bedford who commented on Chapter 9. My thanks also go to Brenda Carter for typing the manuscript, to Linda Harrison and Anna Moloney for typing the tables and bibliography, to Alister Dyer, Jenny Penman and Tony Shatford who drafted the maps and diagrams. Chantal's company and assistance increased the pleasure and productivity of our travels in 1982 and her subsequent patience and support have enabled the successful completion of the manuscript; I gratefully dedicate this book to her.

Douglas Pearce
Christchurch, April 1985

We are indebted to the following for permission to reproduce copyright material:

American Geographical Society for fig 11.1 from fig 3 (Pearce 1984b); British Tourist Authority for fig 4.6 redrawn from *BTA Newsletter* No 19, Autumn 1976 pv, Tables 2.4, 4.1–2 from Tables 20, 45, 54 (BTA, 1981b), 4.5 from Tables pp 36, 38 (BTA, 1982b); the Author, Dr. S. G. Britton for fig 1.8 from fig 3 (Britton, 1980a); C.H.E.T. for fig 1.10 from fig 3 (Gormsen, 1981); the Editor, *Cornell HRA Quarterly* for fig 1.9, Table 1.1 from pp 13–16 (Plog, 1973); the Author, Dr. P. C. Forer for figs 4.7–9, Table 4.3 from figs 4, 6, 8, Table 111 (Forer & Pearce, 1984); the Author, H. Peter Gray for Table 2.2 from Table p 14 (Gray, 1970); the Editor, *Journal of Geography* for fig 7.1 redrawn from figs 1 & 8 (Mings, 1982); the Editor, *Journal of Travel Research* for Table 4.4. from Table 1 (Pearce & Elliott, 1983); the Author, N. Leiper & the Editor, *Contemporary Issues in Australian Tourism* for Tables 2.5, 2.6 from Tables 3, 6 (Leiper, 1984b); P.A.T.A. for fig 3.3 Table 3.7 from fig 1, Table 1 (Pearce, 1983a), Table 2.1 from p 5 (Opinion Research Corporations, 1980); Pergamon Press Inc & the Authors, for figs 1.4, 1.11 from figs 1, 3 (Pearce 1979, after Miossec 1976), 2.1 from fig 1 (Iso-Ahola, 1982); Pergamon Press Ltd for figs 8.2–8.4 from figs 2, 4, 5 (Pearce & Grimmeau, 1985), 10.1 from figs 6, 7 (Pigram, 1977); the Editor, *Revue de Tourisme* for figs 1.6 redrawn from fig 1 (Lundgren, 1982), 10.7 redrawn from fig 2 (Lundgren, 1974), Table 3.10 from Table 1 (Pearce, 1978a); the Author, T. Cullinan for Table 3.9 from fig 12 (Cullinan et al, 1977); the Editor, Dr. T. V. Singh for Table 2.7 from Table 1 (Pearce, 1982a); the Author, Dr. G. Wall for fig 1.3 from fig 30 (Greer & Wall, 1979); World Tourism Organisation for Tables 3.2, 3.7 from Tables VII, IX (WTO, 1983)

We are also grateful to the National Geographical Institute — 1050 Brussels–Belgium for permission No A 584 to reproduce pl. 5 Aerial photography S189–117 *De Panne-Wenduine*.

Introduction

Tourism is essentially about people and places, the places one group of people leave, visit and pass through, the other groups who make their trip possible and those they encounter along the way. In a more technical sense, tourism may be thought of as the relationships and phenomena arising out of the journeys and temporary stays of people travelling primarily for leisure or recreational purposes. While writers differ on the degree to which other forms of travel (e.g. for business, for health or educational purposes) should be included under tourism, there is a growing recognition that tourism constitutes one end of a broad leisure spectrum. In a geographical sense, a basic distinction between tourism and other forms of leisure, such as that practised in the home (e.g. watching television) or within the urban area (e.g. going to the local swimming pool), is the travel component. Some writers employ a minimum trip distance criterion but generally tourism is taken to include at least a one-night stay away from the place of permanent residence. These travel and stay attributes of tourism in turn give rise to various service demands which may be provided by different sectors of the tourist industry so that in an economic and commercial sense tourism might also be distinguished from other types of leisure activity.

The spatial interaction arising out of the tourist's movement from origin to destination has not been examined explicitly in much of the geographical literature on tourism. The majority of geographical, and other, studies have been concerned with only one part of the system, usually with the destination, as typified by the many ideographic studies which have appeared since the 1960s. A sense of this interaction and a more general spatial structure does, however, emerge from some of the earlier studies. In his seminal work on second homes in Ontario, for instance, Wolfe (1951: 28) observes: 'In ecological terms we have added segments of two zones to the city of Toronto: a buffer zone 50 miles wide, a recreation bridge to cross . . . and a summer dormitory zone seventy miles wide'. In a similar vein Defert (1966), one of the first French geographers to make a substantial contribution to the geography of tourism, writes of an *espace distance* which separates the permanent residence from the seasonal one and of an *espace milieu* where the tourist enjoys his holiday. A decade later, Miossec (1976) speaks of *l'espace touristique* as being both an *espace parcouru* and as an *espace occupé* involving a *lieu de déplacement* and a *lieu de séjour*. Miossec notes, however, that few studies have explicitly attempted to bring together the generating regions (origins), receiving regions (destinations) and the associated linkages.

The aim of this book is to analyse in a systematic and comprehensive manner the geographical dimensions of tourism, not only to increase our understanding of this important and growing industry but also to show how a geographical perspective can contribute to its planning, development and management. The basic framework used is an origin–linkage–destination system of the type outlined above as this provides an effective integrative device for investigating what is inherently a very geographical phenomenon. Geographic scale is a second major organizational feature, with the focus changing from the international to the national, regional and local scales. The links between these scales are also emphasized.

While this book stresses geographical methods of analysis and draws predominantly, but by no means exclusively, on the works of geographers, it is addressed to a much wider audience. An appreciation of the geographical dimensions of tourism and the adoption of a spatial perspective can provide valuable insights into this phenomenon for researchers in allied disciplines – economics, sociology, anthropology, resource management, business administration – as well as for those involved in the planning, development and management of the tourist industry at different levels. At present it appears many organizations responsible for collecting tourism-related data do not exploit them fully or in some cases at all. The effort appears to go into compilation rather than analysis. The examples given here show the wide variety of uses to which this information can be put. It is hoped that these will not only stimulate the relevant organizations to make better use of the material that is available but encourage others to extend or modify their data collection procedures.

Chapter 1 provides a theoretical base and reviews a variety of different concepts and models which give weight to different aspects of the origin–linkage–destination system. Chapter 2 concentrates on demand and motivation and considers what underlies people's desire to leave their home area to visit other places. Selected tourist flows at various scales – international, intra-national and domestic – are examined in Chapters 3 to 6. The focus then shifts to destination areas, with Chapter 7 being devoted to a review of ways of measuring spatial variations in tourism. Subsequent chapters then consider the spatial structure of tourism at various scales, at a national and regional level in Chapter 8, on islands in Chapter 9 and in coastal resorts and urban areas in Chapter 10. Finally, Chapter 11 reviews two major and recurring themes – concentration and spatial interaction – and considers the significance of these. Examples are also given of how geographical techniques and a spatial perspective can be applied in planning, development, marketing and the assessment of

the impact of tourism. Conclusions are then drawn.

Each of these topics is examined systematically, with the emphasis being on identifying general patterns and processes and on distinguishing the general from the specific. In order to understand better the processes involved, an attempt is made to examine the evolution of flow patterns and the changing distribution of tourists and facilities over time. Discussion of patterns and processes, and particularly their evolution, cannot, however, be separated from questions of data and methodology. The weight given to these matters varies from topic to topic depending on the extent and nature of the related literature. As recent reviews have pointed out, the coverage of topics is far from uniform and the literature on the geography of tourism is still very fragmented (Pearce 1979a; Barbier and Pearce 1984; Duffield 1984; Lundgren 1984; Mitchell 1984; Pearce and Mings 1984). In some cases, as with domestic tourist studies at the local level (Ch. 6) or the morphology of coastal resorts (Ch. 10), it is possible to review a wide range of related research results. In other instances, more attention must be given to the availability and reliability of the data, as with international tourist flows (Ch. 3) or methodological issues, for instance measuring intra-national tourist flows (Ch. 4) or analysing domestic tourist travel at the national level (Ch. 6). Given the diversity of data and techniques used in measuring spatial variations in tourism, it is appropriate to review and evaluate these in one chapter (Ch. 7) so as to allow a more fluid discussion of patterns in subsequent chapters. In topic areas which have hitherto attracted little attention, existing studies are complemented by original material or new treatment, such as the discussions of an integrated approach to international travel (Ch. 5), national patterns of tourism (Ch. 8), tourism on islands (Ch. 9) and tourism in urban areas (Ch. 10). Avenues for future research are also identified.

Given the nature of tourism, particularly international tourism, as well as the aim of identifying general patterns and processes, it is appropriate to draw on examples from many parts of the globe. Recent national reviews indicate that the coverage of topics varies considerably from country to country (Barbier and Pearce 1984; Benthien 1984; Duffield 1984; Lichtenberger 1984; Lundgren 1984; Mitchell 1984; Pearce and Mings 1984; Takeuchi 1984). Factors accounting for this uneven treatment include differences in the type of tourism practised, variations in available data, broader disciplinary traditions and emphases (regional studies in France and quantitative analysis in North America) and the interests of individual researchers. Drawing on a geographically diverse range of examples allows the generality of ideas and patterns to be examined in those topic areas which have attracted relatively more attention and enables the evaluation of a wider range of techniques and data sources with reference to those problems which are only just being explored. Inevitably the material selected has been biased by the author's own experiences, contacts and limited access to certain foreign language material. Any generalizations made have therefore to be seen in the light of the examples used. It is hoped nevertheless that the systematic approach adopted will readily enable other researchers to put their own results alongside the patterns and trends identified in this book and to compare and evaluate their techniques and methods with those discussed here.

1
Tourism models

The geography of tourism is not yet underpinned by a strong conceptual and theoretical base. To some extent this is due to the relative recency of tourism as a field of study. Although geographers were first interested in the topic over fifty years ago, it was not until the early 1960s in Europe and later in North America and elsewhere that geographical studies of tourism start to appear frequently in the literature (Pearce 1979a). Moreover there has been an absence of sustained research effort in this field, with much of the published work being carried out by those with only a transient interest in tourism, producing one or two usually ideographic papers before returning to their more established and accepted branch of the discipline or moving on to pastures new. Mitchell (1984: 6) speaks of a 'proclivity to "selectively mine" pristine tourism topics and to neglect the "mass mining" of more normal or mundane subjects or areas . . . The stock pile of research findings do not advance systematically but rather progress spasmodically and in a seemingly random fashion.' In the absence of unifying concepts and theories which are slow to develop in such a context, much research continues to lack direction and the cycle goes largely unbroken.

Nevertheless, since the late 1960s a number of models dealing with various aspects of the spatial structure of tourism have started to emerge. As in other areas of the geography of tourism, these models appear to have been developed independently of one another, with little or no recognition of or attempt to build on previous efforts. Perhaps this is not too surprising given that models have been developed by those working in Europe, North America, Australasia and Japan. This chapter reviews and evaluates these models with the aim of providing a theoretical and conceptual base and general frameworks for examining the spatial dynamics of tourism and analysing and interpreting material in subsequent chapters.

As noted in the Introduction, a few early writers such as Wolfe (1951) and Defert (1966) outlined fundamental aspects of the patterns and processes of spatial interaction inherent in all forms of tourism. Later researchers have attempted to express these relationships more explicitly and to derive increasingly complex models of tourist space. The basis of most of these models remains an origin–linkage–destination system, with various writers giving different emphasis to these three elements and expressing them in different terms. Four basic groups of models might be identified: those emphasizing the travel or linkage component, origin–destination models, structural models and evolutionary models.

Models of tourist travel

The emphasis in the early explicit models of tourist systems tends to be on the linkage or

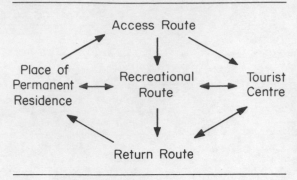

Fig. 1.1 Mariot's model of tourist flows between two locations.

Source: Redrawn from Matley (1976) after Mariot.

travel component. Mariot (cited by Matley 1976), for example, proposes three different routes which may link a place of permanent residence (origin) to a tourist centre (destination) – an access route, a return route, and a recreational route (Fig. 1.1). The access and return routes, which in some cases may be one and the same, essentially provide a direct link between the two places. Those travelling the recreational route, on the other hand, will make use of various tourist facilities along the way, even if the intervening area does not constitute the main goal of the journey. Alternatively, the tourist may use the recreational route for only part of the journey, entering or leaving it at some stage en route between the origin and destination.

Implicit in Mariot's recreational route is the idea of touring, that is in visiting several places on one trip, rather than just a single destination. This notion is developed in Campbell's (1966) model which portrays different patterns of move-

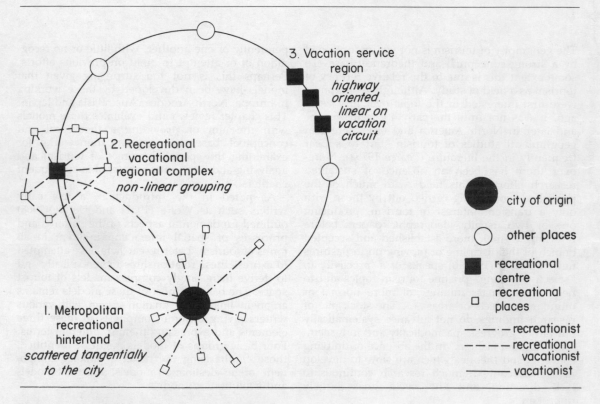

Fig. 1.2 Campbell's model of recreational and vacational travel.

Source: Redrawn from Campbell (1966).

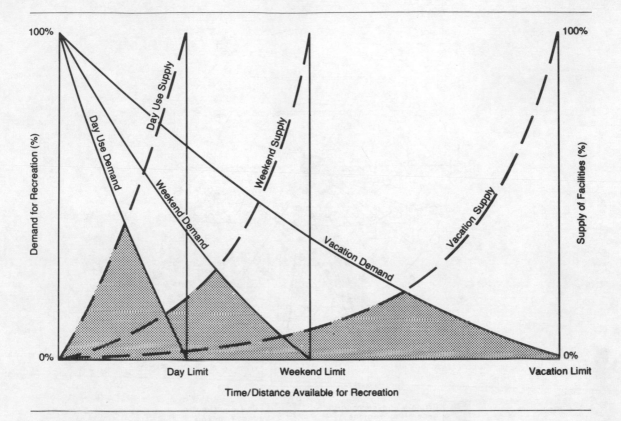

Fig. 1.3 Distribution of recreational uses.

Source: Greer and Wall (1979).

ment away from an urban centre (Fig. 1.2). Campbell distinguishes between various groups on the basis of the relative importance of the travel and stay components of their trip. For the 'recreationist' the recreational activity itself is the main element while for the 'vacationist' the journey as such constitutes the main activity of the trip, with a number of stopovers being made on a round trip away from the city. An intermediate group, the 'recreational vacationist', is shown to make side trips from some regional base. According to the model, 'recreational' travel is scattered radially from the city whereas 'vacation' travel is essentially linear and highway oriented, with 'recreational vacational' travel involving elements of both. Campbell's work is also supported by Rajotte's research on movement patterns in Quebec (Rajotte 1975). While the concept of these different types of travel is useful for analysing tourist flow patterns there are clearly

semantic problems in restricting the term 'tourist' or 'vacationist' to someone whose primary interest is 'invariably in sightseeing and travelling'.

Other writers have been concerned not so much with travel routes and itineraries but with changes in the volume of tourist travel. Both domestically and internationally the volume of traffic is generally held to decrease away from the generating centre as travel costs in time, money and effort increase. Domestic travel is typically seen in terms of concentric zones surrounding the city as defined on the basis of blocks of available leisure time: a day-trip zone, a weekend zone (which often corresponds with a second home belt) and a holiday or vacation zone (Mercer 1970; Rajotte 1975; Ruppert 1978). On the other hand, as Greer and Wall (1979: 230) point out, although demand may vary inversely with an increase in distance from the city, the potential supply of recreational and vacational opportunities will

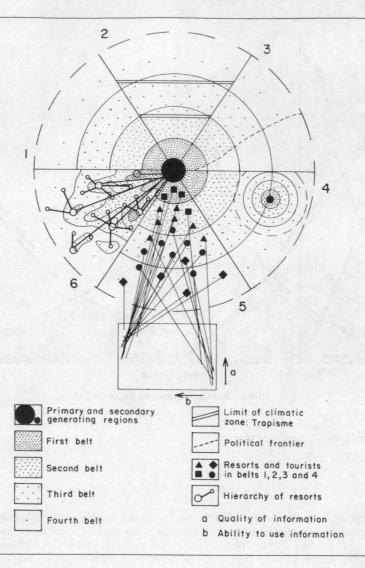

Fig. 1.4 Miossec's model of tourist space.

Source: After Miossec (1976).

increase geometrically 'as each successive unit of distance gives access to increasingly larger areas of land'. This interaction of supply and demand, they argue, would theoretically produce a 'cone of visitation' peaking at some distance from the generating centre with the exact form of the cone depending on the nature of the activity and its sensitivity to distance (Fig. 1.3). The concept of successive, though overlapping, zones is thus retained in Greer and Wall's model, but the notion of a simple distance-decay function within each zone is rejected.

Theoretically, international demand and supply might be expected to interact in a similar manner to produce larger-scale cones of visitation. However, the models of international tourist space which have been proposed (Yokeno 1974; Miossec 1976, 1977) have concentrated on incorporating various modifications to hypothesized regular concentric zones. In Miossec's model

(Fig. 1.4), the origin or core is surrounded by four major belts or zones and travel motives, means and costs change as well (Sector 1). In the real world these theoretical regular concentric zones are subject to modification by 'positive deformations' (low cost of living, favourable climate, historic links) which extend the belts and the 'negative' ones (essentially political) which compress them (Sectors 2 and 3). These positive and negative deformations are not independent. Puerto Rico, for example, benefited from the Cuban blockade, and the development of the Mediterranean is in part due to political barriers in Eastern Europe. Moreover, in reality a series of cores exists giving rise to concurrent spatial demands (Sector 4). Miossec also attempts to incorporate perception of this space in his model, although the schematic representation of this is not particularly clear. In general, knowledge of destinations declines with distance but there may be certain points of reference or evocative names so that the individual's mental map of the tourist space has both concentric and sectoral constraints. Miossec also suggests that the quality of the image will depend on the socio-political-linguistic environment of the points of departure and arrival. Finally, the model incorporates the idea of a hierarchy of resorts, an idea developed in a second model (Fig. 1.11).

Similar notions to these are embodied in Yokeno's model of international travel, a development of his earlier work applying the concepts of von Thunen and Weber to the tourist industry (Yokeno 1968). According to Yokeno, deformations of the hypothetically concentric zones may result from capital city tourism, major transport links and tourism price levels (an intervening country may be bypassed in favour of a more distant one where local costs are lower).

Certain travel models then emphasize the routes taken while others stress the volume, nature and direction of the tourist traffic. A distance decay function characterizes this latter group, whether dealing with domestic or international tourist travel.

Origin–destination models

One of the basic features not considered in the models discussed so far is that most places are, in varying degrees, both origins and destinations. That is to say, as well as sending tourists to some destination or a series of destinations, a particular place may also receive visitors from those same destinations. Likewise, the routes and structures linking one place to another may convey travellers from each place to the other and back again or on to some third place. This double generating/receiving function and this reciprocal interaction is portrayed in the models of Thurot (1980), Lundgren (1982) and Pearce (1981a) as depicted in Figs 1.5 to 1.7 respectively.

Thurot's model concerns tourism at a national and international level. In each of the three national systems A, B and C depicted in Fig. 1.5, Thurot distinguishes between supply and demand and between domestic and international tourism. Part of the demand for tourism generated in system or country B, probably the larger part, will be fulfilled by that country's tourist facilities with the remainder being distributed to countries A and C. At the same time, part of the demand from country A will be channelled to country B (and to country C), which thereby becomes an international destination as well as a source of international travellers. In contrast, no international demand is shown to emanate from country C, although it may generate domestic tourism and receive tourists from countries A and B. Country C is said to represent certain Third World countries where the standards of living may generally be insufficient to generate international tourism (although often a small elite may indulge in a large amount of such travel) and Soviet bloc countries where severe restrictions on international travel may exist. The different national systems, which need not be contiguous, are separated by an *espace de transit*, a transit zone comparable to those of Wolfe (1951) and Defert (1966) noted earlier.

Thurot's model was originally conceived as an aid to analysing carrying capacity (see Ch. 11) but it is equally useful as a means of conceptualizing the different levels of tourist flows and spatial structures. Clearly the model could be made more complex and sophisticated by increasing the number of national systems in the model and by compartmentalizing or classifying in different ways (geographic, qualitative . . .) the supply and demand components in each system. One important question, which will be considered in Chapter 8, is the extent to which domestic and international tourists share the tourist facilities in any given country or region and the extent to which there is a marked separation in the resources and services used by each group.

Lundgren (1982) focuses on the role of different places rather than countries. While he sees places essentially in terms of destinations, their 'degree of mutual travel attraction' (generation vs inflow of tourists) is one of the defining characteristics he uses in positioning destinations within what he calls the 'travel circulation hierarchy' (Fig. 1.6).

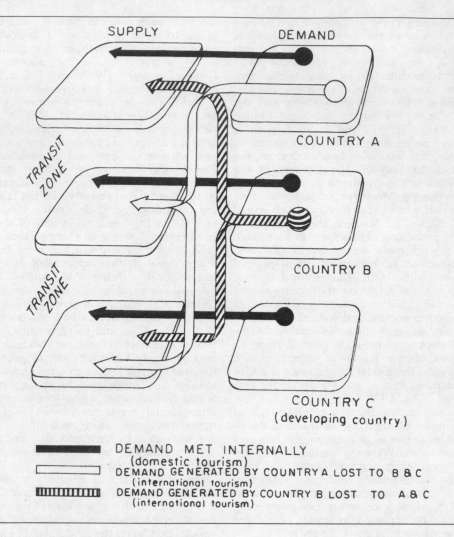

Fig. 1.5 Schematic representation of the supply of and demand for domestic and international tourism in a series of countries.

Source: After Thurot (1980).

The other characteristics used are relative geographical centrality, geographic place attributes (attractions) and the ability of places to supply tourist-demanded services from within their own local or regional economy. Four broad tourist destination types are identified by Lundgren in this way:

1. Centrally-located metropolitan destinations which have a high volume of reciprocal traffic and function both as a generating area and a major destination. These include high-order metropolitan centres well integrated into the international and transcontinental transport networks.

2. Peripheral urban destinations, which have smaller populations, a less important central place function and which tend to have a net inflow of tourists.

3. Peripheral rural destinations, which are less

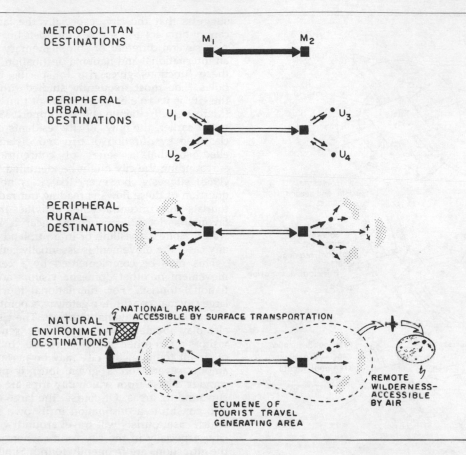

METROPOLITAN
DESTINATIONS

M_1 M_2

PERIPHERAL
URBAN
DESTINATIONS

U_1 U_3

U_2 U_4

PERIPHERAL
RURAL
DESTINATIONS

NATURAL
ENVIRONMENT
DESTINATIONS

NATIONAL PARK-
ACCESSIBLE BY SURFACE TRANSPORTATION

REMOTE
WILDERNESS-
ACCESSIBLE
BY AIR

ECUMENE OF
TOURIST TRAVEL
GENERATING AREA

Fig. 1.6 A spatial hierarchy of tourist flows.

Source: Redrawn from Lundgren (1982).

nodal in character, depending upon a geographically more extensive environment which draws visitors through a combination of landscape characteristics. As the population of such areas is often small and dispersed, a strong net inflow usually results.

4. Natural environment destinations which are usually located at long distances from the generating areas, very sparsely populated and often subject to strict management policies, as in the case of national and regional parks and other reserves. Moreover, Lundgren (1982: 11) suggests, 'as the indigenous economic system for all intents and purposes is non-existent, these destinations can only function through importation into the region of various tourist services. This makes the destination completely dependent upon the tourist generating areas.'

Lundgren's spatial hierarchy is potentially very useful for identifying the functions of a particular place and its associated flows. Unfortunately he only provides a detailed example of the fourth type, the national environment destination, which is illustrated by reference to Nouveau Quebec-Labrador. Some of the features of the other categories require further explanation. Lundgren suggests (p. 11), for example, that some of the peripheral countryside destinations are 'often explored by tourists via some urban centre acting as a staging point', but he does not elaborate on this function. It is also unclear whether or not the flows generated in one metropolitan area are redistributed via a second metropolitan area to lower-order destinations or whether visitors to such destinations essentially originate in the second metropolitan area.

11

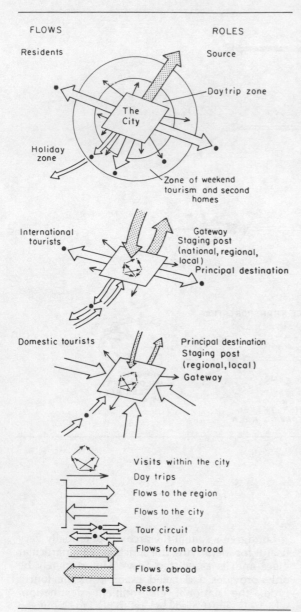

FLOWS

Residents

ROLES

Source

The City

Daytrip zone

Holiday zone

Zone of weekend tourism and second homes

International tourists

Gateway
Staging post (national, regional, local)
Principal destination

Domestic tourists

Principal destination
Staging post (regional, local)
Gateway

Visits within the city
Day trips
Flows to the region
Flows to the city
Tour circuit
Flows from abroad
Flows abroad
Resorts

Fig. 1.7 Schematic representation of tourist flows to and from major urban areas.

Source: After Pearce (1981a).

The joint generating/receiving functions of urban areas and their associated flows have been integrated in the model proposed by this author (Pearce 1981a) as shown in Fig. 1.7. This model

suggests that the city, especially the large city, cannot only act as a source of tourists but can also play several different or complementary roles as an international and national destination. Each of these functions gives rise to specific types of flows. The most frequently studied function of the city is its role as a generator of tourist traffic (Mercer 1970; Rajotte 1975; Ruppert 1978). As noted earlier, the flows of city residents might be classified by duration of trip and distance travelled so that a series of concentric zones surrounding the city might be identified. Yokeno (1968) suggests, however, that it is not just a question of these flows spreading out radially for tourists will concentrate their activities in certain favourable localities, such as near a body of water, along a coastline or in an upland area. In any case, the movement is essentially centrifugal.

This may be complemented by a centripetal movement of other domestic visitors and international tourists. For international tourists, the large city may constitute a gateway, a point of entry into or out of a national territory. The city might also play a regional staging post role, sending the visitors on to other centres or resorts. In the case of circuit tourism, the city may be just one stop among several on a given tour; it may also provide a base from which day trips are made to surrounding areas. Of course, the large city may also constitute a destination in its own right, in which case tourists will travel around within the city, especially in the city centre where many of the attractions are frequently found. Similar functions may also be performed for domestic tourists from other areas, although the relative importance of each of these may differ significantly from the demands being made by international visitors. Indeed, the roles a city plays and the relative importance of each may vary not only from one group of visitors to another but also from city to city depending on such factors as city size, other functions, the nature and degree of development of the surrounding region and so on.

Structural models

Writers examining the impact of international tourism in Third World countries have emphasized the structural relationships between origins and destinations (IUOTO 1975; Lundgren 1972, 1975; Hills and Lundgren 1977; Britton 1980a, 1982; Cazes 1980). Hills and Lundgren and Britton express these relationships in core-periphery terms with the former focusing on the Caribbean and the latter on the Pacific. The models they propose share many common

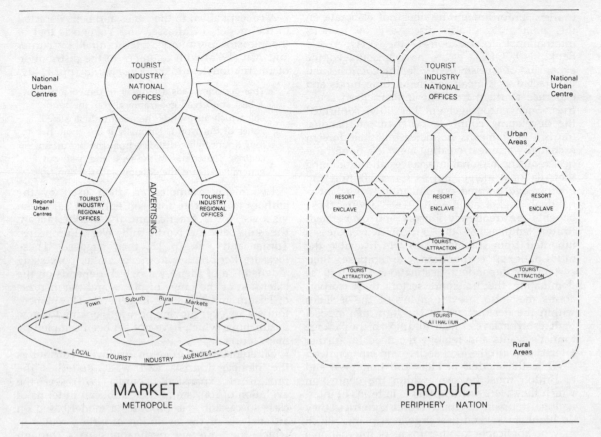

National Urban Centres

TOURIST INDUSTRY NATIONAL OFFICES

TOURIST INDUSTRY NATIONAL OFFICES

National Urban Centre

Urban Areas

Regional Urban Centres

TOURIST INDUSTRY REGIONAL OFFICES

ADVERTISING

TOURIST INDUSTRY REGIONAL OFFICES

RESORT ENCLAVE

RESORT ENCLAVE

RESORT ENCLAVE

TOURIST ATTRACTION

TOURIST ATTRACTION

TOURIST ATTRACTION

Town   Suburb   Rural   Markets

TOURIST ATTRACTION

LOCAL   TOURIST   INDUSTRY   AGENCIES

Rural Areas

MARKET
METROPOLE

PRODUCT
PERIPHERY   NATION

Fig. 1.8 An enclave model of tourism in a peripheral economy.

Source: Britton (1980a).

features and only that of Britton is presented here (Fig. 1.8). In each case the market is concentrated upwards through the local–regional–national hierarchy, with the international transfer occurring between the national urban centres in the generating and receiving countries. Dispersal within the peripheral destination is more restricted, with the tourists moving from their point of arrival out to some resort enclave. Movement may occur between such enclaves but only limited travel to other areas occurs. Cazes (1980) presents a more general origin–linkage–destination model which does not include concentration and dispersion within generating and receiving countries.

These writers generally agree that the basic pattern shown in Fig. 1.8 largely arises out of the control exerted by metropolitan-based multinational corporations over the international tourist industry. Lundgren (1972: 86–7) suggests these relationships 'are basically a function of the technological and economic superiority of the travel-generating, metropolitan core areas as such and the willingness of the destination areas to adopt metropolitan values and solutions in order to meet the various demands of metropolitan travellers'. In particular, he stresses the dominant role of the metropolitan countries as air carriers who can effectively and selectively control the international links between the market and the destination. In this respect the metropolitan-based countries are further advantaged by their direct contact with the market (IUOTO 1975). Although Cazes, like Britton, stresses the role of the 'multinational commercial system' in fostering the tourist traffic to developing countries, he also includes reference in his model to the demand created spontaneously by individual 'pioneer' tourists; unfortunately he does not elaborate on this point. Cazes also discusses how various international organizations – the WTO, World Bank, ILO, OECD etc. – have encouraged the expansion of tourism in developing countries and have acted as a means of channelling funds and expertise to them from the industrialized countries. Such encouragement has often confirmed the developing country's belief in international tourism as a means of increasing their foreign exchange earnings, creating new job opportunities, reducing regional imbalances and promoting their national image. But as Cazes, Britton and others have pointed out, including some international organizations (IUOTO, 1975), these benefits are frequently illusory and over-stated. Britton emphasizes the structural weaknesses inherited from colonial times which enable the multi-national corporations to impose their system on dependent destinations. As well as dominating the transport sector, these corporations may also provide many of the facilities within the destinations in the form of purpose-built resort enclaves which fulfil most of the package tourist's wants and remove the need for further interaction with the local society and environment.

While the models of Hills and Lundgren and of Britton must be seen within the context in which they were written, that is in terms of international tourism in Third World countries, they do highlight several useful general points which may be applicable to other forms of international tourism as well. Particularly useful is the idea of concentration up and subsequently dispersion down the hierarchy. That is to say, international tourist movements commonly involve not just flows between pairs of countries but some prior movement within the generating country and a corresponding distribution within the destination, limited though that may be in the examples given. There is also the over-riding emphasis on the factors giving rise to these structures. In other words, we should not limit ourselves to identifying patterns of movement or spatial relationships but should try to account for them.

Evolutionary models

Models which stress change, whether the evolution of international tourist movements or the development of tourism structures, are also important in drawing attention to explanatory factors and underlying processes. These models again appear to have been developed in isolation with a variety of approaches being adopted and different explanations being proposed.

A concept allied to the zones and belts depicted in the models of Miossec and Yokeno is that of the 'pleasure periphery', a term coined by Turner and Ash (1975) with reference to the distribution of international tourism. They write (pp. 11–12)

> This periphery has a number of dimensions, but is best conceived geographically as the tourist belt which surrounds the great industrialized zones of the world. Normally it lies some two to four hours flying distance from the big urban centres; sometimes to the west and east, but generally toward the equator and the sun.

Two major examples are then used by the authors to illustrate this concept, the Caribbean vis-à-vis North America and the Mediterranean, the sun belt for North and West Europeans. Turner and Ash (p. 12) then suggest: 'These Pleasure Peripheries are never static, possessing a dynamism of their own, which depends on the extension of the range of places and the increase of leisure and affluence in general. The pioneer tourists are ever moving outward looking for new destinations which have not yet been sampled by mass tourism.'

Different views exist on just who constitutes the pioneer tourists and what underlies the process of expansion. Thurot (1973) sees the evolution of tourism in the Caribbean in terms of class succession. He proposes a model based on an analysis of the evolution of airline routes in which the different destinations pass through three successive phases:

- *Phase 1:* Discovery by rich tourists and construction of an international class hotel.
- *Phase 2:* Development of 'Upper Middle Class' hotels (and expansion of the tourist traffic).
- *Phase 3:* Loss of original value to new destinations and arrival of 'Middle Class' and mass tourists.

According to Thurot, the length of this process will depend on the time it takes for the upper middle class tourists to arrive and the speed with which the 'traditionally leisured classes' open up new destinations. In this way the Caribbean pleasure periphery is extended geographically as succeeding waves of tourism spread progressively and selectively outwards from the well-established resorts of Florida. In the Bahamas, for example, the tourist front moves from Nassau out on to the smaller cays and islands. According to Thurot, there is a hierarchy of development in the Commonwealth Carribean, with the development of tourism in Jamaica preceding that of Trinidad and Barbados, which occurs before that of the

Table 1.1
Travel characteristics of psychographic types

Psychocentrics	*Allocentrics*
• Prefer the familiar in travel destinations	• Prefer non-touristy areas
• Like commonplace activities at travel destinations	• Enjoy sense of discovery and delight in new experiences, before others have visited the area
• Prefer sun 'n' fun spots, including considerable relaxation	• Prefer novel and different destinations
• Low activity level	• High activity level
• Prefer destinations they can drive to	• Prefer flying to destinations
• Prefer heavy tourist accommodations, such as heavy hotel development, family type restaurants and tourist shops	• Tour accommodations should include adequate-to-good hotels and food, not necessarily modern or chain-type hotels, and few 'tourist' type attractions
• Prefer familiar atmosphere (hamburger stands, familiar type entertainment, absence of foreign atmosphere)	• Enjoy meeting and dealing with people from a strange or foreign culture
• Complete tour packaging, appropriate with heavy scheduling of activities.	• Tour arrangements should include basics (transportation and hotels) and allow considerable freedom and flexibility

Source: Plog (1973: 15).

smaller Leeward and Windward Islands.

Plog (1973), on the other hand, emphasizes not class but the personalities of different types of travellers. From a series of motivational studies, initially of flyers and non-flyers, Plog suggests that travellers are distributed normally along a continuum from psychocentrism to allocentrism. At the one extreme are the 'psychocentrics', who tend to be anxious, self-inhibited, non-adventuresome and concerned with the little problems in life. In contrast, the 'allocentrics' are self-confident, curious, adventurous and outgoing; travel, according to Plog, is a way for them to express their inquisitiveness and curiosity. The travel characteristics of the two groups differ (Table 1.1) so that different types of travellers will visit different destinations.

Figure 1.9 represents the psychographic positions of destinations visited by American travellers (presumably New Yorkers). Plog suggests that the market for a given destination evolves and that the destination appeals to different groups at different times. The destination will be 'discovered' by 'allocentrics', but as it becomes more well known, develops and attracts more visitors, for example the 'mid-centrics', it will lose its appeal and the 'allocen-

trics' will move on. As the population is said to be normally distributed, this means that an area will receive the largest number of visitors when it is attracting the 'mid-centrics', that is at a stage when it is neither too exotic nor too familiar. But from this point on, the implication is that the market will decline. According to Plog (p. 16), 'we can visualize a destination moving across the spectrum, however gradually or slowly, but far too often inexorably towards the potential of its own demise. Destination areas carry with them the potential seeds of their own destruction, as they allow themselves to become more commercialized and lose their qualities which originally attracted tourists.'

In his recent model of the spatio-temporal development of international seaside tourism, Gormsen (1981) attempts to incorporate not only the ideas of spatial and temporal evolution, but also corresponding changes in the degree of local or regional participation in the development process, in the social structure of the tourist traffic and in the quantity and range of accommodation available (Fig. 1.10). Gormsen's model is based on a study of the historical development of coastal tourism, essentially from a European perspective. Thus the first periphery refers to

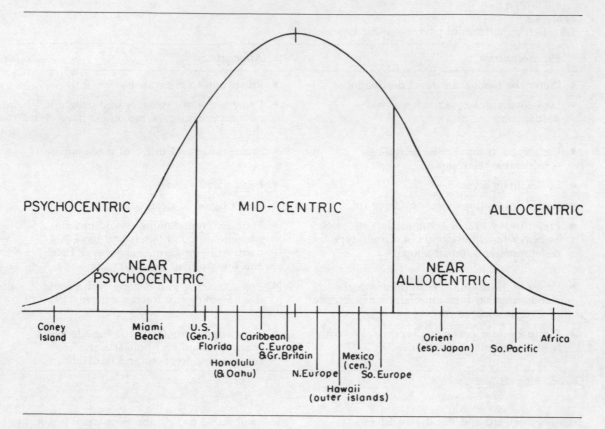

Fig. 1.9 The psychographic positions of selected destinations.

Source: Redrawn from Plog (1973).

resorts on both sides of the Channel as well as those of the Baltic; the second incorporates the coasts of Southern Europe; the third includes the North African littoral and the Balearic and Canary Islands; while the fourth periphery embraces more distant destinations in West Africa, the Caribbean, the Pacific and Indian Oceans, South East Asia and South America. Gormsen also suggests that comparable peripheries can be identified for the USA. In Fig. 1.10, approximate dates are given for the various stages in the development of each periphery.

According to this model, the initiative in the early stages comes from external developers but with time there is a growing local participation in the development process (column A). The extent of local participation shown for the third and fourth peripheries broadly corresponds with the

work of Hills and Lundgren (1977) and Britton (1980a, 1982). These latter writers have not generalized their models as Gormsen has done, but the implication of their work appears to be that the structural characteristics they emphasize would lead to the continued dominance of external developers, at least in the immediate future. Gormsen's model, however, involves a comparatively long time-scale and covers a period of far-reaching social and economic changes. There is also general agreement between the changing social structures suggested by Gormsen (column B) and the processes discussed by Thurot (1973) in the Caribbean (Fig. 1.5). It should be noted, however, that a completely black column B (as in the first periphery since the 1960s) means that tourists from all social classes are participating in seaside holidays and not that the lower

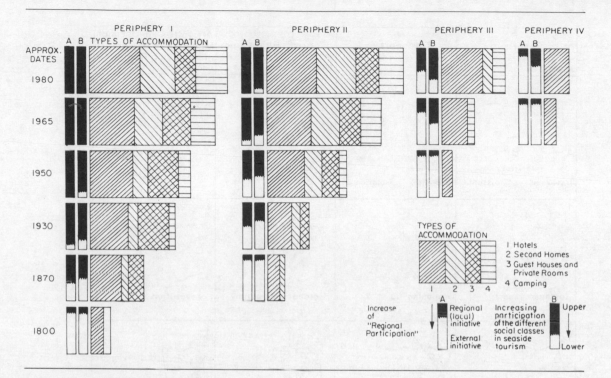

Fig. 1.10 Schematic representation of the spatio-temporal development of international seaside tourism.

Source: Redrawn from Gormsen (1981).

classes have entirely replaced the upper classes. With changes in the social structure of the tourist traffic, which in part results from growing accessibility, also come changes in the types of accommodation demanded and provided, notably an increase in second homes and later in camping facilities.

Aspects of the development process and changes in tourist behaviour were also emphasized by Miossec (1976, 1977) in his second model which depicts the structural evolution of tourist regions through time and space (Fig. 1.11). In particular, Miossec stresses changes in the provision of facilities (resorts and transport networks) and in the behaviour and attitudes of the tourists and the local decision-makers and host populations. In the early phases (0 and 1) the region is isolated, there is little or no development, tourists have only a vague idea about

the destination while the local residents tend to have a polarized view of what tourism may bring. The success of the pioneer resorts leads to further development (phase 3). As the tourist industry expands, an increasingly complex hierarchical system of resorts and transport networks evolves while changes in local attitudes may lead to the complete acceptance of tourism, the adoption of planning controls or even the rejection of tourism (phases 4 and 5). Meanwhile the tourists have become more aware of what the region as a whole has to offer, with some spatial specialization occurring. With further development, Miossec suggests it is tourism itself rather than the original attractions which are now drawing visitors to the area. This change of character induces some tourists to move on to other areas in a manner similar to that suggested by Plog (Fig. 1.9).

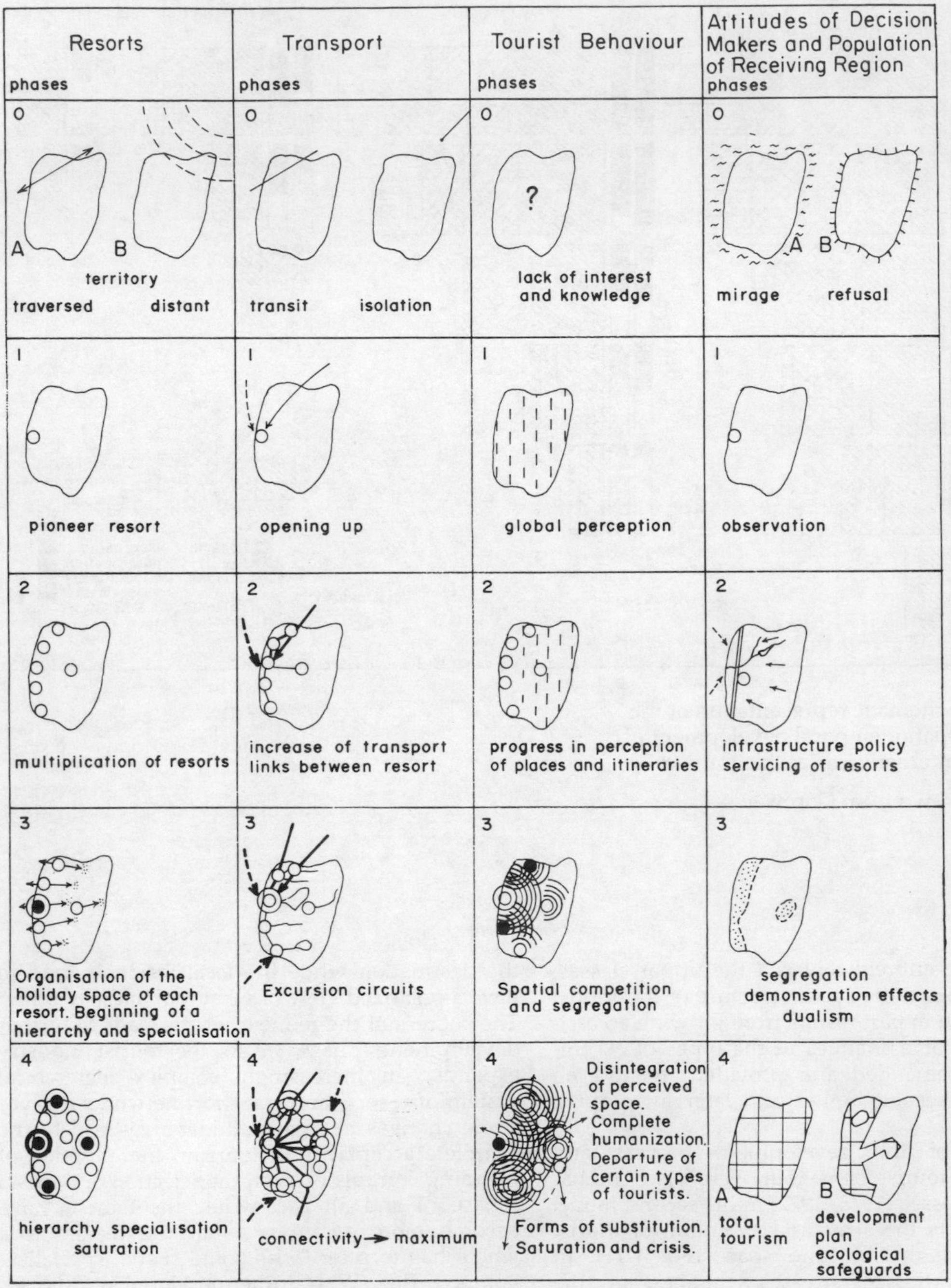

Resorts phases	Transport phases	Tourist Behaviour phases	Attitudes of Decision Makers and Population of Receiving Region phases
0 A B territory traversed distant	**0** transit isolation	**0** ? lack of interest and knowledge	**0** A B mirage refusal
1 pioneer resort	**1** opening up	**1** global perception	**1** observation
2 multiplication of resorts	**2** increase of transport links between resort	**2** progress in perception of places and itineraries	**2** infrastructure policy servicing of resorts
3 Organisation of the holiday space of each resort. Beginning of a hierarchy and specialisation	**3** Excursion circuits	**3** Spatial competition and segregation	**3** segregation demonstration effects dualism
4 hierarchy specialisation saturation	**4** connectivity → maximum	**4** Disintegration of perceived space. Complete humanization. Departure of certain types of tourists. Forms of substitution. Saturation and crisis.	**4** A total tourism B development plan ecological safeguards

Fig. 1.11 Miossec's model of tourist development.

Source: After Miossec (1976).

Conclusions

In the last two decades and in particular the last ten years, a variety of models dealing with particular aspects of tourist flows and the structure of tourist space have been proposed. In most cases these appear to have been developed independently of one another although references to earlier work in the same field are occasionally made and the influence of ideas from other areas of geography, notably the work of von Thunen, can also be detected. Miossec (1976), for example, acknowledges the earlier work of Yokeno (1968), and both writers make explicit reference to von Thunen. There is, however, little evidence of a concerted effort to build up a cohesive body of theory on tourism. Lundgren (1982), for example, refers to the work of Miossec but does not draw any parallels between the dependency of natural environment destinations upon generating areas with his own earlier work which stresses the dependency of Caribbean destinations on metropolitan areas (Lundgren 1974; Hills and Lundgren 1977).

Nevertheless, some general themes do emerge from these disparate studies. The notion of spatial interaction underlies all these models, with a potentially very complex tourist system operating if the various features stressed in individual models were combined. At this stage, however, it is perhaps more appropriate to identify basic concepts and ideas.

The basic geographic concept of distance decay, whereby the volume of tourist traffic decreases with distance away from the generating area, is embodied in several of the models, whether concerned primarily with international tourism or domestic tourism. It is recognized, however, that regular distance decay curves may be deformed in the real world and attention is directed to a variety of factors which may bring about these deformations.

Reciprocity is another important feature, with most areas having, in varying degrees, both generating and receiving functions. In most cases a two-way traffic will exist between pairs of places, whether two countries or two linked cities, although the flows may be stronger in one direction than the other. As most places are linked to a range of other places, a complex system of reciprocal flows may occur, with individual places having a variety of generating and receiving functions. In particular, several of the models draw attention to the receiving functions of urban areas which have often been neglected in the past in favour of more distinct tourist destinations.

Adding to this complexity is the range of links which may exist between origins and destinations, with some places being linked directly to each other, while others may form part of a circuit.

The notion of a spatial hierarchy is also central to many of these models, whether in terms of flows from an international to a national, regional and local level, or the distribution of tourist supply and demand at these different levels. How one flow relates to another and how one level is linked to another are particularly relevant questions. The relationships between domestic and international tourism are especially critical and should not be overlooked.

Spatial hierarchies may change over time, and the idea of evolving flows and structures is central to our understanding of why these developments may come about and what factors influence the nature of distributions and structures at a particular time. Different ideas have been advanced to account for changes in the nature of demand while other writers have stressed variations in the development of destinations. Clearly the changes in demand, flows and the development of destinations are closely inter-related and a variety of different factors acting in different ways and at different scales may play a role.

Some of the models reviewed here have been developed by their creators from work in a particular part of the world and others have been employed by their authors as a basis for examining tourism in specific places. In general, however, they have been little tested by empirical research and none so far has been widely adopted. Several factors may account for this. Firstly, there is the general nature of much tourism research as outlined in the Introduction to this chapter. Secondly, the recency of many of these models has been compounded by the limited distribution of the publications in which many have appeared. The diffusion of ideas between different language groups, in particular, takes some time. The growing popularity of some of Miossec's ideas, for instance, perhaps owes something to an earlier review of his work in a prominent English language tourism journal (Pearce, 1979a). Thirdly, the logic and soundness of the models and concepts themselves may be a factor. There is as yet no comprehensive, all-embracing model of tourism. Rather there is a series of different models which have stressed particular parts of the tourist system. Individually, most give insights into particular areas and together, if they do not as yet offer a full explanation, they at least provide a valuable point of entry into analysis and interpretation. In some cases alternative theories have been put forward but most of the models reviewed complement each other rather than conflict with one another.

The organization of subsequent chapters has been influenced by some of the concepts and ideas outlined above. In other instances, particular topics are examined with reference to these models, which may provide either a framework for analysis or a basis for explaining and interpreting observed patterns. It should be recalled, however, that very few of the studies reviewed in the following chapters have been originally based on the theories and concepts discussed here.

2

Motivations and demand for tourist travel

Research on tourism in generating regions is generally much less developed than destination-related studies. The major focus here is on demand, a subject which is much less tangible than the many more concrete manifestations of tourism in destination areas or even transit regions. A fundamental question, and one which underlies the spatial interaction portrayed in the models in the preceding chapter, is why is it that people leave their home area to visit other areas? This may seem a relatively straightforward question but a review of the literature shows that too often it is a question which has not been asked or has been taken for granted. In any event it remains a question which has not been well answered. Indeed, the whole area of motivation and demand has been one of the least researched areas of tourism to date. It is only comparatively recently that it has attracted serious study, for example from psychologists, sociologists and others (Dann 1977, 1981; Crompton 1979; Leiper 1984a). This chapter examines various aspects of demand in generating regions, namely basic motivations for tourist travel, factors influencing the ability to travel, the measurement and evolution of demand, and spatial variations in the propensity for international travel.

Why do tourists travel?

In many respects our asking why tourists tour is similar to demographers and population geographers asking why migrants migrate, or to transport geographers asking why people in general travel and why goods are sent from one place to another. What have their answers been? In their review of migration, White and Woods (1980: 7) observe: 'Migration occurs because migrants believe that they will be more satisfied in their needs and desires in the place that they move to than in the place from which they come.' Similarly, Lowe and Moryadas (1975: 2) introduce their text on transport geography by noting:

> In the strictest sense, people's wants with respect to goods, contacts, information etc., cannot be satisfied at any one given location. Therefore, it follows that their wants must be met from other locations. Movement occurs to the extent that people have the ability to satisfy their desires with respect to goods, services, information, or experience at some location other than their present one, and to the extent that these other locations are capable of satisfying such desires.'

Following these writers, the question of tourism demand might then be framed in terms of what needs and desires of tourists, or potential tourists, cannot be satisfied in their home area or what can they do elsewhere that they cannot do at home?

Gray (1970), in one of the earlier statements of motivation, saw two basic reasons for pleasure travel – 'wanderlust' and 'sunlust'. Wanderlust, he defines, as 'that basic trait in human nature which causes some individuals to want to leave things with which they are familiar and to go and see at first hand different exciting cultures and places . . . The desire to travel may not be a permanent one, merely a desire to exchange temporarily the known workaday things of home for something which is exotic.' Sunlust, on the other hand, 'depends upon the existence elsewhere of different or better amenities for a specific purpose than are available locally'. One expression of this, as the term suggests, is literally a 'hunt for the sun' as typified by tourist flows to the Caribbean or the Mediterranean.

Wanderlust might be thought of essentially as a 'push' factor whereas sunlust is largely a response to 'pull' factors elsewhere. While development studies and promotional efforts in destination areas have continued to concentrate on the 'pull' factors with respect to the product they offer, recent motivational research has tended to emphasize the 'push' factor, the need to break from routine and to 'get away from it all'.

Leiper (1984a) points out, 'all leisure involves a temporary escape of some kind' but 'tourism is unique in that it involves real physical escape reflected in travelling to one or more destination regions where the leisure experiences transpire'. He continues: 'A holiday trip allows changes that are multi-dimensional: place, pace, faces, lifestyles, behaviour, attitude. It allows a person temporary withdrawal from many of the environments affecting day to day existence'. As such, Leiper argues, tourism enhances leisure opportunities, particularly for rest and relaxation.

Reporting on a motivational study of 39 individuals, Crompton (1979: 415) notes: 'The essence of 'break from routine' was, in most cases, either locating in a different place, or changing the dominant social context from the work milieu, usually to that of the family group, or doing both of these things.' Having established a 'break from routine' as the basic motivation for tourist travel, Crompton then suggests that it is possible to identify more specific directive motives which serve (p. 415) to 'guide the tourist toward the selection of a particular type of vacation or destination in preference to all the alternatives of which the tourist is aware. In most decisions more than one motive is operative.' Crompton goes on to suggest that his respondents' different motives can be conceptualized (p. 415) as being 'located along a cultural-socio-psychological disequilibrium continuum'. The socio-psycholog-

ical motives were often not expressed explicitly by the respondents but Crompton identified seven of these:

1. escape from a perceived mundane environment,
2. exploration and evaluation of self,
3. relaxation,
4. prestige,
5. regression (less constrained behaviour),
6. enhancement of kinship relationships,
7. facilitation of social interaction.

These broadly correspond to Dann's (1977) basic motivations of a reaction to anomie (1, 6, 7), ego-enhancement (4) and fantasy (4, 5). Two primary cultural motives were expressed by Crompton's respondents, novelty and education, though he suggests in many cases these motives were more apparent than real. They would also appear to be closely associated with some of the socio-psychological motives. The search for novelty, for example, might well be a complement to the escape from the mundane environment.

Similar ideas are expressed by Leiper (1984a), but from a different perspective. Leiper distinguishes between recreational leisure which restores and creative leisure which produces something new. He sees the three functions of recreation as being:

(a) rest (which provides recovery from physical or mental fatigue),
(b) relaxation (recovery from tension),
(c) entertainment (recovery from boredom).

These three functions broadly correspond to Crompton's socio-psychological motives while creativity covers aspects of the cultural motives.

Many of these factors are brought together by Iso-Ahola (1982) who proposes a more theoretical motivational model in which the escaping element is complemented or compounded by a seeking component (Fig. 2.1). One set of motivational forces derives from an individual's desire to escape his personal environment (i.e. personal troubles, problems, difficulties and failures) and/or the interpersonal environment (i.e. co-workers, family members, friends and neighbours). Another set of forces results from the desire to obtain certain psychological or intrinsic rewards, either personal or interpersonal, by travelling to a different environment. In general, Iso-Ahola's examples of personal rewards – rest and relaxation, ego-enhancement, learning about other cultures etc. – and interpersonal rewards (essentially greater social interaction) correspond fairly closely with Crompton's specific motivational forces noted above. The point Iso-Ahola

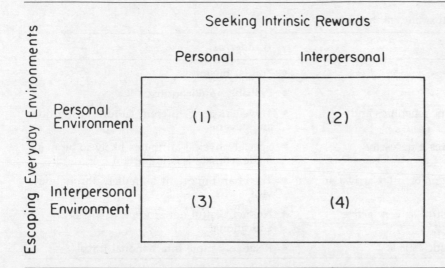

Fig. 2.1 Iso-Ahola's social psychological model
of tourism motivation.

Source: Iso-Ahola (1982).

is making here, and which is conceptualized in his model, is that tourism 'provides an outlet for avoiding something *and* for simultaneously seeking something'. Recognition that elements of both sets of forces, whose relative importance may vary from case to case, may be satisfied at the same time is particularly useful in clarifying some of the issues that arise in motivational research. Iso-Ahola also suggests that in terms of dominant motives, it is theoretically possible to locate any tourist or group in any cell at a given time but notes that this cell may not only differ from one individual or group to another, but for any particular tourist or set of tourists it may change during the course of a trip or from one trip to another.

Evidence from large-scale empirical studies supports many of the points being made in these more theoretical papers. 'Change of environment' was found to be the single most important factor accounting for the desire to travel abroad for vacation in a 1980 survey of over 600 past and potential long-haul travellers in the United States (Opinion Research Corporation 1980). Other factors reinforce this desire for change, notably the 'search for new experiences', the wish to 'see how others live', and the quest for 'adventure/excitement' and new and varied foods and wines (Table 2.1). Nobody acknowledged the

Table 2.1
United States long-haul travellers' reasons for travelling abroad

	%
Change of environment	36
Cultural attractions	31
In search of new experiences	27
See how others live	27
Visit family/friends	24
Adventure/excitement	16
Sense of history	16
Sun, sea, sand	12
New/variety foods and wines	12
Seek own cultural heritage	8
Like to shop abroad	7
Visit religious sites	6
Others have business abroad	6
Broaden education	2
Romance	1
Prestige/status	—
Keeping up with the Joneses	—
Other	15

Source: Opinion Research Corporation 1980.

Table 2.2
The attributes of wanderlust and sunlust travel

Sunlust	*Wanderlust*
• Resort vacation business	• Tourist business
• One country visited	• Probably multicountry
• Travellers seek domestic amenities and accommodations	• Travellers seek different culture, institutions and cuisine
• Special natural attributes a necessity (especially climate)	• Special physical attributes likely to be man-made: climate less important
• Travel a minor consideration after arrival at destination	• Travel an important ingredient throughout visit
• Either relaxing and restful or very active	• Neither restful nor *sportive*: ostensibly educational
• Relatively more domestic travel	• Relatively more international travel

Source: Gray (1970: 14).

prestige aspects of international air travel but this is not surprising in a direct survey of this kind. Similarly, in a 1973 survey of potential air travellers in Canada, 'a complete change of surroundings' was the most frequently cited reason for taking a preferred vacation (Garrett, 1980a). However, a large number of multiple responses were given, indicating that a variety of interrelated factors come in to play.

From a geographical point of view, what is particularly important is the extent to which differing motivations give rise to different types of tourism and create different travel patterns. Gray (1970) suggested that wanderlust and sunlust generate two distinctive forms of travel, the main attributes of which are listed in Table 2.2. From a spatial perspective, one of the crucial differences between the two is the extent to which they are likely to generate international rather than domestic tourism. Wanderlust tourism is more likely to be manifested in international travel than sunlust tourism which in many cases can be realized elsewhere in an individual's country. The extent to which this is true, however, will depend, among other factors, on the size and geographical and cultural diversity of the country in question. Gray also recognizes here that the difference between the two kinds of travel is one of degree and cites as an example a beach resort in a foreign country offering some appeal to wanderlust. Although Gray did not elaborate on it, the suggested difference between the degree of travel associated with wanderlust and sunlust is particularly important to an analysis of travel patterns.

Plog's (1973) work on the psychographic segmentation of tourists discussed in Chapter 1 suggests that tourists with different personalities will seek different travel experiences, selecting particular forms of travel and types of destination (Fig. 1.9; Table 1.1). Since this early work by Plog there has been a growing interest in the application of 'psychographics' to travel research (Solomon and George 1977; Schewe and Calantone 1978; Abbey 1979; Brumbaugh 1983). This typically involves the use of AIO (attitudes, interests and opinions) surveys and its main application has been as a complement to the use of socio-demographic variables in market segmentation studies. A survey of potential New Zealand travellers to Australia, for example, identified in this way four major segments: the 'older relaxation/comfort seekers', 'young excitement seekers', the 'nature/culture' group and the 'unadventurous sightseer' (Burfitt 1983). Different marketing strategies are then designed for each of these groups whose travel requirements differ from one another. While the psychographic approach is useful in marketing, it also offers possibilities for further understanding basic motivations for travel and relating these to particular travel destinations.

Other studies have looked at the motivations for specific types of tourism. In a survey of Grenoble skiers, Keogh (1980) found the 'physical sporting experience' (57.6%) and the 'aesthetic outdoor experience' (33.6%) were the prime motivations in influencing the decision to go skiing, with the opportunity to participate in an activity with family or friends coming a distant third (7.7%). On the basis of these motivations,

Keogh then identified three groups of skiers – the 'sporting', 'contemplative' and 'social' – and found that statistically significant differences occurred between the groups in terms of the resorts they frequented. While this study provides some useful and original insights into skiers' motivations, it does not tell us why those interviewed were seeking either a 'physical sporting' or 'aesthetic outdoor' experience in the first place. Are these two different expressions of the need to escape? Are they two different ways of relaxing? The third factor, the opportunity to participate in an activity with family or friends, however, can be directly related to Dann's and Crompton's need for social interaction.

The ability to travel

To be able to satisfy his desire to travel, the tourist must be able to meet various conditions. In particular, he must be able to afford both the time and money to do so. Tourism requires the ability to get away from school, work, home and social and other commitments. The growth of leisure time in the past century brought about by technological and other improvements has greatly increased the amount of time available for travel, especially in many Western societies. Particularly important here has been the structuring of this time in the form of designated paid holidays to which many groups have been entitled since the late 1930s. Where standards of living have risen and incomes have increased, more people have been able to afford to travel. Spending on tourism is usually regarded as discretionary spending for although travel has been expressed earlier as a response to a desire to escape, in an overall hierarchy of needs this usually comes after more basic ones such as food, housing and clothing have been satisfied. Tourists must also generally be in reasonable health and be able to travel. Age, illness and disability may be significant though not insuperable barriers to travel (Woodside and Etzel 1980); young children may also be a constraint on travel.

International tourism may be subject to more specific constraints. The international tourist must have the right to leave his own country and to enter others. Passports and exit visas are not automatically available everywhere, for instance in Eastern Europe. Stringent currency regulations may be a further bar to overseas travel. The tourist must also be aware of holiday destinations and have the ability to plan and organize his trip. The growth of package tours has relieved the tourist of many of these tasks and, together with the economies they offer, such tours have been responsible for significantly increasing tourist flows in many parts of the world. Moreover,

Table 2.3
Constraints to holiday-taking in France, Spain and Japan

France (1964) Constraint	%*	Spain (1979) Constraint	%	Japan (1976) Constraint	%
Lack of money	39	Lack of money	39	Lack of free time	39.9
Restrained by work	29	Family or health		Health	22.9
Content *chez soi*	16	reasons	23	Couldn't leave home	21.9
Too old	12	Work or study reasons	16	Lack of money	11.5
Family or personal		Prefer to remain at		Couldn't find a	
health	11	home	10	companion	3.5
Restrained by non-		Personal economic		Couldn't buy a ticket	3.5
work duties	7	insecurity	5	Couldn't reserve	
Children too young	4	Lack of civic security	1	accommodation	2.4
Other necessary		Others and no		Couldn't find a	
expenditure	4	response	6	destination	1.4
Nowhere to go, lack				No moral support	
of information	1			from family	1.4
Other	1				
No response	5				

* *Responses exceed 100% due to multiple response.*

Sources: Boyer (1972); Japan National Travel Organisation (1976); Equipo Investigador del IET y CIS (1980).

destinations must be physically accessible to the tourist which implies, at the least, a minimum of transport and accommodation infrastructure.

Few surveys have been carried out to examine specifically why people do not take holidays (or indeed, why they do). Table 2.3 portrays the results of surveys from France, Japan and Spain which indicate the relative importance of these different constraints on holiday-making. At the time of the French survey (1964), some 47% of the French population did not regularly go away on holiday, while 45% of the Japanese sample had not taken a trip of two nights or more away from home during the year (1976). Only a third of the Spanish respondents had taken a holiday in 1979. The results of the three surveys have been classified in different ways but certain comparisons can still be made. Financial constraints were the major factors limiting French and Spanish holiday-taking, while a lack of free time was the single most important handicap for the Japanese. The time factor appears to be compounded in Japan by the practice of many Japanese, for reasons of company loyalty and other cultural factors, not taking all the holidays accorded them. Work and study ties are also important constraints in France and Spain. Family, home and health constraints are significant limitations shared by all three societies. A number of the French and Spanish respondents indicated they were happy *chez soi*, that is, they did not feel a need to go away. The detailed Spanish survey (Equipo Investigador del IET y CIS, 1980) also reveals fairly predictable variations in the relative importance of these constraints from one socio-economic group to another. There is an inverse relationship, for example, between social class and the importance of the financial constraint – nearly half the workers gave lack of money as their principal constraint against only 14% of the upper middle class. Similarly, family ties and health constraints are twice as important for the over 64-year-olds as for any other age group.

While most national tourism surveys have not looked directly at travel motivation and why people do or do not take holidays, many such surveys do present socio-economic profiles of travellers and non-travellers. A selection of these profiles is portrayed in Fig. 2.2. The data presented are not entirely comparable due to variations in the definition of a holiday or trip from one country to another and to differences in class intervals, but certain general tendencies can be identified. For each of the nationalities there is an almost constant decline of trip-taking with age. Conversely there is a positive relationship between the propensity to travel and income

and occupation. The more specific occupational data from France suggest that people in some occupations are more constrained than others, even allowing for a general association between income and occupational category. In particular, the lower propensity to travel among the *patrons* and those engaged in agriculture may reflect ties to businesses and farms. The data in Fig. 2.2 also indicate that the propensity to take a holiday increases with the size of urban area. Why this should be is not altogether clear. It may be that rural populations are more elderly or that average incomes are greater in larger cities. However, in one of the few examples in the literature where one variable is related to another, Baretje and Defert (1972) show that in France the rate of holiday-taking increases with city size even when incomes are held constant. It may be then that the need to escape increases with city size or that larger cities have better transport linkages and that it is easier to get away on holiday. In any event, the nature of the urban hierarchy is likely to exert a significant influence not only on total demand but on the distribution of that demand. Other factors such as the stage in family life cycle or the extent of vehicle ownership may also be factors affecting the propensity to travel, but without more detailed motivation studies much explanation of the patterns identified above must remain largely speculative.

With the analysis of tourism patterns, however, it is not simply a question of taking holidays or not taking holidays. Equally important is the type of holiday taken, influenced by the factors discussed above as well as by motivations. Whether someone holidays in his home region or travels abroad, for example, may depend not only on his motives but also on his capability to undertake and to afford, both in time and money, a short or a longer trip. Table 2.4 shows that not only does the proportion of British adults taking a holiday vary with age and social class, but that marked differences occur in the extent to which different classes holiday at home or abroad. Those aged 45–54 and those in social classes A and B, for example, are proportionately under-represented in the non holiday-takers and markedly over-represented in those holidaying abroad when compared to the distribution of the total adult population in Britain.

A series of Canadian surveys show that marked differences occur in the vacation habits of English and French Quebeckers (Garrett 1980a). English Quebeckers tend to take more vacations, travel more extensively to the United States, the Caribbean and Europe and spend more per person on holiday. French Quebeckers holiday to a much

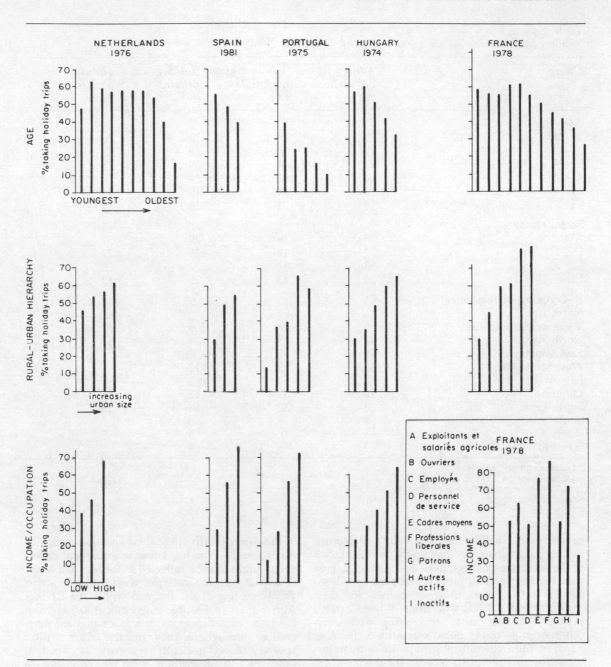

Fig. 2.2 Propensity for holiday-taking in selected European countries.

Data Sources: Centraal bureau voor de statistick, Gabinete de Investigación Turística, Direccão-Geral do Turismo, Hungarian National Council for Tourism, INSEE.

Table 2.4
Profile of British holiday-takers and non-holiday-takers (1980)

Group	Adult population (%)	Adults taking no holiday (%)	Holidays in Britain* (%)	Holidays abroad[†] (%)
Age				
16–24	17	18	13	20
25–34	19	18	19	19
35–44	17	14	19	18
45–54	14	12	14	20
55–64	15	14	18	14
65+	18	24	18	9
Social class				
AB	15	9	20	31
C1	22	17	25	27
C2	33	31	32	29
DE	30	43	23	13
R–G region of residence				
North	6	6	6	7
Yorks & Humberside	9	8	9	7
North West	12	13	11	11
East Midlands	6	7	8	4
West Midlands	10	10	12	7
East Anglia	3	3	3	2
London	14	12	12	16
South East	18	18	18	26
South West	8	8	8	7
Wales	5	6	6	5
Scotland	9	8	9	8

* Holidays of 4+ nights.
† Holidays of 1+ nights.

Source: BTA (1981a)

greater extent within Quebec, with a preference for outdoor activities; those who travel abroad prefer inclusive package tours to a greater degree than the English and favour 'sun-sand-sea' destinations rather than those renowned for their historical and cultural attractions. While Garrett's review contains many interesting points on differences in travel behaviour and preferences between the two cultural groups there is, unfortunately, no attempt to account for them.

Cultural-liguistic factors appear to play a significant role in Belgium where Flemish and Walloon holiday-makers exhibit distinct spatial preferences, especially for international tourism (Institut National de Statistiques 1980). A large-scale household survey in 1978–79 showed almost twice as many of the French-speaking Walloons (32%) took their holidays in France compared to Flemish vacationers (18%). Proportionately more

of this latter group spent their vacation in Spain, Austria and Germany. These international differences might also be reflected at the regional level. Few Walloons, for example, went to the Austrian Tyrol and few of the Flemish visited the Rhone-Alps region in France, suggesting tourists from the two cultural regions may have marked preferences for where they practise their winter sports. More in-depth research is needed, however, to determine whether language is indeed the sole or major element influencing this behaviour or whether other less obvious factors play a role.

Measuring demand

Demand for tourism is expressed and measured in different ways. Most studies refer to what might be termed 'effective demand', that is generally to the number of people who actually participate in a tourist activity or visit a given area. Then there is deferred demand, that is 'those who could participate but do not, either through lack of knowledge, or lack of facilities or both', and potential demand which refers to 'those who cannot at present participate and require an improvement in their social and economic circumstances to do so' (Lavery 1974). This book is concerned almost exclusively with effective demand, with the emphasis being on establishing actual patterns of use and demand rather than on predicting future ones.

Characteristically, effective demand is measured in terms of the number of tourists leaving or visiting a country or region, the number of passengers using a certain mode of transport, the number of bed-nights spent in a particular type of accommodation, the number of people using a given recreational facility or taking part in a specific activity such as skiing and so on. Economically, effective demand might also be expressed in dollars spent on a given activity in a particular region or generated by a specific market. None of these variables lends itself very readily to measurement, and data problems continue to beset most areas of tourism analysis. These issues are examined in greater detail with respect to particular topics in later chapters.

Demand for tourism is also expressed in terms of travel propensity. Schmidhauser (1975, 1976) differentiates between two types of travel propensity, net and gross. Net travel propensity refers to the proportion of the total population or a particular group in the population who have made at least one trip away from home in the period in question (usually a year) and is calculated by the following formula:

$$\text{Net travel propensity (as \%)} = \frac{p}{P} \times 100$$

where p = the number of persons in a country or in a particular population group who have made at least one trip away from home in the given period.

P = total population of the country or group.

Gross travel propensity refers to the total number of trips taken in relation to the total population studied and is expressed by the formula:

$$\text{Gross travel propensity (as \%)} = \frac{T_p}{P} \times 100$$

where T_p = total number of trips undertaken by the population in question.

P = total population of the country or group.

Schmidhauser also discusses the concept of travel frequency which refers to the average number of trips taken by a person participating in tourism in a given period according to the formula:

$$\text{Travel frequency} = \frac{T_p}{p} = \frac{\text{gross travel propensity}}{\text{net travel propensity}}$$

where T_p and p have the same meaning as above.

An increase in effective demand may reflect changes in net travel propensity, gross travel propensity or a combination of the two. Where the net travel propensity is low, for example 30%, growth in tourist demand may come largely through an increase in the proportion of the population who attain a standard of living enabling them to take a holiday. Where the net travel propensity is much higher, for example 60 to 70%, an increase in demand may result mainly from existing travellers travelling more frequently, that is, an increase in gross propensity.

Table 2.5 depicts trends in international travel by Australian residents based on data drawn from inflight surveys conducted by Australia's major international air carrier (Leiper 1984b). The table shows the importance of multiple trips, with the 1,259,000 departures in 1982–83 being generated by half that number of individuals who made an average of two trips each during the year. Cross-tabulation by purpose of visit suggests that although multiple tripping is more prevalent among business travellers, it is by no means limited to this segment. As Leiper points out, the distinction between net and gross travel propensities can provide clues as to why changes occur in the total volume of traffic. He notes, for example, that while total departures in 1981–82 increased by 53,000 or 4.4% over the previous year, the net travel propensity and travel frequency figures show there were fewer not more people travelling. Rather, a smaller number of individual travellers making more trips on average than the previous year appear to have constituted the basis for growth. Why this should occur, however, is not apparent.

Leiper also discusses the number and proportion of 'first-time travellers' obtained from the

Table 2.5
International travel by Australian residents (1978–79 to 1982–83)

	1978–79	*1979–80*	*1980–81*	*1981–82*	*1982–83*
Population ('000)	14,516	14,726	14,925	15,134	15,346
Departures ('000)	1,132	1,205	1,195	1,248	1,259
Gross travel propensity	7.80%	8.18%	8.01%	8.25%	8.20%
No of persons travelling ('000)	605	666	695	564	621
Net travel propensity	4.17%	4.52%	4.66%	3.73%	4.05%
Average travel frequency (12 months)	1.87	1.81	1.79	2.21	2.03

Source: Leiper (1984b).

same inflight surveys. This segment accounted for over a third of all Australian departures in the five years to 1978–79 but then declined to account for 15% in 1982–83. Again, no explanation is given for this downward trend but Leiper (p. 79) points out that 'the 15% share demonstrates that the international travel market was not saturated in 1982–83 in any real sense of that word, for new travellers were present in significant proportions'. Data such as those used by Leiper are not, however, widely available and in general little is yet known about the actual number of individuals making up a given tourist flow and the frequency of travel by individuals within any twelve-month period and from year to year.

The evolution of demand

There can be little doubt that tourist demand has increased dramatically in the post-war period, particularly since the 1960s. World Tourism Organization (WTO) figures (which can only be considered estimates for a variety of reasons discussed in more detail in Chapter 3) indicate that international tourist arrivals have more than trebled in the last two decades, passing from 93 million in 1963 to 284 million in 1981 (Fig. 2.3). The increase in the first half of this period was especially significant, with an average annual rate of growth of 11.6% being recorded over the years 1963–72. This figure dropped to 4.8% for 1972–81, with an absolute decrease being recorded in 1974, the only one experienced throughout this whole period. Variations in the rate of growth occurred from country to country, of course. In the period 1975 to 1981, tourist arrivals in many of the more established destinations in Europe and North America increased at a slower rate than individual countries in parts

of the Caribbean, Latin America and the Middle East (WTO 1983).

Domestic tourism in many developed countries also appears to have expanded dramatically over the last two decades, although few good time-series figures are available. France is one country where national tourism surveys have been regularly undertaken for many years. There, the net travel propensity (*taux de départ*) for summer holidays increased from 43.6% in 1964 to 57.2% in 1981, with the total number of people taking holidays increasing from 20 million to 30 million over this same period (CECOD 1983). Trips abroad accounted for 18% of all French holidays in 1981, compared with 12% in 1964.

Many inter-related factors have contributed to this increase in demand. Absolute population growth and rising standards of living which have resulted in more leisure time and greater discretionary spending have greatly boosted the numbers able to travel, both domestically and internationally. At the same time, both the public and private sectors in many parts of the world have actively fostered this demand and encouraged the expansion of the tourist industry. Tourism, particularly in the 1960s, appeared as a source of unlimited growth and came to be regarded by many as the goose that laid the golden egg. In the market areas, many travel agencies and tour operators appeared, stimulating demand to increase their new businesses. The transport industry also extensively promoted tourist travel while technological improvements, at least for a time, brought down the relative cost of travel. At the same time, the public and private sectors in many areas, attracted by the various economic benefits which tourism appeared to offer (jobs, profits, taxes, diversification, regional development etc.) and as yet unaware of associated negative impacts, embarked on extensive

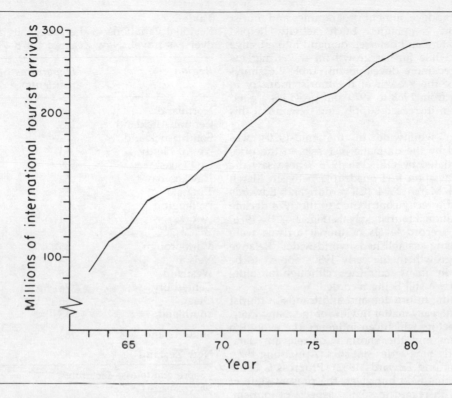

Fig. 2.3 Evolution of international tourist arrivals (1963–81).

Data Source: WTO.

Table 2.6
Evolution of selected aspects of the Australian tourist industry (1968–79)

Sector	Number of firms and organizations	
	1968	*1979*
Retail travel agencies	585	1,557
Foreign tourism organizations	27	43
International on-line airlines	13	23
International tour operators/wholesalers	40	146
International tourists	*1968*	*1979*
Australian departures	252,000	1,132,000
International arrivals	275,800*	793,345

* 1969.

Source: After Leiper (1984b).

31

destination development programmes and tourist promotion campaigns. Such activity helped convert latent and deferred demand into effective demand while further growth in travel markets encouraged more development. Table 2.6 shows aspects of the growth of the tourist industry in Australia from 1968 to 1979 and provides a good example of increased supply and demand at this time.

Growth worldwide in the mid-1970s was tempered by the dramatic increases in the price of oil initiated by OPEC in 1973. These saw the price of aviation fuel quadruple between March 1973 and March 1974 (Cleverdon and Edwards 1982) and directly contributed to the 1974 decline in international tourist arrivals (Fig. 2.4). By 1976, however, record levels of tourist arrivals were again being established world-wide. Relative rates of growth in the early 1980s appear to be slowing in many countries although absolute increases are still being recorded.

Predicting future demand and trends in tourist travel is no easy matter in view of the many inter-related factors which can influence the evolution of tourism and the shortage of relevant data, particularly time-series statistics (Armstrong 1972; Cleverdon and Edwards 1982). Progress is being made in this field but given the present state of the art with regard to spatial aspects of tourism, a better understanding of present and past patterns must precede predictive work.

Intra-national variations in the demand for international travel

For a variety of geographic, demographic and economic reasons, demand for travel abroad or to a particular international destination is unlikely to be generated evenly throughout a country. Studies on variations in international travel from regions within a generating country have been undertaken both in the country of origin and at the destination, although neither are particularly common. The country of origin studies usually attempt to provide some regional measure of the propensity for international travel. Departure cards often require departing nationals to state their home town or state, but even if such information is collected it is often not tabulated or published. Where departures are recorded on a regional basis they can be related to the population of those regions so as to determine the propensity for international travel. Table 2.7, for instance, shows regional variations in the

Table 2.7
Regional variations in the propensity for overseas travel, New Zealand (1978–79)

Region	Departures per 1,000 residents*
Northland	58
Central Auckland	125
South Auckland/ Bay of Plenty	65
East Coast	39
Hawkes Bay	62
Taranaki	55
Wellington	82
North Island	89
Marlborough	55
Nelson	54
Westland	45
Canterbury	76
Otago	56
Southland	48
South Island	64
New Zealand	82

* Short-term tourist departures.
Source: Pearce (1982a).

propensity for overseas travel from within New Zealand expressed in terms of departures per thousand residents. Departure rates are shown to be highest in the regions containing the major metropolitan centres (Central Auckland, Wellington and Canterbury), and lowest in the more rural and isolated regions (East Coast, Westland and Southland). These patterns appear to reflect the location of the international airports (in Auckland, Wellington and Christchurch), the relatively high costs of internal air travel and regional variations in affluence and urbanization (Pearce 1982a).

Information on overseas travel may also be obtained from nation-wide surveys. Table 2.4, for instance, is based on results of the British National Travel Survey. In it the proportion of all British holidays taken abroad are related to the country's adult population to show distinct geographical variations in foreign holiday-taking. In particular, the South East and London generate proportionately more overseas holidays than their population would suggest. This might in part be attributed to the greater accessibility of the South East to the continent.

The destination studies are also usually based either on information obtained from arrival cards or from special surveys. These studies are not so

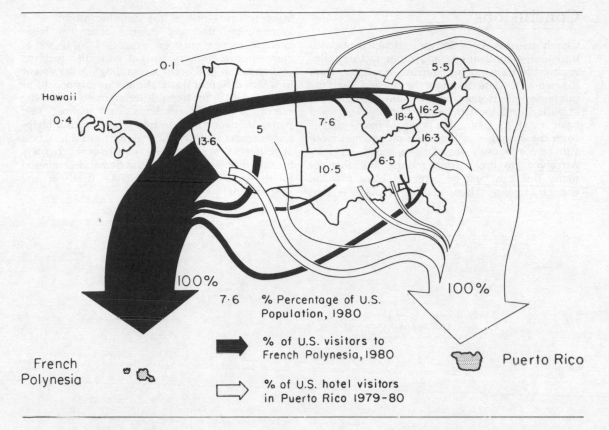

Fig. 2.4 Regional origins of United States visitors to Puerto Rico and French Polynesia.

Data sources: Tourism Company of Puerto Rico and Office de Développement du Tourisme.

much concerned with the total outbound traffic of a given country, as in the two examples given above, but with their share of it. That is to say, the major national flows at a particular destination may be broken down on a regional basis in order to identify markets more precisely for promotional and other purposes. Marked regional biases are found in Fig. 2.4, which depicts the origins of the United States traffic arriving at two tropical destinations, one in the Caribbean (Puerto Rico) and the other in the South Pacific (French Polynesia). Puerto Rico draws heavily on visitors from the east coast, particularly from the Middle Atlantic (44.1%), whereas French Polynesia attracts the majority of its tourists from the Pacific Coast states (57%). These differences in

the regional origins of visitors appear even more significant when compared to the distribution of the United States population. However, it should be borne in mind that in absolute terms the United States traffic to Puerto Rico (359,800 hotel visitors in 1979–80) is much greater than that to French Polynesia (41,200 arrivals in 1980). This means in effect that the actual number of Pacific Coast visitors is greater to Puerto Rico (35,000) than to French Polynesia (24,000) even though the relative share of the Pacific Coast states is far higher in the latter case (57% cf. 9.8%). It may be that one set of factors determines the size of the national tourist traffic to a given international destination while another influences the regional composition of that traffic.

Conclusions

Clearly there is scope for more detailed research into tourist motivations and other factors influencing the demand for tourism. However, from the work to date it might be argued that the interaction between origins and destinations implicit in all tourism arises primarily out of a basic need to leave the origin. What emerges from these studies is that the fundamental motivation for tourist travel is a need, real or perceived, to break from routine and that for many this can best be achieved by a physical change of place. Thus, 'change of place' is seen to be not just one of the defining attributes of tourism, but the very essence of it. The basic need to escape may be expressed in terms of more specific motives so that particular patterns of interaction will occur depending on the extent to which different destinations can respond to or appear to cater for these different motives and the extent to which residents can realize their particular needs and desires. The next four chapters examine in detail these patterns of interaction at different scales while subsequent chapters include discussion of how the demand generated in the market areas manifests itself in the destinations.

3

Patterns of international tourism

International tourism can be considered at a range of different scales. Broad global patterns are established first in this chapter and then more specific tourist flows are analysed. Attention focuses in turn on intra-regional travel, circuit tourism, demographic variations in international travel and the evolution of international tourist flows. Conclusions are then drawn in which the patterns identified are discussed in relation to the models outlined in Chapter 1. At all scales, however, analysis is limited and complicated by the paucity of appropriate data. Major data sources are therefore reviewed at the outset with more specific types of statistics and material being considered in later sections.

Data sources

It is important to recall that what constitutes international tourism is movement across international frontiers while domestic tourism concerns travel within national boundaries. This distinction may be especially significant at a national level, for example in terms of foreign exchange earnings, social impact and immigration control. Clearly too, the fact of being in a foreign country may add something to the appeal of the trip for the individuals concerned, with the differences in culture, customs and so on being a major attraction for many tourists, especially the wanderlust travellers. In such cases, international tourism

constitutes a particular form of tourism and the distinction made by official statistics between international and domestic tourists is an especially useful one. In other instances, as with much sunlust tourism, the reason for and nature of the holiday may be essentially the same whether it involves a German travelling to the Mediterranean coast of France (international tourism) or a New Yorker holidaying in Florida (domestic tourism). Greater distances will in fact be covered by many domestic vacationers in the United States and other large countries such as Canada and Australia than international travellers in Europe. With this type of tourism, the distinction between domestic and international tourist flows is perhaps more official than functional.

The most comprehensive body of international tourism statistics readily available is that published annually by the World Tourism Organization (WTO) in their series World Tourism Statistics. Other international organizations such as the Pacific Area Travel Association (PATA) and the Organization for Economic Co-operation and Development (OECD) also collate and publish statistics concerning tourism in their member countries. In their series the WTO, an intergovernmental organization, compiles and distributes travel statistics furnished by members and some non-member states. While the WTO provides technical guidelines for the collection of these statistics in an attempt to provide internationally uniform and accurate figures (WTO

1978, 1981), it remains dependent on the respective national tourist organizations, immigration or statistics departments for the nature and quality of the data received. These bodies collect travel data in a variety of ways and for a range of purposes. Consequently the type of information and its reliability varies considerably from country to country. Researchers must therefore view the published data carefully, particularly when making comparisons among countries.

Travel statistics world-wide are most frequently expressed in terms of 'frontier arrivals', that is the number of visitors entering a country as determined by some form of frontier check and irrespective of purpose of visit and length of stay; excursionists, that is visitors staying less than 24 hours, are usually included. 'Tourist arrivals', on the other hand, refer to visitors staying at least this minimum length of time. Where the majority of arrivals are by air through a limited number of points of entry, as is the case for example in island states such as Japan, Australia and New Zealand, then the degree of control is usually very high and most related statistics can normally be considered reliable. Where immigration procedures require the completion of an arrival/departure (A/D) card, a range of information is usually obtained including, for example, details on nationality, age, occupation, purpose of visit (however defined) and intended length of stay. In other instances, where there is a large volume of traffic arriving overland through a number of entry points, as is the case in much of Europe, the degree of control is much less and some form of estimate may be used. Not all countries require the completion of an A/D card and, in these cases, periodic surveys may be employed to provide additional information.

A second common source of international travel statistics is that based on accommodation returns. Many countries require international visitors to complete registration cards in hotels and other forms of accommodation, which are then collated and analysed. A number of problems arise here, not the least of which is that the cards are often associated with some form of taxation so that a degree of underestimation might be expected. Conversely, visitors moving around the country would be recorded more than once, thus inflating the figures. Visitors not staying in any form of commercial accommodation would not be recorded at all.

Some of the problems which arise in trying to compare data from different sources can be seen in Table 3.1, which provides some basic data on tourism in Spain. Significant differences occur in the major sources of tourists depending on whether 'frontier arrivals', or 'nights in hotels' are used. The neighbouring countries of France and Portugal constitute half of all 'frontier arrivals', but their numbers are generally considered to be swelled by day-tripping tourists, or travellers passing through Spain from one country to the other, perhaps without an overnight stop. When only hotel nights are considered, the United Kingdom sees its importance increase and West Germany becomes the major source. The significance of the French is considerably reduced on this measure as a larger proportion of French tourists tend to use other forms of accommodation, particularly camping.

The aggregation of the Benelux countries in Table 3.1 is symptomatic of another common problem which affects geographic analyses in particular, that is the combination of various nationalities in the published statistics. The

Table 3.1
Spain: main sources of tourists (1979)

	Country	*Number*	*%*
Visitor arrivals			
Total		36,965,647	
1	France	10,741,682	29
2	Portugal	8,781,176	24
3	United Kingdom	3,427,455	9
Hotel nights			
Total		70,492,951	
1	W. Germany	22,002,050	31
2	United Kingdom	21,054,211	30
3	Benelux	6,279,213	9

Data source: WTO.

degree of aggregation usually depends on their importance at a given destination. In most European countries, other countries from within Europe are listed separately; in more distant destinations, such as much of the Pacific, they are commonly listed together under 'Europe'. Conversely, New Zealanders and Australians, who constitute major markets in the Pacific, appear separately in Pacific statistics but are frequently lumped under 'the rest of the world' as far as many European statistics are concerned. This clearly limits wide-ranging and detailed international analyses. The varying use of 'country of residence' and 'nationality' further complicates geographical and marketing analyses.

The WTO statistics do not usually take into account purpose of visit as all foreigners are usually recorded under 'frontier arrivals' and no distinctions are made in the accommodation figures. International comparisons are therefore limited essentially to studies of 'all travellers'. The originating national body, however, usually does provide some breakdown, for instance into 'holiday and vacation', 'business', 'visiting friends and relations (VFR)', 'education', 'sport' and so on. A more detailed study by the WTO of variations in purpose of visit by major regions in 1979 showed vacation travel accounted for almost three-quarters of all international movements (Table 3.2). Only in the Middle East, where a large pilgrimage traffic is included in the 'other' category and where business traffic is more significant, do holiday-makers account for less than a half of all visits. The composition of visitors to particular countries within these regions may, of course, vary significantly from the regional average. Where possible, differences in the spatial behaviour of particular types of visitors should be taken into account.

Consideration must also be given to what it is that is being measured. Absolute numbers of travellers, even if they can be classified by purpose of visit, do not tell the whole story. Length of stay, for example, is a decisive factor in determining the impact of any one market on a particular destination. McIntyre (1983), for example, has shown that three-quarters of the visitor days in Fiji in 1981 were generated by less than half the arrivals (those staying eight days or more). Throughout the South Pacific, intra-regional travellers tend to stay longer than visitors from further afield so that their contribution to the total number of visitor days spent within the region would be greater than their 45% of all arrivals would initially suggest (Pearce 1983a). Certain groups of tourists also spend more money than others. Increases in total tourist traffic are often the result of destinations becoming accessible to tourists of more modest means. Consequently, as the number of visitors increases, their average expenditure may decrease. These various factors are inter-related. Per diem expenditure, for example, may decline with increasing length of stay so that the overall impact of high-spending short-stay visitors may be comparable to or greater than tourists spending more time but less money per day. Nevertheless, visitor numbers do provide a first approximation of the structure of international tourism at a global scale.

Global patterns of international tourism

Tables 3.3 and 3.4 provide a useful starting point for trying to order international tourist flows throughout the world. These tables portray the major generating and receiving countries as

Table 3.2
Regional variations in purpose of visit (1979)

WTO region	*Purpose of visit (regional averages)*		
	Holidays (%)	*Business (%)*	*Other (%)*
Africa	63	20	17
Americas	76	12	12
East Asia and the Pacific	71	12	17
Europe	68	13	19
Middle East	45	25	30
South Asia	73	14	13
World	71	13	16

Source: WTO (1983a).

Table 3.3
Top 10 tourist-generating countries (4-year average 1973–76)

Generating Country	Global total (millions)	Main destinations						Concentration ratio (%)
		1 Country	(%)	2 Country	(%)	3 Country	(%)	
W. Germany	38.9	Denmark[1]	32.8	Austria[4]	18.8	Spain[1]	9.8	61.4
USA	29.5	Canada[2]	42.7	Mexico[2]	9.5	Italy[4]	6.0	58.2
France	18	Spain[1]	55.4	Belgium[5]	6.0	UK[3]	5.5	66.8
UK	12.2	Spain[1]	27.8	France[6]	12.1	Belgium[5]	9.9	49.8
Canada	11.7	USA[1]	82.5	UK[3]	3.9	France[6]	1.8	87.9
Netherlands	8.9	Belgium[5]	21.8	France[6]	14.7	Germany[2]	14.0	50.5
Belgium	5.3	France[6]*	33.9	Spain[1]	18.9	UK[3]	9.1	61.9
Italy	5.2	France[6]	26.8	Yugoslavia[6]	10.4	Switzerland[6]	8.6	45.8
Japan	3.7	USA[2]	19.8	Hong Kong[1]	11.7	Korea[1]	11.2	42.7
Switzerland	3.6	Italy[6]	17.3	Spain[1]	16.7	France[6]	15.5	49.5

[1] Visitor arrivals at frontiers.
[2] Tourist arrivals at frontiers.
[3] Visitor departures at frontiers.
[4] Tourist arrivals in all means of accommodation.
[5] Tourist nights in all means of accommodation.
[6] Tourist arrivals in hotels.
* Belgium and Luxembourg.

Data source: WTO.

Table 3.4
Top 10 tourist-receiving countries (1982)

Receiving Country	Arrivals (millions)	Origin						Concentration ratio (%)
		1 Country	(%)	2 Country	(%)	3 Country	(%)	
Italy[1]	48.3	W. Germany	21.5	Switzerland	21.3	France	17.5	60.3
Spain[1]	42	France	25.9	Portugal	22	UK	11.6	59.5
France[2]	33.2	W. Germany	24.8	Belgium	17.5	UK	14.5	56.8
USA[2]	22	Canada	47.6	Mexico	11.9	Japan	6.6	66.1
Austria[3]	14.2	W. Germany	59.2	Netherlands	8.9	UK	4.6	72.7
Canada[2]	12.2	USA	85.9	UK	3.5	W. Germany	1.5	90.0
UK[1]	11.6	USA	14.8	France	13	W. Germany	12.4	40.2
W. Germany[3]	9.4	Netherlands	16.6	USA	15.3	UK	10.1	42
Switzerland[3]	9.2	W. Germany	33.3	USA	11.8	France	8.4	53.5
Romania[1]	5.9	Hungary	19.3	Yugoslavia	19	Czechoslovakia	12.8	51.1

[1] Visitor arrivals at frontiers.
[2] Tourist arrivals at frontiers.
[3] Tourist arrivals in all forms of accommodation.

Data source: WTO.

determined from WTO figures. Some of the problems noted above soon become apparent in establishing even these most basic tables. The total number of tourists generated by each country shown in Table 3.3 has been calculated using a variety of different measures and the absolute values shown should be viewed with some caution. Top-ranking West Germany, for instance, owes its position in part to the large number of frontier arrivals recorded in neighbouring Denmark. Many of these represent German excursionists making day trips to Denmark's North Sea beaches. Excursionists are excluded in the case of United States visitors to Canada and Mexico as the figures used in these cases are 'tourist arrivals'. Moreover, many North American movements of a length comparable to those to Denmark's beaches, for instance day trips by New Yorkers to the beaches of New Jersey, are not recorded here as they are, by definition, 'domestic'. Likewise, Table 3.4 cannot be considered a definitive ranking of the top ten receiving countries given the range of measures used. The recorded volume of international tourism in Italy and Spain, if not the relative position of these two countries, has clearly been influenced by the unit of measurement used, visitor arrivals at frontiers. Conversely, other countries such as West Germany and Switzerland whose positions have been determined on the basis of arrivals in accommodation may be disadvantaged in terms of their ranking.

Despite these limitations, two main points emerge from these tables. Firstly, international tourism, both in terms of generating and receiving countries, is concentrated in the developed countries of Europe and North America. WTO figures suggest that South America, Asia, Africa and Oceania account for less than 20% of the world's international tourist traffic. Secondly, international tourism, at least in the main regions, is intra-regional in nature. European countries constitute the main markets and destinations for other European countries and the

tourist traffic in North America is dominated by exchanges between the USA and Canada.

International markets and destinations might also be viewed in relative not just absolute terms. Hudman (1979, 1980) proposes the use of a country potential generation index (CPGI) to assess the relative capability of a country to generate trips. The index is calculated in the following manner. Firstly, the number of trips generated by a particular country is divided by the total number of trips taken throughout the world. Secondly, the country's population is divided by the population of the world. The third step involves dividing the quotient of the first step by the quotient of the second step according to the following formula:

$$CPGI = \frac{N_C/N_W}{P_C/P_W}$$

where N_C = number of trips generated by the country

N_W = number of trips generated in the world

P_C = population of the country

P_W = population of the world

An index of 1.0 indicates an average generation capacity while values greater or lesser than unity show a country is generating respectively more or fewer trips than its population would suggest.

Hudman (1979) then calculates the CPGI for a range of countries using data published in the 1975 *UN Statistical Yearbook* (Table 3.5). These data

Table 3.5
Country potential generation index for selected countries (1974)

Rank	Country	CPGI	Rank	Country	CPGI
1	W. Germany	11.9	16	UK	5.0
2	E. Germany	11.7	17	Jordan	4.0
3	Switzerland	10.1	18	Finland	3.8
4	Netherlands	9.7	19	Syria	3.2
5	Canada	8.0	20	Sweden	3.0
6	Luxembourg	8.0	21	Singapore	3.0
7	Portugal	7.6	22	Australia	2.6
8	Denmark	7.4	23	Kuwait	2.5
9	Belgium	7.2	24	Yugoslavia	2.3
10	Austria	6.5	25	USA	2.1
11	Czechoslovakia	6.1	26	Italy	1.9
12	Hungary	5.9	27	Bulgaria	1.9
13	Poland	5.7	28	New Zealand	1.9
14	Ireland	5.4	29	Spain	1.4
15	France	5.2	30	Norway	1.3

Source: After Hudman (1979).

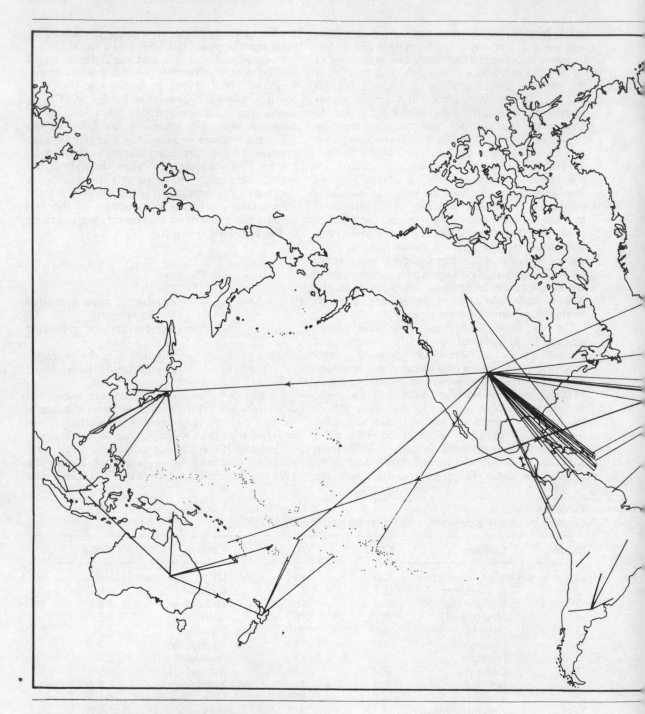

Fig. 3.1 First-order international tourist flows (1979).

Data source: WTO.

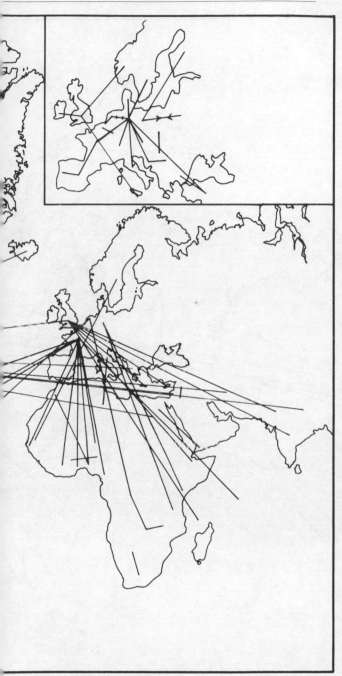

are subject to the same limitations discussed earlier with reference to Table 3.3 and the resultant values must be viewed with some caution. Nevertheless, some interesting points emerge. In particular, the top two ranking countries in absolute values shown in Table 3.3 are now widely separated. West Germany still ranks number one but the United States (25) generates far fewer international trips than its population would suggest. France and the United Kingdom also drop markedly on this measure while some of the other smaller West European countries such as Switzerland, Luxembourg and Denmark produce more visitors than might be expected. Few countries outside of Europe and North America appear in the first thirty countries having a CPGI greater than unity.

Hudman attributes the relative importance of these various countries as generators of international visitors to three main factors: wealth, size and access. The wealth of the developed, industrialized nations accounts for the prominence of European and North American countries in Table 3.5. Size and access appear to explain some of the variation within this group. As Hudman notes, the small size of several of the countries ranking highly in Table 3.5 limits the potential for domestic tourism and allows greater access to other nearby counties. The reverse is true of the United States and, to a lesser extent, of France. A surprising omission from this list is Japan, which has a CPGI of only 0.5. Hudman attributes this low ranking in terms of Japan's large population, its relative isolation and diversity of attractions within Japan.

International tourist flows

Tables 3.3 and 3.4 have identified the major international markets and destinations in the world. A next step is to establish global patterns of flows between generating and receiving countries. At a very broad scale, Hoivik and Heiberg (1980) have expressed these flows in centre–periphery terms. They estimate that in 1981, four-fifths of all international tourism was between centre countries (that is, countries of Europe, North America and Japan) and one-twentieth between periphery countries (the rest of the world). Centre–periphery movements accounted for a further one-twentieth with the remaining tenth going from the periphery to the centre.

At a more detailed level, dominant flows to each country might be identified. Figures 3.1 and 3.2 portray first- and second-order flows (that is, the largest and second largest flows) towards each of the 122 destinations for which appropriate

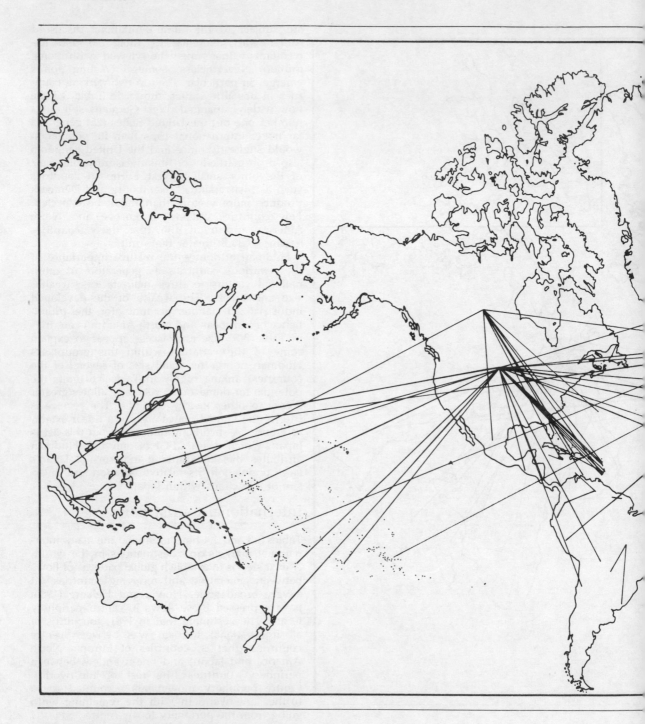

Fig. 3.2 Second-order international tourist flows
(1979).

Data source: WTO.

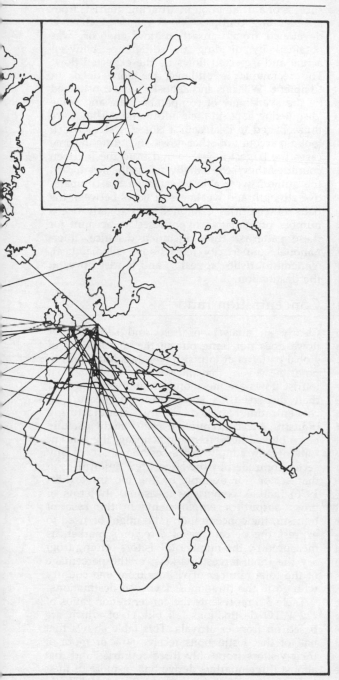

data are available from the WTO for 1979. On this basis, United States visitors are the most dominant group, constituting the major market and generating first-order flows for 32 destinations, or a quarter of those portrayed, while ranking second at a further 22 destinations. Together, the three main European countries – West Germany (12, 12), France (15, 6) and the United Kingdom (7, 13) – generate a comparable number of first- and second-order flows.

The spatial patterns portrayed in Figs 3.1 and 3.2 largely confirm the intra-regional nature of much international tourist traffic. Two-thirds of the destinations where United States visitors are dominant are found in the Americas. The inclusion here of a number of small Caribbean states clearly affects the overall importance of the United States on this measure. Canadians constitute the second largest market after Americans in much of the Caribbean. At the same time, United States visitors generate first-order flows to a wide range of other destinations such as the United Kingdom, Japan, Egypt, Greece and Iran. United States visitors are also seen to play a major role in the Pacific, taking second place in many destinations there to the main South Pacific markets of Australia and New Zealand.

The German traffic too is largely intra-regional, with Germans constituting the largest or second largest market for most West European countries. The volume of many of these flows is much larger in absolute numbers than that of the Americans to the Caribbean. This in part explains the difference in ranking of the two countries in Table 3.3 and Fig. 3.1. Moreover, given the smaller size and continental location of European countries, international travel is easier for Germans than many North Americans. German holiday-makers travelling a thousand or more kilometres could cross a number of international frontiers whereas United States vacationers going the same distance would often remain within national boundaries. However, the selective development of German charter tourism to countries such as Sri Lanka, Kenya and Tanzania has meant that Germans have become the major market for certain more distant destinations as well.

Outside of Europe, the French influence is most apparent in former French West Africa. The influence of formal colonial ties is also seen in many of the cases where the British generate first- and second-order flows and in other specific instances, for example the Dutch to Surinam, Belgians to Zaire and Italians to Libya. It is probable that travellers other than vacationers make up a large proportion of these flows.

The major Japanese flows are again intra-regional, with Japanese visitors constituting the main markets for neighbouring Far Eastern destinations. Likewise, Argentina is the main market for four of the five countries with which it shares its borders. Virtually all other first-order flows are between pairs of neighbouring countries, for example Spain and Portugal, Ecuador and Colombia, Nigeria and Ghana. An interesting exception to this general pattern is the Swedish flow to the Gambia, a further example of selective charter tourism (Holm-Petersen 1978).

The overall impression to emerge from this brief examination of first- and second-order flows is thus one of comparatively short movement between countries in the same region of the globe. Distance clearly plays a major role in shaping international tourist flows. On top of this general pattern are super-imposed some more selective longer-haul flows, particularly from the United States with its large and relatively affluent population. Africa stands out as a continent less frequented by American visitors but one where flows are influenced by former colonial ties and selective charter tourism from Western Europe.

Earlier but less comprehensive studies have identified similar patterns and factors. Guthrie (1961), in an analysis of fifty-eight countries, found that variations in tourist-generated revenue between countries were influenced by: (1) the location of a tourist-receiving country relative to tourist-generating countries (particularly to North America and Western Europe); (2) the level of average income in neighbouring countries (travel between the United States and Canada will be greater than between Portugal and Spain); and (3) the amount of emigration from the tourist-receiving country (basically the VFR market). Almost half of the relative variation in tourist revenue was attributed to the advantages or disadvantages of location, closeness being measured by cost of transportation (one-way minimum available air fare). In an attempt to assess the importance of other essentially qualitative factors whose existence he recognized (for example, scenery and cultural characteristics), Guthrie derived an index of deviations from observed revenues of estimates based on location, exports and emigration. He suggested this index could be interpreted as a measure of subjective preferences by tourists for the particular set of qualitative characteristics offered by various countries. Although he was able to indicate preferred countries (USA, Mexico, Canada, UK), the exercise did little to clarify the nature of the attractions.

A similar approach was later adopted by Williams and Zelinsky (1970) who derived a relative acceptance (RA) index to measure the relative success of a destination in attracting tourists from a generating country. The RA index, which is developed from transaction flow analysis, was obtained by dividing the difference between actual and expected flows by the expected flow. The technique is outlined in more detail in Chapter 6. Williams and Zelinsky were constrained by the availability of comparable data and some 'disquieting gaps' in their information. They were thus obliged to deal with a closed system which took no account of other flows, including in some cases the largest flows, to and from the fourteen countries they selected. By using the RA index, the authors were able to establish the comparative strength and weakness of flows between the pairs of countries examined and to advance a number of 'tentative hypotheses' to account for these patterns. These included distance, international connectivity (e.g. trade, colonial ties), 'general touristic "appeal"', and tourist prices at the destination.

Concentration ratio

Clearly an analysis of first- and second-order flows does not bring out all the complexities of global patterns of tourist travel. It is important to note, however, that market-wise international tourist flows are more often highly concentrated than dispersed. A straightforward measure of concentration applied in the manufacturing industry, the concentration ratio, might usefully be employed here. In manufacturing, the concentration ratio simply expresses the share of any sector controlled by the largest few enterprises in that sector, for example by the top three (Ellis 1976), and is commonly measured in terms of gross output or employment. In the case of tourism, the concentration ratio might be used to express the percentage of a region's market, as measured by the number of visitors coming from say the three largest markets, or the percentage of the total number of visitors from one country who go to the three most favoured destinations.

Table 3.6 represents the concentration ratios of 122 WTO destinations, all but 11 of which are based on frontier arrivals. This table shows that half of the destinations receive 60% or more of their visitors from only three countries and that almost three-quarters derive half or more of their traffic from only three markets. Bermuda (97.4%) and the Bahamas (96.3%) recorded the most concentrated traffic. Moreover, an overwhelming share of their traffic comes from one country alone, the United States, which contributes respectively 96.8% and 75.4% of the visitors. Other Caribbean destinations also record very

Table 3.6
Concentration ratios of visitors to 122 destinations (1979)

Bermuda	97.4	El Salvador	68.8	Iceland	51.4
Bahamas	96.3	New Caledonia	68.8	Yugoslavia	51
Uruguay	93.5	*Barbados	67.2	Netherlands[aa]	50.8
*San Marino	93.4	Chile	67.1	Japan	50.5
Cayman Is.	92.9	Fr. Polynesia	67.1		
Brunei	92.4	Norway	66.5	Belize	49.9
Canada	91.4	W. Samoa	65.9	Israel	48.8
Botswana	90.1	Costa Rica	65.6	Ivory Coast	48.4
		E. Germany	65.5	Romania	47.3
Aruba	89.6	Czechoslovakia	64.9	Hong Kong	46
Jamaica	89.1	Mauritius	64.4	Seychelles	45.6
Br. Virgin Is.	88	Tonga	64.3	Sweden	45.4
Mexico	87.4	*Malawi	63.7	Singapore	44.6
*Hawaii	86.3	Luxembourg[aa]	63.2	W. Germany[aa]	44.4
Guam	85.9	*Algeria	62.7	Sri Lanka	43.8
Dominican Rep.	83.9	Spain	62	*[1]Ghana	41.1
[1]Surinam	82.2	Denmark	61.7	*Zambia	41.2
Ireland	82	Australia	61.5	Kenya	40.7
*Guadeloupe[ah]	81.1	*[1]Philippines	61.1		
Poland	80.5	Portugal	60.9	*Bolivia	37.9
Colombia	80.1	*Venezuela	60.7	[3]Grenada	37.2
Paraguay	80	Guatemala	60.1	UK	37.1
				[3]Bonaire	36.8
Portugal	79.5	Belgium[na]	59.5	Thailand	36.6
[1]Cook Is.	78.8	Malaysia	59.2	Peru	35.9
Malta	78.7	Bulgaria	58.8	Egypt	35
Taiwan	77.3	Jordan	57.4	Indonesia	33.5
*Gambia	77.1	Tunisia	57.1	Togo[aa]	33.2
Fiji	76.8	Morocco	56.8	Greece	33.1
Puerto Rico	76.2	Ecuador	56.1	Pakistan	32.2
Antigua	75.6	Cyprus	56	India	32.1
S. Korea	75.6	Switzerland[aa]	55.6	Turkey	31
Austria[aa]	74.6	Senegal[aa]	55.6	*Iran	30.4
*Haiti	72.3	Panama	55	Nepal	30.1
New Zealand	72.3	Niger	54.6		
*Vanuatu	72.2	Afghanistan	54.3	[4]Cameroon	28.6
Papua New Guinea	70.4	Italy	53.9	[4]Tanzania	28.5
Syria	70.1	Brazil	53.7	[1]Libya	28
USA	70.1	Zaire	52.9	Yemen	26.9
		Monserrat	52.9	[4]Benin	24.4
Comores	69.1	[2]Finland	52.6	*St Vincent	23
Macau	69	*Iraq	51.8	Dominica	21.6
				Ethiopia	16.8

* 1978.

[aa] Arrivals in all forms of accommodation.
[ah] Arrivals in hotels.
[na] Nights in all forms of accommodation.
[nh] Nights in hotels.

[1] Excluding nationals resident abroad.
[2] Arrivals from non-Nordic countries only.
[3] Top 3 countries only – insufficient breakdown of data.
[4] African countries not specified.

Data source: WTO.

high concentration ratios and exhibit the same dependence on the United States market. Other very high ranking destinations – San Marino, Brunei and Botswana – might be classified as 'special cases' which are surrounded by their major market.

A few Caribbean destinations less favoured by Americans, such as Grenada, Bonaire and St Vincent, are found towards the other end of the scale. However, the relative ranking of these is also due to the way some of the statistics are recorded, with countries of the Caribbean region, which together constitute an important market, not being listed separately and thus not included in the calculation of the top three individual markets. This is also the case with a few low ranking African countries such as Cameroon and Tanzania where all African visitors are classified together.

The low concentration ratios of other African countries, e.g. Benin and Ethiopia, appear to reflect their small volume of visitors, the majority of whom are probably not vacationers. Overall, however, there is no statistical correlation between the concentration ratio and volume of visitors. Indeed, with the exception of the generally high ranking Caribbean countries, no regional or other groupings emerge very clearly from this table.

Derivation of accurate concentration ratios for a wide range of generating countries is limited by difficulties discussed earlier, particularly in relation to Table 3.3. This table does show, however, that the outgoing flows from the main generating countries are again fairly highly concentrated.

Intra-regional travel

Analysis of first- and second-order flows has shown that traffic to and from countries within the same region of the globe constitutes an important component of international tourism. The importance of intra-regional tourism will vary depending on the scale of the region considered and the mix of generating and receiving countries it contains. Table 3.7 shows that intra-regional travel is relatively more important in developed regions which generate a large share of the world's total demand for international travel, notably Europe and the Americas. Conversely, the less developed regions of Africa and South Asia depend heavily on inter-regional flows, generating only a quarter of their total traffic themselves. East Asia and the Pacific, along with the Middle East, constitute intermediate cases where the intra- and inter-regional flows are more

Table 3.7
Regional variations in intra-regional tourism (1967–81)

WTO region	Market share of intra-regional tourism		
	1967 (%)	1977 (%)	1981 (%)
Europe	85	86	84
Americas	94	82	75
East Asia and the Pacific	45	63	56
Middle East	68	49	42
South Asia	20	20	24
Africa	16	23	24

Source: WTO (1983a), Table VIII.

balanced. Over the fifteen-year period shown, Europe's market has remained very stable. At the other extreme, Africa and South Asia saw their intra-regional market share increase as the economies of these regions developed. The changes in East Asia and the Pacific are attributed by the WTO (1983a) to a combination of economic development within the region and 'efficient tourism advertising and marketing'. The WTO sees further potential for growth in intra-regional tourism in those regions currently dependent on inter-regional movement as standards of living increase.

The importance of intra-regional tourism, however, is likely to vary from country to country within any given region as well as from one region to another. This section examines more closely the nature and structure of intra-regional travel in the South Pacific (Pearce 1983a). PATA figures shows that in 1981 just under 2 million visitor arrivals were recorded in the South Pacific, of which 45% were generated from within the region itself. This relatively low share (cf. Table 3.7) might be attributed essentially to the low generating potential of South Pacific countries other than Australia and New Zealand.

Considerable variation exists among the twelve South Pacific destinations analysed in terms of the importance of the intra-regional traffic and its composition. In 1981, three destinations – Vanuatu, the Solomons and the Cook Islands – drew over three-quarters of their arrivals from within the region. At the other end of the scale, less than a fifth of the visitors to French Polynesia and just over a third of those to Australia resided within the South Pacific. As Fig. 3.3 shows, there is an inverse relationship between the percentage

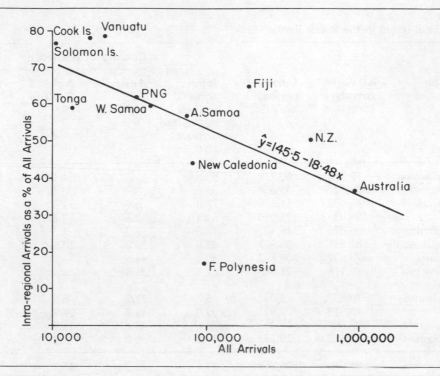

Fig. 3.3 Intra-regional tourism in the South
Pacific (1981).

Source: Pearce (1983a).

of intra-regional arrivals and the total number of arrivals at each destination ($R = 0.6169$). In general, the proportion of intra-regional arrivals decreases as the total traffic to each destination increases. In other words, the small destinations (in terms of visitor arrivals) depend heavily on South Pacific travellers while the large destinations draw proportionately more of their visitors from markets outside the region. A marked exception to this general tendency is French Polynesia, which attracts a much larger proportion of extra-regional visitors than its total traffic would suggest. This appears to be due largely to its French colonial status and its ability to attract North American tourists (see Fig. 2.3).

The composition of the intra-regional traffic also varies significantly from destination to destination (Table 3.8). Australia and New Zealand each generate 18% of the total tourist traffic within the region but Australians constitute the largest market at a greater number of destinations than New Zealanders. This is in large part due to the imbalance in the trans-Tasman traffic, with more

New Zealand arrivals being recorded in Australia (284,372) than Australians arriving in New Zealand (216,621). For a variety of historic and geographic reasons, Australians are particularly dominant in Melanesia (PNG, Vanuatu, the Solomons, Fiji and to a lesser extent New Caledonia) as well as in New Zealand. Other than in Australia, New Zealand residents are particularly important in the Cook Islands and, to a lesser degree, Tonga. The 'New Zealand' share in the latter two cases is boosted by a significant number of expatriates returning home to visit friends and relations. The 'Other Pacific' flow is especially important between the two Samoas and, to a lesser extent, in the Solomons and Vanuatu which receive a significant number of arrivals from Papua New Guinea and New Caledonia respectively. It is also interesting to note that although Australia and New Zealand contributed equally to the region's total arrivals in 1981, South Pacific departures represented about two-thirds of New Zealand's outbound traffic but only about a third of Australia's.

Table 3.8
Intra-regional travel in the South Pacific (1981)

| Destination | All visitor arrivals | Intra-regional arrivals | Intra-regional arrivals / All visitor arrivals (%) | Country of residence | | |
				Australia (%)	New Zealand (%)	Other Pacific (%)
American Samoa*	72,558	50,719	56.6	1.4	4.1	51.1
Australia	936,727	335,664	35.8	—	30.4	5.4
Cook Islands	18,638	14,356	77.0	6.0	54.9	16.1
Fiji	189,935	123,019	64.8	42.6	17.1	5.1
French Polynesia	96,826	16,451	17.0	9.2	3.7	4.1
New Caledonia	81,588	35,801	43.8	26.2	10.5	7.1
New Zealand	478,037	239,162	50.0	44.9	—	5.1
Papua New Guinea	35,116	21,693	61.8	51.4	6.4	4.0
Solomon Islands	10,937	8,392	76.7	37.2	8.6	30.9
Tonga	13,519	7,973	59.0	14.5	27.7	16.8
Vanuatu	22,091	17,365	78.6	43.6	11.9	23.1
Western Samoa	42,608	25,273	59.2	5.0	21.2	37.0
All destinations	1,998,580	895,868	44.8	18.2	18.1	8.5

* American Samoa figures are by nationality, not country of residence. Nationals from American Samoa are not included in the table.

Source: Pearce (1983a).

Circuit tourism

Few data are collected on a systematic basis showing the extent to which international tourists engage in circuit tourism involving visits to more than one country. Most countries record visitor arrivals in isolation and take account only of the part of any trip spent within their frontiers. Likewise, information on departing nationals is usually recorded only in terms of a single 'main destination'. Some A/D cards require both port of embarkation and port of disembarkation but little attempt is made is made to cross-tabulate these to provide information on a given country's place in a larger itinerary (French Polynesia is an exception here, see Ch. 5). The information that is available on circuit tourism frequently comes from more extensive visitor surveys, undertaken on either a regular or ad hoc basis.

Typical of these is a recent New Caledonia survey which included a question of whether New Caledonia was 'your only destination' or 'a stopover in a tour' (OTTN-C 1983). For the vast

majority of visitors, particularly for Australians (87%) and New Zealanders (92%), New Caledonia was their sole destination. The Australian international visitor survey goes further by asking respondents to name those places where they had made a stopover of one or more nights en route to or from Australia. This survey showed that in 1979–80 about a third of all visitors had a stopover on their way to Australia, and a third on leaving the country, with significant variations occurring by nationality and purpose of visit (ATC 1980). In the case of Singapore, a stopover is determined on the basis of length of stay, with visits of at least 24 hours and a maximum of four days being considered a stopover. Respondents staying less than 24 hours were deemed to be in transit while those staying more than four days were presumed not to be on stopover visits. On this basis, about a quarter of all respondents in 1979 were making a stopover visit, with this proportion being higher among respondents from Great Britain and Oceania (Singapore Tourist Promotion Board 1980).

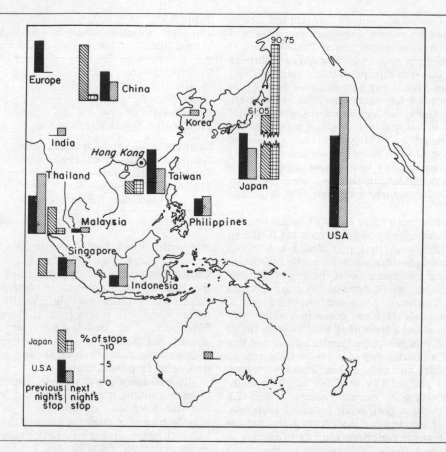

Fig. 3.4 United States and Japanese travel to and from Hong Kong (1982).

Data source: Hong Kong Tourist Association.

The Hong Kong visitor survey provides a good example of the type of detailed data on circuit travel which might be collected by such a survey. Among the questions posed are ones relating to the country in which nights were spent immediately before and after the visit to Hong Kong. Some 60% of American visitors had spent the night prior to arriving in Hong Kong elsewhere within Asia and 60% also intended spending the night following departure in the region (Fig. 3.4). Most of the remainder had either come from North America (26%) or were returning to North America (38%). The majority of the Japanese, on the other hand, spent the night before and after visiting Hong Kong in Japan, respectively 61% and 91%, with virtually all of the remainder

spending those nights elsewhere in Asia. Other information from the survey also confirms Hong Kong's position, at least for non-Japanese travellers, as a stopover on an Asian tour. Visitors to Hong Kong in 1982 had visited an average of 3.68 ports of call, ranging from six in the case of Canadians to two for the Japanese. Although not yet analysed in terms of overall itinerary, the ports of call data appear to lend themselves to such analysis. Overall, visitors spent an average of 3.6 nights in Hong Kong, but this represented less than a fifth of their total trip.

In addition to these destination surveys, studies on circuit tourism have been undertaken in generating countries, notably in the United States. O'Hagan (1979) reports on a US Department of Commerce survey on United States tourist flows to sixteen European countries and analyses trends over the period 1967–77. Circuit tourism does not appear to be a major feature of American travel to Europe as the average number of countries visited per trip declined from 3.9 in 1967 to only 1.9 ten years later. Given these are average figures, a significant number would appear to be visiting just a single country. The data presented by O'Hagan do not enable the combination of visits to be known but the United Kingdom remains the single most popular destination for Americans in Europe, being visited by 43% in 1977 compared to nearly 50% a decade earlier.

A more comprehensive study of circuit tourism in Central America by SRI International (Cullinan et al. 1977) found that just under half of all United States pleasure visitors travelled to two or more of the six countries in the region (Guatemala, El Salvador, Honduras, Nicaragua, Costa Rica and Panama). As about one-third of the survey respondents were pleasure visitors, this means that about a sixth of all visitors were circuit tourists. Of this group, just under half visited two countries, a quarter visited three, a fifth went to four countries and only a small number (respectively 2.7% and 6.7%) visited five or all six countries. On average, circuit visitors visited 2.6 countries in the region, while for all pleasure visitors this figure dropped to 1.9 or a comparable figure to that for American tourists in Europe in 1977 as noted above. Nearly half of the circuit tourists also included other countries outside the region on their trip, notably Mexico.

The SRI study was also able to identify the most preferred country combinations for United States circuit tourists; the ten most popular are shown (in descending order) in Table 3.9. When data on frequency of visits were combined with other information on 'primary destination', Costa Rica and Guatemala were identified as 'prime magnets' in the region and thus important factors in designing strategies for tourism in Central America. While subsequent political events have disrupted the flow of tourists in the region, the SRI study does show how it is possible to structure and identify patterns in international circuit tourism.

Different factors appear to be influencing the nature and extent of circuit tourism in the examples given. The sunlust destination of New Caledonia, for example, contrasts with the wanderlust circuit evident in Central America. Much of the stopover traffic in Singapore and Hong Kong appears to result from a combination of factors including the size, strategic location and nodal

Table 3.9
Ten most popular country combinations for United States circuit tourists in Central America

Costa Rica–Guatemala
El Salvador–Guatemala
Costa Rica–Panama
Guatemala–Panama
El Salvador–Costa Rica

Guatemala–El Salvador–Costa Rica
Guatemala–Costa Rica–Panama
Guatemala–Honduras
El Salvador–Panama
El Salvador–Costa Rica–Panama

Source: SRI International (Cullinan et al. 1977).

role in the South East Asian and Far Eastern air networks and their attraction for shoppers. Changes in tariffs and fare structures which limit the number of stopovers or determine where these may be taken may significantly increase or decrease visits to places such as Hong Kong and Singapore. The development of longer-haul aircraft has also led to the overflying of mid-Pacific destinations such as Fiji and a consequent decline in stopovers there.

The examples given tend to dispel the notion of globetrotting tourists 'collecting' countries as they flit from one destination to another. This may be true of a small segment of the market but the picture to emerge is rather one of tourists restricting their trips to one or two countries. Whether this represents a recent adjustment to travel costs or whether circuit tourism has always been limited to a small but visible group of travellers is not clear. It may be too that the market for international travel has changed, with much of the demand in the 1960s coming from globetrotting 'once in a lifetime' travellers who have since been replaced by tourists travelling abroad more frequently and visiting only one or two countries on each trip. A study of potential travellers to the Pacific region showed three-quarters of the respondents preferred to 'see fewer countries and spend more time in each' (Opinion Research Corporation 1980). In general, little is known about the motivations and preferences of circuit tourists and what distinguishes them from those who visit only one country.

Demographic variations in international travel

Comparative analysis of different groups of international travellers has been hampered by the

Table 3.10

Sex composition of international travellers to selected destinations (1975)

Destination	Definition	Travelling for pleasure* (%)	Male (%)						
			Total	UK	W. Germ.	USA	Jap.	Aust.	NZ
S. Korea	Foreign tourist arrivals		88	85.3	79	77.9	96	81	78.3
Thailand	Tourists		68.2						
Singapore	Visitor arrivals	62.3	67.3	68	67.3	69.7	80.6	55.9	54.6
Japan	Foreigners	61.3	65.3	69.6	73.2	61.2	—	62.9	65.4
Hong Kong	Total visitors	70	64.2	65	70.4	56.7	73.7	53.5	
Tonga	All visitors		62.3			57.4		64	65.6
Ceylon	Tourist arrivals	90.8	60.5	63.9	57.3	57.3	75.9	58.7	
Nepal	Tourist arrivals		60.3						
Australia	International visitors		59	51		59	82		51
W. Samoa	Tourists		54.7						
Fiji	Visitor arrivals	77	54.3	61.6		50.9		52.2	54.1
New Zealand	All arrivals	77	54.1						
	Tourists	100	46.1	40.3		45.5	68.1	44.9	
Bali	Foreign tourists		50	51.4	57.1	44.7	72.4	46.9	46.9
Jamaica	All stopovers		48.6	44.3		50.3		41.2	
Hawaii	Visitors		44.7						

* On vacation or to visit friends/relations.

Source: Pearce (1978a).

limited availability of comparable data. Age and sex statistics, however, do exist for a number of countries and have been utilized by Weiss (1971) and Pearce (1978a) to examine demographic variations in international travel. Both these studies, while being far from comprehensive, suggest that significant variations do occur in the demographic characteristics of international travellers from different countries and that these vary from destination to destination so that male- or female-oriented destinations and those attracting predominantly youthful, middle-aged or elderly travellers may be identified.

The visitor flows to the fifteen destinations (mainly in Asia and the Pacific) examined by Pearce (1978a) were characterized by their male dominance (Table 3.10). The proportion of male travellers ranged from 88% in South Korea, favoured by Japanese tourists for its 'kisaeng tourism' (Kikue 1975), to 45% in Hawaii. The Asian countries on the whole are particularly male-oriented. A more balanced tourist traffic is found in the small tropical and sub-tropical island destinations – Western Samoa, Fiji, Bali, Hawaii

and Jamaica. While some national tourist flows are more male-dominated than others, there appear to be fairly consistent variations in the sex composition of each nationality from destination to destination. That is, there are proportionately more male travellers of all nationalities visiting South Korea and correspondingly fewer in Jamaica and Bali with the proportion of male travellers decreasing between these extremes whatever the nationality concerned. This general correspondence among nationalities suggests that variations in the sex composition of the various flows are a function of the character of the destination, but the critical factors here are not very evident.

Figure 3.5 depicts the age structure of tourists arriving at sixteen destinations in 1975. Three destinations (i.e. those clustered around the centre-point of the graph) have a relatively balanced profile – the small islands of Tonga, Fiji and Bermuda. Hawaii and Israel are shown to attract relatively more elderly tourists. The four East Asian countries stand out as destinations visited by middle-aged travellers whereas Nepal

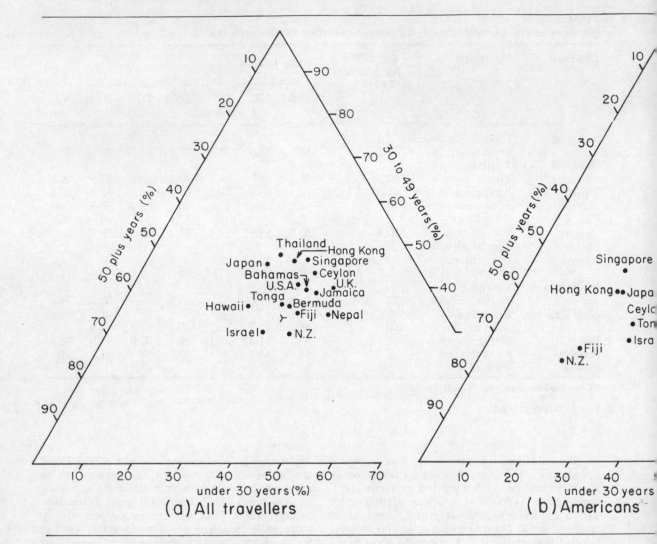

Fig. 3.5 Variations in the age structure of international tourists at selected destinations.

Source: After Pearce (1978a).

is clearly identified as appealing to the young. Jamaica and the United Kingdom attract youthful and middle-aged travellers in approximately equal proportions while the USA, the Bahamas and Ceylon might be regarded as being transitional from 'middle-aged' to 'youthful' destinations. A slightly bi-modal (youthful – elderly) profile exists in New Zealand. The proportion of elderly American travellers is consistently higher

than the norm for all the destinations examined whereas Australian visitors in the countries surveyed tend to be middle-aged.

Interpretation of these patterns is limited by the range of statistics available as data on many of the major destinations for each national flow are missing. Nevertheless, various factors, some not altogether clear, appear to influence these variations in age structure. Differing purposes of visit

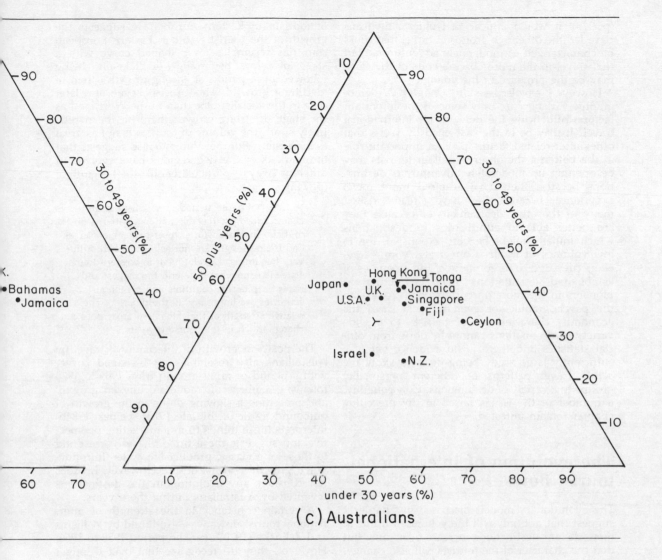

(c) Australians

seem to be reflected by different age structures. Business travellers are predominantly middle-aged while migration links often give rise to a larger proportion of elderly travellers visiting sons and daughters who have emigrated earlier. The 'character' of the destination, as in the case of Nepal, also appears to play a role as does the visitor mix at a particular destination. The bi-modal structure of all visitors to New Zealand results from a combination of elderly American and British visitors (many of whom are visiting kin) and youthful Australians for whom a visit there often represents their first overseas experience, with the two countries being close and not dissimilar socially and culturally. Distance did not appear to play a major role in age selectivity among the tourist flows examined by Pearce. However, Weiss (1971) concluded from her study

(p. 223) 'it would appear that older Americans have led the other age groups in travel that could be characterized as moderately adventurous, but that travel to the more obscure ends of the earth may be the province of the young'.

However, as discussed in Chapter 2, demographic variables are only some of the important factors influencing the demand for international travel. It may be in the case cited by Weiss that other inter-related factors play an important role in the patterns she observes. Older tourists may be opening up moderately adventurous destinations because they have acquired more travel experience, because they have already visited many of the other destinations or because they are better able to afford trips to destinations which initially might be very expensive due to low volumes of traffic. Conversely, young travellers prepared to forgo many of the amenities of established destinations may be acting as pioneers in the more obscure regions. Assessing the psychographic, or even in most cases the economic, characteristics of tourists to a wide variety of destinations cannot be done from official statistics and there is no evidence yet of a sufficiently large study being done to show the actual travel patterns of different personality groups to a variety of destinations. Consequently, a number of the issues raised in the preceding chapter remain untested.

The evolution of international tourist flows

The evolutionary models discussed in Chapter 1 suggest that not only will the volume of traffic to more distant destinations increase over time, but that the character of the tourists will also change. Detailed analysis of the ways in which tourist flows develop over time has been hampered by the lack of a good statistical base. The data difficulties outlined at the beginning of this chapter are commonly exacerbated when statistics for more than one year are required. In the Pacific, for example, the progressive and as yet incomplete changeover to recording visitor arrivals by place of residence rather than nationality frustrates time-series analysis on a region-wide basis. In Vanuatu, for instance, 40% of all arrivals recorded by nationality in 1975 were French, but in 1981 only 2% of all arrivals were recorded as residing in France (some 15% now come from New Caledonia).

Many of these problems are recognized by Vuoristo (1981) in his study of the development of tourism in Eastern Europe. He suggests the growth of the tourist traffic in Eastern European countries resembles an S-shaped curve with a stage of 'slow beginning' or 'take-off' being followed by a period of 'strong growth', then of 'declining growth'. This process began at a later date in the socialist bloc than in the West, and as the stage of strong growth there has been relatively short, the volume of tourism is not as great as in Western Europe. Vuoristo also suggests that the markets of the two regions have evolved in different ways, particularly in the beginning (p. 243):

> . . . the 'take -off' period of socialistic countries is characterized by unstable national patterns of tourists. In other words, tourist catchment areas and their strength are not self-evident from the very beginning. Development in western tourist states is somewhat different: the biggest and richest capitalistic countries and neighbour countries are important all the time . . . The relative strength of the catchment areas does not change much in the course of years

The post-war growth of international travel by Australians also resembles an S-shaped curve, with a period of rapid growth from 1963 to 1976 following a phase of 'moderate uneven growth' and preceding a slowing down in the growth of outbound traffic in the late 1970s. Leiper (1984b) interprets these trends from a marketing perspective and suggests these three phases correspond to those of a classic product life-cycle: 'introduction', 'growth' and 'maturity'. However, he does not consider any evolution in the destinations favoured by Australians during these years.

A certain constancy in the strength of international tourist flows was also found by Williams and Zelinsky (1970) over the period 1958 to 1966. However, they do recognize that over a longer period, changes in the structure of flow patterns might be found. Over periods of a decade or more some significant changes would be expected as demand increases and more countries seek to develop their tourist industries. For some specific flows, time-series data do exist. The example of Japanese travel abroad will be used here to explore ways in which the evolution of international tourist flows might be analysed, with special emphasis being given to changing spatial patterns.

Statistics on the number of Japanese travelling abroad are based on passport applications made to the Immigration Bureau of the Ministry of Justice. These applications require details to be given on purpose of visit and main country to be visited. Passports were initially issued for one

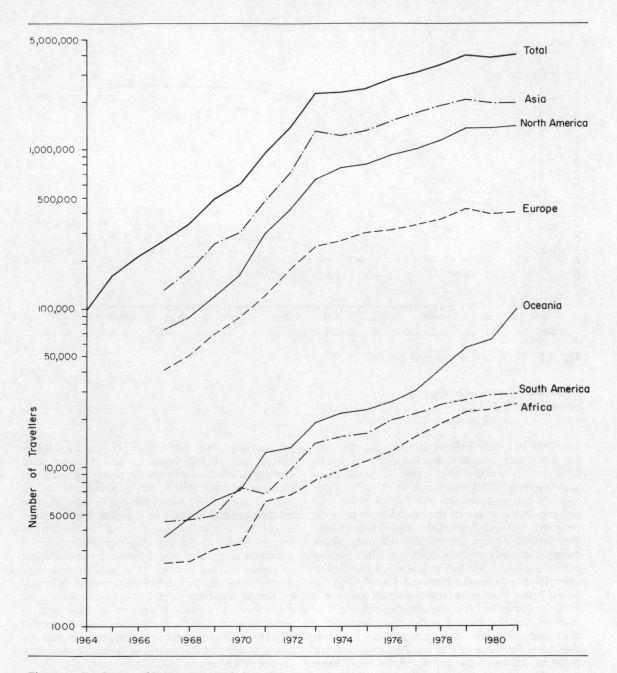

Fig. 3.6 Evolution of Japanese travel abroad (1964–81).

Data source: Japanese Ministry of Justice.

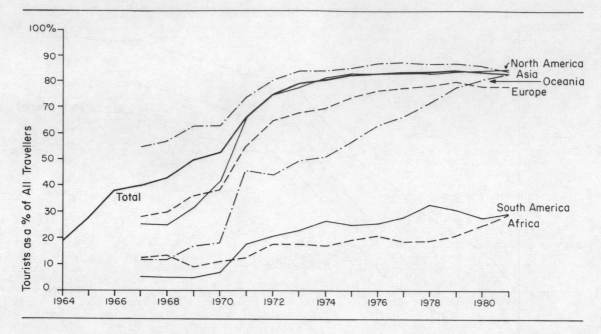

Fig. 3.7 Evolution of Japanese tourists (1964–81).

Data source: Japanese Ministry of Justice.

year only but since 1970 'multiple passports' valid for five years, for both business and pleasure, have been issued. The statistics would thus underestimate total travel due to more than one country being visited on any trip or more than one trip being made in the period for which the passport is valid (especially after 1970). Given that Japanese trips are usually relatively short, multiple country visits should not affect general patterns greatly. Moreover, these are the figures used by the Japanese National Travel Organization. Apart from some regrouping of purpose of visit categories in 1971, the statistics appear to be uniform for the period under consideration. It is argued, therefore, that they provide a reasonable basis for the study of the evolution of travel patterns, although the figures given might more properly be regarded as indicative rather than definitive.

Over the eighteen-year period from 1964 to 1981 the number of Japanese recorded as travelling abroad increased from just on 100,000 in 1964 to over 4 million in 1981. Figure 3.6 shows that trends in Japanese travel to most regions over these years can be likened to the 'strong growth' period of the S-shaped curve discussed

by Vuoristo (1981) and Leiper (1984b). By the late 1970s, Asia, North America and Europe have entered a declining growth phase; growth in Oceania is still strong but Japanese travel to South America and Africa has yet to take off. The marked general increase in Japanese travel abroad might be attributed to a rapid expansion in foreign trade, to the growing personal affluence which accompanied the economic development of Japan in this period, to a long tradition of domestic travel, to the liberalization of currency exchange regulations in 1964, to the easing of procedures to obtain passports in 1970 and to more general developments such as improved aircraft technology and the marketing of package tours which made overseas travel easier and cheaper (Nishiyama 1973; Tokuhisa 1980).

The breakdown of purpose of visit provides some evidence of the evolution of 'tourist' travel in the total travel picture (Fig. 3.7). In this case, tourist travellers have been defined as those giving 'sightseeing' as their prime reason for travelling. Other travel purposes include business, both private and official, study and research, immigration, accompanying spouse or parents. Over the period examined, tourist travellers increased from 19% of all travellers in 1964 to 83% in 1981, with tourists first contributing half of the total traffic in 1969. Comparison of Figs 3.6 and 3.7 suggests that an increase in the total traffic to any region is largely a function of bigger tourist flows. However, it also appears that an increase in the tourist traffic is related initially to existing exchanges between Japan and any given region as evidenced by the volume of other traffic. In the cases of South America and Africa where the total volume of traffic is small, the proportion of tourists has increased much more slowly than the average and tourists still contribute less than a third of all Japanese travellers to these regions. As well as the distance and cost involved, lack of information appears to play a role here (Tokuhisa 1980). On the other hand, in North America and Europe where the total traffic was much greater at the beginning of the period, the proportion of tourists has evolved more rapidly, although

Table 3.11
Evolution of Japanese travel abroad
(a) By major region

	3-year average 1971–73		3-year average 1979–81	
	No.	*%*	*No.*	*%*
Asia	685,683	58.9	1,762,771	52.8
North America	347,944	29.9	1,174,779	35.2
Europe	119,904	10.3	322,522	9.7
Oceania	7,041	0.6	64,617	1.9
South America	2,205	0.2	8,305	0.2
Africa	1,160	0.1	5,950	0.2
	1,163,937	100	3,338,944	100

(b) Within Asia

	3-year-average 1971–73		3-year average 1979–81	
	No.	*%*	*No.*	*%*
Hong Kong	221,775	32.44	335,275	19.63
Taiwan	202,166	29.57	535,922	31.38
S. Korea	189,438	27.71	403,210	23.6
Thailand	31,701	4.64	56,033	3.28
Singapore	12,307	1.8	86,513	5.06
Philippines	10,919	1.6	165,517	9.69
Indonesia	6,340	0.93	35,978	2.1
India	4,555	0.6	10,891	0.64
China	1,371	0.2	56,971	3.33
Malaysia	1,395	0.2	10,965	0.64
Nepal	623	0.1	3,021	0.18
Sri Lanka	287	0.04	4,683	0.27
Burma	395	0.06	1,595	0.09
Vietnam	256	0.04	486	0.02
Laos	37	—	382	0.02
Cambodia	35	—	14	—
N. Korea	33	—	360	0.02
	683,633	99.93	1,707,816	99.95

Data source: Ministry of Justice.

subsequently attaining a plateau around 80% of all travellers. A steady growth in travellers to Oceania throughout this period has been accompanied by a constant increase in the proportion of Japanese tourists visiting the region.

The differing rates of growth of Japanese travel in the regions shown in Fig. 3.6 suggest evolving geographic preferences. These changes can be examined in terms of both relative and absolute market shares. Table 3.11 portrays relative changes in the market shares of the different regions and of the countries within the most important region, Asia, during the 1970s. The market shares have been averaged over three-year periods at the beginning and end of the decade to reduce the effect of any non-regular event affecting distributions in any one year (O'Hagan 1979). Although the number of Japanese visiting Asia has more than doubled in this period, and the region still accounts for half of all travellers, there has been a relative decrease in the share of the market held by Asia. A very slight drop was recorded by Europe while North America and Oceania saw their share of the Japanese market increase.

Within Asia, significant changes were also recorded during the decade (Table 3.11b). Two of the three most important destinations, Hong Kong and South Korea, experienced decreases in their share of the Japanese market. At the same time, the Philippines, Singapore and mainland China emerge as important new destinations. The increase in traffic to China results from a general opening up of that country to tourism and is not of course restricted to Japanese travellers alone. Overall, the trend during the decade is for a greater dispersion of Japanese travellers throughout Asia, with the concentration ratio for the region dropping from 90% in 1971–73 to 75% in 1979–81. Such a trend might be expected during a period of substantial growth. Sustained growth may reflect a combination of experienced travellers exploring new countries while first-time travellers visit established destinations. The ratio of new/experienced travellers and the significance of repeat visits for the latter group could be factors accounting for the extent of the dispersion and redistribution of the tourist traffic through time.

Figure 3.8 portrays in absolute terms the development of Japanese travel abroad in the period 1964–81. In 1964, only three countries, the United States, Hong Kong and Taiwan, were the object of more than one thousand passport applications. Eighteen years later, 41 countries had attained this basic threshold while more than a million tourists were applying to go to the United States

(including Hawaii and Guam). By defining in this way four basic thresholds at logarithmic intervals, it is possible to order and to trace the spatial evolution of international tourism from Japan. In Europe, for example, France is the first country to attain the 1,000 threshold and the only one to reach the 100,000 level by 1981. But in addition to the absolute increases to a core of European countries (France, the United Kingdom, West Germany), there is also a marked dispersal of Japanese tourists within Europe as a growing range of more peripheral countries (e.g. Greece, Spain, Sweden, Poland) attain the first, then subsequently the second, threshold. An average of five to seven years is taken to pass from one threshold to the next. Certain countries such as Denmark and Holland appear not to experience a marked increase, although this may be a function of the statistics as these two countries might be included in a multiple country tour. Similarly in Asia, large increases in the numbers of visitors to Taiwan, Hong Kong and Korea are accompanied by a broadening of the range of more distant Asian countries attaining progressively the first three thresholds (e.g. the Philippines and Singapore). Again, certain countries, particularly India, develop at a slower rate than the average. Brazil and Kenya are the only countries to attain the lower threshold in South America and Africa. Pacific destinations (New Zealand, Tahiti and Fiji) have become important by the mid-1970s, although Australia is the only Pacific destination shown to each the 100,000 level. However, many of the 'United States' visitors are in fact travelling to the Pacific destinations of Hawaii and Guam.

It should be remembered that the trends discussed here are those which have developed in a period of rapid and sustained growth. The opening up of new destinations has led to the expansion of the Japanese 'pleasure peripheries', but this has not apparently diminished travel to established destinations. Monitoring of future Japanese travel may provide insights into whether the established destinations will follow the path postulated by Plog (1973) and start to experience an absolute decline in Japanese arrivals. The gross figures used here do not contain any information on the characteristics of Japanese travellers to particular destinations, other than their purpose of visit, and whether these have changed over time. Other statistics suggest that these travellers are predominantly middle-aged in destinations close to Japan and somewhat younger in more distant countries, but the evidence is far from conclusive (Pearce 1978a). More specific studies are required of the types of visitors to different countries and their evolution. Some of

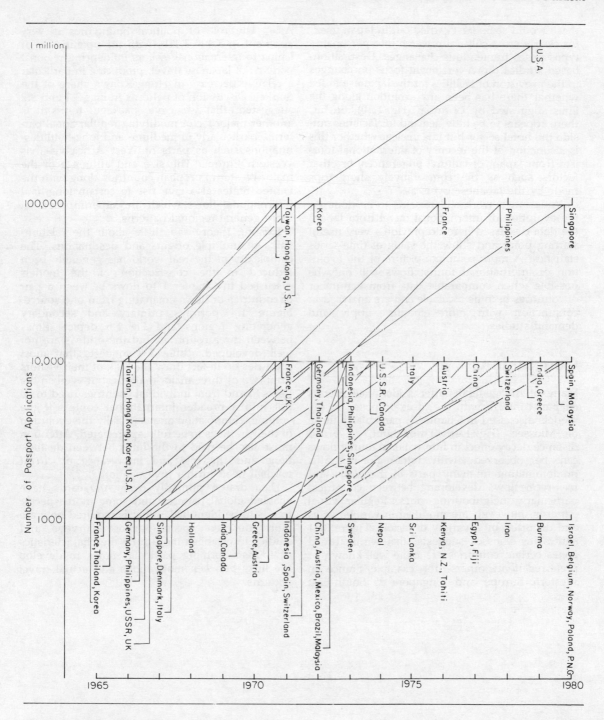

Fig. 3.8 Spatial development of Japanese travel abroad (1964–81).

Data source: Japanese Ministry of Justice.

these would seem best carried out in Japan itself, for clearly cross-cultural research into personality types poses tremendous challenges. Destination-based studies, however, might focus on changes in the provision of facilities for the Japanese to see whether there has been any evolution along the lines suggested by Gormsen (Fig. 1.10). So far, there appears to be little demand for facilities outside the hotel sector but it is unclear whether this is a function of the recency of international tourism from Japan, of cultural preferences, or other factors such as the comparatively short trips made by the Japanese overseas.

While much work still remains to be done on the evolution of international travel from Japan, the data discussed here do provide a very useful starting point and show the value of time-series statistics. A more complete picture of the evolution of international tourist flows will only be possible when comparable data from a number of countries become available and are analysed in conjunction with more specific supply and demand studies.

Conclusions

Many of the general patterns identified in this chapter conform with the ideas proposed in the models discussed in Chapter 1, particularly those of Miossec (Fig. 1.4). Throughout, a broad distance decay effect in international tourist flows can be observed, with intra-regional traffic predominating in many parts of the globe and reciprocal flows developing between countries, particularly neighbouring ones. Regular zonal patterns, however, are modified in various ways and distorted by a variety of factors. Figure 3.11 shows, as Miossec suggests, that within broad zones certain countries are more well-known or preferred than others, for example France in Western Europe and Singapore in South-East

Asia. The role of political boundaries is very apparent in Table 3.11b, with the opening up of China to international visitors influencing regional patterns of Japanese travel, producing in particular a relative decrease in Hong Kong's share of the market. Discussion of patterns in Figs 3.1 and 3.2 suggested that selective package tourism is another major factor modifying regular zonal patterns, particularly in medium- and long-haul destinations such as parts of West Africa vis-à-vis Western Europe. The size and affluence of the major Western European countries along with the United States also give rise to certain long-haul international flows which are superimposed on more general regional patterns.

Existing theory says little about the relationships of multiple origins and destinations. The complexity of the real world has generally been reduced in the construction of the models discussed in Chapter 1 to flows between a pair of countries or flows emanating from one source. Figure 1.4 portrays primary and secondary generating regions and Fig. 1.5 depicts flows between three countries, but these ideas are not well developed. Table 3.6 suggests that most countries do in fact draw the bulk of their visitors from two or three major markets, but even so the flows to and from individual countries need to be put into a broader international context if the volume, composition and especially the evolution of their traffic is to be fully appreciated. Attention must also be paid to the links between destinations and the role and importance of circuit tourism need further investigation.

Data drawn primarily from A/D cards have enabled global patterns and some more specific trends to be identified. What is required now are more detailed special-purpose surveys and studies to establish more fully the characteristics of tourists forming particular flows to develop the links between motivations and actual travel patterns.

4

Intra-national travel patterns

Research on international travel patterns has largely been limited to analyses of flows between sets of generating and receiving countries. There has been little recognition in the literature that these international movements are complemented by two sets of intra-national movements, one in the generating country as tourists leave home and make their way to a port of departure (and subsequently return home via the same or a different port of entry), the other in the receiving country (or countries) as the tourists move to a destination or visit a variety of destinations. In a strict sense these intra-national movements may not be international in the same way that the actual linking trips between countries are, but logically they form integral parts of an international travel system and have been so considered by geographers dealing with other less temporary movements, particularly those associated with international migration (White and Woods 1980).

A certain form of this intra-national travel has been conceptualized by Hills and Lundgren (1977) and Britton (1980a) in their work on the impact of international tourism in the Caribbean and in the Pacific (Fig. 1.8). In each case the market is concentrated upwards through the local–regional–national hierarchy by integrated metropolitan-based enterprises and little dispersion occurs in the destination country where development is essentially concentrated in resort enclaves. To date, these models have been little

tested by empirical research. Nor has travel between developed countries been considered systematically from this perspective. At a more local level, Fig. 1.7 depicts the various functions and flows which might be associated with international tourism in major metropolitan areas. Such areas may act as points of entry into and exit·from a country, constitute major destinations in themselves or act as a staging post sending visitors out into the surrounding region or along a tour circuit.

As Chapter 2 contained a discussion of intra-national variations in the propensity for international tourism and as little is known about the routes taken by international tourists within their own country to reach their port of embarkation, this chapter concentrates on intra-national travel within destination countries. Various demand and supply factors might be expected to influence the travel patterns of international visitors within particular countries. Demand factors will include the volume, origin and types of visitors while decisive supply variables may include the number and location of international gateways, the nature and distribution of the attractions and the development of the transportation network and accommodation. These in turn may reflect government policies and private sector initiatives. Such factors will influence the extent to which travel is concentrated or dispersed and whether itineraries are varied and complex or confined to a limited and well-defined circuit. The travel patterns of

sightseeing visitors in a well-developed continental country accessible by a variety of gateways
are likely to be more varied and diffuse than
those of 'sun–and–sea' tourists visiting a
developing tropical island served only by a single
international airport.

In an attempt to elucidate further these intra-
national travel patterns in destination countries,
this chapter reviews the different approaches
which have been employed to date. Most studies
have focused selectively on specific aspects of
intra-national travel. Some, for instance, have
concentrated on flows into the gateways (particularly in multi-gateway countries), or related ports
of arrival to ports of departure. Others still have
considered the places visited between the two
and a few have attempted to map routes and
itineraries. A limited amount of attention has also
been focused on patterns of movement within
particular cities or resorts. This provides a
particularly challenging area of research and one
which has generated a variety of innovative
methods.

Port of entry/port of departure

The gateway through which the international
visitor enters the intra-national system is often a
useful point of entry into the analysis of intra-
national travel patterns. Knowledge of where a
visitor enters the system may reflect the main
objectives of his visit, particularly if a choice of
gateways is available. Moreover, immigration
statistics are often broken down by port of entry
(and departure), so that the basic dimensions of
traffic through each gateway are available.

Levantis (1981) has used such data to examine
the arrival patterns at Greece's 25 main gateways.
Excluding cruise-ship passengers, 54% of visitors
to Greece in 1975 arrived by air, 25% by road,
10% by sea and 5% by rail. Athens airport was
the single largest point of entry, accounting for
42% of all arrivals (excluding cruise-ship passengers), followed by Evzoni on the Yugoslav border
(19%) and Rhodes airport (7%). Major differences
occur by nationality. Some 90% of all Americans
arrived by air, principally at Athens airport. A
similar proportion of Swedes also arrived by air,
but the majority of these landed at Rhodes airport. Only 56% of British visitors travelled by air,
and of these just over half arrived at Athens, with
the airports of Corfu and Rhodes being other significant points of arrival. The majority of the
Yugoslavs, on the other hand, arrived by road,
mainly at Evzoni. A more balanced pattern is evident among the Italians (sea, 37%; air, 35%; road,

27%). These differences are also reflected in the
composition of the traffic arriving at particular
gateways. A third of the arrivals at Athens airport
are Americans; Yugoslavs account for a similar
proportion at Evzoni; and Scandinavians constitute over half of all arrivals at Rhodes airport.
These differences appear to reflect propinquity
and purpose of visit (the American 'cultural' tourist and the Scandinavian sun-seeker?). The arrivals data also suggest that if the degree of penetration of a country by a particular group is a function of the gateway used, then markedly different
travel patterns within Greece would be found
among the different nationalities.

In the case of Spain, Fernandez Fuster (1974)
qualitatively establishes patterns of intra-national
travel on the basis of the major border crossings
and the connecting highways which channel
foreign visitors throughout the country. But while
such description may convey an overall picture,
no detail on the size of the particular flows is
given, although the absolute number of entries
at each crossing is available from the immigration
statistics.

Elsewhere, more detailed flow patterns have
been obtained in studies of a single or limited
number of gateways. The Aosta Valley in Italy,
for example, appears to be largely a transit zone
for many of the motorists using the Mt Blanc and
Grand-Saint-Bernard tunnels which link Italy to
France and Switzerland respectively. Janin (1982)
has related the number of vehicles passing
through the two tunnels to the number of tourists
of different nationalities recorded in the various
accommodation establishments in the valley. As
Janin recognizes, not all visitors staying in the
area are recorded in the official statistics nor do
they all necessarily arrive by the two tunnels. He
also appears to assume a uniform vehicle occupancy rate of one person per car. Therefore, only
general trends can be inferred from the ratios he
obtains. These suggest that the proportion of
motorists staying in the Aosta Valley increases
with distance from the country of origin. Perhaps
only one in ten French and Swiss motorists actually stay in the area, with the majority of them
either being en route to the Mediterranean or
simply making a day trip. On the other hand,
about half of the British motorists and some 120%
of other European and rest of the world visitors
were estimated to stay in the valley (this latter
ratio is largely a function of arrivals other than via
the tunnels, notably from the south). The accommodation statistics indicate that the stays of
foreign tourists are not scattered throughout the
Aosta Valley but are heavily concentrated in a
few areas, particularly in the major resorts of

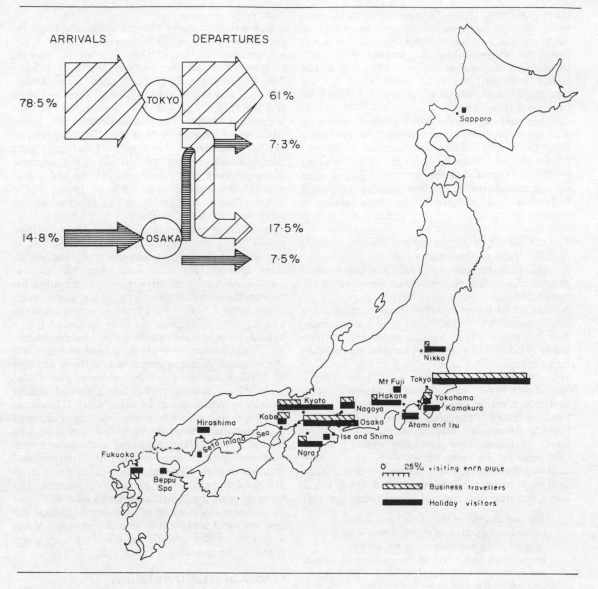

Fig. 4.1   Intra-national travel in Japan.

Data source: Shirasaka (1982).

Courmayeur and Breuil Cervinia.

Likewise in France, Soumagne (1974) has shown that the majority of British motorists arriving by car ferry at Cherbourg were in transit and not heading for Normandy itself (2.5%). Almost a third of the motorists surveyed were making directly for Spain and Portugal, with a further 9% going there after visiting South-West France. Some 8% had South-West France as their main destination. A second major flow was to Brittany (27%), while the remaining 23% had a variety of destinations elsewhere in France or in other countries (Italy, Benelux). Although relatively few of these motorists stay overnight in Normandy, Clary (1978) suggests their role is not negligible in spreading the impact of tourism throughout the region. In particular, this inland traffic provides some counterbalance to the dominant coast-wards movement of domestic holiday-makers (Fig. 5.2).

Other writers have related port of arrival to port of departure in an attempt to get some measure of penetration and a broad picture of routes taken. Pollock, Tunner and Crawford (1975) cross-tabulated the entry/exit points used by American and Canadian visitors to British Columbia and identified four basic types of routes;

1.   the direct route, whereby visitors entered and left through the same zone,
2.   the long traverse, whereby visitors entered at one end of the province and departed at the opposite end,
3.   the short traverse, where visitors made diagonal-type routes across the edge of the province,
4.   the loop, where visitors returned to their point of origin via a different zone to the one they had entered.

The direct route, comparable to Mariot's access and return routes (Fig. 1.1), was found to be the most common, especially with those visitors (mainly Americans) leaving via the Lower Mainland, of whom 66% had also entered British Columbia by the same zone.

The British Columbia data were subsequently analysed further by Murphy and Brett (1982) using discriminant analysis. They found (p. 159):

> The significance of the entry point for most individual regions and its respective signs suggest some peripheral regions act as interceptors to the rest of the province . . . Once the visitors entered British Columbia there was limited evidence of extensive touring . . . these results suggest that the southern regions were not only attracting most visitors but they also absorbed them, allowing relatively few to penetrate further into the province.

The attractive power of the southern regions was seen to lie in the presence of the major metropolitan areas close to the United States border and thus readily accessible to the important West Coast traffic. The authors also showed that these centres attracted a large number of people visiting friends and relations whereas independent vacationers were found in the more isolated northern regions of the province.

In Japan too, many visitors arrive and leave by the same port. A 1979 survey of over 1,000 foreign visitors found that 61% of all foreign arrivals followed the pattern of 'to and from Tokyo' (Shirasaka 1982). Then came Tokyo–Osaka (17.5%), Osaka–Osaka (7.5%), Osaka–Tokyo (7.3%) (Fig. 4.1). Tokyo's dominance is not surprising given the concentration of international air carriers on that city. This dominance is also reflected in the degree of foreign visitor penetration, for other information in the Japanese survey shows that many visitors do not travel beyond the capital: over 40% of those in the Tokyo–Tokyo category, or a quarter of all arrivals, visit no other place.

A different pattern is evident in New Zealand where there is a greater tendency for visitors to depart from a different airport to that at which they arrived (Fig. 4.2). Just over half of the arrivals at Auckland airport, which accounts for two-thirds of all arrivals, left via Auckland, with about a third exiting via Christchurch and a tenth leaving by Wellington. Arrivals at Christchurch exhibit a comparable pattern (59% of departures via Christchurch, 31% via Auckland and 10% via Wellington). A larger proportion of those arriving in Wellington leave via the same airport (73%) with the remaining traffic being shared almost equally by Auckland and Christchurch. This latter pattern is in part a function of the larger share of business and official travel to the capital and its central location. The Auckland and Christchurch patterns reflect the nature of international tourism in New Zealand, much of which is characterized by visits to a number of scenic attractions in both the North and South Islands. Many vacationers thus arrive at one gateway, tour the country, and leave via a second gateway. About a quarter of the arrivals do not even stay overnight in the gateway at which they arrive.

Gateway fragmentation

As intra-national travel is influenced by the number and location of international gateways, any change in these will affect the flow of foreign visitors throughout a country and/or reflect changes in the pattern of demand. In terms of overland travel, most international gateways are well established although some, such as the Mt Blanc (1965) and Grand-Saint-Bernard (1964) tunnels are relatively new and significant (Janin 1982). The closure of particular borders for political reasons has also affected overland travel from time to time, as for example in the case of the Spain/Gibraltar border or the Guatemala/Belize

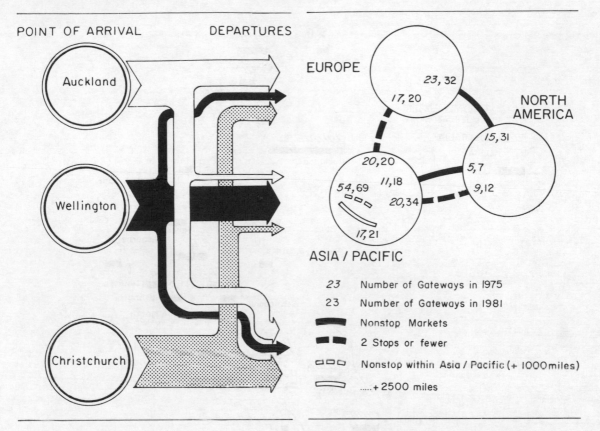

POINT OF ARRIVAL   DEPARTURES

Auckland

Wellington

Christchurch

EUROPE

23, 32

17, 20

NORTH AMERICA

15, 31

20, 20

11, 18

54, 69   5, 7

20, 34   9, 12

17, 21

ASIA / PACIFIC

23	Number of Gateways in 1975
23	Number of Gateways in 1981
	Nonstop Markets
	2 Stops or fewer
	Nonstop within Asia / Pacific (+ 1000 miles)
	.....+ 2500 miles

Fig. 4.2 Departures of international visitors from New Zealand by point of arrival (1981–82).

Data source: NZ Tourist and Publicity Dept.

Fig. 4.3 Gateway fragmentation (1975–81).

Source: After McDonnell Douglas (1981)

border in 1981. Other significant changes internationally have involved an increase in gateway airports.

Scheduled airlines have traditionally been restricted by government regulations and other factors to a limited number of international gateways. The transatlantic traffic, for instance, was for long channelled into the United States largely through New York; as recently as 1978, it was the true origin or destination of less than half of its reported traffic (Lockheed-California 1980). The recent trend, however, has been to gateway fragmentation and route dispersion (Lockheed-California 1980; McDonnell Douglas 1981). Fragmentation is defined in the Lockheed report (p. 1) as:

The process of major on-board traffic flows breaking up into smaller component flows as a new direct service is introduced which more closely matches the true origin-destination of the traffic.

Figure 4.3 summarizes the increase in gateway airports in the major world markets in the period 1975–81. For all the markets studied, the number of gateways increased by 38%, from 191 in 1975 to 264 in 1981. Increases were recorded in all areas except for Asian/Pacific gateways to Europe. The biggest relative increase occurred in the number of transatlantic gateways in North America, which doubled in this period. There was also a 32% increase in market dispersion, as

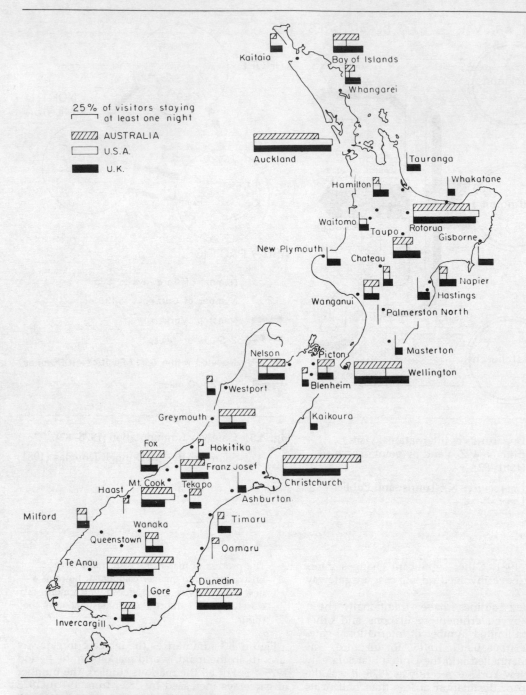

Fig. 4.4 Places visited in New Zealand by country of residence (1981–82).

Data source: NZ Tourist and Publicity Dept.

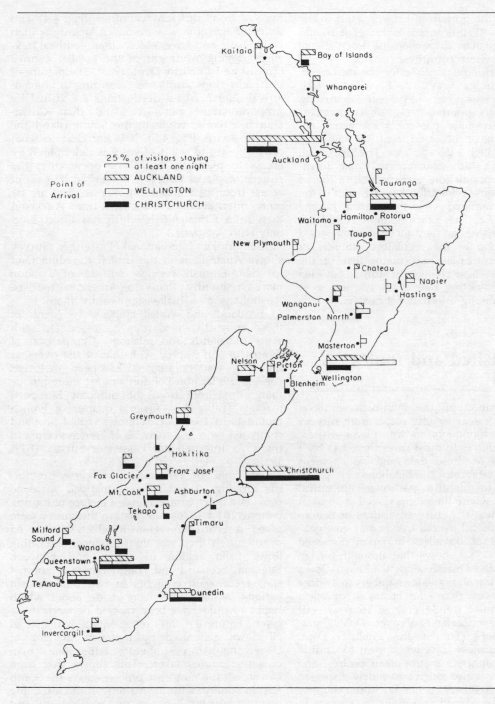

Fig. 4.5 Places visited in New Zealand by point
of arrival (1981–82).

Data source: NZ Tourist and Publicity
Dept.

measured by the growth of gateway pairs in the area studied. As this trend continues it should lead to a greater dispersion of international tourist flows within countries.

A major factor responsible for the increase in the number of gateways has been the overall traffic growth which has put pressure on existing airports and supported new direct services. World-wide, revenue passenger kilometres are estimated to have increased from 327 million in 1969 to 901 million a decade later. The McDonnell Douglas (1981) study also reported some decentralization of population, a dispersion of tourist activity and some re-distribution of wealth in the three areas examined – North America, Europe and Asia/Pacific. These factors alone would not have been effective had they not been accompanied by liberalization in the regulatory attitudes of various governments, particularly that of the United States. These changes in attitude have led to policies promoting new gateways and more competition among international carriers.

Places visited and routes followed

Other information on the intra-national travel patterns of overseas visitors comes from surveys which ask respondents to list 'places visited' while in a country. In most cases there has been little analysis of these data and no apparent attempt to establish combinations of places visited nor to identify particular itineraries. Nevertheless, where the places visited are broken down by particular groups of visitors or nationalities, some useful overall trends may emerge.

The survey of travellers to Japan discussed by Shirasaka (1982) shows that although foreign tourists visit places mainly along the Tokyo–Osaka axis, they do travel in greater numbers to a wider range of places than do business travellers (Fig. 4.1). Similar trends emerge from an exit survey in New Zealand of over 13,000 international visitors (Tourist and Publicity Dept. 1983). Few business travellers appear to venture outside the country's metropolitan centres, and the VFR traffic is also much less widely dispersed than that of foreigners on holiday in the country. Holiday-makers stayed overnight on average in almost seven places, twice the number of the VFR market. The average visiting businessman overnighted in only two places. Furthermore, differences in the numbers of places in which overnight stops were made are found among holiday-makers from different countries (Fig. 4.4) and different age groups, with fewer Americans than Australians and fewer elderly than youthful travellers staying overnight in the smaller centres (Tourist and Publicity Dept. 1983). The pattern of overnight stops also varies according to point of arrival. North Island destinations are visited by proportionately more Auckland than Christchurch arrivals, while in the South Island the reverse occurs (Fig. 4.5). It is not clear to what extent choice of point of entry is determined by access to places to be visited or whether the pattern of places visited is influenced by ease of access from a particular gateway as there are far more international connections from Auckland than from Christchurch which has direct links only with Australia.

The British International Passenger Survey shows Australians in the United Kingdom tend to visit English regions outside of London more frequently than do American tourists. Australians also make significantly more visits to Scotland and Wales (Table 4.1). Many of these more dispersed trips are associated with visits to friends and relations. Comparison of figures in this survey with that of the overseas motoring visitors suggest European motorists concentrate less on London and are more mobile than all visitors from the different European markets (Table 4.2). Over a quarter of French motorists in 1980, for example, visited Scotland compared with less than 5% of French visitors in the 1978 International Passenger Survey (BTA 1981a).

Data from the 1976 survey of overseas motorists arriving in Britain were mapped so as to provide a more comprehensive picture of touring patterns (BTA 1976). Motorists in the survey were asked to record the regions in which they stayed overnight. A map was then produced indicating flows from region to region and between England, Scotland and Wales. Where a motorist stayed consecutive nights in two non-adjacent regions, assumptions were made about which regions would have been crossed between those given. Figure 4.6 thus represents a synthesis of all flows generated by motorists arriving at Dover, the main port of entry, rather than a map of actual routes taken. This shows that from Dover half the motorists proceeded via the South East to London with the majority of the rest being divided initially between the South West and the Thames Valley. A significant proportion ventured on to Wales and Scotland, with traffic being heavier along the western side of Britain than on the east. Some 83% of the touring motorists who entered Britain through Dover also left by the

Table 4.1
Overseas visitors to UK: regional pattern of tourism from leading countries, staying visits (1978)

Total visitors ('000)	Total	Country of residence							
		USA	Canada	France	West Germany	Nether-lands	Belgium/ Luxem-burg	Italy	Australia
	11.730 %	1,964 %	511 %	1,435 %	1,507 %	1,003 %	740 %	358 %	372 %
England:	91.4	97.0	92.0	79.5	92.7	89.1	71.9	97.9	98.0
London	66.1	83.9	65.3	41.2	54.7	53.3	45.7	74.0	78.0
Rest of England	41.9	35.5	54.2	46.7	51.8	49.8	27.5	45.6	60.8
South East	12.7	8.5	19.0	17.9	15.7	20.5	12.4	13.8	12.1
West Country	7.1	8.7	13.2	6.6	9.0	10.0	1.2	5.9	13.9
Thames and Chilterns	6.0	7.0	7.5	7.0	6.6	4.5	5.0	3.0	12.0
Heart of England	5.6	8.8	10.9	6.0	5.8	2.6	1.3	5.2	14.3
North West	5.3	5.9	9.9	1.1	7.8	2.8	1.3	5.5	13.0
East Anglia	5.0	5.0	6.6	5.2	5.4	5.3	3.0	6.5	12.2
Southern	4.7	4.1	6.8	7.0	5.9	4.6	2.3	3.1	8.2
Yorkshire and Humberside	4.4	4.7	7.9	2.9	5.0	3.8	2.5	3.4	9.8
East Midlands	2.5	2.5	3.4	3.4	1.6	3.5	0.3	1.9	5.9
Northumbria	2.4	1.5	4.6	0.2	2.5	3.0	0.7	5.8	3.8
Cumbria	1.8	2.8	4.1	0.4	1.6	2.5	0.2	1.6	4.1
Channel Islands	0.1	0.1	0.5	—	0.3	—	—	—	0.1
Isle of Man	0.1	—	0.1	—	—	—	—	—	0.3
Unspecified	2.5	2.8	3.1	1.7	2.8	1.0	0.5	2.1	5.7
Scotland	9.7	14.6	22.6	4.3	8.9	9.2	2.7	8.9	25.6
Wales	5.2	5.4	7.9	3.7	7.2	6.7	0.5	4.8	21.0
Northern Ireland	0.8	0.6	2.4	0.6	2.4	—	0.4	—	1.5
Nil nights in UK	4.9	0.4	0.3	14.5	3.0	6.2	27.5	0.9	0.3

Note: Figures exclude residents of the Irish Republic and visitors exiting via Irish Republic. The percentages refer to staying visits: columns add to more than 100 as some visitors stay in more than one region/country.

Source: BTA (1981a).

same port, with a further 7% departing via the three other South East ports of Folkestone, New-haven and Southampton. Similar touring patterns were shared by motorists arriving by these ports. In other cases there is evidence of regional biases occurring, though the samples involved are re-latively small. Preferences for the western part of the country were shown by motorists arriving at Plymouth while those entering through Sheer-ness tended to head for the South West and Wales. Motorists arriving at Harwich and Felix-stowe exhibited the most varied travel patterns.

A similar study had earlier been undertaken in the Highlands and Islands of Scotland, with information on overnight stops and itineraries being obtained from a cordon survey of motor-ists, both domestic and overseas, as they left the region (Carter 1971). Data on route links were analysed to construct a flow map showing weekly volumes of 'tourist vehicle journeys' along each part of the Highland road network. The pattern to emerge is one of two main feeder routes chan-nelling traffic into a series of 'spur' routes, with traffic flows on the remaining roads decreasing with increasing distance from there. Some infor-mation on directional movements was also obtained, indicating balanced flows on one of the major feeder routes but a tendency to clockwise or anti-clockwise movements in other parts of the network. Traffic volumes throughout the network also varied by country of origin. Although the region involved is quite a complex one, it is surprising to learn that when data on the sequence of links were retrieved and analysed no more than 1% of the holiday-maker parties took exactly the same route.

Comprehensive surveys, particularly cordon surveys, demand a lot of resources to acquire the

Table 4.2
British regions stayed in by overseas motorists (1980)

Region stayed in	Total (%)	Belgium (%)	France (%)	Germany (%)	Netherlands (%)	Scandinavia (%)
South-East	34	30	36	32	37	28
London	33	31	41	36	17	43
West Country	26	18	27	29	25	20
South	21	17	24	20	19	24
Yorkshire and Humberside	18	9	14	19	22	19
Heart of England	17	11	19	15	14	21
East Anglia	15	9	13	15	15	21
Cumbria	13	7	12	14	13	18
Thames and Chilterns	11	7	14	10	8	12
North West	9	10	11	10	8	8
Northumbria	8	8	6	8	7	22
East Midlands	8	3	8	8	6	9
Scotland:						
Highlands & Islands	20	14	23	21	17	25
Edinburgh	16	10	19	18	10	26
Rest of Scotland	22	10	22	22	22	31
Total Scotland	26	15	27	27	25	39
Wales	17	10	20	21	14	16
N. Ireland	1	2	1	2	1	1
Republic of Ireland	3	3	4	4	2	3

Source: BTA (1981a).

necessary flow data. Forer and Pearce (1984) used a different data source in their study of package tourism in New Zealand and analysed the tour itineraries published in the brochures of New Zealand coach tour operators. This, of course, limited their analysis to one segment of the market, albeit a very important one in the case of New Zealand. Virtually all these coach tour passengers are from overseas. Problems were experienced in deriving actual coach tour numbers from the brochures due to the marketing device of providing a variety of package tours from a basic set of component tours. However, when these were disentangled, the actual number of tours identified corresponded very closely with data obtained from independent sources in specific localities. The coach tour data were then analysed in a variety of ways to provide a comprehensive picture of coach tour circuits throughout the country.

Figure 4.7 (see page 72) depicts the distribution of major and minor nodes in the circuit according to the number of coach nights recorded in each. This reveals a very distinct pattern with two major centres, Queenstown and Rotorua, and a clustering of other nodes based on the scenic attractions of the South Island. To facilitate an analysis of the flow patterns, the 58 separate nodes were amalgamated to form twenty regions. Figure 4.8 (see page 73) shows the inter-regional links of over 150 tours per year. The North Island is characterized by a series of linear routes between the major cities of Auckland and Wellington. The South Island pattern is much more complex and is based on a series of loops. Further analysis of net flows identified northbound or southbound biases in the flows between particular regions. A marked relationship was also found between the importance of each node (expressed in the number of coach nights recorded) and its relative connectivity in the total system (determined by the number of links to other nodes). The residuals in Fig. 4.9 are readily explained. The gateway cities of Christchurch, Auckland and Wellington register fewer nights than their high connectivity suggests as nights spent in these cities before or after a tour are often not registered as part of the formal tour package. Te Anau, on the other hand, records more overnight stays than its connectivity suggests as it is commonly

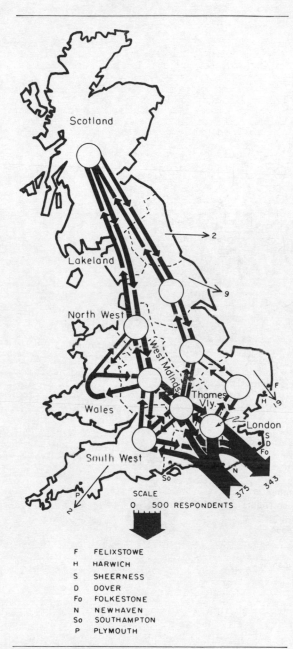

F   FELIXSTOWE
H   HARWICH
S   SHEERNESS
D   DOVER
Fo FOLKESTONE
N   NEWHAVEN
So SOUTHAMPTON
P   PLYMOUTH

Fig. 4.6 Touring patterns of overseas motorists entering Britain via Dover (summer 1976).

Source: After English Tourist Board.

the base for day trips into Milford Sound, which thus generates a large number of two-night stays.

Finally, a typology of nodes was derived using a *k*-mean clustering algorithm. The five variables employed were: tour nights, connectivity, average length of tour visiting the node, stopover function (proportion of second-night stays) and relative impact (ratio of tour nights to local population). Five major groups of nodes were identified on the basis of the nodes' location relative to other major nodes and their own limited attractions (Table 4.3).

This more comprehensive approach, involving the classification of different types of nodes as well as an analysis of the flows between them, begins to offer insights into the functioning of the tourist circuit which might be incorporated into tourism plans. Nodes depending on different lengths of tour, for example, will see their fortunes vary with changes in the composition of the market as well as with changes in total demand. In terms of supply, bottlenecks in the gateways and major generators will have greater repercussions on flows throughout the circuit than shortages in the secondary centres.

Where resources do not allow a detailed analysis of tour circuits, specific places might be examined in terms of whether or not they constitute a main destination in themselves or function as a stopover on a larger itinerary. The place of a given destination in a total trip or vacation might be established by use of the Trip Index (Pearce and Elliott 1983). This relates the nights spent at the destination (Dn) to the total number of nights spent on the trip (Tn) according to the formula

$$\text{Ti} = \frac{Dn}{Tn} \times 100$$

Thus where the Trip Index is 100, the entire trip is being spent at the one destination. On the other hand, were the index 10, the destination would account for only 10% of the total trip, indicating it was but one stop among several or played only a small role in the overall holiday. An index of 0 would show, of course, that no overnight stay at all was made in the study area and that it was being visited either in transit or on a day trip.

Table 4.4 gives Trip Index values for two different places in New Zealand, one a rather isolated national park, the other a major urban centre (Pearce and Elliott 1983). It highlights the role of Westland National Park as a stopover on

1 KAITAIA	34 CHRISTCHURCH
2 WAITANGI	35 FOX GLACIER
3 PAIHIA	36 MT. COOK
4 RUSSELL	37 HAAST
5 KAIKOHE	38 LAKE TEKAPO
6 WHANGAREI	39 MAKARORA
7 AUCKLAND	40 LAKE OHAU
8 WAITOMO	41 OTEMATATA
9 ROTORUA	42 MILFORD SOUND
10 WHAKATANE	43 WANAKA
11 TE ARAROA	44 KUROW
12 TE KUITI	45 OAMARU
13 ORAKEI/KORAKO	46 QUEENSTOWN
14 TAUPO	47 ALEXANDRA
15 TURANGI	48 TE ANAU
16 CHATEAU TONGARIRO	49 MANAPOURI
17 NEW PLYMOUTH	50 DUNEDIN
18 MT. EGMONT	51 GORE
19 GISBORNE	52 INVERCARGILL
20 WANGANUI	53 TIMARU
21 NAPIER	54 GERALDINE
22 PALMERSTON NORTH	55 OMARAMA
23 MASTERTON	56 WHITIANGA
24 WELLINGTON	57 HICKS BAY
25 KAITERITERI	58 TAURANGA
26 NELSON	
27 PICTON	
28 BLENHEIM	
29 WESTPORT	
30 GREYMOUTH	
31 HOKITIKA	
32 HARI HARI	
33 FRANZ JOSEF	

Number of
Coach Nights

5000

1000

100

Fig. 4.7 New Zealand coach tours: distribution
of coach nights by node (1977).

Source: Forer and Pearce (1984).

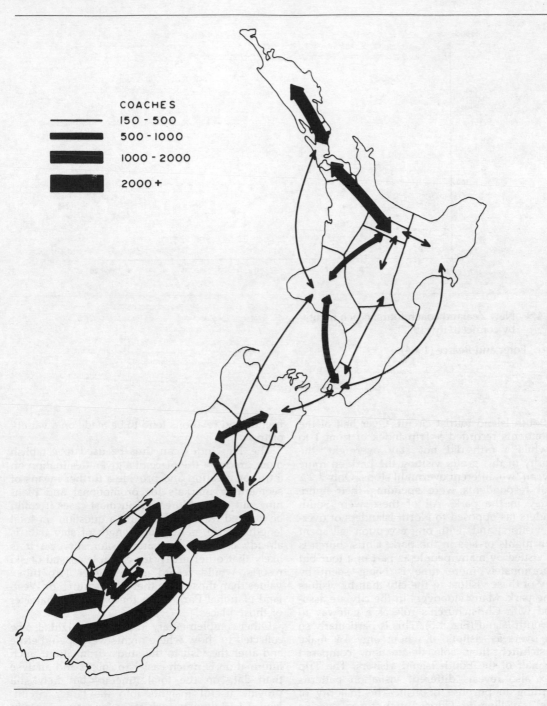

COACHES

150 - 500

500 - 1000

1000 - 2000

2000 +

Fig. 4.8 New Zealand coach tours: major inter-regional flows (1977).

Source: Forer and Pearce (1984).

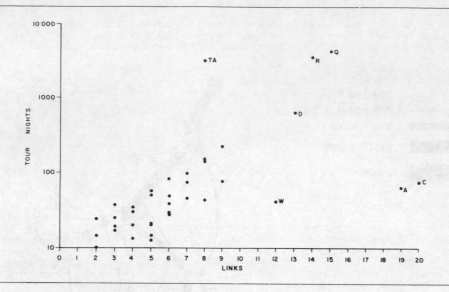

Fig. 4.9 New Zealand coach tours: coach nights by connectivity (1977).

Source: Forer and Pearce (1984).

the South Island tourist circuit. Over half of the respondents recorded a Trip Index of from 1 to 10 while a fifth did not stay overnight, the majority of this group visiting the park en route between two different overnight stops. Only 2.2% of all respondents were spending their entire holiday in the park. All of these were South Islanders (as opposed to North Islanders or overseas visitors) and, with one exception, all spent seven nights or less in the park. Christchurch is also visited by many people as part of a tour but proportionately more time is being spent by many of these visitors in the city than by visitors to the park. Many stopovers in the city are associated with Christchurch's role as a gateway to the South Island (Fig. 4.5). This is particularly so with overseas visitors of whom only 4% make Christchurch their sole destination, compared with half of the South Island visitors. The Trip Index also reveals different visitation patterns according to purpose of visit. The majority of those travelling to Christchurch for a specific purpose (business, convention, sport, special event) spend more than half of their trip in the city, with a significant number making it their sole destination. Christchurch is very much a stopover for those on holiday, while visits to

friends and relations tend to be made on a variety of trips.

The Trip Index can thus be used to establish more precisely the place of a given destination on a trip or vacation and provide a further means of segmenting markets for promotional and planning purposes. Moreover, in most cases it could be derived by simply adding a question on total length of trip as absolute length of stay data is already collected in many visitor surveys. It is likely that other areas, for example coastal or ski resorts, would record much higher Trip Index values than those for either Christchurch or Westland National Park given the particular character of those places.

Other complementary information might also be collected to show where nights were spent before and after the visit to the study destination. Such information is much easier to collect and analyse than data on the total itinerary but may still provide useful insights into the larger circuit. Figure 4.10 depicts such stops for respondents in the Westland National Park survey who were not staying overnight in the park nor visiting it on a day trip. This shows some quite large distances were being covered between nights with the time allotted for a visit to the park consequently being

Table 4.3
A typology of New Zealand coach tour nodes

Group 1: Gateways and major generators
Wellington, Dunedin, Christchurch, Auckland, Rotorua, Queenstown

Group 2: Isolated major attractions
Milford Sound, Mount Cook

Group 3: Secondary centres with strong impacts and long tour involvement
Te Kuiti, Masterton, Taupo, New Plymouth, Picton, Nelson, Greymouth, Fox Glacier, Haast, Invercargill, Oamaru, Tekapo, Blenheim, Timaru, Geraldine, Palmerston North

Group 4: Secondary centres with short tours and above average stopover proportions
Kaitaia, Waitangi, Paihia, Russell, Lake Ohau, Franz Josef Glacier, Te Anau, Otematata

Group 5: Secondary centres with weaker impacts and shorter tours
Whakatane, Napier, Gisborne, Chateau Tongariro, Wanganui, Westport, Hokitika, Hari Hari, Wanaka, Gore, Alexandra, Omarama, Hicks Bay, Tauranga, Kaikohe, Waitomo, Whangarei

Group 6: Small centres with short tours and high relative impact
Te Aroha, Whitanga

Nodes with an overflow function:
Omarama, Te Anau, Manapouri, Tekapo, Otematata, Te Kuiti, Gore, Lake Ohau

Source: Forer and Pearce (1984).

Table 4.4
Trip Index: Westland National Park and Christchurch

Trip Index	Westland National Park (n = 1,028) (%)	Christchurch (n = 756) (%)
0	20.8	2
1–10	55.5	23
11–20	16.3	25
21–50	4.5	21
51–99	0.7	9
100	2.2	17
Not stated	—	3

Source: Pearce and Elliott (1983).

Intra-destination travel

Comparatively little is known about what international visitors do and where they go once they arrive at a particular resort, city or node on a tourist circuit. Figure 1.7 suggests a pattern of within destination travel might be complemented by day or half-day trips away from the resort or city. These movements might also be seen in terms of the visitors' activity space which, following Aldskogius (1977), might be defined as the aggregate spatial pattern of places and areas visited by an individual or group of individuals during his/their visit to a given locality.

If an attempt is made to examine this issue, it usually takes the form of asking visitors what attractions or sites they have visited or intend to visit. This approach can shed some light on the most frequented attractions but generally suffers from the same limitations noted earlier with regard to places visited in that it rarely provides details of the combination or sequence of visits.

A typical example is the British Tourist Authority's survey of overseas visitors to London (BTA 1981b). Table 4.5 lists the 'major tourist sites' and 'other tourist attractions' of London most frequently visited during the summer of 1981. It is interesting to note that some of the 'other attractions', notably Oxford Street, are visited more frequently than many of the designated 'major tourist sites'. The most frequented areas are found in inner London which, of course, reflects the structure of the city and the nature of its attractions with many of the historic sites, major shopping streets and cultural centres being found there. The results depicted in Table 4.5 may also reflect the sampling system used, with respondents in the survey being interviewed at

very limited. Similar details were obtained in a survey of visitors to York (ETB n.d.a). These showed (p. 4) that 'compared with British visitors who arrived in York, either from home or from places fairly near York, overseas visitors arrived in York from places much further away and left York for similarly distant places'. Some directional bias was also apparent with York being included more often in a northbound (largely from London) than a southbound journey. The survey also found that the overseas visitors to York were, on average, staying in seven or more places in Britain and that their trips were on average longer (23.2 nights) than those of all overseas visitors to Britain (average 15.5 nights).

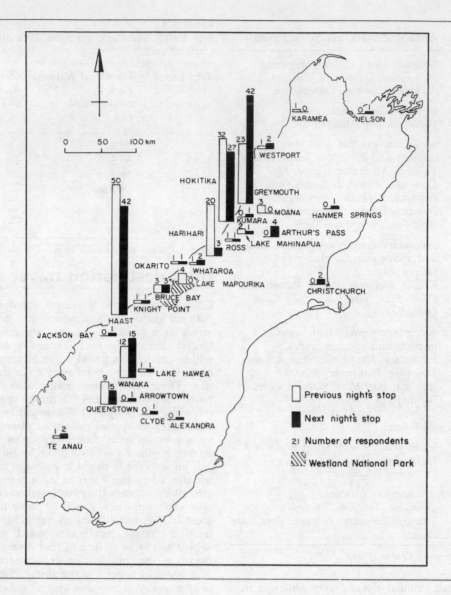

Fig. 4.10 Patterns of travel to and from Westland National Park (1970–80).

Source: Pearce (1982b).

thirty sites 'where visitors to London might be found in some numbers'. As the report notes, this may lead to certain types of overseas visitor, such as business travellers and those staying with friends and relations, being under-represented. The survey also found about a tenth of the respondents had been on a half-day or day coach tour to places near or outside London, with

Windsor being the most popular of these.

In an attempt to reduce any bias in her survey of visitors to Christchurch, Elliott (1981) limited her analysis of attractions to respondents interviewed in different types of accommodation and at various transport termini. Elliott found a third of her respondents had visited three to six of twenty designated sites and attractions, with a

Table 4.5
Places visited by overseas tourists in London (summer 1981)

| | Major tourist sites | |
	Visited (%)	Intend to visit (%)
Piccadilly Circus	92	11
Trafalgar Square	68	10
Buckingham Palace	59	15
Westminster Abbey	55	15
Tower of London	49	12
St Paul's Cathedral	44	18
Houses of Parliament/Big Ben	43	19
National Gallery	30	15
British Museum	27	16
Madame Tussauds/Planetarium	24	15
Westminster Cathedral	24	10
Tate Gallery	16	14
Victoria and Albert Museum	15	9
Science Museum	15	9
London Zoo	13	8
National Maritime Museum	7	7
Museum of London	6	8
London Transport Museum	3	3
None of these	7	29
Don't know/not stated	—	6

| | Other tourist attractions | |
	Visited (%)	Intend to visit (%)
Oxford Street	66	14
Regent street	57	11
Soho	40	13
Knightsbridge	35	8
Bond Street	33	10
Carnaby Street	29	12
High St. Kensington	28	5
Covent Garden	24	12
King's Road	21	12
Shaftesbury Avenue	20	3
Portobello Road	14	13
Petticoat Lane	8	9
St Katherine's Dock	4	4
None of these	12	37
Don't know/not stated	3	11

Source: BTA (1981b).

further third visiting seven or more of these. Inner-city attractions were visited more frequently than outer-city ones. This was especially the case with overseas visitors for whom the accessibility of the clustered inner-city attractions appears to be an important factor given their short visits to Christchurch. However, 13% of all respondents had not visited any of the designated sites and attractions, with this figure increasing among those visiting friends and relations (21%), attending conventions (28%) or on business (34%). Some 9% of the overseas respondents had visited none of the attractions listed compared with 16% of domestic visitors, many of whom

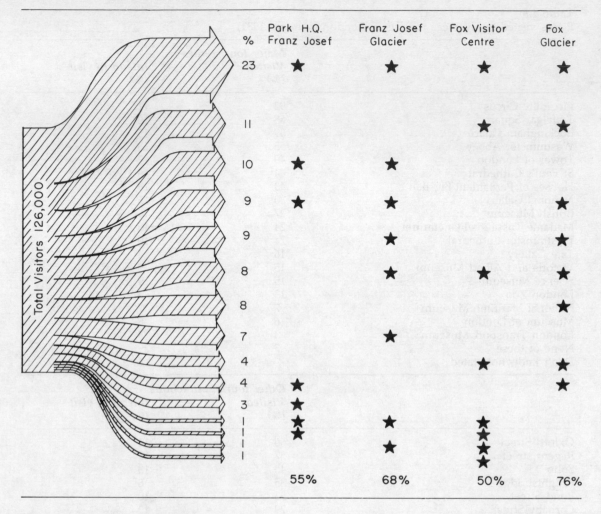

Fig. 4.11 Pattern of visits within Westland National Park (1979–80).

Source: Pearce (1982).

were making repeat visits to the city. Sixty per cent of the respondents staying in Christchurch did not make any day trips out of the city. Of those who did, most made a single trip. The frequency of day trips increased with length of stay and with repeat visits to the city. Day tripping was also more popular among sightseers and those visiting friends and relations, but few differences occurred between domestic and overseas visitors.

Pearce (1982b) estimated the number of visitors to four major places of interest in Westland National Park, two glaciers and two visitor

centres, and was able to determine the popularity of different combinations of places visited. A sample of visitors was interviewed at each site and asked to indicate which of the four places they had visited or intended to visit. From the percentages derived for each combination of visits and the total recorded number of visitors at that site, it was possible to calculate the total number of visitors for each combination of sites visited (for a more detailed explanation of this procedure, see also Pearce 1981b). Figure 4.11 shows that just under a quarter of all park visitors visited all four sites, with the next popular combinations

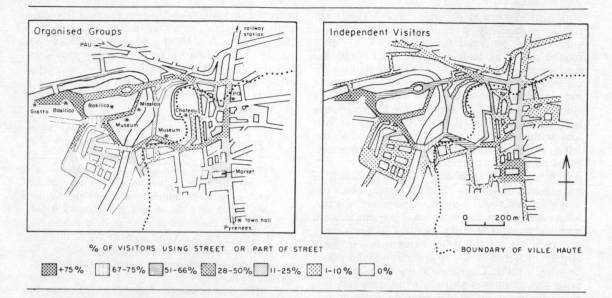

% OF VISITORS USING STREET OR PART OF STREET

⋮⋯⋅ BOUNDARY OF VILLE HAUTE

▓ +75%   ▦ 67-75%   ▤ 51-66%   ▧ 28-50%   ▥ 11-25%   ░ 1-10%   ☐ 0%

Fig. 4.12   The activity space of visitors to
Lourdes.

Source: After Chadefaud (1981).

involving visits to one glacier and the corresponding visitor centre, visits to both glaciers, and visits to both glaciers and one visitor centre. Altogether, 95% of the park visitors visited a glacier and approximately three-quarters of all visitors went to a visitor centre. In Yosemite National Park, van Wagtendonk (1980) cross-tabulated entries and exits to build up a picture of visitor use patterns within the park. The traffic was fairly evenly distributed among the four major entry/exit points surveyed, with approximately 40% of the visitors leaving via their point of entry.

A completely different approach was used in a study of short-term visitors to Victoria, B.C. (Murphy 1980). A survey of pedestrian traffic at various sites in the central area of Victoria showed a strong correlation between the arrival of the ferries and an increase in pedestrian volumes within the Old Town. A decline in afternoon pedestrian volumes with increasing distances from the Inner Harbour was also recorded. The pedestrian survey was complemented by the 'unobtrusive' following of visitors as they left the ferry terminal, which revealed them walking very slowly, making an extensive tour of the district difficult. The slow progress of the visitors was attributed (p. 67) to the 'confusion, lack of sense of direction, crowds, pamphlet pushers and some problems with vehicles'.

Chadefaud (1981) provided details on the activity space of visitors to Lourdes by mapping the intensity of pedestrian use of the town's streets. His maps (Fig. 4.12) show that pilgrims travelling in organized groups confine their movements, or have them confined, to the lower part of the town, to the zone between the major hotels and the religious sites. The activities of pilgrims travelling independently and of other visitors are also concentrated in the lower part of Lourdes, although their movements are more dispersed, particularly around the commercial centre. Chadefaud attributes these differences to a variety of factors. In addition to a full programme of pious activities, many of the group pilgrims were aged and infirm and put off by the climb up to the *ville haute*. The independents, on the other hand, incorporate a greater element of sightseeing and non-pilgrimage activities and may need to support themselves by shopping for food and items other than the religious souvenirs found in abundance in the lower zone.

Aerial photography has been used in coastal areas, for example Brittas Bay in Ireland (An Foras Forbatha 1973), to record directly the distribution of visitors at particular times. This technique, particularly if combined with a visitor survey, has potential for further use in other coastal areas, as well as in ski resorts and the countryside, but obviously has limitations in urban areas where many tourist activities occur indoors and where the presence of residents confuses the issue. In general, the literature says nothing about the pattern of movements of visitors within seaside and ski resorts. Within the latter, it should at least be possible to determine gross patterns through the use of ski-lifts.

If little is known about the actual pattern of movements of visitors within a resort, then even less is known about why those movements occur. Murphy (1980) and Chadefaud (1981) put forward various reasons to explain the patterns they observed but in the other cases these are seen largely in terms of the distribution of the places or sites visited. Cognitive studies exploring the spatial awareness of tourists in the same way that the activity spaces of day-tripping recreationists have been analysed would appear to be a potentially fruitful avenue of future research, although deriving a representative sample of visitors poses more problems than interviewing day-tripping householders (Elson 1976; Aldskogius 1977).

One of the few behavioural studies referring specifically to tourism is that by Murphy and Rosenblood (1974), who examined the spatial search behaviour of first-time visitors to Victoria, B.C. Respondents in their survey were interviewed at one of the mainland ferry terminals prior to their departure for Victoria and then asked to complete and return a diary of their holiday activities. Information on five groups of variables – personal characteristics, activities, planning, spatial relationships and intervening opportunities (information sources, change of plans, weather) – were collected in this way and then subjected to smallest space analysis. A two-dimensional solution suggested that the variables might be grouped into four relatively distinct clusters: planning, personal characteristics and two activity types (shopping and sightseeing). From their analysis, the authors concluded (p. 208) that: 'The distinctive planning cluster and over-all accuracy of prediction on the part of the tourist indicate that their search pattern is closely related to their prior mental image and motivation. In addition, the link between intervening variables, particularly the information sources, and shopping suggests that inter-trial learning has a relatively strong association with this activity.'

A similar approach has been used by Cooper (1981), who asked visitors to the island of Jersey to record their movements over the first five days of their holiday, each day being split into five time periods. A hierarchy of sites on Jersey was then determined on the basis of facility provision, and the accessibility of each site was calculated using network analysis. On analysing the pattern of visits in terms of the site hierarchy, Cooper (p. 365) found:

> The sequence of visits over the 5 days represents a progressive filtering down the hierarchy of sites. The first day of the holiday sees the hotel site or the major touring centre (St Helier) dominating visits. By the second day tourists are leaving the major touring centre and visiting the large beach sites (Gorey and St Brelaude's Bay) or touring the island in general. By the third day, they are beginning to reach the small sites and the initial pulse of visits from St Helier weakens as it dissipates among progressively more sites . . .
>
> The tourists' search strategy appears to use the hierarchy of site size as a surrogate for information. Tourists progressively reduce uncertainty at the expense of effort.

Cooper likens this pattern to 'a wave of visits which spreads down the hierarchy, decreasing among increasing numbers of sites'. Cooper also found differences in the touring patterns of different groups. Visitors from the upper social class, for example, tended to be more mobile and adventurous, reaching a large number of more remote sites. Those from the lower social grades were more inclined to limit their visits to the major sites. Middle-aged visitors tended to be more mobile than the young or elderly.

As both these studies show, the time-budget approach offers much scope for examining the spatial search process among visitors. It may also help determine more precisely their actual pattern of visits, for the indications from other visitor surveys are that visits to specifically designated sites and attractions do not account for all, or in some cases any, of the time spent at the destination.

Conclusions

Research on intra-national travel patterns is characterized by a diversity of approaches. In part, this stems directly from the lack of a common source of data such as the A/D card which provides the cornerstone for much of the work on international tourist flows at a more global level. More importantly, the field of intra-national travel has scarcely been recognized as such.

Several of the larger-scale studies such as those by Shirasaka (1982) and Forer and Pearce (1984) explicitly tackle the question of where overseas visitors go within a given country, but many of the other examples cited refer to intra-national patterns of movement, sometimes incidentally, as part of a more general and traditional case study. Likewise, few of the studies providing material on intra-destination travel are set explicitly within this more general problem area.

As a result of the variety of approaches used and the absence of common goals pursued, it is difficult to identify general patterns and themes. Individual studies, however, do indicate signifi-cant differences in the intra-national travel patterns of different groups of tourists and high-light the various roles and functions which particular places may have. While studies of travel within particular destinations indicate the movements of tourists are spatially concentrated, others indicate a tendency to over-simplify the places sought and visited by them. Taken together, these divergent studies do enable a broad definition of the area of intra-national travel, and the diverse approaches reviewed hold out rich possibilities and inviting challenges for future research in this domain.

5

An integrated approach to international tourist flows

As the preceding three chapters have shown, most studies of international travel flows deal with a single scale of analysis. A few have considered regional variations in the propensity for international tourism, a number have focused on flows between countries, others have looked at intra-national travel patterns within destination countries and some have concentrated on movements within cities and resorts. In practice, international travel involves, in varying degrees, movements at each of these scales so that it is appropriate to attempt a more integrated approach which links one part of a trip to another and which combines the various levels of flows (Fig. 1.8). Two examples of such an integrated approach, drawing on different data sources and employing different methods of analysis, are given here. The first concerns travel to and within French Polynesia, with particular attention being paid to the extent of inter-island movement associated with circuit tourism and destination travel. Brief comparisons are made with Hawaii. An attempt is also made to assess the tourists' daily activity patterns within French Polynesia. The second example deals with package tourism between the United Kingdom and Spain, with emphasis being given to the linkages between multiple gateways in the two countries and the catchment areas served by the British airports. The time-budgets of coastal tourists in Spain are also discussed briefly before the evolution of the charter flight network is examined.

French Polynesia

The number of tourists visiting French Polynesia increased from 1,472 in 1959 to a total of 98,826 in 1981. The United States constitutes its single largest market, providing 43% of all tourists in 1981, followed by metropolitan France (14%) and Australia (9%). Since 1980 the usual information collected on international A/D cards has been supplemented by a short questionnaire which, among other questions, requests visitors to indicate their intended length of stay on the three main islands and to note other islands to be visited. Data from these two sources provide an integrated picture of travel to and within the territory (Pearce 1984a).

A distinction between destination and circuit tourism is made by the Tahiti Tourist Development Board on the basis of port of disembarkation/embarkation. Where these ports are the same, for example a visitor arrives at Papeete from Auckland and subsequently returns to Auckland, then French Polynesia is considered to be his sole destination. If, however, he arrives from Auckland and then leaves for Los Angeles, then he is considered to be visiting French Polynesia as part of a larger circuit. Unfortunately, no data are collected to show what the other stops in the circuit are.

Perhaps surprisingly, given Tahiti's mid-Pacific location, the majority of visitors are making French Polynesia their sole destination for, in

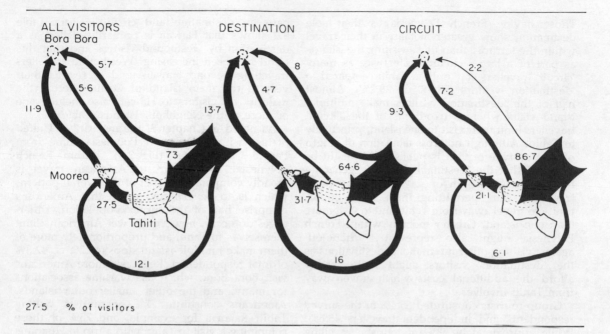

27.5 % of visitors

Fig. 5.1   Patterns of travel within French
Polynesia (1981).

Source: After Pearce (1984a).

1981, 61% of those surveyed returned to the port
from which they embarked (Table 5.1). This is
particularly so with the two major markets, the
USA and metropolitan France, where two-thirds
of the visitors are 'destination' tourists. Other
Europeans and South Americans, on the other
hand, tend to visit French Polynesia more as part
of a larger circuit.

Given the nature and extent of French Polynesia, a wide variety of possible places to visit
exists within the territory. However, half of all
classified hotel rooms are found on Tahiti which
has more than half of the territory's population
of 140,000 and its only international airport
(Faaa). Moorea, with 28% of classified hotel
rooms, and Bora Bora (12.5%) are the only other
islands to have experienced significant hotel
development. The patterns of visits within French
Polynesia reflect this distribution, particularly the
dominance of Tahiti (Fig. 5.1). Some 40% of visitors spend their entire stay in Tahiti and a similar
proportion spend part of their time there. Moorea
is also visited by about 40% of international travellers, mainly as part of a combination of islands,
and about a quarter of all travellers visit the more
distant Bora Bora. A little over 40% of all visitors

Table 5.1

Distribution of destination/circuit visitors in
French Polynesia (1981)

Origin	Destination (%)	Circuit (%)
USA	70.1	29.9
France	65.1	34.9
Australia	62.7	37.3
Others	61.5	38.5
New Zealand	59.6	40.4
Japan	55.9	44.1
South America	47.3	52.7
Canada	45.3	54.7
Europe (excl. France)	34	66
All visitors	61.2	38.8

Source: Pearce (1984a).

stay at more than one island, Tahiti–Moorea
being the most favoured combination, followed
by Tahiti–Moorea–Bora Bora.

As might be expected, these patterns change
when the tourists are grouped by type of visit.

Those having French Polynesia as their sole destination show greater mobility in their travel within the territory than those visiting the islands as part of a larger circuit. Fully twice as many 'circuit' travellers stay only in Tahiti compared to 'destination' visitors (58.4% cf. 28.2%). Almost half of the 'destination' visitors make multiple-island visits whereas two-thirds of the 'circuit' travellers limit their visit to one island, principally to Tahiti. Although no cross-tabulation of length of stay by type of visit is published, it might be assumed that the 'destination' visitors generally have a greater length of stay than the 'circuit' travellers, thus permitting them more opportunity to travel away from Tahiti and to visit more than one island. Greater mobility within French Polynesia might also represent a 'trade-off' against visiting other international destinations as the 'destination' visitors might more readily afford the additional costs which travel away from Tahiti involves.

Group tourists constituted 55.4% of the survey respondents and independent travellers 45.6%. While approximately 58% of tourists travelling independently or with a group visited only one island, there was a much greater tendency with independent travellers for this island to be Tahiti (51.5%). In contrast, a significant number of group tourists made one-island stops in Moorea (19%) and Bora Bora (8.3%); many of these would appear to be on Club Méditerranée packages. Only 30.6% of group tourists restricted themselves to Tahiti. The pattern of multiple-island visits was very similar for both classes of tourist.

Data from the Hawaii Visitors Bureau (HVB) surveys suggest similar patterns to those found in French Polynesia also occur in the Hawaiian group. The HVB distinction between 'visitors to Hawaii' and 'visitors beyond Hawaii' is comparable to the French Polynesian differentiation

between 'destination' and 'circuit' visitors. Table 5.2 shows that Hawaii is primarily visited as a destination by westbound visitors and that this trend has been increasing. Westbound travellers travelling beyond Hawaii tend to restrict their visit to the main island of Oahu whereas the majority of 'visitors to Hawaii' also include one or more of the Neighbour Islands (Table 5.3).

As noted in Chapter 2, the majority of United States visitors to French Polynesia come from Pacific Coast states (Fig. 2.4). Within French Polynesia, the pattern of American travel is broadly comparable to that of the overall pattern, which is to be expected given that Americans comprise half of the survey population. Differences do occur, however. Fewer Americans limit themselves to Tahiti and proportionately more of them make multiple-island stops (48.2% cf. 42.3% of total respondents). Relatively more Americans visit Bora Bora, which has wartime associations for many, and the other smaller outer islands. Americans constitute 77% of tourists visiting Tahiti–Raiatea, for example, and 75% of those combining a visit to Tahiti with a trip to Huahine; the numbers involved in such cases are relatively small (respectively 360 and 183). The more dispersed pattern of American travel within French Polynesia is clearly related to the proportion of American visiting the territory as their sole destination. The majority of American tourists are choosing to travel within French Polynesia rather than visiting Tahiti as one stop on a Pacific circuit.

Figure 5.2 represents an attempt at portraying in an integrated fashion the different aspects of Australian tourist flows to and within French Polynesia. The within-origin flows have been able to be related to the within-destination travel patterns, but the published data do not enable the movements of particular groups of visitors to

Table 5.2
Visitors* to and beyond Hawaii (1960–80)

	1960		1970†		1980†	
	No.	%	No.	%	No.	%
Visitors to Hawaii	213,670	72.8	995,680	84.8	2,718,863	89.3
Visitors beyond Hawaii	79,914	27.2	179,025	15.2	327,269	10.7
	293,584	100	1,174,705	100	3,046,132	100

* Westbound travellers only.
† Excludes in-transit visitors.

Data source: Hawaii Visitors Bureau.

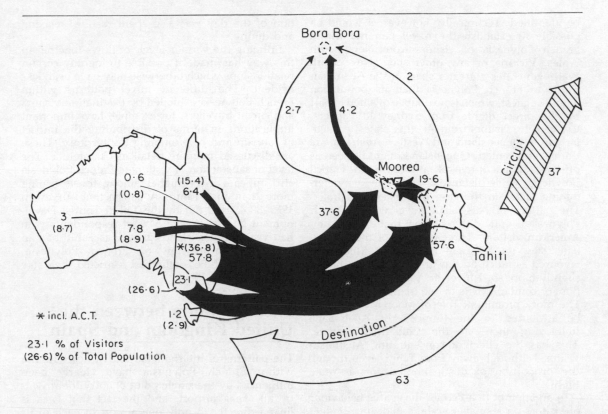

Fig. 5.2 Australian travel to and within French
Polynesia (1981).

Source: After Pearce (1984a).

Table 5.3
Distribution of westbound visitors in Hawaii (1969–80)

	Visitors to Hawaii			Visitors beyond Hawaii		
	1960 (%)	1970 (%)	1980 (%)	1960 (%)	1970* (%)	1980* (%)
Oahu only	23.9	37.8	29.6	71	87.9	84
Oahu and other islands	54.8	62.2	50.5	11.2	12.1	12.5
Neighbour Islands only	1.2	—	19.9	0.6	—	3.5
Undecided	20.1	—	—	17.2	—	—

* Excludes in-transit visitors.

Data source: Hawaii Visitors Bureau.

be identified. Technically, however, it would be possible to establish the travel patterns within French Polynesia of visitors from New South Wales, Victoria or any other state. New South Wales generates a greater share of the Australian traffic to French Polynesia than its population would suggest, which is no doubt explained in part by the direct flights from Sydney to Papeete. Conversely, visitors from all other states, particularly from Queensland and Western Australia, are under-represented. Queensland might be seen as offering similar physical attractions to French Polynesia, while distance is undoubtedly a determining factor in the case of Western Australia. The pattern of Australian travel within French Polynesia is quite different from that exhibited by American visitors. Three-quarters of the Australians stay on a single island, but Moorea is favoured as much by this group as Tahiti, indeed slightly more so. Far fewer Australians visit Bora Bora or combine visits to one island with another. The more prominent role of Moorea can largely be attributed to the numbers of Australians holidaying there at the Club Méditerranée. This has the effect of concentrating Australian visitors, although away from Tahiti, even though the proportion of destination visitors is quite high.

In an attempt to ascertain the spatial behaviour of visitors on a smaller scale, a pilot time-budget study initiated by the author was undertaken in Tahiti during September and October 1984. Hotel guests were requested to record their activities and the location where these took place for each of six two-hour periods during the course of the day for up to the first five days of their stay. This approach achieved a very low response rate, approximately 5%, with a total of only 20 respondents completing their diaries satisfactorily. It is unclear to what extent the low response rate represents problems in the distribution and recovery of the diaries or an unwillingness on the part of the guests to record their activities. In any event the gross results obtained can only be seen as indicating possible patterns which might be pursued in subsequent research. Just over half of the time recorded was spent in and around the hotel itself, with a further quarter being spent in Papeete. Other time was devoted to circle island tours and visits to other places in Tahiti, as well as day visits to other islands. Excluding the evening meal slot, a fifth of the time was spent sunbathing, swimming or pursuing other watersports. This was only marginally more than that devoted to sightseeing, which is somewhat surprising if it were to hold true for the total visitor population. A fair propor-

tion of the day was also spent resting, relaxing and dining.

Bringing the various levels of flows together in this way has made it possible to identify certain relationships which otherwise may have been less evident. The different travel patterns within French Polynesia exhibited by destination visitors and circuit travellers, for example, have important implications in terms of distributing the impact of tourism and of promoting the territory. These are discussed in more detail in Chapter 11. The level of satisfaction of visitors to French Polynesia also appears to be higher among those visiting more than just Tahiti. A satisfaction survey in 1979–80 carried out by the Taihiti Tourist Development Board showed 54% of respondents who had visited other islands as well as Tahiti had an 'excellent' impression of French Polynesia, compared with 36% who had restricted their stay to Tahiti (ODT 1980).

Package tours between the United Kingdom and Spain

The patterns of international tourist flows to and within French Polynesia have clearly been influenced by the single point of entry for arrivals by air, Faaa airport, and the fact that Faaa is linked directly to only one airport in each of its major markets. In this respect, French Polynesia exhibits the characteristics of many small destinations, particularly insular ones. In other cases, both generating and receiving countries may have several points of entry and departure and a variety of linkages is possible, particularly where different modes of transport are available. Patterns of package tourism by air between the United Kingdom and Spain have been selected to exemplify these multi-gateway flows. In 1980 the United Kingdom–Spain traffic accounted for a fifth of all chartered inclusive tour passengers carried within the European Civil Aviation Conference system.

The development of package tourism has been a very significant feature of the post-war expansion of tourism, especially in the Mediterranean (Burkart 1971; Estrada 1973; Burkart and Medlik 1974; Spill 1976). The few geographical studies of international package tourism that have been undertaken to date have largely focused on country-to-country flows. Vanderheyden (1979), for example, used tour operators' brochures to identify the countries most frequented on package tours from Belgium, while Gillmor (1973) used similar data to examine the destinations of chartered inclusive tours from Ireland. Both writers also comment on the concentration of package tours within the destination countries but do not detail the flows to these. Since the early 1970s, however, many European civil aviation authorities have published statistics on non-scheduled air traffic (that is, charters) on a city-pair basis (Cambau and Lefevre 1981). Using these data it is possible to establish a much more detailed picture of flows between specific points of origin and destination although assumptions have to be made regarding the direction of the traffic as this is not specified. In the case of flows between England and Spain, this presents few problems, but in other instances, such as England–Germany, the proportion of the traffic generated in each country is less evident.

Civil Aviation Authority (CAA) figures for the mid-1970s suggest that approximately two-thirds of British leisure inclusive tour passengers departed from the three London area airports (Heathrow (12%), Gatwick (35%) and Luton (16%)) while the remaining third passed through thirteen provincial airports.[1] Of these, Manchester (15%), Birmingham (7%), Glasgow (4%) and East Midlands (4%) handled the largest volume of traffic. Data from the CAA's ultimate origin/destination surveys show that each of the provincial airports serves a fairly localized catchment area (Fig. 5.3). The Scottish airports, for instance, derive virtually all their CIT passengers from Scotland, while Cardiff and Bristol generate business almost exclusively from within Wales and the South West. Manchester and Birmingham also rely heavily on the large populations of their home regions but, in addition, draw passengers from neighbouring regions through the greater variety of tours operated out of them. This is also the case with the London area airports which derive about two-thirds of their passengers from within the South East, principally from the Greater London Metropolitan Area, while the remaining third is drawn from throughout the country. The total volume of extra-regional traffic passing through the London airports and, to a lesser extent, those of Manchester and Birmingham mean that while the provincial airports depend heavily on passengers from their home market, a significant proportion of tourists may nevertheless use airports in other regions. In addition to East Anglia which has no international airport, the regions where less than half the traffic generated passes through the regions' own airports are: Yorkshire/Humberside (1%), the South West (17%), the East Midlands (29%) and Wales (30%).[2] The London area airports appear to capture much of the traffic from these markets.

While the London area airports serve virtually all chartered tour destinations operated out of the United Kingdom, data compiled by the Institut de Transports Aériens (Cambau and Lefevre 1981) indicate tours from the provincial airports are essentially limited to destinations within Spain. Spanish civil aviation figures reveal that 2.6 million passengers arrived in Spain from England in 1979 on non-scheduled flights. Figure 5.4 shows that in 1979, 16 Spanish airports were linked to 16 English airports by 113 different flows of greater than 1,000 incoming non-scheduled passengers. In contrast, that same year, just over half a million passengers arrived in Spain from the United Kingdom on scheduled flights, all of which originated in London. Half of the non-scheduled passengers left from the London area airports from which flights were operated to each of the Spanish airports. Palma de Majorca received almost a third of the total, being linked to all but one of the British airports (Prestwick). Alicante, Malaga, Tenerife and Ibiza were the next most popular destinations, being linked to all but the smallest British airports in the network. In general, the pattern is the smaller the total number of passengers, the fewer the number of linkages. At one end of the provincial scale, airports such as Bournemouth, Exeter and Southampton only have one or two flows greater than 1,000 passengers and their links are primarily with Palma. Belfast, Bristol and Cardiff are linked to the five or six most popular Spanish destinations while the larger airports such as Birmingham and Manchester also serve such places as Gerona, Menorca and Reus.

With a few exceptions, notably flights between the London area airports and Madrid, Santiago (essentially pilgrims) and Zaragoza, all flows are to coastal or insular destinations. Unfortunately, ultimate destination figures similar to those provided by the CAA surveys are not available in Spain to complete the picture by showing the dispersion of these non-scheduled passengers at their point of entry. However, the economics of tour operation suggest that each Spanish airport serves a localized area. Most non-scheduled passengers arriving at Malaga airport, for example, would appear to be destined to nearby Torremolinos or perhaps Fuengirola and Marbella, while Alicante airport mainly serves Benidorm.

Results from a time-budget study which formed part of a survey of over 3,000 foreign and domestic tourists at 16 different Spanish beaches Gaviría et al. (1974) suggest the package tourist activities within these resorts are likely to be spatially constrained.[3] This study showed that 29% of the respondents' time, outside of that devoted to sleeping at night (which averaged 7

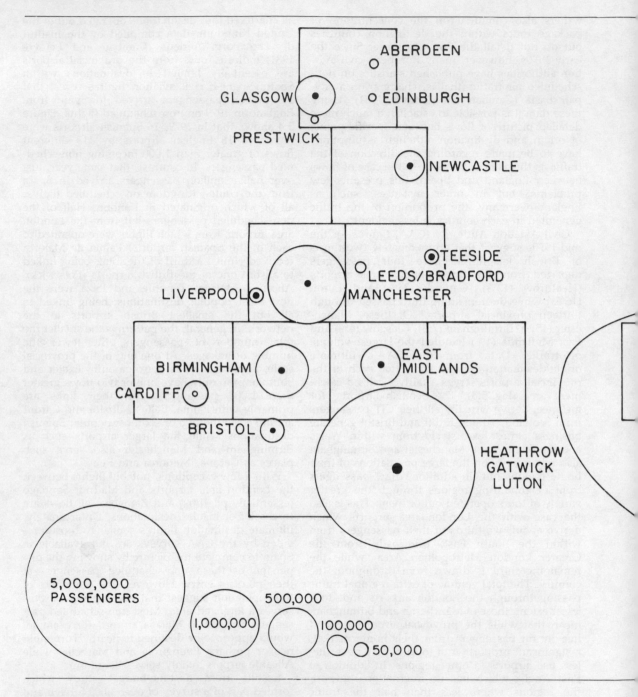

Fig. 5.3 Inclusive tour catchment areas of British airports.

Data source: CAA.

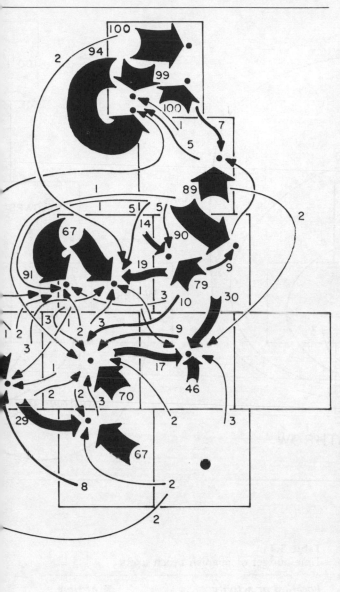

to 9 hours), was spent in and around their accommodation, including time spent around the swimming pool, on the terrace, in the bar or having a siesta in their room (Table 5.4). The beach accounted for a quarter of the time spent, with other major activities occurring on the streets (walking around, shopping, on public terraces etc.) and in places of entertainment (cafes, bars, restaurants, discotheques etc.). Relatively little time was spent on excursions or other activities organized by the tour operator or travel agency, or on private motoring. In an earlier study, Gaviría et al. (1974) suggest that such patterns of tourist behaviour must be seen in the light of the commercial strategies of the hoteliers and tour operators which aim at retaining as much as possible of the tourist's spending within the hotel (p. 112):

> The best way of doing this . . . is to do all that is possible to see that he doesn't leave the hotel, enclosing himself if necessary in the hotel, in an hotel transformed into a factory which uses him as raw material to be processed into cash. This is why hoteliers are interested in hotels located away from recreational centres . . . .

The dominant pattern which emerges from Fig. 5.4 is one of a multiplicity of links between the generating country, the United Kingdom and the receiving one, Spain. In many cases the market and the destination are linked directly by these non-scheduled flights. Half of the non-scheduled traffic entering Spain from the United Kingdom originates in one of the provincial airports and, as Fig. 5.3 has shown, these generally serve a fairly localized catchment area. There is indeed some movement up the urban hierarchy, particularly in the case of the London area airports, but given the larger population of the South East region, this movement does not appear particularly pronounced in the case of tours to Spain. However, it does become much more important in the case of charter flights to other (non-Spanish) destinations. Within Spain, there is little dispersion down the urban hierarchy, as the package tourists proceed from provincial airports directly to the 'resort enclave' where they appear to spend most of their time in and around their hotel or apartment and at the beach. Madrid accounts for just over 1% of the non-scheduled British traffic while Gerona airport handles some 50% more non-scheduled passengers than nearby Barcelona.

Neither the British nor the Spanish civil aviation statistics are sufficiently detailed to trace the spatial development of the network shown in Fig. 5.4. Little detail exists on the formative

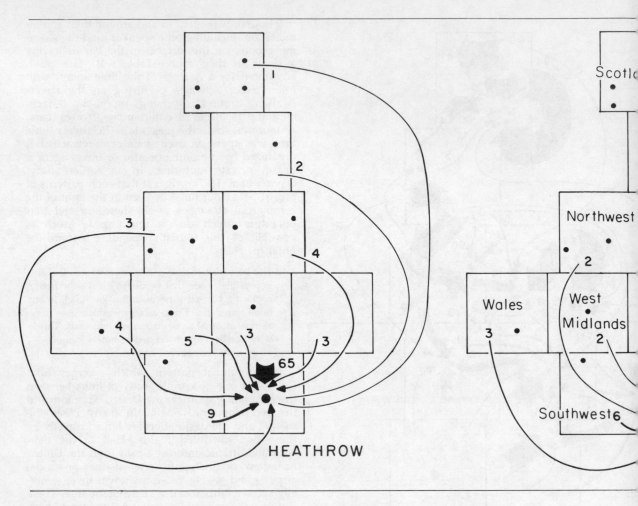

Fig. 5.3 (*Contd.*)

decade of the 1960s as city-pair statistics only became available in the mid-1970s when the network is already well established. However it seems there has been a progressive decentralization of charter tours away from the London area airports. An ITQ study (Anon 1971a: 71) observes: 'one of the most significant trends in the charter inclusive tour industry in the United Kingdom is the extent to which departures from provincial airports have become important in terms of the numbers of tours sold'. Two years later a follow-up study found 'the trend towards extending the network has continued, and most major tour operators offer flights from several provincial airports, as well as from Luton and Gatwick, which remain the prime departure points' (Anon 1973: 24). Later still, the Spanish

Table 5.4
Time-budget of Spanish beach users

Location or activity	% of time
In and around accommodation	29.5
At the beach	25.7
On the streets	21.9
Places of entertainment	13.9
Private motoring	3.2
Activities organized by operator or agency	3.0
On a boat	1.2
Practising a sport other than swimming	1.1

Source: After Gaviría et al. (1975).

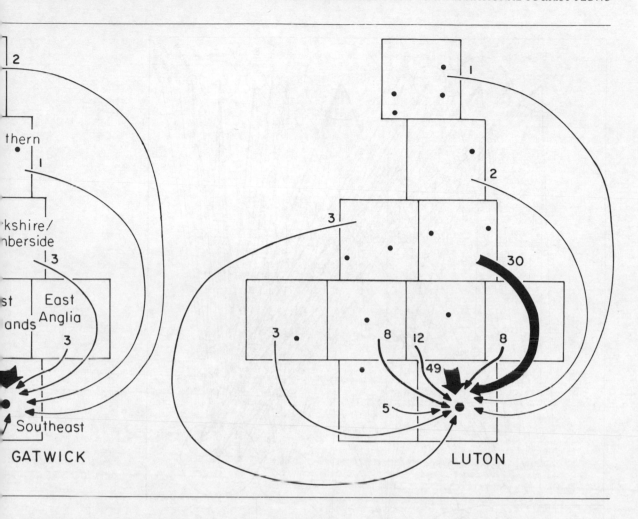

GATWICK

LUTON

civil aviation figures show the proportion of British non-scheduled traffic originating in the London area airports dropped from 55% to 50% in the period 1975–79. A similar trend has been observed in Sweden, where the number of charter flights leaving Arlanda airport (Stockholm) dropped from 65% in 1974 to 56% in 1978 (Eriksson 1981). Eriksson also expected this trend to occur in Finland.

The decentralization of charter flights to the provincial airports appears to reflect attempts at increasing the size of the market by broadening the market base. As Fig. 5.3 has shown, each of the provincial airports serves a predominantly local clientele and as the total number of charter flights has increased it seems logical to assume that a large part of this expansion is due to

package holidays becoming more accessible by reducing internal travel costs and increasing regional promotion. At the same time, the existence of a large number of commercial airports in Britain and the relatively small size of the aircraft originally used in charter operations has meant that this strategy has been technically feasible. Some airports, of course, have been better able to handle the charter traffic than others. The ITQ study (Anon 1971a; Part II, 53) notes in the case of Manchester's Ringway airport that 'because of its importance for scheduled services, its runway and terminal facilities are well able to meet the requirements for handling a substantial volume of ITC holiday traffic'. Completion of a new terminal building and runway extensions at East Midland's Castle Donnington airport in 1970 saw

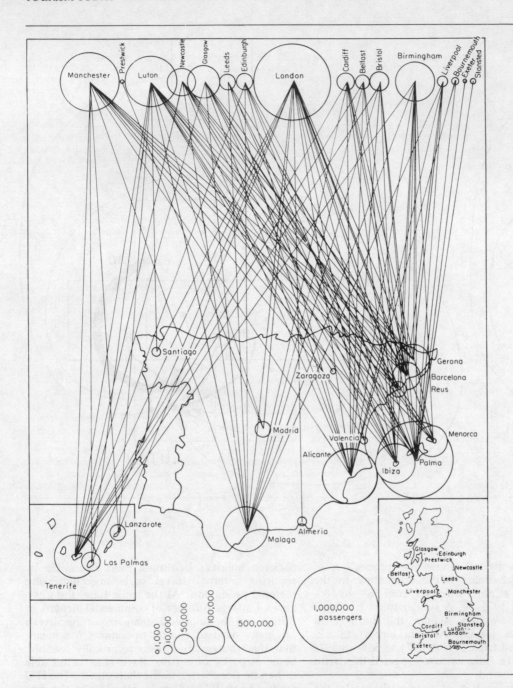

Fig. 5.4 Non-scheduled traffic flows between
the United Kingdom and Spain (1979).

Data source: Ministerio de Transportes Y
Communicaciones.

a four-fold increase in charter passengers the following year (Anon 1973).

The ITQ studies (Anon 1971a, 1973) also examined the commercial organization of package holidays through the provincial airports. They found that the major national companies 'have organized provincial departures within the activities of the main tour operation organizations' (Anon 1971a: 56). Other companies, however, organized their provincial ITC holidays through the operations of various subsidiary or associate companies which were often regional in origin. Some changes were also noted between 1971 and 1973 with various operators adding or deleting flights from particular airports from one season to another. The 1973 study (Anon 1973: 57) also suggests that 'as provincial departures develop further, some smaller tour operators may well decide to pool resources in order to establish a significant provincial operation', but this trend is not re-examined in later reports.

Within Spain, similar commercial and technical factors have led to the operation of charter flights to a number of airports. Tour operators have sought to expand their market by increasing the range of destinations offered so that 'new' packages could be made available each year. In addition, tour operators' financing of hotel development proved lucrative and encouraged the opening up of new destinations (Gaviría et al. 1974). At the same time, the technical demands of the charter flights were rather less than regular scheduled international flights so that charter operations were possible on a seasonal basis using modest facilities and domestic or military airfields, at least in the initial stages. Later, airports were developed specifically to encourage the charter traffic, for example the Gerona airport which serves the Costa Brava. The relatively liberal Spanish policy towards charters plus such positive action as providing this new infrastructure are other important factors. Elsewhere, Spill (1976) and Marenne and Puissant (1979) note how charter operations have pioneered international connections and have permitted the spatial diffusion of tourism beyond the traditional gateways, for example Djerba and Al Hoceima in Morocco, Rimini and Krk in Yugoslavia, Corfu in Greece. In the case of Corfu and Djerba, the unscheduled flights have subsequently given rise to the establishment of regular international services. The international traffic to many of the Spanish airports, however, remains almost exclusively non-scheduled (Lanzarote, 100%; Tenerife Norte, 100%; Gerona, 99%; Alicante, 95%).

Conclusions

The examples of French Polynesia and the United Kingdom and Spain show that it is possible to develop a more integrated approach to international tourist flows, although in the latter case the analysis has been limited to a particular form of tourism between a single pair of countries. In adopting such an approach, researchers cannot rely on a single source of data but must seek, and subsequently integrate, statistics and other information on the various stages of the trip. This is not a straightforward task as statistics compiled in different ways are not necessarily directly comparable, as with the British and Spanish civil aviation figures. In the case of French Polynesia, excellent use has been made by those compiling the visitor statistics of the A/D card. This has been used as a source of data on regional markets, on destination and circuit travel and as a means of collecting supplementary information on inter-island movements. Movements at the local level remain the most difficult to record.

The extent of inter-island movements in French Polynesia and the limited results of the Tahitian time-budget study indicate a greater mobility within the territory than the models of Hills and Lundgren (1977) and Britton (1980a, 1982) might suggest (Fig. 1.8). In the case of charter flights between England and Spain, significant linkages occur between regional urban centres in both countries. Half of the British non-scheduled traffic to Spain still leaves from the London area airports but Madrid receives only a minute fraction of this as the bulk of the traffic is distributed among a large number of coastal and insular airports. The geographic characteristics of the market in the United Kingdom and the resources in Spain combine with the relatively short distances between the two and a variety of historic and technological factors to produce this pattern. More empirical research on the patterns of movements at the local level is needed to test the nature and extent of tourist activity within or beyond the 'tourist enclaves'. Time-budget studies offer potential here, providing methodological difficulties can be overcome. Ideally, a time-budget study at a destination would also include questions relating to other aspects of the visitor's trip, for example whether it involved circuit travel or simply a stay-put holiday, but this may be pushing the visitor's co-operation to the limit.

Notes

1. These figures can only be regarded as indicative as they are based on composite data drawn from the CAA's ultimate origin/destination surveys which were carried out at a sample of airports in three different years, namely 1975 (the Scottish airports, Birmingham, East Midlands and Manchester), 1976 (Newcastle, Teesside, Leeds/Bradford, Liverpool, Cardiff, Bristol) and 1978 (the London area airports – Heathrow, Gatwick and Luton). The effect of this may be to give further emphasis to the London area airports, but the proportional flows through each airport shown in Fig. 5.3 should not vary significantly over the four-year period.

2. These figures are also indicative in nature for the reasons outlined in note 1.

3. All the methodological details of this survey are not discussed in the book but it appears respondents, who had to have spent at least three days at the resort, were approached on the beach and asked to complete a questionnaire on the spot. The respondents apparently had to recall the amount of time spent on various activities and in particular places but it is not clear what period was covered.

6

Domestic tourist flows

The volume of domestic tourism world-wide is estimated by the WTO to be about ten times greater than international tourism (WTO 1983b). Despite the magnitude of this activity, little systematic research has been undertaken into domestic tourist flows. In part, this might be attributed to the less visible nature of much domestic tourism and a consequent tendency by many government agencies, researchers and others to regard it as being less significant than international tourism. At the same time, research on domestic tourism has been plagued by data problems similar to those relating to intra-national travel by foreign visitors. Quite simply, there are few regular records kept of domestic travel and none comparable to the international A/D card, inadequate as that may be for many purposes. Consequently, most domestic tourism research has been ideographic in nature, focusing either on the flows generated by a given town or city or on the origins of visitors to a particular destination. Such studies have usually been based on either household or destination surveys. Studies of domestic tourist flows at a national and regional level are much less common and for this reason the discussion in the first part of this chapter concentrates on methodological issues rather than general patterns.

National patterns

Given that both demand and supply are unlikely to be evenly distributed throughout a country, it may be useful to begin a study of domestic tourism with a nation-wide perspective. A national study might identify the basic dimensions of domestic tourism and outline its broad geographic structure through an analysis of inter-regional flows. This information can then provide the background against which more detailed regional and local studies might be developed in the same way that an analysis of global patterns of international tourism can put flows to and from a given country in context. The value of providing a national perspective prior to a more detailed regional study is well illustrated by Owen and Duffield (1971) with reference to caravanning in Scotland and by Rogers (1977) with regard to second homes in Wales. For the purposes of analysis, a domestic tourism region in a given country might be considered in similar terms to that country in a larger global system or network of countries. A range of approaches comparable to those applied in Chapter 3 might thus be used here.

The utility of national surveys has been recognized for some time. Piatier (1956), in perhaps the earliest review of tourism surveys, cites examples of national surveys from the United States and Great Britain which feature maps of regional tourist flows. In the first case, the maps depict the regional origins of visitors to particular United States regions; in the second, the destinations of holiday-makers from eleven regions in Britain. Despite this early interest, there are still few examples of comprehensive inter-regional studies where the analysis is based on a complete matrix of both origin and destination regions, however broadly defined they might be. The reason for this is not difficult to find. Unlike migration or commodity flow data (White and Woods 1980; Smith 1970), few appropriate and reliable sets of tourism statistics exist which might be used to construct such a matrix. Considerable investment in time, money and effort are required to undertake nation-wide surveys which are sufficiently representative and reliable that the sample results might be weighted by some population factor to arrive at an estimate of total flows between regions.

France is one country where nation-wide tourism surveys are undertaken annually and where the data collected have been expressed in the form of the matrix described above. The following section focuses on ways of analysing this matrix to determine patterns of inter-regional tourist flows. Comparisons are then made with Italy.

Inter-regional tourist flows in France

In France, national surveys are undertaken each year by the State's statistical agency, the Institut National de Statistiques et d'Etudes Economiques (INSEE). The main surveys are limited to summer holidays, with a holiday being defined as a trip away from home for four consecutive nights or more for purposes other than those of business, study or health. A standard unit of measurement, number of holidays, is thus available for all regions, which greatly facilitates analysis compared with the varying definitions found in international tourism statistics. The INSEE expresses some reservations regarding the sample size on which the absolute inter-regional flows have been estimated for any one year, and the matrix used in this study employs average figures for the four-year period 1973–76 (Secrétariat d'Etat au Tourisme 1977). Even here, small absolute values in any region must be viewed with some caution. Origin and destination data are presented for each of the 21 planning regions in France so as to give a 21-by-21 matrix.

As with the analysis of other large bodies of data, it is useful to begin by identifying broad trends in domestic tourism before proceeding to a more detailed examination of flow patterns. The identification of major generating areas and destinations might be a first step here. Gross values for the number of holidays generated by and spent in each region in France are given in Table 6.1 but, for the purposes of cartographic

representation, the origin/destination data might be brought together by calculating net flows into or out of each region. Those regions with a net positive flow, that is where the number of holidays spent within the region exceeds those spent by that region's holiday-makers elsewhere, might be thought of primarily as destinations. Conversely, those regions experiencing a net negative flow might be considered essentially as generating areas or sources.

Figure 6.1 depicts the net flows for France in the period 1973–76 and shows that the country falls neatly into two broad zones. The north and east are primarily generating zones while the south and west are basically destinations. With the exception of the Rhône-Alpes and Provence-Côte d'Azur-Corsica (henceforth referred to as Provence), this pattern parallels the traditional geographic division of the country along the Le Havre–Marseille axis. The industrialized, urbanized and highly populated regions to the north of the line contrast with the agricultural, rural and more sparsely populated regions to the south. These characteristics clearly influence the sign and size of the net flows. The population weight of the north and east coupled with the generally less attractive urban/industrial environment contribute to the zone's net negative flows. The smaller populations of much of the south and west, together with the more appealing rural and coastal environments, result in net positive flows. Climate also affects this broad pattern, favouring the south in particular. On the whole, the destination zone is more evenly balanced than the source zone. There the Ile-de-France (Paris) region is overwhelmingly dominant and, with the exception of the Nord region, the net flows of the other regions are relatively small. The dominance of the Ile-de-France is not only a function of its population, containing 9,878,500 inhabitants in 1975 or 19% of France's population, but also the greater propensity of Parisians to take holidays (78.2% in 1976 compared to the national average of 51.5%). Moreover, the Ile-de-France tends not to be favoured by other French vacationers in summer.

Similar sized net flows may, however, result from different situations. Such is the case with the Limousin and Rhône-Alpes which have comparable net positive flows in absolute figures. The poor, slightly populated Limousin region generated the smallest number of holidays of any region (only about 1% of the national total), whereas the Rhône-Alpes is second only to the Ile-de-France. In this latter case, the populous Lyons agglomeration is compensated by an attractive alpine environment elsewhere in the

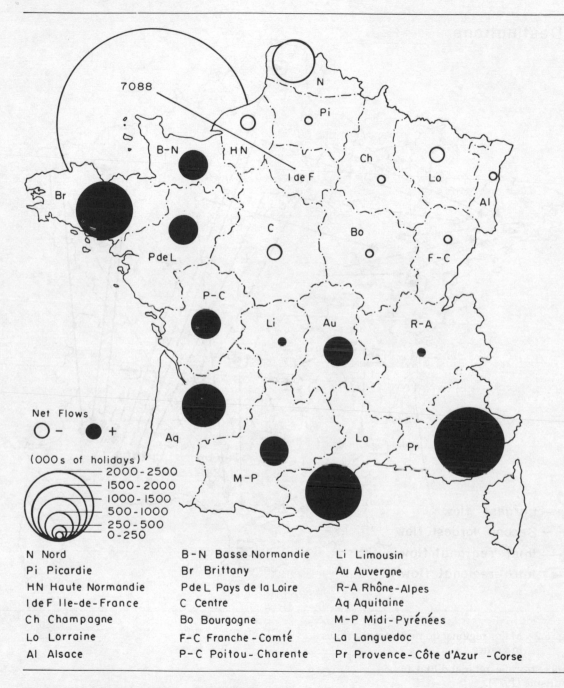

Fig. 6.1 Net domestic tourist flows in France (summer, 4-year average 1973–76).

Data source: Secrétariat d'Etat au Tourisme (1977).

Destinations

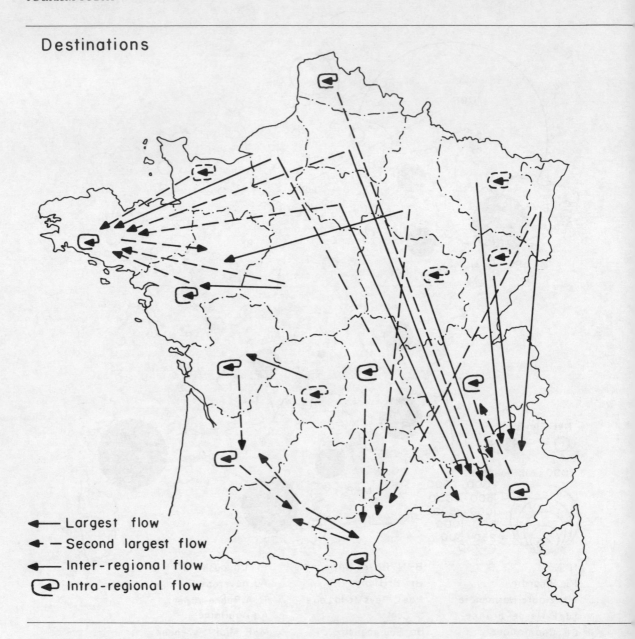

Largest flow
Second largest flow
Inter-regional flow
Intra-regional flow

Fig. 6.2 Major regional domestic tourist flows
in France.

Data source: Secrétariat d'Etat au
Tourisme (1977).

Origins

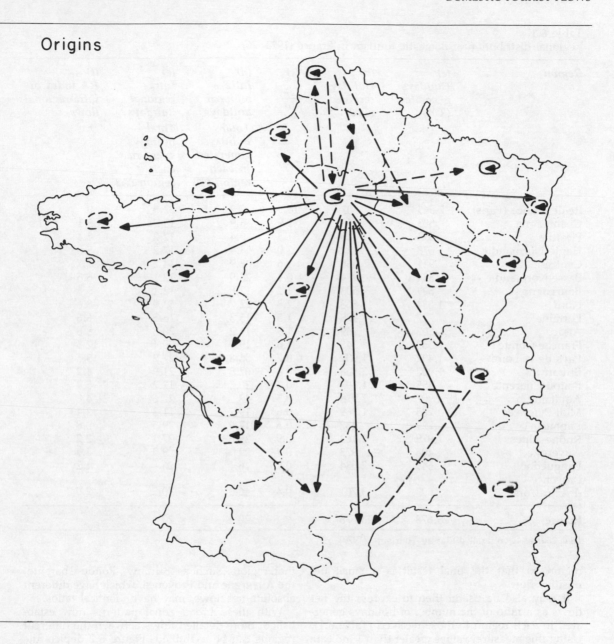

Table 6.1
Regional distribution of domestic tourism in France (1973–76)

Region	(a) Holidays generated ('000)	(b) Holidays received ('000)	(c) $\frac{(a)}{(b)}$	(d) Intra-regional holidays / Total holidays generated in each region (%)	(e) Intra-regional holidays / Total holidays spent in each region (%)	(f) RA index of intra-regional flows
Ile-de-France (Paris)	7,545	507	14.9	2.2	32.3	0
Champagne	505	268	1.9	6.9	13	5.1
Picardie	533	410	1.3	9.4	12.2	4.4
Haute Normandie	678	332	2.0	8.4	17.2	5.0
Centre	921	565	1.6	8.9	14.2	2.7
Basse-Normandie	384	914	0.4	28.9	12.1	6.5
Bourgogne	599	503	1.2	12.8	12.1	5.1
Nord	1,584	563	2.8	22.7	63.9	8.6
Lorraine	727	475	1.5	15.3	18.5	6.6
Alsace	502	269	1.9	11.2	20.8	8.8
Franche-Comté	357	348	1.02	19.9	20.4	12.5
Pays de la Loire	1,432	1,939	0.7	36.8	27.2	3.5
Brittany	1,002	2,838	0.4	62.5	21.9	4.2
Poitou-Charente	455	1,108	0.4	30	12.2	5.4
Aquitaine	907	1,918	0.5	47	22.6	4.8
Midi-Pyrenees	785	1,369	0.6	19.7	11.3	2.4
Limousin	229	432	0.5	17.9	9.5	8.8
Rhône-Alpes	1,979	2,162	0.9	29.6	27.1	2.2
Auvergne	408	973	0.4	22	9.2	4.4
Languedoc	549	2,084	0.26	46	26	4.2
Provence-Côte d'Azur-Corse	1,597	3,701	0.4	46.3	20.2	2.0
France	**23,678**	**23,678**		**20**	**20**	

Data source: Secrétariat d'Etat au Tourisme (1977).

region so that the final result is a small net positive flow.

It may also be useful then to express the net flows as a ratio of the number of holidays generated in each region to those received (Table 6.1). Using this measure, values greater than 1 indicate source regions and those less than 1 destination regions (column c). Again the same basic north–east/south–west division is evident. The Franche-Comté appears as a balanced region, receiving almost as many holidays as it generates, while at the extremes the Ile-de-France's role as a source area is fifteen times greater than its function as a destination, and Languedoc generates only one holiday for every four it receives. This index also discriminates between the Limousin and the Rhône-Alpes but at the same time shows that regions such as Brittany, Poitou-Charente, the Auvergne and Provence, which have different absolute net flows, may have identical ratios.

With these broad zonal patterns now established, more detailed flows between the different regions can be examined. Figure 6.2 depicts the two largest flows of holiday traffic generated by each region. Two main directional trends are evident, both of them towards the coast – one to the south-east, to Provence and to a lesser extent Languedoc, the other to the west, notably to Brittany. The only major inter-regional flows inland are from the coastal regions of Aquitaine, Languedoc and Provence.

Figure 6.2 and Table 6.1 (column *d*) indicate the localized nature of much domestic holiday-making. One-fifth of all holidays spent in France occur in the vacationer's home region, with that region being the dominant or second most important destination for 14 of the country's 21 regions. Vacationing in the home region is particularly noticeable in the major coastal regions (Brittany, 62.5%; Aquitaine, 47%; Provence, 46.8%; Languedoc, 46%) and much less significant in the Paris basin, especially in the Ile-de-France (2.2%). The home region is again prominent when the origin of holiday-makers to each region is considered (column e). However, with three exceptions, the sheer volume of Parisian vacationers makes the Ile-de-France region the most dominant source of visitors throughout France (Fig. 6.2). Two of the three exceptions, Nord and Rhône-Alpes, themselves have large populations and constitute secondary source areas. The Nord received almost two-thirds of its holiday-makers from within the region itself, but these account for less than a quarter of all holidays generated within the region. Intra-regional flows account for a significant proportion of both origins and destinations in regions such as the Pays-de-la-Loire (27.2%, 36.8%), Languedoc (26%, 46%) and the Rhône-Alpes (27.1%, 29.6%), but overall there is no correspondence in the rankings of the 21 regions on these two measures ($r_s = 0.07$).

While the preceding analysis has identified major patterns in the actual flows, it is also useful to measure the magnitude of these against some predicted value in order to identify flows which might be stronger or weaker than expected (Smith 1970; Britton 1971). The Relative Acceptance (RA) Index, employed by Williams and Zelinsky (1970) in their study of international flows, might therefore be applied here, with the advantage that it is being used with reference to a total domestic tourism matrix. In this instance, the relative success of a region in attracting tourists from a generating region will be a function of all domestic tourist flows not just a selection of them.

The RA index is obtained by the formula:

$$RA_{ij} = \frac{A_{ij} - E_{ij}}{E_{ij}}$$

where RA_{ij} is the relative acceptance from origin i to destination j,

A_{ij} is the actual flow from origin i to destination j,

E_{ij} is the expected flow from i and j.

Calculation of the expected flow (E_{ij}) is based on an assumption of origin destination independence or indifference which holds that the flow from i to j reflects the total flow to j. It is obtained by the formula:

$$E_{ij} = \frac{n_i n_j}{n}$$

where n_i is the observed number of visitors from region i in the country as a whole,

n_j is the observed number of visitors in region j.

n is the total number of visitors in the country as a whole.

Thus in the case of France, as Provence received 15.6% of all French holidays, the model predicts it should receive 15.6% of the holidays from each of France's 21 regions.

This technique has the advantage of eliminating the effects of absolute size and enables the identification of unusually high or low flows. The RA index has a range from -1 to plus infinity, with positive values indicating a greater than expected flow and negative values the reverse. Given this range, determination of threshold values for salient positive and negative flows is, however, arbitrary.

Figure 6.3 depicts the flows of those regions having an RA index of unity or greater. This further highlights the importance of intra-regional tourism, for in each case, with the exception of the Ile-de-France region, RA index values are greatest for flows within regions, ranging from 12.5 in the case of the Franche-Comté to 2 for Provence (Table 6.1, column f). With a value of 0, the Ile-de-France received as many holidays from within the region as predicted by the hypothesis of indifference. Overall, there is little correlation ($r_s = -0.27$) between the rankings of the regions in terms of their RA index for intra-regional flows and the proportion of all holidays originating within the region. Much stronger than expected intra-regional flows are found in the north-east (Franche-Comté, 12.5; Alsace, 8.8; Lorraine, 6.6), in the Nord (8.6) and in the Limousin (8.8). Figure 6.3 also reveals patterns of relatively strong interaction among regions in the north-east and in the centre/south-west where the Limousin again features prominently. Together, these two patterns revealed by the RA index suggest holiday-making in the north-east and centre/south-west is much more regionalized than might be expected from the overall national patterns. Or, it may be that the RA index here is in effect revealing the relative inability of these

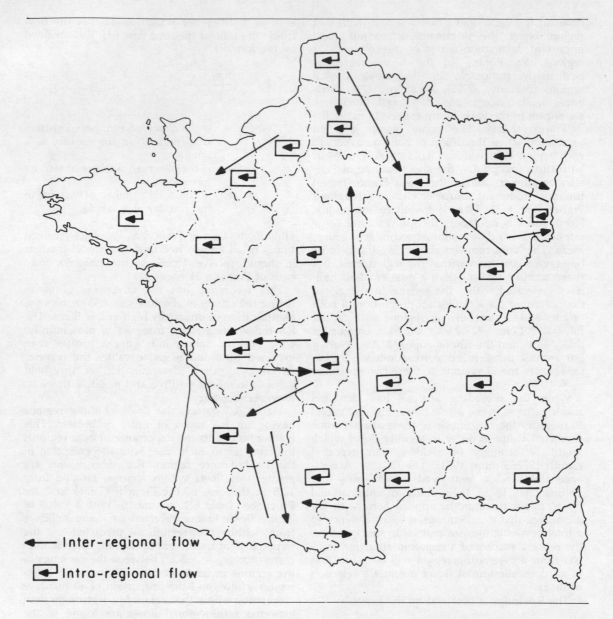

Fig. 6.3 Regional domestic tourist flows in France with an RA index of unity or greater.

Data source: Secrétariat d'Etat au Tourisme (1977).

Table 6.2
Regional distribution of domestic tourism in Italy (1975)

Region	(a) Vacation days generated ('000)	(b) Vacation days received ('000)	(c) $\dfrac{(a)}{(b)}$	(d) Intra-regional days / Total days generated in each region (%)	(e) Intra-regional days / Total days spent in each region (%)
Piedmont	40,308	19,291	2.1	24	47
Aosta Valley	694	6,001	0.1	13.5	1.6
Lombardy	96,833	23,683	4.1	19.7	80.6
Trentino-Alto Adige	5,497	14,212	0.4	41.3	16.0
Veneto	27,653	30,736	0.9	60.7	54.7
Friuli-Venezia Giulia	6,857	8,161	0.8	52.4	40.9
Liguria	14,192	38,171	0.4	29.9	11.1
Emilia-Romagna	33,613	50,466	0.7	57.2	38.1
Toscana	27,129	35,018	0.8	53.5	51.3
Umbria	3,338	3,407	1.0	5.3	5.2
Marche	3,991	12,772	0.3	53.1	16.6
Lazio	48,162	28,519	1.7	49.7	72.2
Abruzzi	3,644	12,147	0.3	65.2	19.6
Molise	1,024	1,605	0.6	28.3	18.1
Campania	23,163	24,733	0.9	62.5	58.5
Puglia	18,334	21,394	0.9	59.3	45.3
Basilicata	2,273	3,118	0.7	23.4	17.7
Calabria	9,438	20,270	0.5	71.1	33.1
Sicily	14,164	19,438	0.7	64.5	47.0
Sardinia	5,450	10,555	0.5	75.9	39.2
Italy	383,697	383,697		42.3	42.3

Data source: Instituto Centrale di Statistica (1977).

regions to attract extra-regional holiday-makers rather than their success in drawing intra-regional vacationers and those from adjoining regions. In other words, regional holiday-makers have been shown to be more important in the north-east as fewer than expected vacationers have been drawn from outside the region. Given the character of the north-east, this appears the more probable explanation. The majority of strong negative flows, that is those where the traffic between regions is rather less than expected, are northerly in direction.

Inter-regional tourist flows in Italy

Comparative data on inter-regional tourist flows in Italy are provided by a 1975 survey undertaken by the Central Institute of Statistics (Instituto Centrale di Statistica 1977), based on a stratified sample of more than 80,000 households. Survey results were then weighted by the population in each stratum to give, among other results, total flows to and from each of the country's twenty regions in the form of a 20-by-20 matrix of the number of vacation days generated or spent in each region. When analysed in the same way as the French data, the Italian survey provides some interesting comparisons and contrasts.

When net flows are considered, only three generating regions are identified: the wealthy industrialized and highly populated northern regions of Piedmont and Lombardy, and Lazio, which contains Rome, Italy's capital and largest city. These three regions together account for almost half of the vacation days generated within Italy, with a quarter of the total coming from Lombardy alone (Table 6.2). The top two destination regions, in both absolute and net terms, are Liguria and Emilia-Romagna, which provide coastal facilities on the Mediterranean and

Destinations

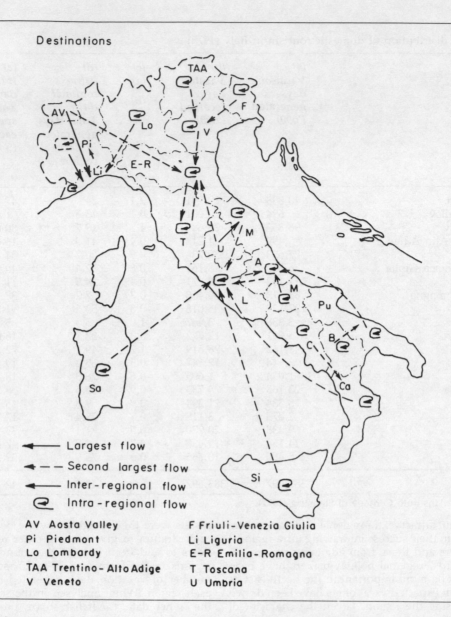

Fig. 6.4 Major regional domestic tourist flows in
Italy (1975).

Data source: Instituto Centrale di
Statistica (1977).

Origins

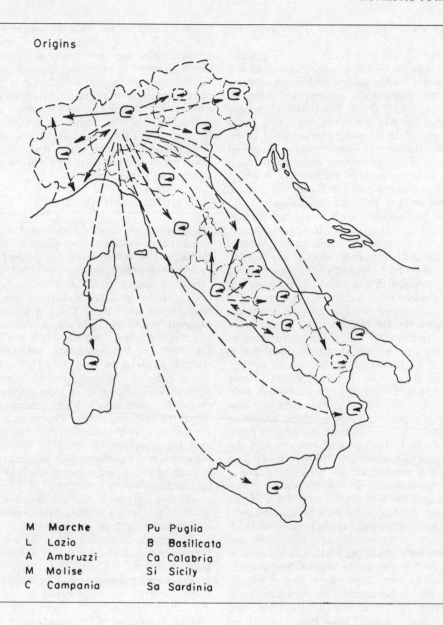

M	Marche	Pu	Puglia
L	Lazio	B	Basilicata
A	Ambruzzi	Ca	Calabria
M	Molise	Si	Sicily
C	Campania	Sa	Sardinia

Adriatic in close proximity to Piedmont and Lombardy.

The impact of the two geographically distinct generating regions becomes very evident in Fig 6.4 which portrays the largest and second largest flows to and from each region. In terms of origins, vacationers from Lombardy dominate inter-regional flows in the north, the south, Sicily and Sardinia, while a smaller central zone is the domain of Roman holiday-makers. Regional development plans promoting tourism in such regions as Calabria may be influencing flows to the south, but much of the Lombardy traffic there is no doubt related to earlier migration to the north. The pattern of flows to destinations is more complex, with flows to neighbouring regions being common. Lazio and Abruzzi join Liguria and Emilia-Romagna as regions attracting first- and second-order flows from several regions. On this measure, Lazio is shown to have important roles as both a generating and receiving region and in this respect contrasts markedly with the Ile-de-France in France.

Perhaps the most outstanding feature in Fig. 6.4 is the importance of intra-regional flows. Over 40% of all the vacation days spent in Italy were confined to the holiday-makers' home regions, compared with 20% of all French holidays, although differences in the units of measurement may account for some of this variation. Intra-regional flows constituted the largest destination flows in 16 of Italy's 20 regions and the second largest in two others. The two exceptions to this general pattern are the small land-locked regions of Umbria and the Aosta Valley which received only 5.3% and 13.% respectively of the vacation days generated by their holiday-makers. Holiday-makers from the highly populated land-locked regions of Lombardy and Piedmont also spend a relatively small proportion of their vacation days within the home region (respectively 19.7% and 24%) even if the single largest flow in each case is intra-regional. In contrast, vacationers from Sardinia, Sicily, Calabria and Abruzzi tended to restrict their holidays to their home region (Table 6.2, column d). Isolation, particularly in the case of the islands, and the existence of local vacation opportunities (a function of Italy's elongated shape and long coastline) may be factors accounting for this tendency to holiday in the home region.

Table 6.2 also shows that the proportion of the total number of days spent in each region which are intra-regional in origin varies widely from 1.6% in the Aosta Valley to 80.6% in Lombardy (column e). In the first case, the low propensity for Aosta Valley residents to holiday at home is compounded by the valley's winter sports facilities which draw skiers from throughout the country. The low propensity for Lombardy residents to holiday at home appears to reflect the relative lack of appeal which the region has for other holiday-makers. Conversely, a high propensity to holiday in the home region may reflect favourable conditions for tourism there. Regions in this situation, such as Calabria, Abruzzi and Marche, may thus receive only a small proportion of their total vacation days from within the region itself.

A national perspective

The examples of France and Italy demonstrate the value of a national perspective on domestic tourism. The progressive analysis of the matrix of inter-regional flows has enabled the identification of major national flow patterns. These highlight the localized nature of much domestic tourism, as shown by the importance of intra-regional flows, and the national dominance of the major generating regions. Here the primacy of the Paris region contrasts with the bi-nodal pattern evident in Italy (cf. Figs 6.2 and 6.4). These national patterns provide some yardstick against which flows to or from particular regions might be measured. Much more information about the national role of Provence and Brittany, for instance, is provided in Figs 6.1 and 6.3 than can be obtained from the more traditional separate, and usually disparate, survey of visitors to each of these two regions. Such information is invaluable for a variety of planning and marketing purposes, such as defining the market share of particular regions and positioning these in the domestic tourism system.

The approach employed in the analysis of the French and Italian data is not without its limitations, however. As with the international flows, only general inferences can be made about why these patterns have appeared for no details are available regarding motivations and the decision-making behaviour of the vacationers. The level of analysis is such that it may conceal significant variations in flows of tourists within individual regions. Is the behaviour of intra-regional holiday-makers the same as that of visitors from outside the region? The itineraries which link origins to destinations are also unknown, although certain inferences might be made on the basis of transport networks. Multiple-region visits, however, cannot be determined in this way. In many instances, it may be more feasible to investigate these questions, for example motivation and itineraries, at a different scale and use a series of local and regional studies in combination with the national matrix to build up an overall picture.

While comparable patterns to those found in France and Italy might be expected in other countries, it is impossible to extrapolate from one country to another due to variations in the resource base, in demand and in other factors. The massive coastwards movement of domestic holiday-makers evident in France, Italy and many other countries is simply not possible in such nations as Switzerland, Austria and Hungary. Alternatives there include focusing on some other body of water, for example on Lake Balaton in Hungary, non-water-based recreation or international travel. Cultural differences may also be a significant determining factor as Robinson (1972) has observed in relation to the Orient, and Ritter (1975) with regard to the Islamic world. After commenting on the 'neglect of the seacoast in Lebanon and elsewhere in the Middle East', Ritter (p. 59) observes that failure to take into account cultural differences may give rise to misguided developments:

> Egypt persistently tries to develop the Marmarican coast west of Alexandria for European tourists. But while this coast by virtue of its cool summer breeze and location is ideally suited to Egyptians it has nothing to offer Europeans.

Other variations from country to country may be more a function of definitions and units of measurement. The apparently greater propensity for intra-regional travel in Canada (58% in 1980) (CGOT 1981) and Australia (approximately 75% in 1981–82 according to the Domestic Tourism Monitor, Morgan Research Centre 1982) compared with France (20%) and Italy (40%) can partially be attributed to the larger size of Canadian provinces and Australian states. Moreover, in the case of Australia all trips greater than one night were considered, while in France only vacations of four consecutive nights or more were taken into account.

Regional studies

Few surveys have been undertaken which reveal patterns of domestic tourist travel within regions. This might be attributed to the limited research functions which most regional level organizations responsible for tourism have as well as to the more general difficulties associated with domestic tourism research discussed in the preceding section. The paucity of research at this level is unfortunate as the studies which have been

undertaken indicate that important differences may occur in the flows of inter-regional visitors to different destinations within a given region. A survey of tourists visiting the province of Quebec in 1975 found that the major metropolitan areas of Montreal and Quebec were the most favoured destinations of all Canadian visitors to the province (Service de la Recherche Socio-Economique 1977). The proportion of visitors to other parts of the province varied markedly according to their origin, with proportionately more visitors from New Brunswick and the Maritime provinces being found in the Lower St Lawrence-Gaspé area and more Ontarians travelling to the Outaouais and North-West areas. A similar pattern emerges from the Australian Domestic Tourism Monitor (Morgan Research Centre 1982). This shows, with one exception, that the state capital is the most favoured destination in each state for all inter-state travellers. Flows to other parts of the state may vary by state of origin. In the case of New South Wales, Queenslanders tend to favour the adjoining coastal region of Tweed Heads–Byron Bay, while Victorians are drawn to the southern border region of the Murray.

These two surveys indicate that large urban areas are the main focus for inter-regional travellers while areas bordering on to other regions may attract proportionately more visitors from the regions in question. In the first case, the strength of the flows appears to reflect the special character of the attractions of the big city, particularly where business and VFR travellers are included (as is the case with the Australian survey). Urban areas appear to be able to draw visitors from outside their region to a much greater extent than other domestic destinations which compete less successfully with intra-regional destinations offering similar features. Border areas, however, might be considered an extension of particular regional hinterlands. Propinquity is the major factor here for in the examples given the state or provincial boundaries are much less significant in practical terms than international ones.

In Australia the major urban areas (Sydney, Melbourne, Brisbane etc.) are also the prime focus for intra-regional (intra-state) travellers. Sydney and Melbourne respectively account for about a quarter of the visits generated by residents from New South Wales Country and Victoria Country. As for the residents of the major urban areas, their visits tend to be rather dispersed but the most favoured destinations are in adjoining coastal areas.

Figure 6.5 is a schematic representation of

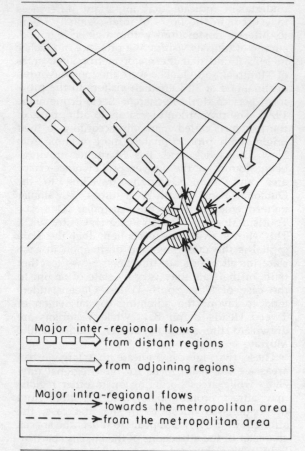

Major inter-regional flows
□ □ □ ⇨ from distant regions

⟹ from adjoining regions

Major intra-regional flows
→ towards the metropolitan area
- - - - ⤍ from the metropolitan area

Fig. 6.5 Schematic representation of domestic tourist flows at a regional level.

major domestic tourist flows seen from a regional perspective and based on the Australian example. The model shows the major metropolitan area to be the main focus for both inter- and and intra-regional flows, with border areas attracting a share of the traffic from adjoining regions, and areas surrounding the metropolitan area being favoured by metropolitan holiday-makers. Further empirical information is needed to test the generality of this model. It should be stressed, for instance, that all Australian states have a coast-line and that the major urban areas are located on or near the coast. In this respect, Australia contrasts markedly with France, discussed earlier in this chapter. The prominence of the metropolitan centres for certain forms of domestic tourism suggests Christaller's (1964) view that tourism is

an activity which avoids central places is not universally true and at the same time supports the hierarchical classification proposed by Lund-gren (Fig. 1.6).

Local studies

Studies of tourist flows are much more numerous at the local level, not only because of the greater range of possibilities there but also because data collection is generally much more feasible at this scale. Local studies normally focus either on flows emanating from a particular city or on the origins of visitors to a particular destination. The flow data are usually collected as part of a larger visitor survey although a range of other data sources have been used, including mailing lists (Wolfe 1951), car licence plates (Sarramea 1979) and social columns (Carlson 1978). In the one case, details are sought on destinations visited so as to define the vacational hinterland of particular towns or cities (Cribier 1969; Greer and Wall 1979), in the second, place of origin or home town are used to delimit the market areas of particular resorts or destinations (Wolfe 1951; Deasy and Griess 1966). A limited amount of research has also dealt with travel routes and patterns.

Vacational hinterlands and market areas

Most studies of vacational hinterlands and market areas concentrate on aggregate origin/destination flows, either for the population at large or for specific groups of travellers, including: second home owners (Coppock 1977); campers (Gibson and Reeves 1972); honeymooners (Carlson 1978); and pilgrims (Chadefaud 1981). Other researchers have compared the hinterlands of different groups defined in terms of accommodation used, purpose of visit and activity patterns or intra-urban residential areas. A few have also considered changes in vacational hinterlands over time.

Vacational hinterlands or market areas are most frequently portrayed by dot distributions or some system of zoning. The general pattern to emerge is that of a decline in the intensity of flows with distance from the origin or destination. Various factors may affect this distance decay pattern, notably the distribution of recreational opportun-ities in the case of source areas or the distribution of population in the case of destinations. As noted in Chapter 1, Greer and Wall (1979) argued that theoretically visitation should peak some distance from the source area due to the interaction of supply and demand (Fig. 1.3) before declining. They graphically illustrated their point with empirical evidence from Toronto. Carlson (1978) showed that aside from distance and financial resources, scenery, particularly that found in national parks, played a significant role in concentrating honeymooners from rural North Dakota and Wisconsin in certain localities.

Different quantitative techniques have been used by various writers to analyse further the role of distance and other factors. Gibson and Reeves (1972), for example, used regression analysis but their efforts were hampered by the size of their samples. A much more widely tested technique incorporating the friction of distance factor in relation to tourist flows is the gravity model. The basic gravity model proposed by Zipf (1946) expressed the interaction between an origin and a destination as a function of the population of each and the distance between them. Tourist flows, however, are not necessarily reciprocal, as Wolfe (1970) points out in the case of second homes where the traffic outward from an urban area to a cottage resort is frequently not complemented by a reverse flow to the city. Consequently, when applied to tourist flows, the gravity model has been modified in various ways. Such modifications include the incorporation of variables measuring the attractiveness of the destinations (the number of ski lifts, the ratio of water to land area), intervening opportunities or the measurement of distance in terms of time or travel cost. Modified gravity models have been applied with some success to specific cases such as tourist travel to Las Vegas (Malamud 1973), the demand for second homes (Bell 1977) and travel to skifields (McAllister and Klett 1976). For a fuller review of methodological issues and for other applications of gravity models, see Archer and Shea (1973) and Smith (1983a).

One of the earliest comparative studies was that by Cribier (1969) who delimited the vacational hinterlands of the major metropolitan centres in France then found, within each hinterland, spatial variations in the type of accommodation used. Non-commercial accommodation (second homes, visits to friends and relations) predominated close to home, while those travelling further afield tended to stay in hotels. Greer and Wall (1979) established the hinterlands of Toronto residents day-tripping, owning cottages, camping and staying in commercial resorts. Different distance decay curves were found for each category but there was also a considerable degree of overlap in the zones frequented by each group.

In their survey of Canterbury (New Zealand) holiday-makers, Johnston, Pearce and Cant (1976) found social visiting and sightseeing to be the major objectives of those travelling to the North Island. Those pursuing water-based activities or seeking general relaxation usually found suitable holiday destinations closer to home. However, in a study of Dayton area households, Etzel and Woodside (1982) found no significant differences in terms of purpose of trip between distant and near-home travellers (defined as travellers within Ohio or to destinations in adjacent states). The two groups did differ though on a number of demographic and psychographic variables. Different activity preferences between local and extra-regional visitors have also been found in destination studies. Jackson and Schinkel (1981) examined the activity preferences of local and 'tourist' campers in the Yellowknife region of Canada and concluded (p. 361): 'Local residents expressed a stronger preference than tourists for activities such as resting and relaxing, swimming, boating and canoeing, while tourists more frequently preferred activities such as sightseeing, hiking, photography, visiting and meeting people.'

Wolfe (1951: 29) argued that it was necessary to disaggregate visitors from major urban areas, suggesting, in the case of Toronto, that 'the zonation of the city finds a rough extension in the zonation of summer resorts'. He later showed a significant directional bias among Toronto cottage-owners from different parts of the city, with residents tending to buy cottages in Ontario in locations that avoided cross-town travel (Wolfe 1966, cited by Smith 1983a). Despite the early recognition by Wolfe of the need to investigate variations in travel from different parts of the city, little serious work has subsequently been undertaken in this area. Washer (1977) showed a close association between the location of permanent residence in Christchurch and ownership of second homes on Banks Peninsula. Mercer (1971) examined the role of urban mental maps in producing directional bias in beach usage from different residential areas in Melbourne. The main handicap in developing this line of research with regard to vacation travel appears to be the need for an enlarged sample so that meaningful comparisons could be made among different parts of the city.

As yet, comparatively little is known about the extent to which vacational hinterlands and market areas expand or contract over time. Rajotte (1975) has shown, historically, how developments in transport technology have extended the vacational hinterland of Quebec, but inadequate time-series data and the absence of baseline studies mean little detailed information is available on how local tourist flows change through time. Chadefaud (1981) has used a series of different sources (diocesan records, hotel registers, surveys) to map long-term changes in the catchment area of French pilgrims to Lourdes. In 1880, a quarter of a century after the appearance of the Virgin Mary before Bernadette Soubirous, the majority of French pilgrims came from South West France, from a zone corresponding to that serviced by the regional railway. By 1925, with the development of a national rail network, pilgrims were arriving from all over the country, but principally from the North, the West and the southern Massif Central, that is, from rural and conservative France. Data from 1972 show an increasing dominance of the faithful from the North and West, with a noticeable absence of Parisians. There had also been a marked increase in foreign pilgrims who now constituted 60% of all visitors to Lourdes.

A certain amount of interest, particularly in North America, was shown in changes induced by the increase in fuel prices and the shortage of petrol supplies experienced at particular times in the 1970s (Corsi and Harvey 1979; Kamp, Crompton and Hensarling 1979; Williams, Burke and Dalton 1979). These indicate some decrease in the distance travelled on holiday trips and even cancellation of vacation travel plans, but these effects appear short-lived and the overall picture is rather inconclusive. The surveys in question have relatively small samples, often low rates of return, and other methodological limitations (McCool 1980).

Flow patterns may also change throughout the year as, for example, the emphasis switches from the coast in summer to the mountains in winter. But the picture may be more complicated than this. Sarramea (1978) concludes from his studies of visitors to Frejus and Saint Raphael on the French Riviera that north–south movements predominate in summer, with visitors from neighbouring departments being more significant at other times of the year.

Travel routes and patterns

Despite the comparatively early models of Mariot and Campbell (Figs 1.1 and 1.2), few domestic tourism studies have examined itineraries or routes, with most surveys concentrating solely on aggregate flow patterns. However, the methodologies used in the analysis of intra-national travel by foreign tourists can in most cases be applied to studies of domestic travel patterns. Indeed, several of the examples cited in Chapter 4 embraced domestic as well as international tourists, for example the study of tourist movements in Scotland (Carter 1971) and the analyses using the Trip Index (Pearce and Elliott 1983).

Information from national travel surveys suggests that most domestic tourism, at least in Europe, does not involve multiple-stop touring but consists mainly of stay-put holidays at a single destination. Three-quarters of British 'main holidays' in 1970 were spent 'staying in one place', notably at the seaside (ETB n.d.b). A 1976/77 survey of Swiss holiday-makers found that 'circuits, expeditions and voyages of discovery' comprised only 3% of domestic holidays compared with 9% of foreign vacations, although there is no information on the actual number of stops made on this or on other types of holidays (Schmidhauser 1977). Circuit tourism (as opposed to stays on the coast, in the mountains, the countryside or towns) accounted for about 4% of French domestic holidays in 1980 and 1981 (CECOD 1983).

In a study of the vacation hinterlands of residents of Dunedin, New Zealand, Goldsmith and Forrest (1982) attempted to establish more directly the proportion of holidays corresponding to the different types of tourist and recreational travel postulated in Campbell's model (Fig. 1.2). Their survey showed 61% of the respondents had holidays involving trips to a recreational–vacational complex, 9% of these being in the metropolitan hinterland and 52% in the regional hinterland. A further 17% involved tours of different regions, for example of Central Otago or of the North and South Islands. Goldsmith and forrest also suggest a fourth category of travel not inherent in Campbell's model, the 'there and back' trip to a single urban centre. Such trips, however, correspond directly with the flows between major metropolitan areas depicted in Lundgren's model (Fig. 1.6). In the case of Dunedin holiday-makers, they constituted 21% of all trips and were primarily associated with visiting friends and relations. This type of travel is also evident elsewhere, for example in the visits to Canadian and Australian metropolitan centres discussed earlier in this chapter (Fig. 6.5).

Goldsmith and Forrest do not comment on the nature of the vacation circuit nor on trips within the recreational–vacational regional complex. Although not conceived in such terms, patterns from a study of visitors to Albury–Wodonga in Australia (P. A. Management Consultants 1975) lend support to Campbell's concepts. Figure 6.6

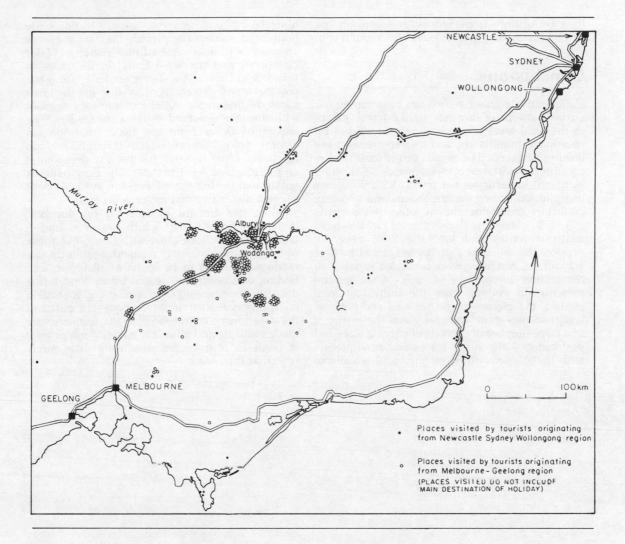

Fig. 6.6 Places visited by visitors to
Albury–Wodonga originating from
Newcastle–Sydney–Wollongong and
Melbourne–Geelong.

Source: After P.A. Management
Consultants (1975).

depicts places other than main destinations
visited by tourists originating in the
Newcastle–Sydney–Wollongong area and from
Melbourne–Geelong who visited and were interviewed in Albury–Wodonga, which constituted
the main destination for 72% of the respondents.

Two distinct patterns emerge, one of linear
highway-oriented travel in the case of the former
group, the other of a regional vacation complex
centred on Albury–Wodonga. The
Albury–Wodonga area would appear to be
regarded more as a destination by the Victorians

111

than by visitors from Sydney and surrounding cities who are to a greater extent on a round trip.

Conclusions

Comparatively little research has been carried out on the patterns of domestic tourist travel, except at the local level where a variety of studies on vacational hinterlands and market areas have been undertaken. The results of the local studies confirm the existence of a distance decay function in much domestic tourist travel, with variations being found among certain groups and a variety of factors modifying the hypothesized patterns (Fig. 1.3). The few local studies which have analysed routes and itineraries also generally support the different patterns suggested by Figs 1.2 and 1.6, but more work is needed to establish the relative importance of each. While general patterns do emerge from the individual local studies, the picture at the regional and national level becomes more complex given the existence of a large number of markets of varying sizes and preferences – the cities, towns and rural areas – and the consequent overlapping of vacational hinterlands and market areas. Nation-wide household surveys can provide the data to enable an analysis of inter-regional flow patterns. Major directional patterns were found in the cases of France and Italy and a strong tendency for intra-regional travel also emerged, confirming the often sharp decline in the volume of domestic tourism with distance observed in the local studies. The impact of flows from the major metropolitan centres were, however, felt throughout both countries. Little research has been undertaken at an intermediate level to determine flow patterns within regions but the information available does suggest distinct spatial patterns do exist.

While the amount of research on domestic tourism is limited, that which has been undertaken clearly indicates that such flows, like those of international tourists, are neither uniform nor random. Order is to be found at all levels, and finding that order is essential for understanding domestic tourism and for planning and managing it. Appropriate analytical techniques do exist and the data can be collected when the resources are made available and when the role and importance of domestic tourism are recognized. It is surely time that they were.

7

Measuring spatial variations in tourism

The preceding four chapters have focused on the interaction between origins and destinations through an analysis of tourist flows at various scales. The nature, intensity and direction of these flows can provide important insights into the spatial structure of tourism. Further understanding can be gained by examining the location and distribution of various tourist-related phenomena. Given the multi-faceted nature of tourism, a wide range of factors have been analysed in this way. In most cases an attempt is made to describe and account for spatial variations in the nature and intensity of tourism. The emphasis here has been on the delimitation of formal rather than functional regions, that is on regions defined by the uniformity of characteristics or homogeneity of content rather than in terms of their economic coherence or the interdependence of their parts (Robinson 1953; Price 1981). In a few instances, the delimitation of tourist regions has been a first step in examining particular problems or broader questions, but in general the contribution of such studies to planning, marketing and management has not been fully explored. Nor, in most cases, is there more than a cursory mention of why the measures and techniques used have been employed and what it is they are actually measuring.

This chapter reviews and evaluates a range of factors and approaches which have been used to define and describe spatial variations in tourism. Four major sets of factors are identified – those

relating to accommodation, to attractions, to the economic impact of tourism and to the tourists themselves. Composite studies incorporating a range of different variables and emphasizing different types of tourism are then discussed. Not included in this section, however, are regional resource evaluation techniques used in planning and development as these have been reviewed by this writer elsewhere (Pearce 1981c). Finally, studies which seek to distinguish tourist regions from those characterized by other forms of socioeconomic activity are outlined. Subsequent chapters contain comparative studies of tourism at different scales as an attempt is made to identify common trends and patterns using a selection of these factors and techniques and so develop a more general understanding of the spatial structure of tourism.

Accommodation

The distribution of accommodation is the most widely used measure of spatial variations in the tourist industry. A major reason for this is that accommodation is one of the more visible and tangible manifestations of tourism. Accommodation is generally readily inventoried, with statistics on commercial accommodation being compiled for fiscal and other reasons in many countries while data on second homes are often collected as part of a household census. If necessary, the researcher can also go out and physically count the number of accommodation units in a given area, a task more readily accomplished than the enumeration of visitors to the same area, though one which is not without its problems.

Accommodation statistics tend to be used mainly to indicate spatial variations in the importance of tourism or to identify regions of different types of tourist activity; some studies incorporate elements of both. As a measure of the importance of the tourist industry, the use of accommodation is a logical one, a stay away from home being one of the defining characteristics of tourism. Except where a great deal of day-tripping occurs from a tourist base, the distribution of accommodation does provide a fair measure of actual demand. As a measure of impact, it is also reasonable, given that expenditure on accommodation usually accounts for a third to a half of a tourist's budget and that provision of accommodation plant contributes a similar or even greater proportion of tourism investment in most cases (Pearce 1981c).

Published accommodation statistics should not be used uncritically and note must be taken of the definitions employed and of the manner in which they are compiled. Conflicting figures from different sources are not uncommon, even for comparatively small regions or resorts (Barbier 1978; Vanhove 1980). Comprehensive studies are often complicated by variations in the availability and reliability of data from one sector to another. In particular, statistics on the less formal sector (camping, caravanning, second homes etc.) tend to be less common and less reliable than those for the more commercial and structured hotel industry. Visits with friends and relations are also not recorded in accommodation inventories, yet surveys show a significant proportion of visitors may stay in private homes, particularly in urban areas. Where statistics are not available for all types of accommodation, some assessment should be made, for example through a visitor survey, of the significance of the missing sectors as these may vary widely from place to place and from market to market. Hotels, for example, may well account for virtually all the accommodation in some international resorts but play only a minor role in many areas of domestic tourism.

Accommodation statistics are usually expressed either in the number of units in each sector (e.g. the number of hotels or second homes) or some measure of capacity, commonly beds or rooms. Given that hotels in particular can be of widely varying size and that the mix of sizes may vary from one locality to another, significant differences may occur in the distribution of the number of hotels and the distribution of hotel rooms or beds. In most cases, the capacity figures will be more meaningful. Where comparisons are being made, capacity figures are also to be preferred, with the capacity of each sector being expressed in some standard unit, usually beds. Hotel and motel capacity is often so expressed in official statistics but for other sectors, such as holiday homes, camping grounds or caravan sites, a survey may be necessary or some more arbitrary decision may have to be made. Not all beds, however, are equal. Some will be filled virtually every night of the year while others will be used in certain seasons only. In general, occupancy rates will be higher in the hotels and lower in camping grounds, second homes and other less formal sectors. Occupancy rates also vary from one area to another, with metropolitan centres usually experiencing more consistent demand throughout the year than coastal or alpine resorts. Where the length of the season is known, adjustments might be made in terms of annual bed or room capacity (Keogh 1984). Actual use figures expressed in monthly or annual bed nights are compiled in some countries, for example Belgium and Spain, and provide a valuable measure of demand, particularly where they are classified by origin (see below), and of impact.

Accommodation inventories may also provide data on the quality available. Information on the type and quality of the accommodation may suggest who the users might be, but inventories alone do not provide any direct information in this respect. It should be borne in mind, particularly in interpreting distribution patterns, that not all accommodation is directed at or used by tourists, in the sense of those travelling primarily for pleasure purposes. Indeed, in their study of the United States lodging industry, van Doren and Gustke (1982) report that the major market for hotels there in 1978 consisted of 43% of business travellers, 32% tourists and 17% conference participants.

Spatial variations in the importance of tourism are commonly depicted by or inferred from maps portraying the distribution of one or more types of accommodation. The distribution of absolute numbers of units is usually portrayed by dot distribution maps (e.g. Vuoristo 1969; Bielckus 1977) or some form of shading by administrative area (Boyer 1972; Thompson 1971; Gutiérrez Ronco 1977). Capacity is usually depicted by proportional circles, spheres or bar graphs with these being used as the scale of resorts, towns or administrative units (Ashworth 1976; Coppock 1977; Ishii 1982). In other instances, the percentage of total national bed capacity has been mapped by region (Poncet 1976).

Although data on the distribution of all accommodation units or total bed capacity give a useful indication of where tourism is important in terms of a country or region as a whole, absolute figures do not necessarily reflect the significance of tourism within particular areas. As a result, several indices of the relative importance of tourism have been proposed.

The index which has gained most acceptance, although still not in widespread use, is Defert's tourist function index (Defert 1967; Baretje and Defert 1972). The tourist function T(f) of an area is taken by Defert as a measure of 'tourist activity or intensity' as reflected in the juxtaposition of two populations – the visitors and the visited. It is derived by comparing the number of beds (N) available to tourists in the area with the resident population (P) of that area according to the formula:

$$T(f) = \frac{N \times 100}{P}$$

The theoretical limits of the index are T(f) = 0 where no tourist accommodation exists and T(f) = ∞ where there is no resident population. A value of 100 indicates that the number of tourists would equal the number of local residents, assuming all beds available to tourists were being used.

Boyer (1972) proposes a six-fold classification of French communes based on their T(f) values:

T(f) > 500 = recent 'hypertouristic' resort
T(f) 100–500 = large tourist resort
T(f) 40–100 = predominantly tourist commune
T(f) 10–40 = communes with an important but not predominant tourist activity
T(f) 4–10 = little tourist activity or tourist function 'submerged' in other urban functions
T(f) < 4 = practically no tourist activity

While initially applied to towns and cities, the T(f) index has also been calculated for regions such as Colorado (Thompson 1971), Normandy (Clary 1977), Sao Paulo (Langenbuch 1977) and New Brunswick (Keogh 1984) and at a national level in New Zealand (Pearce 1979b). Values tend to decline with the increase in the scale of the spatial unit as the role of tourism is diluted by other activities.

As a measure of tourist intensity, the T(f) index can be a useful discriminating variable. In the case of New Zealand, there was little correlation in the rankings of the 22 regions in terms of their absolute accommodation capacity and their T(f) value (r_s = 0.27). The region which ranked last in terms of capacity, Fiordland, recorded the highest T(f) value (103). Conversely, the major metropolitan regions which had a large number of beds tended to have low T(f) values. Differences in the population base of the regions account for much of the variation, but the T(f) index does indicate that whereas tourism is only one activity among many supporting a large population in places like Auckland and Wellington, it is a mainstay of the economy in Fiordland.

As a relative measure of tourist intensity or 'tourist ascendancy' (Ryan 1965), the T(f) index provides a useful complement to the traditional absolute capacity figures and should be used more widely. Given that population statistics are normally readily available, the additional calculation should pose few problems. At the same time, the limitations of the capacity statistics should be borne in mind, particularly if there is much variation in the mix of accommodation types and the occupancy rates of these (Keogh 1984).

A number of variations on this approach have been offered. In his study of tourism in Quebec, Lundgren (1966) uses a ratio exactly the opposite of Defert to obtain an index expressed simply in terms of the number of local residents per hotel unit. Places with a low numerical ratio are seen to have 'a more tourist-geared local economy' than those with a higher numerical ratio. In mapping spatial variations of tourism in the province, Lundgren effectively combines capacity and intensity by depicting the capacity of each place with proportional circles and then shading these according to the ratio of population to hotel units (see, also, Mirloup 1974). Plettner (1979) advocates the use of bed nights rather than capacity and proposes an index of the 'intensity of tourism' which is the quotient of the number of bed nights and the local population. In studies of the distribution of second homes, maps are often prepared depicting the ratio of second homes to permanent residences (Ryan 1965; Coppock 1977).

Measures of the density of tourist activity have also been suggested. Girard (1968) has mapped the number of hotel beds on Guernsey by half mile squares and, in the Pacific, Rajotte (1977) has depicted the number of tourist days recorded at each destination in relation to their area as well as to the size of the local population. Marsden

(1969) derived 'holiday homescape indices' for the Gold Coast of Australia based on the number, proportion and density of unoccupied dwellings as measured in unoccupied dwellings per square mile. In his study of second homes in Czechoslovakia, Gardavsky (1977) suggests it is not total area but rather the potential recreation area available in each district which should be taken into account. This latter consists of (p. 67) 'areas of woodland and water, in addition to orchards, parks, meadows and pastures which contribute to the attractiveness of the environment for recreation'. He then proposes a modification to Defert's basic formula such that

$$Rp_1 = \frac{L \times 100}{O} \cdot \frac{1}{Rp}$$

where Rp_1 = recreation index
L = the number of second homes multiplied by four, representing the average number of occupants
O = the number of permanent residents
Rp = the potential recreation area of the area surveyed

Studies which employ variations in accommodation as a means of deriving regions or of identifying areas specializing in particular types of tourism are usually of two kinds. Some focus on a single accommodation sector and examine variables such as quality or comfort. Others are concerned with a variety of accommodation types but usually only one variable, normally capacity. In many of the single accommodation studies, particularly those dealing with second homes, the main objective may be more with analysing the distribution of that particular sector than with determining the spatial structure of tourism in general. Coppock (1977: 6), for example, notes that the main factors controlling the distribution of second homes appear to be: 'the distance from major centres of population; the quality or character of the landscape; the presence of sea, rivers or lakes; the presence of other recreational resources; the availability of land; the climates of the importing and exporting region'.

In a number of countries, hotels, camping grounds and other types of accommodation are officially classified by grade or quality and this provides a first basis for categorization. In most cases, capacity is first represented by proportional circles, these then being subdivided and shaded according to the proportion of beds, rooms,

hotels and so on in each category (Stang 1979; Chadefaud 1981; Fig. 10.5). Mirloup (1974) prefers a single comfort index for each locality based on the formula

$$RCI = \frac{(0.25R_1 + 0.5R_2 + 0.75R_3 + R_4)}{TC} \times 100$$

where RCI = Room Comfort Index
R_1 to R_4 = the number of rooms in 1 to 4 star hotels
TC = total capacity of the resort or town

In using this index in his study of hotels in the Loire Valley, Mirloup distinguishes between low-quality rural hotels and high-quality hotels in towns near the chateaux or main roads, with the major cities falling between the two. He also proposes a diversification index based on the distribution of rooms in each category compared to the national average. Dewailly (1978) suggests a comfort index for second homes based on ten criteria such as the proportion of homes in each area being serviced with water and electricity or having a garage. He raises the question of weighting the variables but sees no consistent way of doing so. Use of this index showed that not all the second homes in the Nord-Pas de Calais region of France were equal, with those on the coast generally being of superior quality to those located in inland areas.

Types of accommodation have also been classified and mapped according to size distribution (Chadefaud 1981), type of location (Mankour 1980) and national or foreign ownership (Berriane 1978).

Where a series of variables or indices is used, these may be presented in sequence, an attempt may be made to synthesize them through some form of classification, or both approaches may be used. Mirloup (1974) presents a series of maps of the Loire Valley depicting variations in the different indices he uses and then derives a more general classification based on threshold values for three measures – capacity, diversification and tourist function index.

Studies which examine a range of accommodation types tend to do so either by examining the distribution of each in turn, or by combining different types of accommodation at different scales and analysing spatial variations in the composition of these. Typical of the first approach is Carlson's (1938) early study of the recreation industry of New Hampshire in which he presents a series of maps showing the number of summer residences and the capacity of hotels, lodgings, cabins and juvenile camps by county.

Different spatial patterns emerge for each type of accommodation. Hotels, for example, tended to be located at or nearby railway junctions while cabins were found mainly in the lake and mountain districts. Carlson's emphasis is on the factors accounting for the distribution of each type, but some more general geographical statements are also made as a result of 'grouping various accommodations by recreation regions'.

Vuoristo (1969) too, in his examination of the geography of tourism in Finland, looks in turn at the distribution of different accommodation types and proposes a division of the country into six tourist regions based on a 'cartographic synthesis'. In concluding, he notes (p. 45):

> The differences between the regions are due to many factors, among which are a) differences with respect to the distribution of population and points of interest to tourists, b) differences with respect to the natural conditions needed to promote the tourist trade, c) the concentration of the points of entry into the country for foreign travellers in certain areas, d) the attraction of Lapland to foreigners, e) the formation of travel routes running north–south, f) differences in the distribution of various types of lodging and camping establishments, g) differences in the length of tourist seasons, etc. In a number of these cases, there can be observed as a background factor the elongated shape of Finland in a north–south direction.

Researchers who combine accommodation types usually do so by presenting the amount and proportion of accommodation, expressed in a standard unit of measurement such as beds, available in each resort or administrative unit by means of pie charts or bar graphs (Barbier 1976; Huetz de Lemps 1976; Berriane 1978; Pearce 1979b). This can be an effective means of visually presenting differences in capacity and composition from one area to another (Fig. 8.5). Resorts or regions can usually be identified which are composed of one or two dominant types of accommodation or even a balanced mix, but in most cases little attempt at synthesis is made, for example by combining like regions.

A notable exception is found in the ambitious, comprehensive and more analytical French project involving a detailed examination of 318 coastal resorts (Cribier and Kych 1977). Cribier and Kych adopted an original approach, that of estimating the actual number of holiday-makers in all types of accommodation on the coast during the peak summer period (the first two weeks of August 1974). This was achieved through mobilizing a substantial number of researchers who

Table 7.1
Distribution by accommodation of tourists during the peak summer season in 318 French coastal resorts

	% of tourists
Second homes	41
Camping and caravanning	27
Permanent residences	17
Hotels	6
Children and youth holiday camps	5.1
Other 'collective' accommodation*	3.4

* Includes clubs, family holiday camps (VVF), tent villages etc.

Source: After Cribier and Kych (1977).

combined a comprehensive inventory of accommodation plant with field surveys. The latter, among other factors, ascertained, for a sample of the resorts, the number of holiday-makers staying in permanent residences and second homes. The proportions obtained were then used to calculate figures for the coast as a whole. The results of this exercise are instructive even if, as the authors stress, they are strictly applicable only to the survey period and do not reflect year-round usage or overall impact (Table 7.1). Nearly 60% of all coastal holiday-makers were being accommodated in permanent or second homes: hotels accounted for only 6% of the total.

Seven categories of resorts were then identified on the basis of their accommodation profiles by means of factor analysis. Three categories were distinguished on the basis of the predominance of a single type of accommodation (second homes, permanent residences, camping); three according to a mix of two major types (camping and permanent residences; camping and second homes; hotels and second homes); while the seventh included those resorts whose profile approximated the average for the coast as a whole. Similar categories might also have been derived by a visual scanning of the profiles themselves but, given the large number of observations, the use of factor analysis should have led to a more consistent classification of the 318 individual resorts. Even so, the authors recognize that the classification of some resorts is rather marginal; some even appear surprising, such as the inclusion of La Grande Motte in the category typified by the 'omnipresence of camping'.

Each of these seven categories was found to correspond closely with a recognizable type of

117

resort. A mix of mainly hotels and second homes, for example, was characteristic of well-established 'name' resorts such as Deauville, Biarritz, Saint-Tropez and many of the resorts of the Côte d'Azur. Camping, on the other hand, was largely a feature of small rural communes.

Further investigation showed a marked degree of regional homogeneity, with large and distinct stretches of the coast being characterized by resorts of a single or contiguous categories. Camping, for example, predominates in southern Brittany and along much of the Atlantic coast. Concentrations of second homes are found along sectors of the Channel coast, around the mouth of the Loire and in parts of Languedoc. It should be remembered here that the categories of resorts are based on the relative composition of the accommodation types, not on their absolute distribution. In addition to these regions characterized by specific types of accommodation categories and associated resorts, there are also several regions where different types of resorts are found. In Languedoc, small blocks of communes characterized by camping alternate with others where second homes predominate; in the Var, hotels are interspersed with camping and, in the Contentin, second homes and permanent residences are intermixed.

Cribier and Kych conclude from this regional homogeneity that (p. 124) 'In France the vacation space in destination areas is not primarily a local resort level space, but a regional space. Each tourist region is perceived by the visitors in terms of its historic, climatic and cultural unity.' The emergence of this homogeneity is later attributed to the following factors (p. 158):

> The development of a particular mode of accommodation in each region depends on the size of the permanent population in each resort, on the volume of visitors . . . on physical factors (the size of the communes), but more importantly on the history of tourism, that is on the history of the relationships between supply and demand. We can thus distinguish between the established tourist resorts with important hotel industries, dependent sectors (in the orbit of a metropolitan area) characterized by second homes, sectors where camping has recently developed and those numerous but dispersed resorts where tourism is in the process of developing without a predominant accommodation type emerging or where communes are trying various paths of tourist development.

Cribier and Kych's methodology has much to commend it, combining as it does the regional insights typical of geography in France with a more systematic and analytical approach found less frequently among the French (Barbier and Pearce 1984). The authors also raise the question of whether the particular regions they define would have emerged if criteria other than accommodation types had been employed.

Attractions

A number of researchers have examined various aspects of the spatial structure of the attractions sector. The discussion in most cases is limited to specific forms of tourism or types of recreational facilities and there is often little attempt to incorporate these analyses into a broader examination of tourism as a whole. Usually it is the more distinctive forms of tourism or types of facilities which have been treated in this way.

Defert (1960) has mapped the distribution of thermal resorts in Europe, and Ginier (1974) includes a map of French thermal resorts classified by the number of *curistes* and the types of treatment given. Among a series of maps showing the distribution of accommodation in Colorado, Thompson (1971) includes maps of hunting and fishing licences. Barbier (1978) has compiled statistics on the number of ski-lifts by country, and Ginier (1974) has mapped the distribution of ski resorts in France according to the hourly capacity of their uphill facilities. He also depicts the distribution of casinos and recreational boating facilities in France but makes no attempt to synthesize the various sorts of attractions he describes. Yamamura (1982) and Ishii (1982) deal with a range of recreational resources and facilities in Japan including hot springs, ski fields and national parks.

In his monograph on tourism in the Netherlands, Ashworth (1976) discusses the distribution of natural and man-made resources and includes maps of nature reserves and solitude, landscape evaluation, and two of 'attractions' in Western Europe. The latter are clearly biased towards urban historical and cultural attractions visited primarily by 'sightseers', with one, based on features cited in the Michelin guide books, offering a French perspective and the other depicting attractions recognized by the German tourist geographer, Ritter. Ashworth recognizes difficulties in the identification and assessment of attractions and notes that recorded patterns of use do not always correspond with the apparent distribution of attractions.

Maps of attractions in specific urban areas also tend to be biased towards historic monuments, museums, art galleries and other cultural features (Burnet and Valeix 1967; Burtenshaw, Bateman and Ashworth 1981). Some of the problems which arise in analysing the spatial structure of attractions can be seen in Burtenshaw, Bateman and Ashworth's map of major tourist attractions in Paris. They admit that it is not exhaustive but depict it as being based on 'those selected by the visitors themselves'. By this they appear to mean monuments and museums where an entrance fee is paid and a record is kept by the Secrétariats d'Etat au Tourisme and à la Culture. However, of the listed attractions, only three – the Eiffel Tower, the Louvre and the Musée de l'Armée – recorded more than half a million visits and of these some proportion would have been from Parisians. Even if the figure of 13 million visitors to Paris in 1977, cited by Chenery (1979), might also be viewed as imprecise and as containing a large proportion of businessmen and other travellers, the indications are that the majority of tourists are not visiting the 'major attractions'. The Eiffel Tower can, of course, be viewed without a visit being recorded if the tourist does not actually go up it, but clearly there are many attractions other than these official ones which are drawing visitors to *la ville lumière* (see Ch. 10).

The factors dicussed here do provide a means of establishing the spatial structure of particular forms of tourism and have so far primarily been used in this way. Their value as indicators of the overall importance of tourism appears much more limited, however, unless more rigorous efforts are made to synthesize the many different types of attractions and to derive a composite measure of tourist attractiveness.

Economic impact

With the growing interest in the economic impact of tourism, attention has been directed at establishing more directly spatial variations in the economic importance of the tourist industry. Such research can provide a very useful bridge between national studies of the contribution of tourism to a country's economy, with an emphasis on overseas exchange earnings, and detailed local impact studies, commonly based on expenditure surveys and calculations of tourist multipliers. The reliance in the literature on indirect measures of impact, notably accommodation statistics, reflects, however, the paucity of economic data on tourism at a sub-national scale. The studies of variations in the economic impact of tourism which have been undertaken are rarely comprehensive but relate to specific sectors of the tourist industry or to particular segments of the market.

One of the more detailed studies is that by Britton (1980b) who obtained, through a large-scale survey of tourist businesses, annual turnover figures for the different sectors of the tourist industry in Fiji. Although the majority of the tourist industry's gross turnover was concentrated in urban areas on Viti Levu, significant variations did occur between sectors. Turnover from accommodation was less concentrated than that from the travel and tour and the tourist shopping sectors due to the large numbers of resort hotels along the Coral Coast and on Mamanuca Island (Fig. 9.5). Accommodation accounts for 96.5% of tourist industry turnover in rural areas but only 31.4% in urban areas. Britton's work shows the importance of considering all sectors of the tourist industry, for these figures clearly indicate that examination of the accommodation sector alone would have distorted the picture of the spatial structure of Fiji's tourist economy. Britton also shows that the degree of concentration of the tourist industry in Fiji depends to a certain extent on the economic indicator used. Rural areas generated only 17.5% of gross tourist industry turnover but accounted for nearly 30% of direct employment in tourism.

While Britton examined spatial variations in the economic impact of different sectors of the tourist industry, he did not assess how the relative importance of tourism in the economy as a whole varied throughout Fiji. As with the accommodation statistics, it is useful to obtain a measure of tourism dependency or the relative contribution of tourism to the economy of different areas by relating absolute economic measures of tourism to some other factor. Several relative measures have been proposed in the United States. Mings (1982) presents a map of travel-generated employment as a percentage of non-agricultural employment by state and suggests a number of 'dramatic' differences are evident when this is compared with a base map of person nights by state (Fig. 7.1). The New England states, for example, are shown to be much more dependent on tourism than their share of total person nights would suggest, while the opposite occurs in California. Size and population are clearly important factors here. Florida, on the other hand, is one of the top-ranked states on both measures. Van Doren and Gustke (1982) analysed the evolution of the lodging industry in the United States from 1963 to 1977 by ranking states in terms of lodging receipts and then considering changes in state per capita income over the period. Unfortunately the two measures

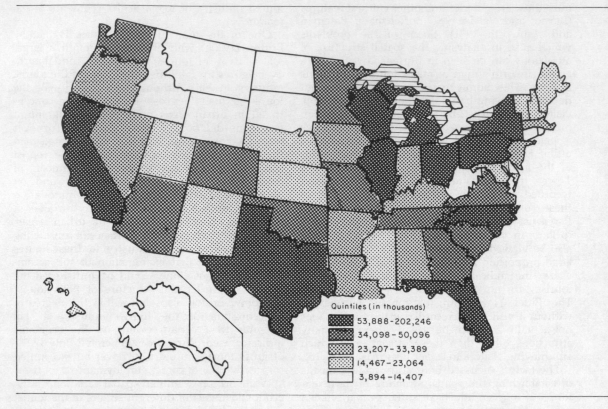

Fig. 7.1   Spatial variations in tourism in the
            United States
            (a) person nights by state (1977)

Source: Redrawn from Mings (1982).

cannot be directly compared, but the general picture which emerges is that the pattern of growth on a per capita basis differed significantly from the changes in total revenue, with many of the Sunbelt states becoming more prominent on this relative measure.

Other United States writers have discussed the use of slightly more refined measures than simple per capita traveller expenditure (PCTE). Royer et al. (1974) proposed two such measures:

1.   A Tourism Impact Factor (TIF), derived by dividing per capita traveller expenditure by per capita personal income and multiplying the result by 100.

2.   A Tourism Proportion Factor (TPF), calculated by dividing the total travel expenditure in each state by its gross state product and multiplying the quotient by 100.

The traveller expenditure data in each case came from the 1972 National Travel Expenditure Survey and refer only to domestic tourism. Doering (1976) subsequently revised and expanded this study on the grounds that the authors had not fully considered the implications of the other

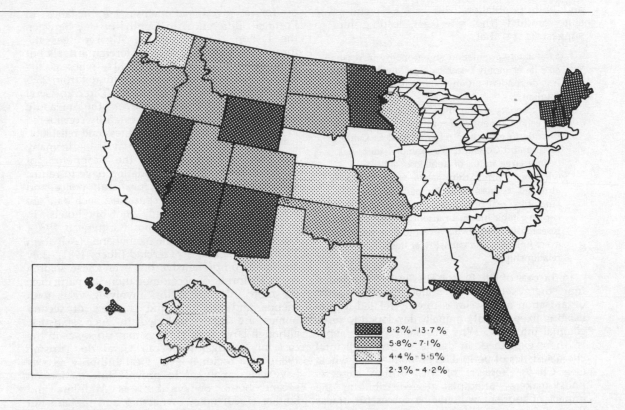

▓▓	8·2% – 13·7%
▒▒	5·8% – 7·1%
░░	4·4% – 5·5%
☐	2·3% – 4·2%

(b) travel-generated employment as a percentage of non-agricultural employment by state (1975)

data they had used. Doering found a high inter-correlation between the three measures and concluded (p. 15) that 'per capita traveller expenditure [is] at least as good a measure as the TIF or TPF and one that is certainly more communicable to both professional and lay audiences'. In a similar study in Australia, Cooper (1980) also found strong though not quite so significant relationships between these three measures.

This work on the spatial patterns of the tourist economy, more than the research on the distribution of accommodation, emphasizes that the identification of these patterns is not an end in itself but rather a means of answering both specific and more general questions relating to society and the economy as a whole. Royer et al., for example, had derived their measures at the time of the 1973 energy crisis in order to identify states which might be hit the hardest by petrol rationing. Doering's revised figures suggest these would be the Mountain and South Atlantic states. He then goes on to examine other relationships between tourism and the economy using PCTE figures at the state level. He found a negative correlation between state tourism dependency and both population (rho = −0.51) and gross state product (rho = −0.54), leading him to suggest (p. 14) that:

> as a state's population and economy increase in size its economy becomes more diversified and less dependent on any one sector including tourism.

> A corollary to this may be that in some states the establishment of a tourist sector is often a prelude to growth in other sectors. In California, Florida and Colorado, for example, there has been a large influx of 'footloose' activities (electronics firms, think tanks, etc) which were attracted to these states by many of the amenities, real or imagined, associated with the earlier establishment of a tourist industry. More research is needed, however, to determine the exact linkages and causality of these relationships.

In the case of Fiji, Britton (1980b: 159) concluded that 'there seems little doubt that the spatial organisation of tourism is directly related to pre-existing fixed capital originally developed to serve colonial interests'. Why this should come about is then explained in terms of the structural characteristics of peripheral economies as a whole (see Ch. 9). Because of this, Britton suggests policy-makers' attempts at redistributing the impact of tourism will not be successful unless there is some change in these underlying structures.

Tourists

While studies of accommodation and economic impact may reveal the general spatial structure of the tourist industry, they rarely say much about the tourists themselves. Where possible, such studies should be complemented by direct analyses of the spatial preferences of different groups of tourists and of geographical variations in the composition of the tourist traffic. These analyses also complement the studies of tourist travel patterns discussed in the earlier chapters.

Many countries, unfortunately, do not collect areal data on the composition of the tourist traffic. Where they are collected, the most common variable recorded is the origin or nationality of the visitor, although details on seasonality and length of stay may also be available (Ashworth 1976; Plettner 1979; Herbin 1982; Mings 1982). Information on nationality is usually expressed either in arrivals or bed nights and sometimes both. Bed nights generally give a better picture of total demand in a given region

or for a given nationality. For instance in Portugal, differences in lengths of stay between the Lisbon region and the Algarve sees the former account for 27% of all foreign arrivals but only 23% of foreign bed nights, whereas the latter's share of foreign tourism jumps from 25% of arrivals to 36% of bed nights (Direccao Geral do Turismo 1980). Whatever the measure selected, the data have to be carefully considered in terms of their comprehensiveness and reliability.

Regional bed night data are available in many European countries where the proprietors of different forms of accommodation have to return statistics on their guests for fiscal, police and other purposes. In some countries, such data are limited to one sector only, notably hotels. In others, for example Belgium (Grimmeau 1980), Bulgaria (Poncet 1976), the Netherlands (Ashworth 1976), Austria and Switzerland (Ilbery 1981), they are more comprehensive but even these seldom cover all forms of accommodation. In particular, the more informal sectors involving visits with friends and relations and the use of second homes are rarely included in such statistics, although large-scale surveys may do so, as in the case of Portugal (Direccao Geral do Turismo 1980). At a regional level, local authority records have been analysed to provide information on second home owners but, as Andrieux and Soulier (1980) note, ownership and use are not necessarily the same, particularly where second homes are bought primarily as an investment and for renting to other users.

Ashworth (1976) sees three main sources of error in the official Dutch tourism statistics: inaccurate information provided by the visitors, non-inclusion of smaller commercial establishments and omission of non-commercial accommodation. He estimates that (p. 2) 'in practice just under 80% of hotel beds, around 50% of pension beds, and only just over 3% of camp site accommodation in the Netherlands are included in the C.B.S. Survey'. Qualifying the statistics used in this way is essential for interpreting the patterns subsequently established. If the data used cover only one or a limited range of accommodation types, then this should be clearly stated and the representativeness of the patterns so derived explored. Plettner (1979), for example, shows that significant differences occur in the distribution of foreign tourists in Ireland depending on whether hotel or accommodation figures are used. Even within a given sector, consideration should be given to whether biases occur from one group to another. It may be, for instance, that hotel receptionists are less rigorous in recording domestic guests than foreign arrivals.

Ashworth (1976) observes that in the Netherlands the regions used are 'traditional Dutch holiday areas but are not always equally relevant to foreign visitors'. In most other countries the units in which tourist data are presented are the formal administrative ones, such as provinces in Spain, departments in France or arrondissements in Belgium.

These data on the composition of the tourist traffic have been analysed in different ways and with varying degrees of refinement. A basic approach is to prepare separate maps showing the distribution of domestic and foreign tourists (based on their percentage distribution in each category), as Poncet (1976) has done for Belgium and Pearce (1978b) has done for France. A more detailed series of maps showing the distribution of foreign visitors in the Netherlands has been prepared by Ashworth (1976), who derived location quotients for all foreign visitors and each of the major nationalities. Location quotients provide a measure of concentration and in this case were derived by relating the percentage of bed nights to the percentage of land area in each region. Values greater than unity indicate a region is receiving more tourists from a given nationality than the national average; values less than 1 show it is below the national average. Ashworth then provides a map of 'nationality mix' using pie charts depicting the percentage distribution of six nationality groups in each region. Other writers, e.g. Steinecke (1979) in Ireland and Ilbery (1981) for Austria and Switzerland, have also used pie charts involving proportional circles to show the size of the tourist traffic in each region as well as its composition. Ilbery limits his maps to a breakdown of domestic and international tourism although he does provide more detailed data in accompanying tables, neither of which is particularly easy to assimilate.

While maps such as Ilbery's may be appropriate for a regional geographic text, a more analytical approach might be expected in specialized studies of the geography of tourism. If, for purposes of synthesis, nationalities are to be grouped together, then this should be done on the basis of identified shared spatial preferences rather than on some basic assumption such as all European countries following the same pattern. Likewise, where the composition of the tourist traffic is comparable, administrative units might logically be amalgamated into larger formal regions. Where the matrix of origins and regions is reasonably large, principal components analysis has proved an effective means of identifying major patterns in the spatial preferences of tourists. Using this technique, Grimmeau (1980) identified three major groups of tourists to Belgium and nine distinct regions from a 9-by-30 matrix of origins and arrondissements. Similarly in a study of the structure of hotel demand in Spain (Pearce and Grimmeau 1985), principal components analysis suggested the nine nationality groups might be reduced to three, and that ten formal tourist regions might be identified among Spain's 52 provinces on the basis of similarities in their tourist traffic (Figs 8.2 and 8.3). In each case, the principal components analysis was performed on the deviations of the recorded bed night values from a matrix of expected values constructed on the basis of an equal distribution of bed nights by nationality throughout the country.

The degree of concentration or dispersion of different groups of tourists can be depicted effectively by means of localization curves. These are constructed by ranking the areal units in descending order of their location quotients and calculating, then plotting, cumulative percentage values of the target variable (e.g. foreign tourist bed nights) against the base variable (e.g. area). If there were a perfect correspondence between the distribution of the target variable and the base variable, then a straight diagonal line would result. The greater the divergence between the localization curve and this diagonal, the greater the degree of localization or concentration present in the distribution of the target variable. Thus if localization curves are plotted for different periods, it can be determined whether tourists are becoming more or less concentrated over time or whether dispersion patterns are relatively constant. The distribution of different groups of tourists within a country can also be compared in this way, as can the extent of concentration between countries (Ashworth 1976). Only general comparisons can be made, however, where the number of areal units varies from country to country, as the form the localization curves take depends in part on the number of units used. It should also be borne in mind that particular geographic areas can no longer be identified from the localization curves. It may be, for instance, that two groups of tourists show a comparable degree of concentration but are concentrated in different regions. The use of localization curves for comparative purposes will be explored more fully in the following chapter (Fig. 8.1).

Composite studies

The majority of the studies cited so far have dealt primarily with specific aspects of tourism,

Table 7.2
Classifications of tourism in Romania
(a) Molnar, Mihail and Maier's typology of tourist localities

Type	Sub-type	Variant	Sub-variant	Other typological characteristics		
				Geographic position	Tourist traffic	Importance of inter-national tourists
(A) Health resort	Resort I Thermal–Climatic II Climatic	Market (a) National year round (b) National seasonal (c) Local year round (d) Local seasonal	Centre 1 Urban 2 Rural 3 Collection of cabins	Carpathians ≤500 m >500 m >1,000 m Sub-Carpathians ≤500 m >500 m >1,000 m Zone of contact (between plateau, Carpathians and Sub-Carpathians) Plain and plateau	Bed nights I >500,000 II >250,000 III >100,000 IV >20,000	% of foreign tourists 1 >30% 2 >20% 3 >10%
(B) Tourist town or city	Functions I Visits and inter-national transit II Visits	Functions (a) Comple-mentary coastal (b) Indirect tourist		Along the Danube On the coast		

Source: After Molnar, Mihail and Maier (1976).

particularly with types of accommodation and groups of visitors. In other cases, authors have considered in turn several different facets of the tourist industry. Ashworth's (1976) maps showing the distribution of foreign tourists in the Netherlands, for example, are complemented by others dealing with the distribution of accommodation and attractions, and Ishii (1982) deals with a range of recreational resources and facilities in Japan. Herbin (1982) has produced maps showing the distribution of resorts in the Austro-German Alps classified by accommodation capacity, the importance of winter tourism and visitor origin. These are but parts of a larger series which also includes maps of tourist intensity, ski-lifts, communications, occupancy rates and length of stay. A whole series of regional maps depicting types of accommodation, attractions, visitor origin and intensity appear in the *Atlas de Provence Côte d'Azur* (Barbier 1975). Similar maps have also been produced at a national level in France (Conseil Supérieur du Tourisme 1978).

Such maps can, individually, provide a lot of useful information. They could also contribute to a broader picture of the spatial structure of tourism but, in the cases cited, there is little or no attempt at synthesis. Other writers have endeavoured to produce such a synthesis by

Table 7.2 (*Contd.*)

(b) Swizewski and Oancea's classification of types of tourism

I *Structural types*	II *Dynamic types*	III *'Stay-put' types*
Mountain	A. On foot	Thermal–climatic
Grottos	*alpine*	Climatic
Cultural	*mountain*	Water sports
Thermal–climatic		Winter sports
Climatic	B. Transit and itinerant	Scientific–artistic
Sporting	International and national	Commercial
Commercial	*by rail*	Customs
	by road	
	by river	
	by access routes into	
	potentially important tourist	
	areas	
	National	
	by rail	
	by road	

Source: After Swizewski and Oancea (1978).

devising classification schemes or typologies to enable them to integrate a variety of tourism characteristics.

Plettner (1979) has classified resorts in Ireland according to the following factors: prevailing kind of tourism, intensity of tourism, type of accommodation, bed nights, seasonality, average length of stay, visitor origin. A composite symbol, featuring proportional pie charts embellished with other graphics, has been derived for each resort. Unfortunately, the key to the resultant map is a little obscure. No attempt is made to group like resorts although Plettner (p. 44) does identify general patterns:

> Most of the tourist resorts are situated along the coastal fringes of Ireland. The places on the west coast have on average a greater number of overnight stays, though their size is generally smaller than in places on the east coast. Correspondingly, the intensity of tourism increases from east to west. . . . The most marked spatial and behavioural patterns are shown by the British who prefer angling, guest-house and supplementary accommodation and stays in the Midlands Region and by the North Americans visiting preferably the Mid-West Regions and having 'touring' as main holiday interest.

A similar approach has been followed by Molnar, Mihail and Maier (1976) who derived a typology of Romanian tourist centres based on the main types of tourism and variations on these. Geographic position, size and composition

of the tourist traffic are other criteria used (Table 7.2). A map of tourist centres in Romania is then presented but, like Plettner's map of Ireland, its utility is limited by an inadequate key. And, like Plettner, the authors attempt to identify the salient features of the distribution of the different centres. They note, for instance, the role of the Black Sea coast, particularly for foreign tourists, and observe how the tourist towns are to be found mainly along the major arteries. A second map of tourism in Romania has been prepared by Swizewski and Oancea (1978) who define three categories of tourism types: structural, dynamic and 'stay-put' (Table 7.2). The structural category is based on an area's tourist resources while different travel patterns determine the dynamic types. The 'stay-put' types are said to be based on length of stay, but statistical difficulties apparently occurred and different functional types (e.g. winter sports, water sports) are depicted. The resultant map is rather detailed and not readily assimilated; moreover, no interpretation is given by the authors. The lack of a measure of capacity or intensity also makes it difficult to appreciate variations in the scale and importance of tourism throughout Romania. In particular, the importance of the Black Sea coast is lost on Swizewski and Oancea's map.

In Belgium, Piavaux (1977) classified and mapped tourist units in the province of Luxembourg by combining data from a visitor survey with a detailed examination of physical and socio-economic features. Although the details on how this was achieved are not too clear, the dominant forms of tourism practised appear to have played a significant role. Piavaux identified three main forms of tourism: transit tourism, weekend tourism and destination tourism (*le tourisme de séjour*). This latter category was sub-divided into two classes depending on whether the stay was spent in one locality (*le séjour fixe*) or whether that locality was used as a base to visit other sites (*le séjour mobile*). Piavaux then goes on to propose specific measures to promote tourism in the units he has identified.

Despite their shortcomings, the Romanian examples and that of Piavaux are interesting in that they attempt to incorporate types of tourism defined in terms of travel patterns as discussed in earlier chapters. The notions of circuit and destination travel, for example, are embodied in each of these examples. In spite of their different origins, Piavaux's *séjour mobile* is almost identical to Campbell's 'recreational vacational regional complex' (Fig. 1.2). What is required now is work integrating the studies of travel patterns with research on the distribution of tourism features. It may be that those concerned with the distribution of different types of tourism would find that some concise measure of circuit/destination travel, such as the Trip Index, could be incorporated into their classification. Conversely, researchers examining travel patterns should be encouraged to develop their work further to identify the function of different places in their networks and circuits, as Forer and Pearce (1984) have endeavoured to do in their study on package tourism (Table 4.3).

Tourism vs other regions

The studies reviewed in this chapter have concentrated on different types of tourist regions. Many of these, particularly those incorporating some measure of tourist intensity, considered variations in the relative importance of tourism but did not directly relate tourism to other types of economic and social activity. As Jackowski (1980: 86) observes: 'In geographical-tourist studies . . . the typology of tourist localities was usually carried out independently of the whole settlement network of a given region.' Jackowski and a few others have thus sought to discriminate not simply between different types of tourist regions but between tourist and other socio-economic regions. This has involved extending the number and range of variables examined and analysing them quantitatively.

Eighteen variables were selected by Jackowski in his analysis of 453 settlements in the Polish vovoidship of Nowy Sacz. These he divides into two groups, one 'characterising the level of economic development' (agricultural population and area of agricultural land) and the other 'covering features of social development'. This latter group covers an intriguing range of 16 variables, some of which might be considered direct measures of tourism, e.g. restaurants and sleeping facilities, while others include shops, cinemas, length of paved roads, total telephone subscribers and private telephone subscribers. Eight types of localities were then identified by Jackowski using nearest neighbour analysis. Over half of the 453 settlements were classified as agricultural localities or farming-service localities. The remaining six types are characterized by a varying mix of agricultural and tourism functions.

In their study of 74 coastal cantons in Brittany, Bonnieux and Rainelli (1979) chose 28 variables – five demographic, fifteen covering employment in different sectors and eight relating to accommodation – and subjected the resultant matrix to factor analysis. Four major types of cantons were identified in this way: agricultural, urban and peri-urban, tourist and maritime. Two or three sub-groups were found in each type, e.g. summer tourism, and summer tourism and retirement. The authors then list and map the cantons belonging to each category. However, neither Bonnieux and Rainelli nor Jackowski go on to explore and account for the patterns they have identified.

As consistent statistical data are required in analyses such as these, it is inevitable that existing administrative units will form the basis of the analysis. However, where the concern is more with functional than formal regions, other boundaries and divisions may be needed which differ from one activity to another. Sprincova (1968) demonstrates this point well in her study of the structure of tourism in the mountainous region of Hruby Jesenik in Czechoslovakia (p. 209):

> The investigation of the area has shown that the central ridge of the Hruby Jesenik . . . had been a serious obstacle for a number of territorial and industrial relations and especially for the formation of a unified network of communications, as well as for the formation of a uniting centre. . . . In the economic and administrative development of the examined territory it has always formed a natural dividing line and therefore a very constant one. Only in tourism it is different, here the ridge is no more a division but its very axis, its most attractive

component part. All the other territorial units derive their function in tourism according to their relations to it.

Conclusions

Geographers and others have used a wide range of data sources, techniques and approaches to examine spatial variations in tourism. While in some respects healthy, this diversity appears to reflect a general lack of direction in the literature and common purpose among researchers, both in terms of questions addressed and approaches adopted, rather than a conscious striving to select and develop the most appropriate techniques for particular problems. Nevertheless, the many and varied ideographic studies reviewed do provide the base on which to develop a more systematic approach to the spatial structure of tourism. Such an approach is attempted in the following three chapters which consider in turn national and regional patterns (Ch. 8), the spatial structure of island tourism (Ch. 9) and then of coastal resorts

and urban areas (Ch. 10).

In each case an attempt is made to identify basic patterns through comparative studies and to explain these so as to develop a more general understanding of the processes at work. Two types of comparisons are used. Where suitable data are available from a range of countries, regions or other areas, these are analysed using the same technique or approach. Thus in Chapter 8, localization curves are used to examine the concentration of domestic and international tourism in selected European countries, and in Chapter 9 the distribution of accommodation provides a means of establishing regularities in the spatial structure of tourism on islands. In others instances, case studies which use different techniques or data sources but which address common problems are systematically compared, as in the discussion in Chapter 8 of variations in the distribution of international tourism within countries and regions and of the functional structure of coastal regions. Particularly with this latter approach, there are limitations in the extent to which generalizations can be made.

8

The national and regional structure of tourism

In this chapter the spatial relationships between domestic and international tourism are explored. This is a field which has attracted little attention to date (Poncet 1976; Ilbery 1981; Pearce and Grimmeau 1985). As with the studies of tourist flows discussed in Chapters 3 to 6, most researchers dealing with the spatial structure of tourism have confined themselves to one sector, in this case usually to international tourism (e.g. Ashworth 1976; Plettner 1979; Grimmeau 1980). To a certain extent this may reflect the availability of data, but often it seems that international tourists are regarded as being more important economically than domestic holiday-makers and are thus worthy of closer study. But in many instances domestic and international tourism can best be seen as being complementary (United Nations 1970): 'in some countries development of domestic tourism might lead to a development of foreign tourism, whilst in others, as yet undeveloped, but well endowed with tourist attractions, the encouragement of foreign tourism would lead in due course to growth in domestic tourism'. How does this complementarity, if it does exist, manifest itself geographically? Do domestic and international tourists share the same preferences or do certain tourists favour particular parts of a country or region while others take their holidays elsewhere?

The basic spatial relationships between domestic and international tourism are implied in Fig. 1.5. There, Thurot (1980) distinguishes between supply and demand and between demand generated domestically and that originating externally. The question now on the supply side is to what extent these two markets seek and use the same resources or whether distinct spatial differences exist. Moreover, if the demand originates from several foreign countries, is it distributed in the same way in each case or do different patterns exist from nationality to nationality? If spatial variations do occur, is this essentially at a regional level or are different structures also to be found within regions?

These questions are examined at a national level in the first part of this chapter with reference to a range of European countries for which adequate comparable data were available or where common approaches in different case studies enabled general patterns to be identified. The focus in the second part then switches to the regional level and is broadened to include a discussion of functional structures generated by different forms of tourism. The regional examples are drawn primarily from coastal regions in the Mediterranean.

The spatial structure of tourism at a national level

Domestic and international tourism

The basic features of domestic and international tourism in the countries of Europe to be studied in this section are depicted in Table 8.1.[1] This shows that the countries to be considered include relatively large ones such as France and Spain which have varied tourist resources and smaller land-locked countries like Luxembourg and Switzerland which have a more limited range of attractions. These countries are also at various stages of development, particularly with regard to international tourism, with the established tourist industries of countries such as France and Switzerland contrasting with those of comparative newcomers like Bulgaria. The volume of tourist traffic also varies considerably from country to country. In this respect it should be borne in mind that while data for four of the countries are expressed in total bed nights, statistics for the remainder relate either to hotel and camping bed nights or to hotel bed nights alone. In Spain, hotels account for about half of the recorded bedspace, but regional differences do occur in the distribution of different types of accommodation there (Pearce and Grimmeau 1985). Hotels account for about half of the foreign bed nights in Portugal, with camping contributing a further 12% (Direccao Geral do Turismo 1980). Hotel demand in France is much less representative of domestic tourism in general than international tourism. These differences in comprehensiveness limit and complicate crossnational comparisons but, through the use of relative measures such as localization curves, it is possible to identify general patterns.

Table 8.1 shows considerable variation in the relative importance of domestic and international tourism, with the extremes in the countries selected being found in neighbouring Belgium and Luxembourg. Important differences are also found in countries with much larger tourist industries such as France and Austria. Interrelated factors contributing to these differences include population size and the national propensity for travel, which together influence the size of the domestic market, and the nature, extent and degree of development of the tourist resources which affects the volume of foreign visitors. France, for example, experiences one of the largest influxes of foreign visitors in Europe but it also has a large and relatively affluent population which generates an even bigger domestic demand. Austria, on the other hand, has a comparatively small population along with alpine attractions favoured by its much more populous neighbour, West Germany. These national differences in the size and share of domestic and international tourism will be reflected in its spatial structure within these countries.

The first question considered in this respect is to what extent are domestic and international tourism concentrated or dispersed, and Fig. 8.1 depicts the localization curves for these in the countries listed in Table 8.1. In addition to the limitations outlined earlier, it should also be noted that the number of spatial units varies from country to country. The number of units, however, is consistent in each case for both domestic and international tourism and from one year to another when time series data are used.

Three general trends can be identified in Fig. 8.1. Firstly, the tendency is for both forms of tourism to be spatially concentrated. Only in the case of Switzerland do the two curves approach the diagonal, indicating that tourism there is

Table 8.1
International and domestic tourism in selected European countries

Country	Year	International bed nights	Domestic bed nights	International bed nights / Domestic bed nights
Austria (all)	1977	78,374,000	26,826,000	2.92
Belgium (all)	1977	2,484,149	14,745,362	0.17
Bulgaria (all)	1973	12,555,000	16,495,000	0.76
France (h)	1973	43,792,000	117,783,000	0.37
Luxembourg (h)	1980	859,567	46,636	18.43
Luxembourg (c)	1980	999,519	138,270	7.22
Portugal (h)	1980	6,240,989	5,700,853	1.09
Portugal (c)	1980	1,857,797	5,530,780	0.33
Spain (h)	1980	58,654,442	37,783,625	1.55
Switzerland (all)	1977	19,380,000	12,920,000	1.5

c Camping only.
h Hotels only.

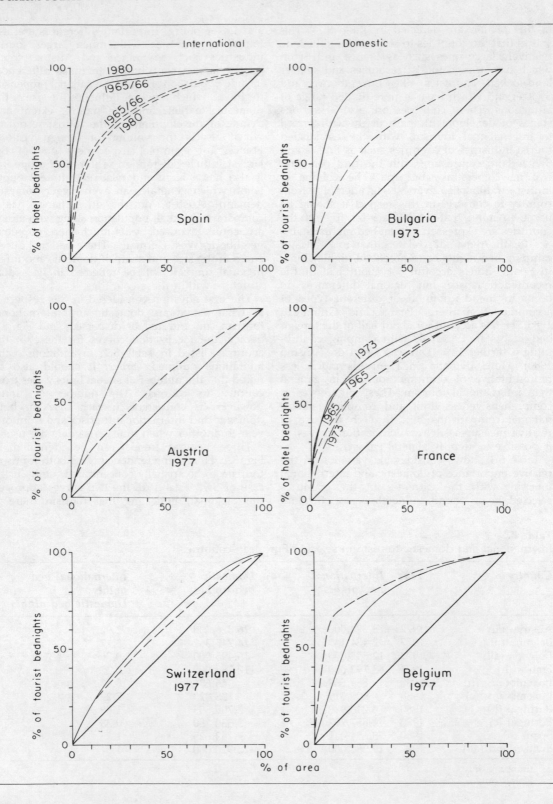

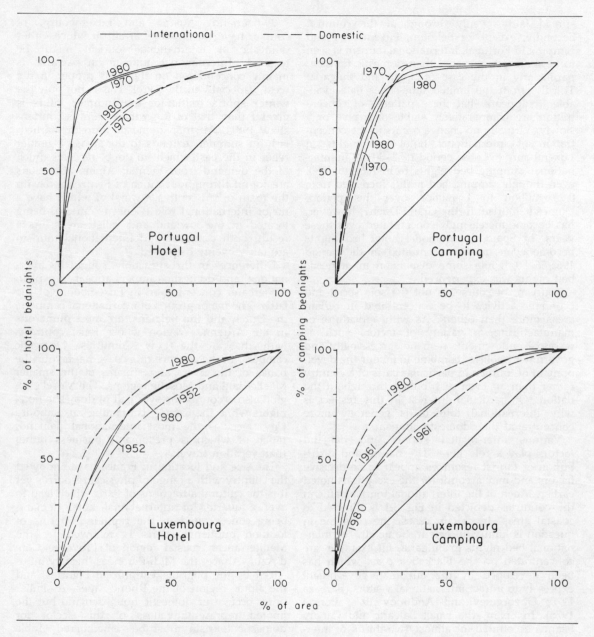

Fig. 8.1 Localization curves for domestic and international tourism in selected European countries.

spread fairly evenly throughout the country. Secondly, except for Belgium, Luxembourg and camping in Portugal, international tourism is seen to be more concentrated than domestic tourism, particularly in the case of Spain and Bulgaria. Thirdly, from the limited time-series data available, it appears that these patterns of concentration are comparatively stable or evolve only slowly. Virtually no change occurs in the concentration of international hotel bed nights in Luxembourg over the period 1952–80 nor in international camping bed nights from 1961 to 1980, even though camping bed nights increased from 0.25 million to 1 million over this period. Domestic tourism in the Grand Duchy, however, has become increasingly concentrated over these years. In Spain, international hotel bed nights become even more concentrated in the period 1965/66–80, while some dispersion in domestic bed nights was experienced.

Tourism, of course, is not the sole social and economic activity to be concentrated in certain areas more than others. As with agriculture or manufacturing, a variety of factors such as resource endowment, demand, accessibility and government policies combine to favour the development of tourism in particular parts of a country rather than an even distribution throughout the nation. Of particular interest in this respect is why international tourism is generally more concentrated than domestic tourism.

Various inter-related supply and demand factors play a role here. The nature and distribution of tourist resources appear to be decisive factors and may account for the exceptions noted earlier. Much of the international tourist traffic in the countries depicted in Fig. 8.1 is directed to coastal areas. In certain cases, the coastline in question is limited in extent. Some 80% of international bed nights in Bulgaria, for example, are concentrated on the Black Sea coast which has been developed by the Bulgarian government expressly to attract international visitors (Barbaza 1970; Gueorguiev and Andonov 1974; Poncet 1976). In Spain, the small Balearic and Canary Islands accounted for almost two-thirds of international hotel demand in 1980 but only 2.5% of the country's surface area. In Portugal it is the sunnier southern coast of the Algarve which is most attractive to holiday-makers. The extremely small stretch of the Belgian coastline, 67 km for 10 million inhabitants, has led to the concentration of two-thirds of domestic tourism in the province of West Flanders. The Belgian coast is also frequented by foreign holiday-makers, but other international visitors are attracted to Brussels and Antwerp (Grimmeau 1980).

Switzerland, Austria and Luxembourg, of course, have no coastline at all on which either domestic or international tourism might be focused. International tourism in Austria is mainly concentrated on the Alps proper in the west, especially in the Tyrol. This is not only the winter sports traffic for the summer influx is greater than that of the winter months (Burtenshaw 1981). Austrian domestic tourism, particularly in summer, extends to the areas of gentler relief in the east which no doubt receives much of the demand from Vienna. Alpine attractions are found throughout much of Switzerland with the main urban centres, several of which have a major international role (Geneva, Zurich), being located in the lowland and valley areas. As a result, both domestic and international tourism are fairly evenly dispersed.

Differences in the attractions sought by international and domestic campers appear to explain the greater concentration in Luxembourg of the latter. The major groups of international campers, the Dutch and the Belgians, are most numerous in the Ardennes region whose relief contrasts with that of the Low Countries. Domestic campers, in the absence of a coastline, favour the banks of the rivers and streams of the smaller Moellerdahl and Moselle regions. The Moselle region also accounts for over half of domestic hotel nights while the Centre, containing Luxembourg City, receives the most international demand, much of which is presumably business rather than vacation travel.

The size and location of France have endowed the country with a range of physical resources yet it is the cultural attractions of Paris which lead to over a quarter of international hotel demand being concentrated in the capital. In terms of location quotients, Paris is followed by the Mediterranean coastal region of Provence–Côte d'Azur, Alsace, the Midi-Pyrénées (heavily influenced by the pilgrimage traffic to Lourdes) and the alpine region of the Rhône-Alpes. A similar order occurs for domestic hotel demand but the limited representativeness of this sector for domestic tourism must be remembered (Table 7.1). In particular, Fig. 6.2 indicated that Paris was not a major destination for French holidaymakers.

These regional variations in resource endowment are reinforced by different patterns of demand and accessibility. The quality of the resource or experience sought by the international tourist will normally be higher and perhaps more specific than that of many domestic tourists. In leaving his own country, the international tourist is generally investing more time, money and effort to get to his destination. The sites and sights he seeks are thus likely to be much less common and therefore more localized than those sought by, or at least able to be afforded by, many domestic tourists in the destination country. Non-vacation travel by international visitors, for example those attending conferences or on official or private business, is also likely to be more concentrated than that of their domestic counterparts, notably in capital cities and major urban areas. In Chapter 6 it was shown that much domestic tourist travel is intra-regional in nature with the volume of travel decreasing with distance from each market area (Fig. 1.3). Although patterns of settlement and urban hierarchies vary from country to country, in most of the cases studied there is a reasonable number of these markets, the main urban centres, scattered throughout the country, each giving rise to a regional pattern of demand. In contrast, international gateways, which were shown in Chapter 4 to influence the intra-national travel patterns of international visitors, are generally much fewer in number, particularly where arrivals are by air. Moreover, economies of scale in development and operations are achieved by focusing on a limited number of development areas. This is particularly the case with international tourism, whether in terms of constructing international airports, developing mass tourism or of selectively promoting particular areas once a country's image has been established in the international market-place. For these and other reasons suggested by Miossec (1976), the international tourist is also less likely to be aware of the full range of vacation opportunities than the domestic holiday-maker (Fig. 1.4).

These factors may also contribute to the contin-uing concentration of the tourist industry in already developed parts of the country. The payback period on tourist plant, e.g. airports and hotels, is relatively long, encouraging continuing efforts to promote these areas (Burkart and Medlik 1974). This is not true to the same extent with condominium construction where the developer is often more interested in the initial sale of the apartment. But even here, the desire to reduce investment risks will frequently lead to new projects being located in or near areas which are already well known and which have an established servicing and infrastructural base. An informal feedback system will also develop, with many marketing surveys showing the 'influence of friends and relations' as a major factor affecting the selection of a holiday destination. As the market grows, so the amount of information feedback will increase, especially important where the quality of the experience is satisfactory. McEachern and Towle (1974) suggest that even where there is a decline in environmental quality a decrease in the tourist traffic is not inevitable:

> As the character of the tourist island changes from 'unspoiled' to 'spoiled' (e.g. more urbanized) the influx of tourists does not stop. Due to various stimuli, such as man's advertising and other publicity, it continues and may even accelerate according to a positive feedback loop that reinforces the degree of urbanization and the influx of new tourists with different tastes.

The concentration of tourism may thus develop from a process of circular cumulative growth similar to that observed in industrialization and economic development (Myrdal 1957; Pred 1965) or in agricultural specialization (Moran 1979).

Table 8.2
Rank correlation coefficients of the regional distribution of international and domestic tourism in selected European countries.

Country	Measure of regional distribution	
	Location quotient (r_s)	% of bed nights (r_s)
Portugal (hotels)	0.8972	0.8090
Portugal (camping)	0.8772	0.8845
Bulgaria	0.8500	0.7400
Spain	0.8304	0.7798
France	0.8422	0.8072
Luxembourg (camping)	0.7000	0.5000
Austria	0.5334	0.0800
Belgium	0.5222	0.5080
Switzerland	0.3590	0.4720
Luxembourg (hotels)	0.3000	0.4000

Certain types of tourism, unlike these other industries, however, are characterized by a search for novelty. Developing or maintaining the more allocentric or perhaps fashionable segment of the market may depend in part on opening up new areas. Given that the measures of concentration used here are relative ones, the development of new areas does not necessarily mean an increase in dispersion. In absolute numbers, the traffic to the new resorts may be offset nationally by an expansion in the volume of visitors to or on the fringe of the more traditional areas. Where, however, the expansion of the tourist traffic has come about through the concerted development of a specific attraction or a new area, such as the Black Sea coast of Bulgaria, a marked increase in the degree of concentration might be expected. In Romania, the Black Sea coast's share of advertised hotel accommodation increased from 33% in 1967 to 76% in 1975 as a result of 'vigorous efforts to develop tour business with Western operators' (Turnock 1977: 53).

Although the localization curves depicted in Fig. 8.1 show how domestic and international tourism are concentrated in differing degrees in the countries examined, they do not show directly the extent to which the two groups of tourists favour the same regions. In other words, are domestic tourists concentrated in the same regions as international visitors? Table 8.2 depicts the rank correlation coefficients of the two sets of regions – domestic and international – in each country ranked in terms of their location quotient and share of each market. Caution is needed in making cross-country comparisons, however, given the variations in the degree of concentration and the number of units involved in each country. In some countries where the rank correlation is very high, as in Portugal and Spain, important differences may occur in the actual numbers involved due to differing degrees of concentration and the size of each market. For example, in Portugal the Faro region (the Algarve) was the top ranked region for international bed nights and second for domestic tourism. In the first case it accounted for 47% of the bed nights, in the second for only 12%. Similarly in Spain, the top ranked Balearic Islands accounted for 47% of international bed nights in 1980 but, although coming second for domestic tourism, took only 7% of that market's bed nights. Conversely, in Switzerland, variations in the domestic/international structure of each region are not as great as they might seem from Table 8.2, given the general degree of dispersion of both types of tourism throughout the country (Fig. 8.1). One or two predominantly international tourist re-

gions, notably Lake Geneva and north-east Switzerland, can be distinguished along with predominantly domestic ones such as Zurich but the remainder are reasonably balanced (Ilbery 1981).

It is thus difficult to make any generalizations about the location of domestic and international tourist regions in the countries examined except to note that, among the major tourist regions in each country, there are some which cater predominantly for domestic tourists and others which depend mainly on international visitors. The particular orientation of specific regions will depend on the same factors as those influencing the degree of concentration, notably the nature and distribution of the tourist resources, accessibility and the location of centres of domestic demand. Minor tourist regions, on the other hand, rely mainly on domestic visitors.

Domestic and international tourism in Spain

Detailed examination of the spatial coincidence of domestic and international tourism might therefore be best undertaken at the level of the individual country, as Pearce and Grimmeau (1985) have done in the case of hotel demand in Spain. Their analysis of 1975 hotel bed nights by province and nationality yielded two principal components (see page 123), which respectively account for 75.5% and 13% of the variation (Fig. 8.2). The first component opposes the domestic market against that of the European countries, particularly the major European markets, while the second isolates demand from beyond Europe. These results suggest that the tourists in each of these three categories – Spain, Europe, rest of the world – exhibit similar preferences in the provinces they visit and that the bed night data might logically be regrouped in this way. Reasonably distinct clusters of provinces also appeared when the factor scores of the observations (the provinces) on the first two components were plotted. Figure 8.3 represents a synthesis in which the major structures identified in terms of the first two components are portrayed graphically.

The synthesis provided by Fig. 8.3 suggests that there are marked differences in the spatial patterns of domestic and international hotel demand in Spain. Domestic demand predominates in the urban and historical centres, notably Madrid, Barcelona and the Moorish cities of Sevilla, Granada and Cordoba, as well as in the inland and Atlantic coastal provinces. Much of the urban-centred demand appears to be related

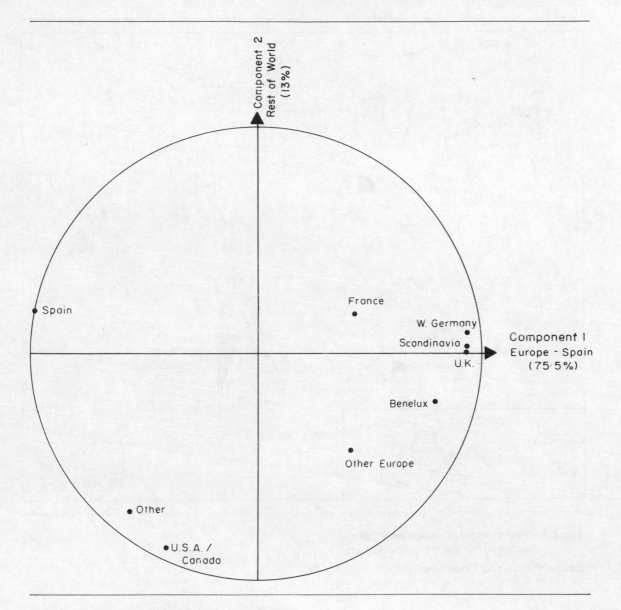

Fig. 8.2 Spain: vector diagram depicting the loadings of the variables (the nationalities) on the first two components.

Source: Pearce and Grimmeau (1985).

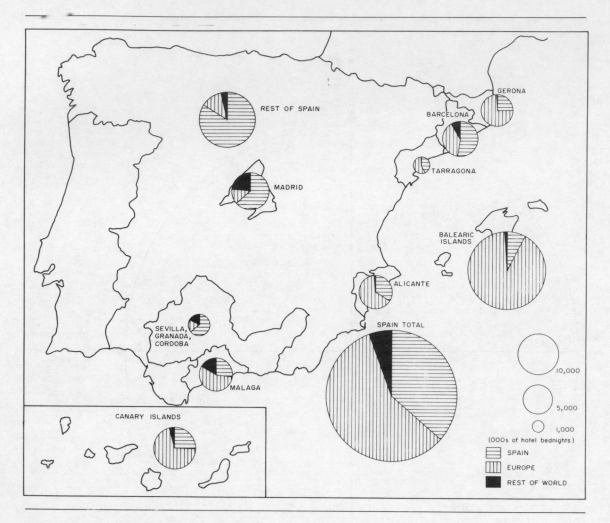

Fig. 8.3 Spain: regional variations in hotel demand by major national groups.

Source: Pearce and Grimmeau (1985).

to non-vacation travel. The general dispersion of the domestic demand is perhaps a function of regionalized trip-making in a country where holiday-making has not yet developed to the same extent as in other European countries. The distribution of European and rest of the world bed nights typifies to a large extent two contrasting types of tourism – sunlust and wanderlust (Plates 1 and 2). Demand from European visitors is highly concentrated in the islands and major Mediterranean coastal provinces where

charter tourism plays a significant role (Fig. 5.4). Visitors from beyond Europe, on the other hand, focus primarily on the urban and historical centres which are visited by many as part of a cultural circuit. Madrid's traffic is also augmented by its gateway role and central place functions.

The intra-national travel patterns which Gray (1970) associated with sunlust and wanderlust (Table 2.2) are evident in other research results. Over 40% of respondents in a survey of 1,500 foreign visitors to Spain in the period December

Pl. 1 Sunlust tourism: the Playa de Levante,
Benidorm.

1980–January 1981 indicated that the locality in which they were interviewed constituted the sole place visited on their trip (Equipo Investigador del IET 1981). The proportion varied from insular and coastal zones (Canary Islands, 75%; Costa Blanca, 65%) to urban and historical centres (Madrid, 24%; Barcelona, 11%; Sevilla, Cordoba and Granada, 6%). North Americans were much more mobile than Germans, with only 9% of the former group making a single stop compared with 63% of the latter.

Pearce and Grimmeau also sought to establish whether there had been any noticeable changes in the spatial preferences of hotel guests over a period which had seen a marked expansion in the tourist industry in Spain. To do this, they took data for four years (1965/66, 1970, 1975, 1980) and subjected it to principal components analysis in the manner outlined earlier. In this case the number of variables had been increased from 9 to 36, that is the nine nationalities for each of the

four years considered. The variable loadings on the first two components, which respectively accounted for 69.2% and 12.7% of the variation, are depicted in Fig. 8.4.

Figure 8.4 suggests a pattern of comparative stability as the four related variables for each nationality load on the components in a consistent manner, indicating little change in the overall preferences of any nationality from one year to another. The French, and to a lesser extent the Scandinavians, constitute exceptions to this pattern, with a constant evolution towards the preferences of the main West European markets being recorded throughout the period; attributed to changes in charter tourism. Pearce and Grimmeau then show that while the spatial preferences of each nationality have remained remarkably constant over the period 1965–80, growth rates have differed significantly from market to market. As a result, marked regional differences in demand occurred, with the number

137

Pl. 2 Wanderlust tourism: a group of tourists pass through the Courtyard of the Lions, the Alhambra, Granada.

of bed nights increasing much more rapidly in the coastal and insular provinces favoured by the Europeans than in the regions more heavily dependent on the 'rest of the world' and domestic markets. In this way it is possible to translate changes in specific markets into impacts in particular regions.

Spatial variations in international tourism

Trends in the distribution of international tourism similar to those identified in Spain have also been observed in other parts of Europe. The general tendency is for tourists from neighbouring countries or other short-haul markets to be associated with sunlust tourism and to concentrate in areas of natural resources, whether coastal or alpine.

Such resources complement or extend those found in the generating country. The longer-haul visitors, on the other hand, tend to exhibit the characteristics of wanderlust tourists and non-vacation travellers and focus more on urban, historical and cultural centres. The distribution of the different nationalities may also be influenced by accessibility, either in terms of proximity to the markets or the location of major gateways.

In Spain's neighbour, Portugal, some two-thirds of the British, Dutch and German bed nights (in all forms of accommodation) are concentrated in the Algarve (Direccao Geral do Turismo 1980). Particularly in the case of the British, much of this demand is channelled through Faro airport. Proximity is a factor in the case of the French, many of whom travel overland by car and who head as much to the Costa

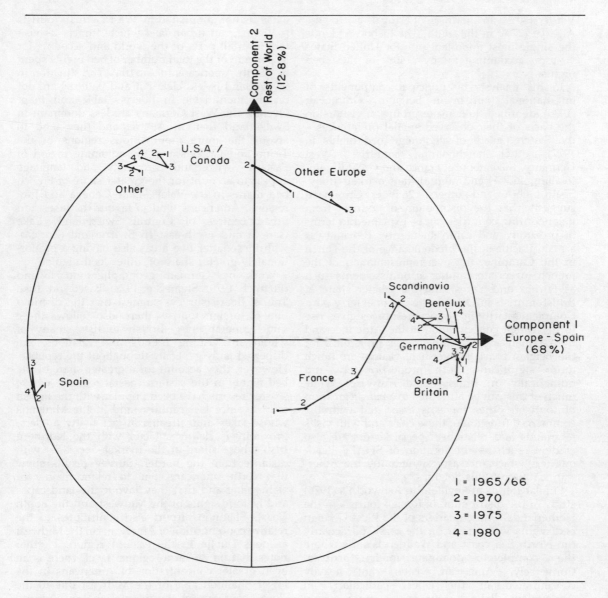

Fig. 8.4 Spain: vector diagram depicting the evolution of the spatial preferences of the major national groups.

Source: Pearce and Grimmeau (1985).

Verde (30%) in northern Portugal as to the Algarve (27%) in the south. The Lisbon region is the single most important one for United States visitors, accounting for over 40% of their bed nights.

In his analysis by principal components of international tourism in Belgium, Grimmeau (1980) identified three major groups of visitors on the basis of their observed spatial preferences – the Dutch (26.8% of all foreign bed nights in 1977), other neighbouring countries (West Germany, Luxembourg, France and Great Britain, totalling 46.7%) and more distant markets (Italy, Spain, USA and others, 26.5%). Grimmeau suggests that the distribution of tourists from neighbouring countries can be explained in terms of proximity and complementarity. Proximity is a major factor in the predominance of the Dutch in the Campine, the over-representation of the French in certain frontier arrondissements such as Furnes and Ypres, and the greater share of British tourists in Ostend, the Channel ferry port. Complementarity in physical resources gives rise to the Dutch concentration in the Ardennes and the German and Luxembourgeois preference for the Belgian coast. Longer-haul visitors are much more significant, both proportionately and numerically, in Brussels and Antwerp. While much of this can be attributed to a *villes d'art* form of tourism, other travel is associated with the commercial function of these cities and with visits to friends and relations. Special factors are also evident, such as the location of SHAPE head-quarters which increases significantly the American traffic to Mons-Soignies.

Similar trends are evident in Ashworth's (1976) study of the distribution of foreign tourists in the Netherlands. Three-quarters of the West German bed nights were spent on the coast, particularly the North Sea coast and Wadden Islands where they completely dominate foreign arrivals. Conversely, American visitors are heavily concentrated in the cities, particularly in Amsterdam. Belgian tourists are more evenly dispersed, visiting not only the coast, particularly the southern part, and the cities, but also the inland areas. The British and French constitute an intermediate group for as Ashworth (p. 39) points out, they 'fall between the extremes of German concentration on the coast and American concentration on the cities, and also between the extremes of Belgian dispersion and American concentration'.

Comparable patterns appear to exist in Austria and Switzerland where the basic natural resource changes from the coast to the mountains. As Ilbery (1981: 127) notes, the only Austrian *land*

which is not dominated by West German tourists is Vienna, 'an urban *land* which attracts its visitors from all parts of the world and accounts for 36 per cent of the total number of bed nights spent by North Americans in Austria'. The situation in Switzerland is less clear-cut and patterns are not readily identifiable in Ilbery's table and map. Overall, the West Germans are less dominant in Switzerland than in Austria and they tend to favour the more mountainous regions of the Ticino and Grisons and the adjoining region of Eastern Switzerland. Proximity and language appear to account for the greater share of French bed nights in the Valais, Lake Geneva and Jura regions. Americans tend to favour the lakes and urban centres of Central Switzerland, Lake Geneva and north-eastern Switzerland (Zurich), with these latter two areas also having a proportionately greater share of 'other' bed nights.

Work by German geographers in Ireland (Plettner 1979; Steinecke 1979) based on Irish Tourist Board surveys suggest that the distribution of foreign tourists there also follows these same general lines. British tourists, many of whom are visiting friends and relations, are dispersed fairly generally throughout the republic. However, they account for a greater share of the bed nights in the eastern coastal regions, whose seaside resorts have been popular with the British tourists since last century, and in the Midlands whose lakes and streams attract many anglers. Proximity is clearly a factor with the Northern Irish whose share of the market decreases with distance from the border. Survey results show that North Americans come to Ireland mainly for sightseeing and that they favour the landscapes and historic sights of the Midwest and the South Coast. Shannon airport also contributes to the relative concentration of Americans in the Midwest as does Dublin in the eastern region. Plettner notes that on an intra-regional level, there is an even greater concentration of Americans in the lower Shannon area of the Midwest due to the close association of the international airport and such nearby castles as that at Bunratty. The south is also especially favoured by Continental Europeans, many of whom are seeking an 'active' holiday, participating in a range of sporting activities such as walking, riding and sailing. An above-average share of European bed nights is also recorded in the east, in part a function of the transport links there between Ireland and Great Britain. Unfortunately, the data are presented in aggregate form and it is not possible to detect any differences in the preferences of different groups of Europeans.

The specific patterns described in these examples are in part due to each being a European country with a range of different attractions. Similar structures have also been identified in other contexts. Writing on the expansion of tourism in Kenya, Jackson (1973) notes:

> Until the early 1960s, the coast was the resort chiefly of up-country expatriates . . . But from 1962 onwards, increasing numbers of foreigners began to take advantage of the first package tours to be organised to this new tourist frontier. Almost all the newcomers were from Europe, thus establishing a dichotomy that has continued to be more marked between a European-dominated coastal tourism, with shop signs and hotel menus in German, Italian and French, and American dominated game lodges attended by zebra skins, camera accessory shops and higher prices.

These lines of research could be profitably extended to include comparable studies of countries such as Canada, Mexico and Caribbean destinations where Americans constitute the neighbouring short-haul tourists and Europeans the travellers from further afield. Are their respective roles and patterns reversed there? Likewise, studies on essentially sunlust or wanderlust destinations would shed further light on the general structure of international tourism.

The spatial structure of tourism in regions

Studies of the extent to which differences occur in the structure of domestic and international tourism at the regional level are far less common than the national ones discussed in the preceding section. In part this appears to be a function of the data available. Although the national studies are often based on bed night returns made at a local level, the data are seldom published or made available at this scale. As a result, the regional studies of variations in market composition have usually been based on specific surveys or analysis of second home ownership records. Studies at this scale have tended to be concerned more with the functional structure of tourism, giving attention to the nature and location of tourist facilities and their relation to landscape features and other forms of land use. Such an approach is in keeping with the regional focus of much European geography in general (Barbier and Pearce 1984) but it is one which has been adopted by few Anglo-American tourist geographers. This is no doubt a reflection of general trends in their discipline in recent decades which have favoured more systematic and quantitative methods. Studies of the spatial structure of tourism in regions, however, can provide a useful bridge between national analyses of tourism and the many more detailed case studies of individual resorts and cities (Ch. 10).

This section reviews examples of different types of regional studies drawn from coastal regions in the Mediterranean and from Belgium. The studies from France focus on spatial variations in the composition of different geographic markets, those from Spain and Morocco emphasize the structure of various forms of tourism, and the example from Belgium contains elements of both supply and demand. The functional structure in each case is examined in terms of the various factors outlined in Miossec's model of the development of a tourist region (Fig. 1.11) to provide some basis for general comments on the spatial structure of coastal tourism at a regional level.

The Belgian coast

Despite its limited length, significant differences occur in the structure of tourism along the Belgian coast, both in terms of supply and demand. With over twenty resorts located along its 67 km, virtually the entire length of the coastline has been developed to some degree for tourism. Rarely, however, does the tourist zone extend for more than a kilometre inland, the urbanized area being abruptly terminated in many instances where the polders are reached. The oldest resorts – Ostend, Blankenberg and Knokke – were already well-established by the end of the nineteenth century (Vanhove 1980). While these resorts benefited from early rail links, the construction of a coastal tramway later opened up access to other parts of the littoral. This tramway, now paralleled by the road system, continues to play a significant role in unifying the region. Many of the new resorts were coastwards extensions of existing communities which have been separated from the sea by large dune systems, e.g. Koksijde-Bad and Koksijde, Oostduinkerke-Bad and Oostduinkerke. These dune systems are still responsible today for breaking up the ribbon development of the coast, separating, for instance, De Panne from St Idesbald and St Idesbald from Koksijde-Bad.

Figure 8.5 shows that for the coast as a whole, camping, rental accommodation (villas and apartments) and second homes each account for about a quarter of the total bedspace along the coast, with the remainder being shared by hotels and

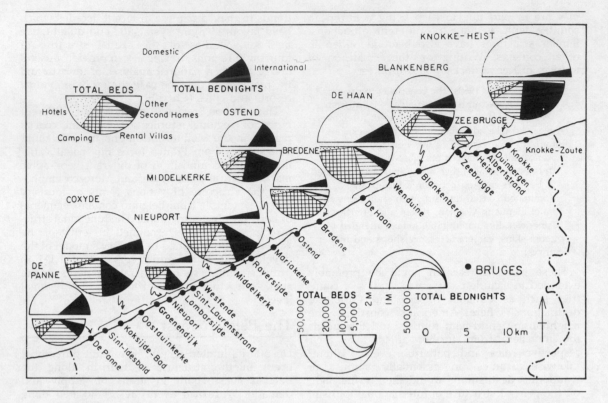

Fig. 8.5 Spatial variations in the composition of tourism along the Belgian coast.

Data source: Vanhove (1980).

other forms of accommodation (essentially holiday villages and various forms of 'social' tourist centres). However, as Fig. 8.5 shows, the composition of the accommodation varies from commune to commune. According to Flament (1973), the coast has traditionally been divided into three distinct sectors on the basis of the accommodation available and the history of tourist development. Hotels are relatively more important in the eastern zone with its old, established aristocratic resorts of Knokke, Heist and Blankenberg. But even here hotels have long been surpassed by the bedspace available in villas and second homes, the latter often taking the form of apartments in high-rise buildings along the beach-front. With the exception of Ostend, which shares a similar structure to Knokke and Blankenberg, the central zone (from De Haan to Middelkirke) has attracted tourists of more modest means. Camping is the dominant form of

accommodation here, particularly at Bredene where tents were first pitched in 1912 (Vanhove 1980). The western zone, where tourism expanded in the inter-war period, is characterized by its broad beaches, developed beachfront, villas, holiday villages and social tourism centres. Here the twinning of resorts with established settlements is particularly noticeable (Flament 1973).

Figure 8.5 also emphasizes the role of domestic tourism along the coast, with Belgian holiday-makers accounting for about 90% of all estimated bed nights in 1978 (Vanhove 1980). However, the domestic share fell to 68% at Ostend and 77% at De Panne, largely as a result of the concentration of British tourists in the former, the ferry port, and of French holiday-makers in the latter, a border resort. Flament (1973), commenting on the results of a more detailed survey in 1969, showed that visitors from the north of France, the largest group, tended to favour De Panne and Koksijde, while Parisians were relatively more numerous in the renowned resorts of Knokke and Ostend. The Parisians favoured hotels and pensions while the majority of holiday-makers from the north rented villas or apartments. This latter tendency has attributed to the greater facility which those in the north had for establishing contact directly with rental agencies and individuals. Flament also suggests that the presence of the French along the western part of the coast is in part responsible for a greater concentration of French-speaking Walloons in this zone. Flemish holiday-makers are particularly dominant in the east, while vacationers from the Brabant (Brussels) are more equally distributed along the length of the coast. Proximity, communications (e.g. the rail links from Bruges to Blankenberg and Knokke) and habit are factors contributing to these variations in domestic tourism.

Finally, it should be recalled that the coast accounts for two-thirds of domestic bed nights and over half of all tourist bed nights in Belgium. It is this tourist function which sets the Belgian coast apart from the adjoining industrialized Channel coast of France whose physical attributes are however very similar. As Dewailly (1979) notes, these differences must be seen in a national context. France's long coastline provides a range of much better opportunities elsewhere for tourist development as well as space for other forms of economic activity. In Belgium, the choice is strictly limited. Although some industrial development has occurred at Zeebrugge, it is Antwerp on the Schelde estuary which has assumed the major port–industrial role, thus fortunately reducing the potential for conflict with tourism along the coast itself. That one can stand on the promenade at St Idesbald and look out to the industrial smoke stacks at Dunkirk is in large part due to the intervening political frontier and to decisions taken in two inland capitals.

Provence and Languedoc-Roussillon

Tourism has developed in different ways and at different rates along the Mediterranean coast of France. Provence, to the east, has a well-established tourist industry which grew up gradually last century, and has since experienced substantial spontaneous expansion to become the country's foremost tourist region (Fig. 6.2). Languedoc-Roussillon, on the other hand, has been the object of a major, highly planned programme of development initiated in the early 1960s which has been responsible for lifting the area from one of regional importance to national and even international significance (Pearce 1981c:

Ch. 6). Given these and other differences, e.g. in the urban network, it is not surprising that variations occur in the patterns found in each region. At the same time, however, certain common tendencies exist.

In Provence, significant differences occur in the origins of second home owners along the coast and between the coast and the interior (Barbier 1975). The highest rates of foreign ownership are found from Saint Tropez to the Italian border, a zone where extra-regional ownership, particularly by Parisians, is also the most significant (Fig. 8.6). Classified hotel capacity, both in absolute and relative terms, is also generally much greater along this part of the coast. Further west, notably in Cassis and in the lower reaches of the Rhône Valley, most of the second home owners are from the region itself, particularly from Marseille. History and geography contribute to this division. International tourism has been important on the Côte d'Azur proper (from Cannes to Menton) since the area first began attracting tourists during the winter months in the late eighteenth and early nineteenth centuries. Cannes' origins as a winter resort date from 1839 when the Englishman, Lord Brougham, was obliged to spend some time in the village on his way back from Italy due to an outbreak of cholera in Provence. He found the locale and climate agreeable and returned the following year to build his villa; his English friends soon followed suit. Cassis, on the other hand, owes its development to its proximity to the largest metropolitan area in the south of France as well as to its charming port and *calanques*. Most of the second homes in interior Provence are owned by coastal dwellers from within the region, with foreign and extra-regional ownership being noticeable in the immediate hinterland of Nice and Cannes and in the more accessible Rhône Valley. Proximity, complementarity and sunlust are factors contributing to this pattern.

A different pattern of second home ownership west of the Rhône is suggested by Andrieux and Soulier's (1980) study of Languedoc-Roussillon. Their figures indicate that about half of the second homes belong to owners living within the region, another 40% from owners residing elsewhere in France, with about 8% being in foreign ownership. Proportionately more of the second homes on the coast belong to local (within the same commune) and regional residents, many of whom have purchased them as an investment and for rental to other users. As a result, differences in the origins of owners and users appears to be greater here than on the Côte d'Azur. Further inland, foreign ownership is about twice

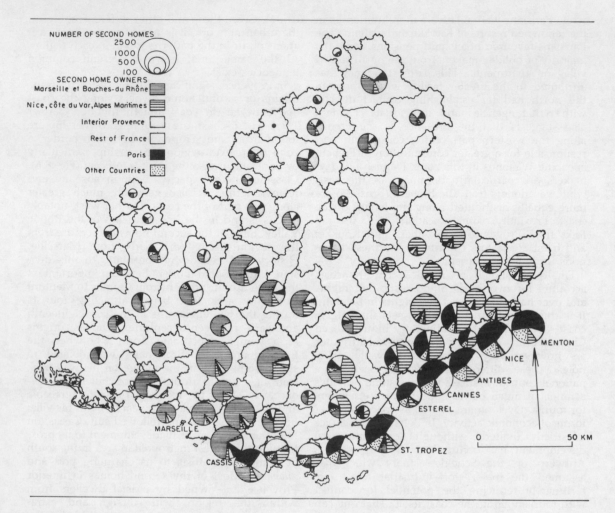

Fig. 8.6 Origins of second home owners in Provence.

Source: After Barbier (1975).

the regional average in the Garrigues-Soubergues district – 'an area which is not important agriculturally, is not densely populated but which is still relatively close to the coast'. Differences are also found throughout the region in the composition of the international sector. Germans, for example, are over-represented on the coast, while Belgians are relatively more numerous along the margins of the Rhône Valley and Massif Central, with Dutch second home owners being dominant in other upland areas. In the absence of absolute figures, these trends must be regarded with caution, but it does seem that the complementarity

of resources plays a role in the distribution of international demand within regions as well as between them.

Other research suggests that significant differences occur in the structure of demand along the Languedoc-Roussillon coast. Fornairon (1978) carried out an extensive survey of the origin of cars at different beaches throughout the region during the summer of 1977. Such an approach is likely to overestimate regional demand, through a greater likelihood of nearby beach users travelling by private car rather than some other mode of transport and through the inclusion of regional day-trippers, but the general trends are nevertheless interesting. These indicate that the pattern of usage reflects the history of tourist development in the region. Regional demand is proportionately greater in the older resorts, many of which, through access and proximity, have long-established ties to cities located further inland, e.g. Grau du Roi to Nimes, Palavas and Carnon to Montpellier. Foreigners who accounted on average for 12% of the car registrations, are over-represented both in the large modern resorts and in the underdeveloped areas, the *plages sauvages* (L'Espiguette, 15.6%; Les Aresquiers, 16.8%). Overall, there was little variation in demand from Parisians throughout the region and no systematic variation in the demand from elsewhere in France was apparent.

The Costa Brava, Costa Blanca and Costa del Sol

Much tourist expansion along the Mediterranean coast of Spain occurred over the same period that Languedoc-Roussillon was developed (since the early 1960s), but there the growth of tourism has been much more spontaneous and unplanned. Research at the regional level in Spain, notably by French geographers, has focused on the functional structures which have resulted from this development rather than on variations in the origins of visitors. Different types of structures and forms of development do, however, reflect different types of tourism which are discernible, if not always quantifiable, along various stretches of the Mediterranean coast. Three areas are examined here: the Costa Brava, the Costa Blanca and the Costa del Sol.

Barbaza (1970) notes that prior to the development of tourism, the Costa Brava was rather isolated and had not been dominated by any large city, neither Gerona, further inland, nor Barcelona, further along the coast. The rapid and massive development of tourism in the 1960s ended this isolation, linking the coast, by means of flows of workers and capital as well as the new transport infrastructure (new motorways and the Gerona–Costa Brava airport), to the rest of Catalonia, to other parts of Spain and even to neighbouring countries. At that time (1970), a fully developed hierarchy of urban areas along the coast had not yet emerged but, as Barbaza observed (p. 451), 'tourism introduces a powerful unifying element and leads to the development of a truly functional region, *l'espace touristique'*. Cals, Esteban and Teixidor (1977: 200) identify two major markets on the Costa Brava: 'in several

centres, Lloret, l'Estartit, Tossa, Rosas et Blanes, etc, the dominant form of tourism, which has expanded rapidly since 1965, is that of the tour operators. Elsewhere, on the contrary, the tourist clientele, continues to be basically private and individual.' The first form of tourism is typically reflected in large densely-settled resorts, comprised of high-rise hotels and apartments, the second by sprawling sub-divisions of villas known as *urbanizaciones* (Plates 3 and 4).

Further south, in the region of Alicante (see Fig. 8.3), Dumas (1976: 45) observes: 'One of the major characteristics of the Costa Blanca is the juxtaposition of very varied types of tourism: family style villas as at certain French beaches, or organised, industrial tourism linked to the tour-operators.' Benidorm is the classic example of the latter. Popular originally with well-to-do Madrileños, being the closest resort to the capital, Benidorm during the 1960s, 'became part of the tourist space of the North European tour operators, in particular the British and Germans' (Fig. 5.4). By the mid-1970s, with a resident population of only 12,000, Benidorm was able to accommodate 120,000 visitors at the one time. Factors accounting for its development include a splendid physical site (two long curving sandy beaches separated by a promontory), access via the N332 and later the Valencia–Alicante motorway and proximity to the Alicante airport (40 km away) which was modernized in 1967 (Plate 1).

North of Benidorm, *urbanizaciones* sprawl over the broken relief of the Cap de la Nao, as hillsides have been progressively colonized by villas, many owned by German families (Plate 3). Sub-divisions here tend to be smaller in scale and larger in number than those found to the south of Alicante. Construction of apartments and villas has also occurred around existing coastal communities such as Denia and Moraira.

The coast south of Alicante to Cabo de Palos is more sparsely populated. Development there has been more recent and taken the form of a series of large Centros de Interes Turistico Nacional (CITN), resort enclaves in which the activities of the tour operators have been linked with those of the real estate promoters. As CITNs, these developments benefit from generous credit facilities and fiscal assistance (Vila Fradera 1966). With the exception of Santa Pola del Este which has been grafted on to a fishing port with some established holiday homes, the others – La Zenia, Dehesa de Campoamor and La Manga del Mar Menor – have been developed *ex-nihilo* on large agricultural holdings at the initiative of the land owner. Dumas (1976: 48) describes the development of La Zenia and Campoamor thus:

Pl. 3 The colonization of hillsides by tourism: villas sprawl across Punta Ifach, Costa Brava.

The property along the coast (between the road and the sea) is subdivided and several apartment buildings and bungalows and villas are built. Other serviced sections are put up for sale and to rapidly attract clients [and to give some life to the resort] a large hotel is built and filled by tour operators. In the same way, a large number of apartments are rented through German, Dutch and French agencies.

The process at La Manga del Mar Menor has been similar but on a larger scale and with more tour operator involvement (Dumas 1975). Development there has occurred along a sandy bar, 300 m wide and 22 km long, which separates the Mar Menor from the Mediterranean (Plate 7). Both in its physical setting and its scale of development, La Manga recalls other recent tourist projects, notably the new resorts of Languedoc-Roussillon and Cancun in Mexico (Pearce 1983b).

A similar mix of resorts filled by package tourists and *urbanizaciones* is found along the Costa del Sol where Malaga is the major urban centre and Torremolinos the counterpart of Benidorm (Fig. 8.7). Villegas Molina (1975) shows Torremolinos had almost twice the hotel bedspace of Malaga in 1970, with the capacity of Marbella exceeding that of the provincial capital as well. Three major structural elements are identified by Mignon and Heran (1979) along the Costa del Sol:

(a) the *front de mer* featuring a promenade and dominated by a wall of high-rise hotels and apartment buildings,

(b) the commerical axis bordering the N340 and containing shops, travel and real estate agencies, restaurants,

(c) villas and *urbanizaciones* which cover the lower slopes beyond the resorts.

146

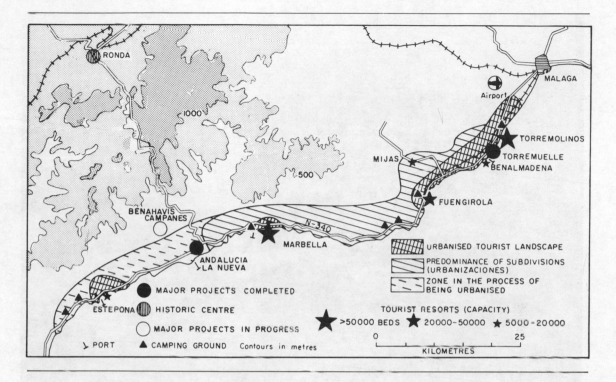

Fig. 8.7   The structure of tourism along the Costa del Sol.

Source: After Mignon and Heran (1979).

Between the first two zones, residential quarters and more modest hotels mix with boutiques and occasionally the remnants of the original residential quarters. In most cases, however, local residential areas have been pushed further inland, aside from the resort itself.

These three elements do not assume the same importance along the coast with the density of development decreasing westwards, away from Malaga and its airport (Fig. 8.7) to Andalucia La Nueva and Estepona where new *urbanizaciones* dominate (Plate 4). In some cases, inland towns have been incorporated into the regional structure, as in the case of the hilltop town of Migas, which has experienced considerable residential development, and Ronda, an historic town famed for its ravine and bridge, and now, after the construction of a new sealed road from the coast, the focus of day tours. Other excursions are organized to the major Andalucian cities of Sevilla, Granada and Cordoba.

Morocco

The Mediterranean coast of Morocco was 'launched' in the mid-1960s as the country's 'future Costa del Sol' (Berriane 1978) with the aim of capturing part of the European 'sun-sand-sea' market. In 1964, this coastal region, east of Tangiers to Alhoceima, was sparsely populated and accounted for only 2% of Morocco's hotel capacity. Physical difficulties of access and its recent political history had meant that its series of sandy beaches had not yet been exploited (Péré 1975). By 1977, however, the Mediterranean coast had 13% of the country's bedspace (7,365 beds) and accommodated 130,000 visitors annually. With Agadir it had become one of the country's two major sunlust destinations but as Berriane points out, in Morocco, unlike Tunisia, circuit or wanderlust tourism based on centres such as Casablanca, Marrakesh and Meknes-Fes is more important.

Pl. 4 An *urbanización* developed around a golf course inland from Marbella, Costa del Sol.

Foreign tour operators, benefiting from generous financial incentives and infra-structural assistance from the state, were responsible for much of the development of the Mediterranean coast. While hotels and second homes are found there, the bulk of the capacity is in the form of holiday villages such as those of Club Méditerranée. Tourist development along the coast is essentially characterized by isolated enclaves of which Berriane (1978) recognizes three distinct forms (Fig. 8.8):

1.   the juxtaposition of a tourist enclave alongside an existing urban centre with, however, little interaction between the two (e.g. Midiq and Alhoceima),
2.   a new tourist centre located away from the highway where several types of tourist facility (a hotel, apartments, villas, serviced sections . . .) are clustered together as in many Spanish *urbanizaciones* (e.g. Capo Negro),
3.   isolated resorts, situated some distance from

each other and from the main road to give a 'comb' structure (e.g. Kabyla, Club Méditerranée at Smir).

This isolation, appealing in the beginning because of the freedom to develop which it has allowed, has meant that the resorts have not become integrated economically and socially into the region. Moreover, these resorts have suffered from a lack of activity and *animation*, leading the operators there in recent years to concentrate on a limited season and to favour other areas, notably Agadir, where they have been able to develop a year-round traffic.

While this type of development shares some of the structural characteristics of other new tourist regions in the Maghreb, notably the Nabeul–Hammamet region of Tunisia, it contrasts markedly with the recent expansion in Algeria. There, much of the new hotel construction in the 1970s was associated with other more major forms of development, industrial and commer-

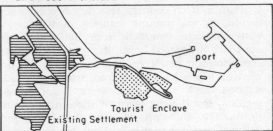

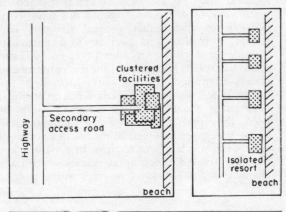

Fig. 8.8 Types of tourist development along the Mediterranean coast of Morocco.

Source: After Berriane (1978).

cial, and occurred around the major urban areas, particularly Algiers (Mankour 1980). Due to a general shortage of housing, many of the new hotels effectively act as a form of residential overflow, being occupied by officials, consultants and workers on other development projects.

Regional structure

The limited number of examples examined show that differences occur in the composition of the tourist traffic not only between but also within regions. In the cases of the Belgian coast, Provence and, to a lesser extent, Languedoc-Roussillon, variations were found in the distribution of domestic and international tourists. Distinct

spatial preferences may also exist within these two markets. Flemish and Walloon vacationers, for example, tend to take their holidays along different parts of the Belgian coast while French and British tourists there favour the resorts most accessible to them. Different forms also reflect different types of tourism along the Mediterranean coasts of Spain and Morocco. These variations are less quantifiable, but certain resorts or zones are dominated by hotels and apartments oriented towards package tourists with *urbanizaciones* and camping grounds catering more for domestic tourists and independent foreign holiday-makers.

These regions are clearly at different stages of maturity in terms of Miossec's model (Fig. 1.11). The coasts of Belgium and of Provence have undoubtedly reached a very mature stage, being well developed or even saturated for virtually their entire length, with a dense and well-integrated transport network being established and tourism coming to shape and even dominate the urban and economic structure of each region. Market specialization occurs in both cases, distinct variations in types of accommodation are found and a hierarchy of resorts and urban centres is apparent, especially on the Côte d'Azur. Languedoc-Roussillon, the Costa Brava, Costa Blanca and Costa del Sol are at an earlier stage of development. A range of resorts has been developed in each case, the communications network has been expanded to include regional motorways and, especially in the Spanish case, international airports and an overall regional structure is starting to emerge. In Languedoc-Roussillon, a formal hierarchy of resorts was imposed by the official development plan while in Spain major resorts such as Torremolinos and Benidorm, which started to expand dramatically in the 1960s, have been complemented by smaller resorts. The development of excursion circuits is illustrated in Fig. 8.7 by the road link to the inland town of Ronda. The Mediterranean coast of Morocco is at an even earlier stage, perhaps Phase 3 of Miossec's model. The number of resorts there has multiplied as package tourism expanded but a coherent, hierarchical regional structure has yet to develop and there are indications that this may not occur given the difficulties experienced by some of the isolated tourist enclaves there.

In each of these cases, major resorts and indeed tourist regions have grown up in relatively undeveloped areas, often some distance away from the large urban centres. This appears to be the case especially with those areas catering for international visitors and non-local domestic tourists.

In Provence, for example, international and inter-regional domestic tourism has developed over a long period along the easternmost part of the coast, essentially outside Marseille's zone of influence and recreational hinterland. Likewise the Costa Brava, where tourism has developed much more recently, fell outside the zone of influence of both Gerona and Barcelona, and little settlement at all had occurred along the Mediterranean coast of Morocco. In many cases, small fishing and other villages formed the nucleus of resorts, but from the 1960s a number of large projects were created *ex-nihilo* on sparsely populated parts of the coast. Factors contributing to this pattern include historical accident (as at Cannes), the non-compatibility of coastal tourism and industrial and other urban uses, variations in the resource base, the availability of relatively cheap land and the development of package tours to self-contained resorts. Land appears to have been a particularly important factor in Spain where property speculation fuelled much of the expansion of tourism, particularly in the form of *urbanizaciones*. Even in the state-planned project to develop the coast of Languedoc-Roussillon, the existence of large blocks of undeveloped land was a major criterion in the selection of sites for the new resorts. Given the relatively isolated and undeveloped nature of these regions, the willingness of the state to provide infrastructural assistance was a significant development factor, not only in Languedoc-Roussillon but also in Spain and Morocco. At times in Spain, major problems emerged when the provision of infrastructure did not keep pace with the demand-led tourist expansion. This new infrastructure and the scale of tourist development have clearly had a marked impact on the geographical structure and character of each of the regions studied. In Provence and along the Belgian coast, this character is now well defined; elsewhere, there is evidence that a new formative period is still underway.

Conclusions

Significant spatial variations occur between and within regions in terms of the composition, volume and relative importance of domestic and international tourism. While the structure of tourism in each country and region reflects local conditions and unique features, certain general patterns have emerged from the comparative approach adopted here: the generally greater concentration of international tourism, the preference of long-haul tourists for wanderlust destinations and short-haul tourists for sunlust regions, the development of some major tourist destinations in comparatively isolated and undeveloped coastal regions. Without this comparison, the definition of specific objectives and questions at the outset (prompted in part by existing models) and the use of a common method or framework of analysis, it would not have been possible to distinguish general patterns and trends from situations peculiar to a particular country or region. An attempt has also been made to explain and account for the patterns and trends identified in this way. Although the patterns described and explanations given must be seen in the light of the range of examples used, they perhaps advance our understanding of the processes involved in tourist development and our appreciation of tourism in general more than the isolated, ideographic studies which have characterized this field of research in the past.

Note

1. The basic bed night data in Table 8.1 and Fig. 8.1 have been drawn from the following sources: Austria and Switzerland (Ilbery 1981); Belgium (*Annuaire de Statistiques Régionales*, Brussels, 1978; Bulgaria (Poncet 1976); France (*Annuaire Statistique de la France*, INSEE, Paris); Luxembourg (*Statistiques du Grand-Duché*, STATEC, Luxembourg); Portugal (*O Turismo em 1980*, Direccao Geral do Turismo, Lisbon); Spain (*Movimiento de Viajeros en Establecimientos Turisticos*, Instituto Nacional de Estadistica, Madrid).

9

The spatial structure of tourism on islands

In Chapter 3 it was shown that in absolute terms the largest international tourist flows are within Continental Europe, in North America and between these two regions. The developed countries on both sides of the Atlantic also experience large-scale domestic tourism. However, in relative terms international tourist flows are also very significant in many islands in the Caribbean, in the Pacific and the Indian Ocean. On many small islands, the ratio of tourist arrivals to the host population, and particularly to the land area, is much greater than in North America and in many parts of Europe (Bryden 1973). Moreover, in several countries within these latter regions the insular parts of the national territory constitute significant destinations, for example Spain with the Balearic and Canary Islands and the United States with Hawaii.

As with tourism at other scales, research on the spatial structure of tourism on islands has largely been confined to case studies of particular ones, in which the spatial aspects, depicted in the main by the distribution of tourist accommodation, form part of a general overview of tourism. Exceptions to this include the comparative study of Corsica and Majorca by Richez and Richez-Battesti (1982) and the more conceptual work of the structure of tourism in peripheral economies, noted in Chapter 1, by Hills and Lundgren (1977) and Britton (1980a, 1982) who exemplify their work by reference respectively to islands in the Caribbean and in the Pacific.

This section identifies systematically the various inter-related factors which influence the spatial structure of tourism on islands, particularly those which distinguish tourism on islands from that in other areas. Examples are drawn from a range of islands, which differ in their location, size, resource base, political status and their degree of tourist development (Table 9.1). The emphasis, however, is on comparatively small islands, rather than on the larger and more developed island nations such as the United Kingdom, Japan and New Zealand.

Basic patterns

Many of the major features of the spatial structure of island tourism are shown in Figs 9.1 to 9.6 which depict the distribution of tourist accommodation on selected islands in the Mediterranean, the Caribbean and the Pacific. The general pattern is one where tourist accommodation is concentrated in a small number of coastal localities in or close to the major urban centres and near to the international airport. Metropolitan San Juan accounted for almost three-quarters of the 9,300 tourist rooms in Puerto Rico in 1980 while Santo Domingo provided over half of the 4,000 hotel rooms in the Dominican Republic in 1982. In the western part of Hispaniola, 95% of Haiti's, 1,700 international hotel beds are located in Port-au-Prince et Petionville (Girault 1978). In

Table 9.1
Major features of selected islands

Island or island group	Political status	Area (km²)	Population 1980	Density per km²	Tourist arrivals 1980
Bahamas	Independent	11,396	223,000	20	1,118,000
Grand Bahama		1,126			884,980*
New Providence		155			378,242*
Balearic Islands	Spanish province	5,012	680,000	136	3,800,000†
Majorca		3,639	n.a.	n.a.	2,947,034‡
Barbados	Independent	431	249,000	577	370,000
Canary Islands	2 Spanish provinces	7,270	1,430,000	197	1,972,000‡
Corsica	French department	8,720	240,000	28	1,300,000
Fiji	Independent	18,272	634,000	35	190,000§
Viti Levu		10,386			
Vanua Levu		5,535			
French Polynesia	French overseas territory	4,000	140,000	35	96,826§
Tahiti		1,041			
Guadeloupe	French overseas department	1,625¶	316,000¶	194¶	156,000
Hawaii	State of USA	16,638	965,000	58	3,935,000§
Hawaii (the Big Island)		10,414	92,200	9	
Kauai		1,427	39,000	27	
Maui		1,886	63,000	33	
Oahu		1,526	762,000	499	
Hispaniola					
Dominican Republic	Independent	48,734	5,431,000	111	383,000
Haiti	Independent	27,750	4,330,000	156	134,000
Puerto Rico	Commonwealth associated with USA	8,897	3,188,000	358	1,679,000
Sicily	Italian region	25,708	4,936,000	192	n.a.

* 1976.
† Arrivals in hotels, 1979.
‡ International arrivals by air.
§ 1981.
¶ Including Marie Galante (150 km²), Désirade (27 km²) and Les Saintes (14 km²) but not St Martin or St Barthelemy.

other instances, clusters of hotels are located outside the major urban centres, as in Guadeloupe where most of the hotels are situated along the Riviera Sud, with little tourist accommodation being found either in Pointe-à-Pitre itself or the capital, Basse Terre. Elsewhere, hotels are shared between the major urban centre(s) and nearby coastal sites, as in Tahiti and on Viti Levu where the bulk of accommodation is to be found in Nadi, Suva or along the intervening Coral Coast. In both these cases this represents a second level of concentration, with each of these islands accounting for a major share of tourist accommodation within, respectively, French Polynesia and Fiji. The clustering of tourist accommodation within the Bay of La Palma on Majorca represents a third level of concentration, with Majorca accounting for approximately three-quarters of all hotel and apartment beds in the Balearic Islands (Bardolet 1980), and the Balearics in turn having a disproportionately large share of Spain's tourist industry (Fig. 8.3). This, however, is not the case in Corsica where several major tourist zones occur on an island which plays a lesser role in the tourist industry of France.

Other tropical and semi-tropical islands also exhibit similar general patterns to those shown in Figs 9.1 to 9.6. Virtually all tourist accommodation in Barbados is on the western coast of the island, notably immediately to the north and south of the capital, Bridgetown (Potter 1981). Over 80% of hotel rooms in the Bahamas in 1975 were located on New Providence – Paradise Island (44%) and Grand Bahama (38%). In the first case, hotels are clustered in Nassau and on Paradise Island while Freeport and nearby Lucaya account for all but three of the 23 hotels on Grand Bahama (Bounds 1978). Development in Hawaii has been on a much grander scale but concentration of accommodation is still very apparent, both within the group and on individual islands (Farrell 1982). In 1980, Oahu accounted for 60% of the state's accommodation, and almost three-quarters of Oahu's 34,000 rooms were concentrated on the 144 hectare site which constitutes Waikiki.

It should be borne in mind, however, that the use of accommodation statistics, the only comparable figures readily available at this scale, may accentuate or under-estimate the degree of tourist concentration on particular islands (see Ch. 7). In Guadeloupe, tourist-related employment at the level of the commune is more widely dispersed than accommodation capacity. In this case, the hotels lie outside the main urban area, Le Raizet airport in another commune generates a large number of jobs and restaurant-related employment is scattered throughout the island (Baptistide 1979). Conversely, as was noted in Chapter 7, the turnover of the accommodation sector in Fiji is less concentrated geographically than that of other sectors of the tourist industry (Britton 1980b).

Economic structures

The basic pattern shown in Figs 9.1 to 9.6 and evident elsewhere in the literature generally supports the conceptual models of Hills and Lundgren (1977) and Britton (1980a, 1982) which highlight the role of the main urban centre and a limited number of resort enclaves (Fig.1.8). The emphasis in each case, however, is on the resort enclaves, with the urban centre seen as providing a point of arrival, and associated tourist facilities. Hills and Lundgren write (p. 259) of 'a structured descent within the tourist product, via the arrival mechanism . . . to the resort-accommodation

facilities where the dispersal tends to stabilize'. Interaction at this level is limited and 'illustrates an enclavic, institutionalized tourist circulation between resort facilities, a process often actively promoted by hotel management, or a certain type of resort hotel'. In a similar vein, Britton (1982: 341–3) writes:

> In physical, commercial and socio-pyschological terms, . . . tourism in a peripheral economy can be conceptualized as an enclave industry . . . Tourist arrival points in the periphery are typically the primary urban centres of ex-colonies, now functioning as political and economic centres of independent countries. Within these towns are located the national headquarters of foreign and local tourism companies and retail outlets of travel, tour, accommodation, airline, bank and shopping enterprises. If on package tours, tourists will be transported from international transport terminals to hotels and resort enclaves . . . Tourists will then travel between resort clusters and return to the primary urban areas for departure. While resident in the resort enclaves, tourists will make brief excursions from their 'environmental bubbles' into artisan and subsistence sectors of the economy for the purchase of shopping items, entertainment, and sightseeing.'

Goonatilake (1978: 7), discussing tourism in Sri Lanka, sees tourist enclaves as 'islands of affluence within the country, walled in and separate from the rest of the population'. A tourist enclave then is not just a physical entity but also a social and economic structure. Indeed, these writers have focused primarily on the economic structure of tourism. Accordingly they have sought their explanations essentially in economic terms, emphasizing the broader economic and political structures of peripheral or Third World countries rather than the insular character of the examples they have chosen. Such a perspective does provide valuable insights into the spatial structure of tourism but by itself is incomplete, as it fails to take into account other basic features which arise out of the size and insularity of small islands.

Smallness

Islands, although cited frequently as examples, have not been treated separately from other small territories in the general literature on smallness, where tourism is usually considered only in passing if at all (Knox 1967; Ward 1975; Shand 1980). Nevertheless, the main characteristics of smallness identified by these writers have an important bearing on the structure of tourism on islands. In particular, a small land area usually implies a less diverse resource base while a small population means a limited domestic market. This in turn gives rise to a heavy reliance on foreign trade based on a limited number of products and a narrow range of markets. Diseconomies of scale, which may also extend to the public sector, are also apparent.

Most islands lack the diversity of resources to attract a broad range of international tourists and depend overwhelmingly on the three S's – sun, sand and sea. These may be augmented by other attractions such as gambling (the Bahamas), duty-free shopping (Fiji), historic features (the Dominican Republic), and the ubiquitous folklore concert and day or half-day circle island tour. However, except in the cases of gambling and where the islands form convenient stopovers on a larger circuit, such attractions will usually generate relatively little demand by themselves. Singapore, with its shopping, and Easter Island, with its archaeological interest (Porteous 1981), are exceptions to this pattern. Cultural differences may distinguish one island from others within a region, for example the French influence in Guadeloupe and Martinique, but they rarely lead to internal differentiation on individual islands except where political divisions occur (Haiti/Dominican Republic, St Martin). Moreover, the number of attractive coastal sites may be limited and sites suitable for development few. Despite the images conveyed by brochures and posters and a ratio of coastline to surface area greater than most other places, few islands are encircled by continuous stretches of white sand. On volcanic and other mountainous islands, land suitable for building may be restricted to a narrow coastal strip. For ease of access, a circle island road will often be located along this same strip. In other instances, broken relief will isolate parts of the island.

These factors, stemming from the limited resource base, contribute significantly to the coastal location and concentration of tourist accommodation characteristic of islands. Potter (1981: 47) notes in the case of Barbados that 'The principal beaches and hence tourist accommodation zones are all located on the sheltered leeward . . . coast of the island'. In Tahiti, Donehower (1969: 85) observes 'as all roads closely follow the coastline, hotel location on the coast or beach implies also location on the main roadway'. Attractions and access, two of the main locating factors for tourism (Pearce 1981a), thus go hand in hand here and on many other islands.

In Majorca, Richez and Richez-Battesti (1982) see the coastal range 'protecting' the north-west coast from tourist development and the small surface area limiting the island to a single international airport whose location has favoured development in the Bay of La Palma. In Corsica, on the other hand, they attribute the emergence of three major tourist zones rather than a single concentration to the *compartimentage du relief* and to the well-established multiple gateways which have in part arisen out of the difficulties of overland travel on the island. Mass tourism on the Canary Islands has developed around the existing urban network but has been conditioned by the physical characteristics of the different sites. In the case of the two main tourist centres, Odouard (1973: 65) notes 'one [Las Palmas] has been able to adapt to present day tourism which demands space, sun and beaches, while the other [Puerto de la Cruz] has difficulty meeting these three requirements'. As a consequence, other sites are being developed on Tenerife, while on Gran Canaria tourism continues to accentuate the imbalance between Las Palmas and the rest of the island and to dominate the group as a whole.

On many islands, a small land area and a small population contribute to limited domestic tourism. Where distances are not great, overnight stays are not warranted and beach usage, fishing and other recreational activities are accomplished on day trips. In island groups, domestic tourism may, however, involve inter-island travel but there informal accommodation is often used. On some of the larger islands with a mountainous interior, movement inland to hill stations may occur in the hot season, particularly where there is or was an important expatriate community. Larger islands, particularly when under colonial rule, may also see a certain amount of business travel, both official and private, as in Fiji (Britton 1980b). In any event, any numbers involved in these forms of domestic tourism are usually not very great given the size of the population and the levels of economic development of many islands.

This lack of domestic tourism makes the concentration of foreign tourism more pronounced and contrasts markedly with the situation in Europe discussed in Chapter 8. There foreign and domestic tourists share, in varying degrees, the major tourist regions. Moreover, the domestic demand, which may exceed foreign demand (Table 8.1), also tends to be distributed to a range of minor regions. On many islands this recreational interaction may be limited to local day use of hotel beaches. Even this may be discouraged or prohibited in some places. The sharing by foreign and domestic guests of tourist destina-

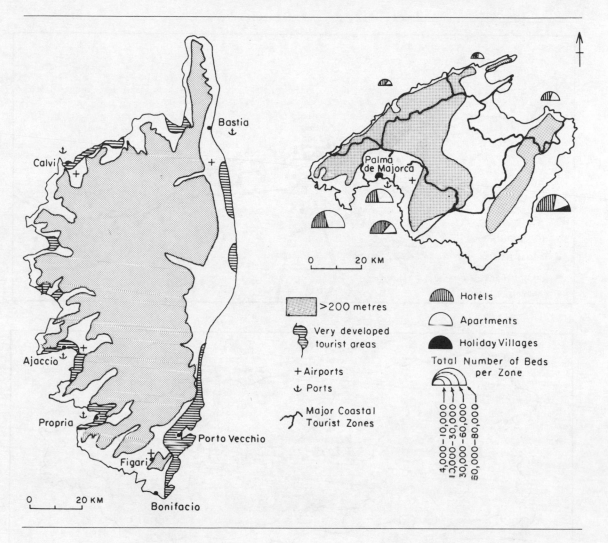

Fig. 9.1 Distribution of major tourist zones on
          Corsica and Majorca.

Source: After Richez and Richez-
Battesti (1982).

tions reduces social conflicts and lessens economic differences in mainland resorts. However,
in physical terms such resorts, particularly those
like the third-generation winter sports resorts in
France (Knafou 1978) and the new coastal resorts
of Languedoc-Roussillon (Pearce 1981a), are as
much tourist enclaves as the hotel clusters on
developing islands.

Where the island is not a nation state in itself,
domestic tourists from the mainland may play a
more significant role. Such is the case in Corsica
where only a quarter of the arrivals on the island
are foreigners, with the remainder holiday-
makers from the *métropole*, including a significant
number of returning Corsican migrants. However,
in general, through the dependence on foreign
tourists attracted primarily by a 'sun-sand-sea'
holiday, tourism is not dissimilar to other sectors
of island economies which also rely on an
external market and a limited range of products.

155

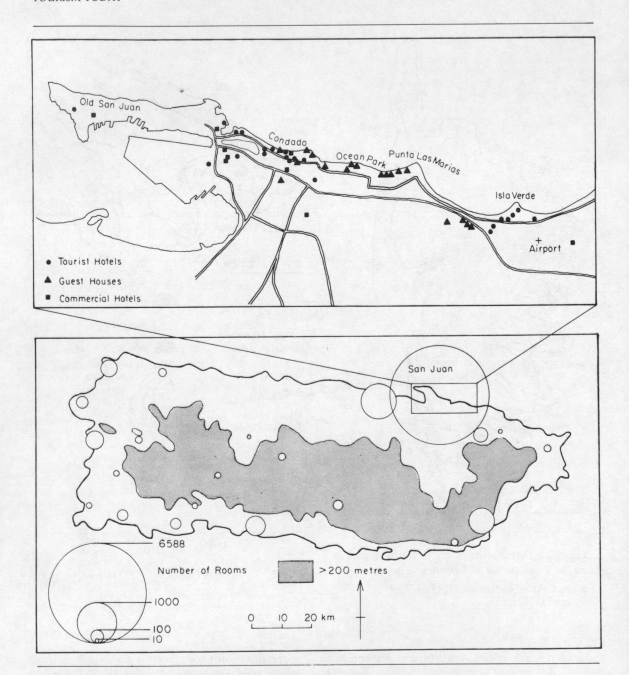

Fig. 9.2 Distribution of accommodation in San Juan and in Puerto Rico (1980).

Data source: Tourism Company of Puerto Rico.

Large-scale foreign or metropolitan involvement in the provision of tourist plant is in part a function of the small size of island economies. A lack of experience in catering for a domestic tourist market has also meant a more difficult entry by local entrepreneurs into the international tourist industry, particularly in the face of competition from large, well-established foreign or metropolitan developers. However, the activities of this latter group have also been influenced by the small size of the public sector. In particular, the provision (or lack of provision) of sealed roading, electricity and adequate water supply has often furthered the trends towards concentration.

The lack of public services on the island at the time of the development of mass tourism to Puerto Rico in the 1960s was a major reason for the concentration of hotels in metropolitan San Juan. Hotel construction there was part of a more general process of urban expansion which saw the city's share of Puerto Rico's population increase dramatically in the 1960s while 'the urban fringe exploded by 213% in one decade' (Cross 1979). New hotels were located on beach-front sites in the Condado, Ocean Park and Punta Las Marias among highrise quality residential accommodation. There guests enjoy the advantages of both an urban and coastal location. Further out, lower land values, proximity to the airport and a good beach site have led to another cluster of hotels at Isla Verde. A similar process was later evident in Santo Domingo, while in Haiti the general lack of development has restricted hotels to the capital. In Fiji, an unwillingness to extend public utilities has effectively discouraged the construction of hotels on more isolated sites. In Sicily, the general lack of services has led, paradoxically, to a juxtaposition of new tourist areas and industrial zones (Ciaccio Campagnoli 1979: 137):

> . . . the dominance of private interests in the tourist industry led to the planning of new tourist facilities in areas which were already developed and were already furnished with auxiliary services which private investors were not willing or able to finance. Therefore, tourist installations were often concentratd by their planners in areas adjoining large industrial establishments producing high degrees of pollution, and the major part of financial aid was granted with a total lack of interest in the existing socio-economic structure.

A similar situation occurs in the south-east coast of Barbados where the Holiday Inn is separated from the Hilton Hotel by an oil refinery and power and light company. Elsewhere, Ciaccio Campagnoli (1975: 86) cites the example of the Sicilian motorway network. Rather than facilitating the dispersion of tourism by linking Messina, the bridgehead to Continental Italy, with five designated tourist development zones, the first motorway ran between Catania and Palermo 'in order to facilitate contacts between the regional capital and the domain of Montedison'.

In French Polynesia and Guadeloupe, administrative decisions have markedly influenced the concentration of tourist plant at different scales. Official policy in French Polynesia in the 1960s favoured the construction of large, luxurious *hôtels d'impact* on Tahiti, with 90% of public credit to the tourist industry in the period 1960–69 going to that island (Blanchet 1981). A significant sum went to the construction of the Maeva Beach Hotel on a reclaimed site near Faaa airport. The following decade saw a shift in emphasis to bungalow type accommodation on other islands, notably Moorea and Bora Bora, so that by 1977, Tahiti's share of public investment in tourism had dropped to two-thirds. In 1981 the island still accounted for half of all classified hotel rooms in French Polynesia.

Baptistide (1979) shows that in Guadeloupe too the administration favoured large international class hotels aimed at the American market and sought to establish economies of scale through concentration:

> As experience has shown that the success of hotels depends on their concentration, the need to achieve a satisfactory return on infrastructural investment, implies that the southern coast of Grande-Terre must be the sole focus for their development. (Extract from the Sixth National Plan 1971–75, cited by Baptistide, p. 18)

This policy was in part a reaction to the difficulties experienced by three relatively isolated hotels built in the 1960s, at Sainte Anne, Deshaies and at Moule (Fig. 9.4). The first two were later taken over by Club Méditerranée and the third was converted into apartments. Isolation was not solely responsible for their failure, however, other contributing factors cited by Baptistide being: poor management, the emphasis on luxury hotels in lower quality sites and the fact that Guadeloupe was still a relatively unknown destination. Club Méditerranée, on the other hand, has frequently sought comparatively isolated sites to foster self-contained holiday villages by providing a full range of activities on site (and thereby also retaining maximum visitor expenditure). In the Dominican Republic, for instance,

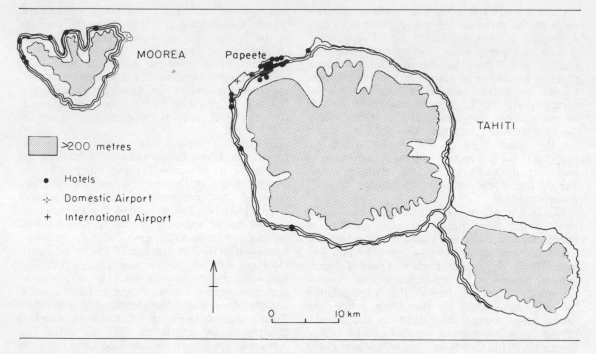

Fig. 9.3 Distribution of hotels on Tahiti and Moorea (1982).

Club Méditerranée is located at Punta Cana on the most easterly part of the island (Fig. 9.6).

In Guadeloupe, local political interest and the availability of land at St Francois were important factors which led to the concentration of hotels on the Riviera Sud. The more extensive development at Gosier (eight 3-star hotels) is a function of its proximity to Pointe-à-Pitre and to the airport at Le Raizet rather than the physical attributes of the site. Ironically, extensive infrastructural works involving the creation of artificial beaches were required here.

Insularity

Islands usually generate a positive image for the tourist. In contrast to many mainland regions, they possess a distinct and readily recognized and marketable identity. Garcia (1976: 88), for example, writes:

> Being islands, the Balearics provided a suitable place both for political and military exiles and for exotic trips in keeping with the romantic ideal prevailing at the time [the nineteenth century].

Famous travellers . . . were the first to provide an image of the island at the international level, an image which was seized upon by the elite tourism of the period . . .

And later, during the period of isolation which followed the Spanish Civil War:

> Majorca, which was the best prepared for tourists, managed to attract to itself what little domestic tourism there was in the period 1940–50. Once again, its island character proved to be a decisive attraction since, for the domestic tourist, this was the nearest thing to going abroad, which was out of the question.

Similarly, in the case of Guernsey, Girard (1968: 186–7) notes:

> Probably Guernsey's most important asset is the fact that it is an island. This alone conjures up a special image in the mind of the average Briton, living in one of the many industrial towns of England, particularly when the island is in a southerly position with suitable sea and air communications with the mainland of Britain.

From a structural point of view it is this reliance

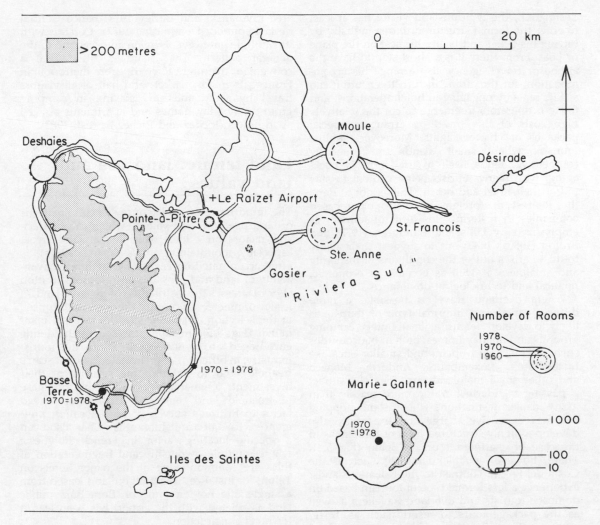

Fig. 9.4   Distribution of hotels in Guadeloupe
(1960–78).

Source: After Baptistide (1979).

on sea and especially air communications which distinguish islands from mainland destinations where, depending on the distances involved, overland travel usually plays a significant role. An immediate effect of this dependence is a reduction in the number of gateways, commonly to a single international airport. A sole point of dispersion constrains the amount of internal movement (see Ch. 4). Reduction of internal travel costs, in time and effort as well as money, becomes especially important in mid-ocean locations where airline schedules often impose late

night and early morning arrivals and departures. For the tour operator, reducing internal travel also enables the cost of the package he can offer to be kept as low as possible. For small islands in particular, low traffic volumes will normally mean higher fares over equivalent distances to larger countries so that reductions in travel cost become very important.

Reliance on air travel also means that the type of tourism which develops on islands is generally more structured and less diversified than that found in many mainland regions. To arrive at his destination, the typical island visitor has at least to enter the formal structured tourist industry by buying his ticket and taking his seat on the plane or boat. From there it is a short step to have the airline or travel agency also arrange his accommodation, for the airline in turn to ensure it can sell its seats by engaging in hotel operations, and for tour operators to emerge to cut the relatively high costs of this travel by arranging special packages or charter flights. Moreover, sunlust tourism, where small islands are especially competitive, lends itself to this form of packaging, with many tourists being content to stay put at their hotel and beach. This is not to deny the interest of foreign- or metropolitan-based companies in fostering this form of tourism as emphasized by Hills and Lundgren (1977) and Britton (1980a, 1982) but to suggest their ability to do so arises out of the conditions of insularity and smallness as well as because of economic, political and technological dominance.

Where overland travel is possible, a more diffuse, varied and informal type of tourism is likely to develop, featuring small hotels, camping grounds and holiday homes, both in big countries such as France and Spain, and smaller ones like Luxembourg. Luxembourg, Andorra, Monaco and other small mainland territories also attract a passing wanderlust traffic more readily than many insular destinations where island hopping becomes expensive. Large countries may also develop a highly structured form of tourism as in the case of chartered tours to Spain (Fig. 5.4). There, however, mainland regions such as the Costa del Sol, in contrast to the Balearic Islands, experience a less formal type of tourism based on domestic tourists and overland travellers as well as the package tours to resorts such as Torremolinos (Fig. 8.7). Where, however, overland travel is difficult, the major markets are long-haul ones and the levels of economic development are relatively low, tourism in continental regions, for example in many parts of Africa, may share many of the features characteristic of tourism on islands.

In terms of spatial organization then, the general effect of insularity is to reinforce the tendency towards concentration noted earlier, and in particular to encourage the location of hotels close to the international airport. This in turn is often, but not always (e.g. Tonga, Western Samoa), close to the major urban centre. Such a pattern is clearly seen in Majorca, Puerto Rico, Guadeloupe, Tahiti and Fiji. In the case of the Dominican Republic, construction of an international airport in the north of the country (La Union) was essential to the development of the Puerto Plata area (Symanski and Burley 1973; Banco Central de la Republica Dominicana 1977). Corsica, with its multiple gateways, is again an exception to the general pattern. The island is situated at a convenient overnight ferry trip from metropolitan France, its major market, and half of all visitors travel by ferry and car, staying in camping grounds, holiday homes and apartments as well as in hotels (Richez and Richez-Battesti 1982).

Land tenure, land use and land values

The importance of land tenure systems, patterns of land use and land values, which can be decisive factors on a local scale in mainland areas, especially mountainous ones (Pearce 1981a), is often accentuated on islands by the limited availability of land and pressure on resources. Britton (1980b) stresses the distribution of freehold land, 'a legacy of nineteenth century European enterprise', in the selection of specific sites for tourism plant in Fiji (Fig. 9.5). In some cases a freehold title encouraged an owner to move into the tourist industry; in others, foreign investors sought scarce freehold land to enhance the security of their investment. 'Ownership or favourable purchase of freehold land' emerged as the top-ranked factor in Britton's survey of hotel location preferences. Ease of acquisition of land has also been a specific locating factor in French Polynesia where multiple ownership and fragmentation of titles are common. One of the major hotels on Tahiti, for instance, was built on land leased from a single title holder while on Bora Bora public land associated with the airport has been leased for hotel construction.

At Waikiki, changing land values fuelled the rapid growth of tourism and exacerbated the concentration of hotels and condominiums as Farrell (1982: 35–6) notes:

> In the 1940s, before the real impact of air travel, Waikiki's beautiful golden beach provided the stage for several low, elegant and charming hotels, green lawns and well-cared-for parks . . .
>
> Tourism's development was dramatic. It grew from an enthusiastic roar by the 1950s to a resounding crescendo in the 1960s when concrete monoliths were constructed in every available space. Still, from a room count of 10,700 in 1967, the number grew to 25,000 in a little more than a decade. The rate of increase was unbelievably fast until 1971 when growth flattened out after most prime areas, zoned appropriately, had been taken up. By this time two new regulations were

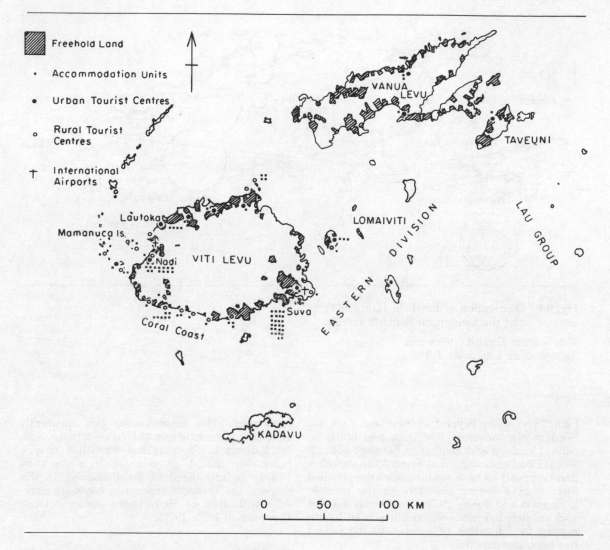

Fig. 9.5 Distribution of accommodation and freehold land in Fiji.

Source: After Britton (1980b).

enforced; apparently foreknowledge of these encouraged the earlier frantic activity.

Land values and taxes rose so high that spindly highrises grew from handkerchief-sized lots, and older hotels were dismantled to allow for new structures:

In the Dominican Republic, land ownership and land use have given rise to an enclave within an enclave at La Romana (Fig. 9.6). By absorbing the South Puerto Rico Sugar Company in 1967, Gulf and Western, the American giant, acquired 1,118 square kilometres of land, chiefly cane-fields, in the east of the country. This represented 2% of all Dominican territory and, depending on the definition used, 5–10% of the country's arable land. In a process of diversification, the sugar factory management's club was transformed into a hotel (Hotel Romana) and a large luxurious country club complex, La Casa de Campo, was

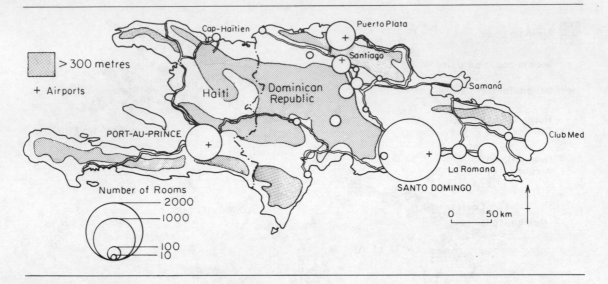

Fig. 9.6 Distribution of hotels in Haiti (1977) and the Dominican Republic (1982).

Data sources: Girault (1978) and
Secretario de Estado de Turismo.

built. Diversifying beyond their enclave, Gulf and Western also acquired and built two hotels in Santo Domingo and another in Santiago (Girault 1980). Hotel construction at Samaná, on the other hand, appears to have resulted from the personal interest of a former president of the republic (Symanski and Burley 1973). Despite his support and an attractive site, Samaná has been handicapped by difficulties of access and the project has been unsuccessful.

The development of Freeport represents another but more successful form of tourism and one which has been responsible for spreading the flow of tourists throughout the Bahamas. Bounds (1978: 179) observes: 'While it took Nassau a full century to reach 200,000 tourists per year, Freeport went from no tourists and no citizens in 1955 to more than 200,000 tourists in 1966.' The mechanism for this rapid growth was the 1955 Hawksbill Creek Act which enabled an American financier to develop a huge block of land, attracting foreign investment by generous tax freedoms. According to Bounds (p. 178), Freeport 'is probably a first for the international tourist profession, a new town with a combined industrial, commercial, and tourism function all in the same immediate area and all under the same leadership'. This co-ordination has apparently enabled a successful mix of land uses to develop, for tourism in Freeport has flourished despite being 'set amidst an area which is the most heavily industrialized in the Bahamas'. In this respect, the Freeport experience contrasts markedly with that of Sicily noted earlier (Ciaccio Campagnoli 1975, 1979).

Evolving patterns

The spatial concentration of accommodation continues to be a dominant feature of tourism on small islands, but time-series data show a significant reduction in the degree of concentration in several cases since the 1960s. In island groups such as Hawaii and French Polynesia, the rate of construction of accommodation has been greater on the neighbour and outer islands causing a relative drop in the share of the main island, respectively Oahu and Tahiti (Tables 9.2, 9.3). Factors accounting for this dispersion include: reaction to concentration on the main island (particularly in Hawaii), the attractiveness of the outer islands, a desire to generate new demand through multiple-island visits, improved access to

Table 9.2
Hawaii: distribution of tourist rooms* (1955–80)

Island	1955		1960		1970		1980	
	Rooms	%	Rooms	%	Rooms	%	Rooms	%
Oahu	2,628	76.1	5,716	83.8	21,217	70.6	34,173	61.3
Hawaii	451	13.1	581	8.5	3,486	11.6	6,299	11.3
Kauai	152	4.4	237	3.5	2,609	8.7	4,707	8.5
Maui	222	6.4	291	4.2	2,720	9.1	10,521	18.9
	3,453	100	6,825	100	30,032	100	55,700	100

* Hotels, condominiums, apartments.

Source: After Farrell (1982).

Table 9.3
French Polynesia: distribution of accommodation (1960–80)

Island(s)	Classified hotel rooms						Rooms in family units	
	1960		1970		1980		1980	
	Rooms	%	Rooms	%	Rooms	%	Rooms	%
Tahiti	48	79	894	73	1,133	54	32	10
Moorea	13	21	243	20	593	28	11	4
Iles Sous le Vent	—	—		7	313	15	91	30
Other islands	—	—		—	75	3	169	56
	61	100	1,230	100	2,114	100	303	100

Source: After Blanchet (1981).

and within the island group, and changing official attitudes (Blanchet 1981; Farrell 1982; Bush and Lipp 1983).

In French Polynesia, official emphasis has gone from luxury hotels on Tahiti to bungalow type accommodation on Moorea and Bora Bora to encouragement for small family units on the more distant islands, particularly in the Tuamotu archipelago. This latter policy was designed to maintain the population in these islands, but the small units developed through state subsidies have proved difficult to market. In Guadeloupe, the Riviera Sud maintains its dominance (Fig. 9.4) but recent policy also stresses diversification, both in plant and location. Official encouragement and assistance is now being given to the development of small units, private and communal, initially on the Ile des Saintes and later on Marie-Galante and La Désirade. The scale of these units, 20 rooms in the case of *gîtes communaux*, is to be in keeping with the small size of these islands and the emphasis is on water sports, walks and other activities rather than on the beach. Alternative accommodation on the island, notably villas and small *paradores*, have also been encouraged in Puerto Rico. This has accounted for some decrease in the dominance of San Juan in terms of overall accommodation, but the city retains its share of tourist hotels (Table 9.4).

In other island groups, governments anxious to limit certain social and cultural impacts of tourism have developed rather more cautious policies towards the spread of tourism. These concerns are expressed clearly in Fiji's Eighth Development Plan, 1981–85 (Central Planning Office 1980: 198):

Tourism development is different in the Eastern Division [the small islands of Lau, Lomaviti, Kadavu] when compared with the other parts of the country. The islands which constitute the Division face specific problems and display very

163

Table 9.4
Puerto Rico: distribution of rooms by type of accommodation (1968–80)

			San Juan	Island	Puerto Rico
Tourist hotels	1968	no.	5.347	1,461	6,808
		%	78.5	21.5	100
	1980	no.	5,680	1,606	7,286
		%	78	22	100
Commercial hotels	1968	no.	933	313	1,246
		%	74.9	25.1	100
	1980	no.	830	305	1,135
		%	73.1	26.9	100
Guest houses	1968	no.	308	57	365
		%	84.4	15.6	100
	1980	no.	268	54	322
		%	83.2	16.8	100
Tourist villas on the island	1968	no.	—	—	—
		%	—	—	—
	1980	no.	—	392	
		%	—	100	
	1968	no.	—	—	—
		%	—	—	—
	1980	no.	—	195	195
Paradores		%	—	100	100
Puertorriqueños	1968	no.	6,588	1,831	8,419
		%	78.3	21.7	100
	1980	no.	6,788	2,552	9,330
All accommodation		%	72.6	27.4	100

Source: After Tourism Company of Puerto Rico.

different needs. The social and cultural context of island life and the potential impact of tourism necessitates a more controlled approach to the development of any tourism facilities.
Government shall not allow the development of any 'tourist resort' islands providing accommodation of the 'international' type. However, the Eastern Division may prove to be suitable for the development of small scale facilities, (rest-houses etc) run by villagers under the 'alternative tourism' programme. In some cases low-key developments may be allowed.

Similar concerns and policies are evident in Vanuatu's First National Development Plan (National Planning Office 1983: 199):

– Government will seek, through involvement in planning the development of the sector, to limit the impact of tourism on cultural and traditional lifestyles of the island communities,
– the future development of tourism will occur mainly in Efate, Espiritu Santo and Tanna.

Elsewhere it will be developed only after full consultation and agreement has been reached with the local people.

Thus for very different reasons, the strategies of these newly independent nations may reinforce the pattern of spatial concentration which derives in part from the activities and policies of their former colonial rulers.

Conclusions

Many inter-related factors influence the amount, nature and distribution of tourism on small islands, but the combination of smallness and insularity produces spatial structures which are more evident there than in most mainland countries and destinations. In particular, tourist accommodation on islands tends to be concentrated in a small number of coastal localities in or adjacent to the major urban centre and close to the international airport. The predominance of sun-sand-sea tourism, especially on tropical and sub-tropical islands, is a direct consequence of an insular situation and the limited range of other possible tourist resources. The absence of relatively low-cost land access reduces the range of possible markets and the types of development which may occur. This pattern is reinforced by the limited local demand which stems from the size of the islands' own markets and the small distances involved. The emphasis on air travel and structured holidays for foreign tourists not only leads to the concentration of hotels close to the airport and major urban centre (the two usually go together) but increases the likelihood that the island tourist industry may be controlled by external developers.

The effect of these factors on small islands may also be reinforced by relatively low levels of economic development which in turn result in varying degrees from the conditions of smallness and insularity. Elsewhere, notably in many parts of Africa and Asia, low levels of economic development may produce pattterns similar to these. Very low standards of living in a number of contiguous continental countries will not only give rise to very small domestic markets but also

to a limited demand for short- and medium-haul international travel. The tourism which has developed under these circumstances has often involved structured air travel from more distant, developed markets (Fig. 3.1) and the development of coastal enclaves for package tourists (Fig. 8.8). Nevertheless, in many such cases other national and cultural resources may also be exploited and an alternative form of lower budget overland travel creating different demands and patterns of development may also emerge, as in parts of South-East Asia and South America. More systematic work is needed in these areas, however, on past and present processes of tourist development and the resultant spatial structure before these issues can be clarified and the factors and patterns compared to those on islands or in more developed countries.

Some island governments have recently encouraged alternative forms of tourism, especially on outer islands. While such projects may correspond to local development needs, they have often met with limited success as it has not been easy to overcome some of the constraints and conditions which insularity has imposed. The general structure of tourism on many islands thus appears unlikely to change in the near future.

10

Coastal resorts and urban areas

Earlier chapters have shown that the tourist industry at the national and regional level is comprised of a network of different resorts, urban centres and rural areas. This chapter focuses on the spatial structure of tourism at the local level, and in particular on two major and contrasting types of tourist areas, coastal resorts and major urban centres. The former, based on sunlust tourism, have generally developed a distinctive form and function and have attracted a certain amount of attention from geographers and others over the last fifty years. Urban tourism is more diverse in character, its significance has been recognized rather more recently and a smaller and less coherent body of literature has been devoted to it. Finally, some comparisons between the structure of coastal resorts and of tourism in urban centres are made. While some of the effects of such developments on surrounding rural areas are discussed here, no attempt is made to review the structure of tourism in the countryside, in national parks or in alpine areas. Nevertheless, the general approach adopted in this chapter might be applied, with relevant changes in emphasis, to such areas.

Coastal resorts

Although the Romans frequented towns such as Frejus primarily for recreational purposes, the modern coastal resort has its origins in the seaside towns which began to develop in England, France and other parts of Europe in the late eighteenth and early nineteenth centuries. Later last century New World resorts started to emerge on the Atlantic coast of the United States. Domestic resorts have proliferated along the coasts of developed countries throughout this century while international tourism, often on a large scale, has become widespread in tropical and sub-tropical regions.

Gormsen (1981) suggests that variations in the extent and length of development of tourism will give rise to different types of resorts (Fig. 1.10). Variations are seen to occur not only in the range of accommodation offered but also in the degree of involvement of local and external developers and in the extent to which the resorts cater for different social classes. These differences are seen to be part of an evolutionary process with an implicit progression along the same path from different starting points. Other writers have commented more explicitly on the nature of this evolution. Stansfield (1978), in the case of Atlantic City, refers to a 'resort cycle', a concept developed subsequently by Butler (1980). Six stages are identified by Butler: exploration, involvement, development, consolidation, stagnation and rejuvenation or decline. However, as Wall (1982: 190) points out, although Butler's model provides a concise and useful framework, 'the existence of the stages has yet to be demonstrated empirically in a rigorous fashion'.

Of particular importance for the spatial structure of the resorts, however, will be the date or period at which development begins as much as at what stage the process has reached, whether in Gormsen's or Butler's terms. Technological changes, whether in transport or the building industry, might be expected to have important morphological implications. Attitudes and expectations have also changed over the past century. Demand has multiplied rapidly in the past three decades as a holiday at the coast, both within the home country and increasingly abroad, has come within the reach of a larger proportion of householders in developed countries. Mass tourism has brought with it the development of large-scale resorts, virtually overnight.

Discussion of resort structure is further complicated by definitional problems, with a variety of coastal urban centres having some tourism function. In most cases, tourism has been grafted on to some existing centre, whether a small fishing port, as at St Tropez, or a much larger and growing city such as San Juan. Tourism may have subsumed these earlier functions or remain dominated by them. Other resorts have been planned as such. Some of the most striking examples of these are the large new resorts created *ex-nihilo* in the 1960s and early 1970s – La Grande Motte, Cancun, La Manga del Mar Menor. It should be recalled, however, that a number of the nineteenth-century resorts were planned and developed specifically for tourism, e.g. Deauville in France and Atlantic City in New Jersey. Over the years such centres have gradually acquired other functions, particularly residential zones. Then there is the case of Freeport, which was developed as a multifunctional centre from the outset (see Ch. 9). It is debatable too whether clusters of hotels, as for example at Gosier in Guadeloupe (Fig. 9.4), constitute resorts in themselves for they depend on the services and other functions of nearby cities, in this case Pointe-à-Pitre. In effect, a spectrum of coastal resorts exists, ranging from those with a wholly tourist function, notably the new planned resorts, to those where a significant amount of tourist activity occurs alongside a variety of other urban functions.

Examples from different parts of this spectrum are found in the literature. The most frequently cited studies deal with what might be called the traditional seaside town, particularly those of England (Gilbert 1939, 1949; Barrett 1958; Wall 1971; Robinson 1976) and the United States (Stansfield 1969, 1978; Funnell 1975; Stansfield and Rickert 1970). Detailed descriptive accounts of established resorts in France have come from

Burnet (1963) and Clary (1977), while Pearce (1978c) has considered newer developments there. Elsewhere in Europe, aspects of Spanish resorts have been examined by Garcia (1976), Mignon and Heran (1979) and Dumas (1982), while Young (1983) has presented a generalized model of the 'touristization' of Maltese villages. The morphology of Australian resorts has been discussed by Pigram (1977) and Baker (1983). Franz (1983) has examined the growth of seaside resorts in South-East Asia while, in Mexico, the new resort of Cancun has received attention (Gormsen 1982; Pearce 1983b).

Whatever the resort, analysis of its morphology needs to take account of three main sets of factors: tourist elements, other urban functions and site characteristics. The tourist elements include the type of attractions, the range of accommodation, the means of circulation, tourist-related shops and services, and accommodation for those providing these services and facilities. The role and range of other urban functions will depend on the size of the centre and how much it is oriented towards tourism. Factors to be considered here are more general residential and commercial functions, industrial activities, the transport network and other forms of land use. While individual site characteristics may affect the layout or structure of any urban centre, much of the distinctiveness of coastal resorts arises from their location along the beach or seashore for, as Stansfield (1969) points out, growth outwards from a coastal core is limited to approximately 180° as opposed to a full 360° in most urban centres. Some writers, e.g. Burnet (1963) and Pigram (1977), have adopted a fairly comprehensive approach while others have focused on particular features, for instance commercial functions (Stansfield and Rickert 1970, Dumas 1982) or the location of hotels (Franz 1983).

Given the factors outlined earlier, the morphology of coastal resorts might be expected to vary widely from place to place and period to period. The literature, however, suggests that while details do differ, the basic structural features are frequently repeated from resort to resort. Imitation, particularly within countries, may account for some of these similarities but the form of these resorts generally reflects their specialized function. The basic structure to emerge from these studies is the seafront or *front de mer*. Linear in form, this typically consists of a parallel association of the beach and maybe port, a promenade, road or railway and a first line of buildings comprised of the densest and most expensive forms of accommodation and a core of tourist-related shops, bars and restau-

Pl. 5 An aerial view of Nieuport on the Belgian coast showing a gradation in the density of development from top to bottom right, with a zone of villas separating the high-rise apartments overlooking the *digue* from the polder land below. A camping ground is evident in the lower left.

Source: Institut Géographique National.

rants. A gradation of accommodation in terms of height, density and price occurs behind this seafront as high-priced hotels and high-rise apartments give way to smaller and less expensive hotels, pensions, villas, camping grounds and merge with residential accommodation and other urban functions.

A classic example of this linear structure is given in Plate 5, an aerial view of Nieuport on the Belgian coast (see Fig. 8.5). Immediately adjacent to the beaches is the *digue* or *dijk*, a pedestrianized protective sea wall, the Belgian equivalent of the promenade. Given the vicissitudes of the Belgian summer, the *digue* has assumed a major role in the life of Nieuport and other Belgian resorts (Plate 6). It is a zone of activity where holiday-makers walk, meet, shop, eat their *frites* and where children play a variety of games. The *digue* has even spawned its own transport, a range of pedal-driven *cuistax*. For much of the day, however, the adjoining high-rise apartment buildings cast their shadows across the *digue* and out on to the beach. The first two blocks back from the beach are densely built-up, development in the third is intermittent, then the grid-like street pattern gives way to a less uniform zone of villas among the dune land. In parts, the more extensive dunes break up development completely, although several centres of social tourism have encroached on the open dunes to the south. The transition from the tourist-occupied dunes to the farmland of the polders is generally abrupt, but along an inland road a large camping ground has developed. The coastal tramway runs along the main street, one block back from the *digue*. This pattern, with minor variations, is repeated the length of the coast.

The linear form of the coastal resort or seaside town reflects its orientation towards the main centre of attraction, the beach. The gradation in land use and density away from the beach is in large part a response to economic forces. In general, land nearest the attraction commands the highest rent and thus generates a more intensive form of land use. Further away, prices decline, density decreases and forms of accommodation yielding a lower return become viable. Planning regulations, such as those in force along the Belgian coast, may reinforce these economic factors. The price of land will be higher in zones where high-rise buildings are permitted, and the higher the building allowed, the higher the price of land will be (personal communication, N. Vanhove 1985). Variations on the general pattern outlined here will occur from resort to resort as the result of the interplay of a variety of factors: the range of attractions, site characteristics, other land uses, dunes, the period at which development began and most growth took place, the extent of planning, size etc.

The seafront

Much of the variation occurs in the sequence and form of the various elements which comprise the seafront or *front de mer*. In the earliest American resorts, the promenade took the form of a 'boardwalk', the first of which was constructed at Atlantic City in 1870. This pedestrianization of the seafront contrasts with many of the English and French resorts where a road separates the promenade from the first line of buildings. Stansfield (1978: 243) attributes this difference to the early dependence of Atlantic City on rail transport:

> . . . the railroad was not eager to encourage stage or wagon traffic to the new resort. Early vacationers thus couldn't drive their own carriages to the resort, a factor which may have encouraged a seafront pedestrian promenade rather than a seafront vehicular drive for the traditional display of fancy coaches and equippages which characterized older resorts such as Cape May, or even such resorts as Brighton and Nice in Europe

The railway was also to shape the morphology of English resorts as it was at the period that railways developed that 'many resorts acquired a characteristic "T-shape", the stem of the T being the main street leading from the railway station to the promenade' (Robinson 1976: 162). In Belgium, Knokke and Blankenberg exhibit, for similar reasons, this same 'T shape', though at Koksijde-Bad the stem is along the main thoroughfare to the inland town of Koksijde.

Later, as the motor car replaced the railway as the dominant means of transport, the coastal road increased in importance, both as a means of access to the resort and for circulation within it. In established resorts the car often contributed to a lengthening of the *front de mer* while in many new resorts, e.g. St Jean de Monts on the Atlantic coast of France, ribbon development along the coastal road was inevitable. As Clary (1977) points out, the coastal drive initially continued the *m'as-tu-vu* aspect of the seafront. However, as traffic volumes increased, major congestion and circulation problems arose. At worst, the motor car has seriously jeopardized the integrating function of the promenade as Garcia (1976) notes in the case of Palma de Majorca:

169

Pl. 6 The seafront at Knokke: the promenade or *digue*, a major zone of activity, is backed by a zone of high-rise hotels and apartments.

The seaside promenade not only links the organization of tourist residential space with the beach and the sea, but becomes in its turn a place of consumption, of both objects and places. To some extent the seaside, beach and hotel are not strictly separate, and all the space is structured as a single entity.

However, planning errors and the proliferation of the motor car have all but destroyed this scheme of things, and have converted the seaside promenade into a veritable wall tending to isolate tourist consumption of natural assets (beach and sea) from the other consumption zones (residential and recreational).

Not all resorts, however, have experienced these problems. The effects of the decision by the developers of Deauville in the 1860s to create a 'calm and aristocratic resort' (Burnet 1963) by directing the main access route outside the new town continues to be felt today. However, many resort planners in the last two decades have reacted specifically to the problems caused by the motor car and have attempted in various ways to limit its impact (Pearce 1978c). In some of the smaller resorts, especially marinas, virtually all vehicle circulation within the resort has been prohibited, with the cars being consigned to parks at the entrance to or on the outskirts of the resort, as at Port Grimaud and the Marines de Cogolin. While some of the larger resorts, e.g. La Grande Motte, certainly have been conceived at the scale of the motor car, the location of the major access route some distance inland has over-

Pl. 7 La Manga del Mar Menor (Costa Blanca): the access road bisects the accommodation zone with apartments and villas to the left overlooking the Mediterranean and those to the right facing La Mar Menor.

come traffic problems along the seafront itself. In other new resorts such as Cancun and La Manga del Mar Menor which have been built on a sandy bar separating a lagoon from the sea, the access road bisects the accommodation zone (Plate 7). Such sites, which essentially have two seafronts, one facing the sea, the other overlooking the lagoon, lend themselves to intensive tourist and residential development, as has been shown at Miami Beach.

The traditional promenade is absent from many of the new resorts, with the hotels and apartments giving directly on to the beach, public or private, a reflection of the hedonistic obsession with the three S's which characterizes many of today's tourists. It should be recalled here that the renowned promenades of the Riviera developed at a time when the winter season was the most important. Significantly, where one or more of the three S's is less attractive or reliable, the promenade continues to play a vital role in the life of the resort, as noted earlier in the case of the Belgian *digue*. The rejection of the interior and the complete orientation to the sea in modern resorts is graphically described by Baptistide (1979: 160) with reference to Gosier in Guadeloupe:

. . . the buildings are built as close as possible to the sea (*pieds dans l'eau*), as if the tourist were disabled and incapable of walking a few metres. The hotel itself, less than 50 metres from the sea, is oriented exclusively towards the water. The tourist's domain is that which separates the room from the beach. The buildings, standardised and soul-less, could have been built anywhere; they take little account of the relief and none at all of the tropical nature of the environment.

The inland facing side is unattractive, an area of car parks, a no man's land of irregularly mown wild grasses . . .

The now widespread obsession with sand and sea has also contributed to the increasingly high-rise construction of seafront apartments and hotels. This trend is especially apparent in those new resorts where the bulk of the visitors arrive by air and have no on-site transport of their own.

Other aspects

Discussion of the seafront, the most distinctive element of the coastal resort, has dominated research on resort morphology. More work is required on other morphological features, particularly in the larger resorts and in those centres where tourism is but one of several urban functions. Burnet's (1963) descriptions of French resorts contain many relevant details but he makes no attempt to generalize from his many examples. His description of Cannes, for example, sheds light on how the resort has developed in size and depth behind the seafront. There the railway lies some 500 m inland, the third of three axes running east–west parallel to the sea, the two others being the rue d'Antibes, on the traditional route from France to Italy, and the boulevard de la Croisette which follows the promenade. His map of hotel location in the early 1960s shows that the better class hotels overlook the Croisette, 2- and 3-star hotels border the route d'Antibes, many of the 1- and 2-star hotels lie between it and the railway, and others are found inland of the railway. The city has grown up a valley whose sides were colonized at an early stage by villas. Burnet also noted that Cannes, unlike its larger neighbour Nice, had neither industrial nor workers' quarters: 'The city exists not to produce but to consume, not to manufacture but to sell.'

The seminal study of the effect of consumption patterns on resort morphology is that by Stansfield and Rickert (1970) who distinguish between general commercial functions found in the Central Business District (CBD) and the more specific ones grouped together in the Recreational Business District (RBD). The latter is defined (p. 215) as 'the seasonally oriented linear aggregation of restaurants, various specialty food stands, candy stores and a varied array of novelty and souvenir shops which cater to visitors' leisurely shopping needs'. In their examples of two New Jersey seaside resorts, the RBD is found along the boardwalk with the CBD and a major shopping thoroughfare located several blocks further back. Stansfield and Rickert also point out (p. 219) that 'the RBD is a social phenomenon as well as an economic one'. The social aspects of the Golden Mile, an English variation on the RBD, are graphically described by Hugill (1975). Dumas (1982) has examined in detail the commercial structure of Benidorm and identified several distinct districts. The old centre on the promontory separating the two bays has virtually been taken over by tourism. Small tourist-oriented shops comprise three-quarters of all businesses here, with an emphasis on bars, night-clubs, restaurants and souvenir shops. The modern tourist quarter lies to the east, overlooking the Levant beach. This is the zone of high-rise hotels, banks, travel agencies, jewellers' shops, fashion boutiques, shops selling leatherware and other luxury goods. On the eastern and western fringes of the seafront are found less hectic tourist districts, where the ground floors of apartment blocks house souvenir shops, restaurants, bars and the occasional supermarket. Further out still, the built-up area gives way to olive groves and camping grounds. The residential and shopping district now stretches inland from the old centre. A similar structure, particularly the displacement inland of the residential quarters, is also found on the Costa del Sol (Mignon and Heran 1979).

In these cases, changing land values resulting from the new or expanded tourist demand have been a major factor in the relocation of pre-existing urban functions and the separation of tourist and residential quarters. Elsewhere this pattern may be reinforced by planning goals and established at the very outset. In Cancun, planners have designated a triangular zone on the mainland for commercial, administrative and residential purposes, with the tourist accommodation zone beginning three kilometres away and stretching along the coastal bar (Gormsen 1982). This separation, presumably designed to maximize the tourist-carrying capacity of the seafront, has added little to the life of the resort, particularly in the evenings. The planners of the new resorts in Languedoc-Roussillon also sought to maximize the amount of on-site tourist accommodation and have not encouraged the devel-

Pl. 8 The port at St Tropez: the quaysides have been invaded by the easels of artists who 'capitalize on the good name of this former painter's corner and on the gullibility of tourists'. Pleasure craft have replaced fishing boats.

opment of a large resident population. But in Languedoc-Roussillon, unlike Cancun which was developed in a sparsely populated area, the new resorts are able to draw on commuting labour from nearby urban centres. These resorts, never-theless, tend to lack a sense of community.

Ports, particularly small fishing ports, are perhaps the most typical of the pre-existing coastal communities which have been trans-formed by tourism and seen traditional functions replaced by new ones. Such resorts have often assumed a crescent-shaped form rather than the linear morphology of the beach-oriented resort.

In many cases, the attraction initially lay in the charm of the site. Some, such as St Tropez, achieved early prominence through being 'discovered' by artists and writers and owed their growth as resorts to subsequent visits by filmstars and other celebrities which conferred on them a certain fame or notoriety (Christ 1971). As pleasure boating expanded in the 1960s, yachts and cabin cruisers began to share the port with fishing vessels, then to replace them or to occupy extensions to the harbour (Plate 8). At St Tropez, in particular, the quaysides have been invaded by the easels of artists who 'capitalize on the good

173

Pl. 9 Albufeira: Portuguese fishermen still draw their boats up on to the central beach but hotels, apartments and villas have progressively colonized the surrounding hillsides.

name of this former painter's corner and on the gullibility of tourists' (Christaller 1964: 103). However, no good beaches are found at St Tropez itself to cater for today's sun worshippers, so they flock to the immense sandy beach at Pampelonne six kilometres away. This separation of beach and port has contributed to the *mitage* of the surrounding hillsides and countryside by second homes.

At Albufeira on the Algarve, Portuguese fishermen still draw their boats up on to the central beach around which the town initially developed but they are now flanked by the bronzed or burnt bodies of scantily-clad British holiday-makers. Much of the initial nucleus of shops and fish-

ermen's houses still remains here, but hotels, apartments and villas have progressively colonized the surrounding hillsides with adjoining areas now being sub-divided at lower densities for second homes (Plate 9). Form and process here are similar to those described by Young (1983) with reference to the transformation of Maltese fishing villages.

As the growth of boating has exceeded the capacity of existing ports, new resorts have been developed expressly for this new demand, with very functional forms (Pearce 1978c). Whether designed around basins or islets, resorts such as Port Camargue, Port Grimaud and the Marines de Cogolin bring together the nautical holiday-

Pl. 10 The Marines de Cogolin: a purpose-built functional marina which brings together the nautical holiday-maker, his boat and holiday home.

maker, his boat and holiday home (Plate 10). Elsewhere, the boat harbour or marina has been used as a second focus of activity to the beach, either to spread the prime real estate sites in new resorts (e.g. La Grande Motte) or to generate new demand in existing centres (e.g. Carnon, Deauville and Brighton).

In other cases, golf courses have been used to develop a new resort in depth. Fairways are constructed behind the seafront hotels, creating both an additional recreational attraction and a pleasant open environment. The developer benefits from this strategy in several ways: by enhancing the attractiveness of the hotels and broadening their clientele, by direct returns from the golf course and, most significantly, by greatly enlarged real estate opportunities, notably for the construction of condominiums and villas. This strategy has been used successfully in Hawaii (Farrell 1982) and is being applied in some of the new *urbanizaciones* on the Costa del Sol (Plate 4) and elsewhere. Valenzuela Rubio (1981) suggests that in the case of the Costa del Sol the golf courses, like the new marinas, are directed at the top of the market, which has been less affected by the economic recession, while the substantial investment required for such projects perpetuates conditions of external dependency.

The evolution of coastal resorts

Many of the studies reviewed so far have recog-

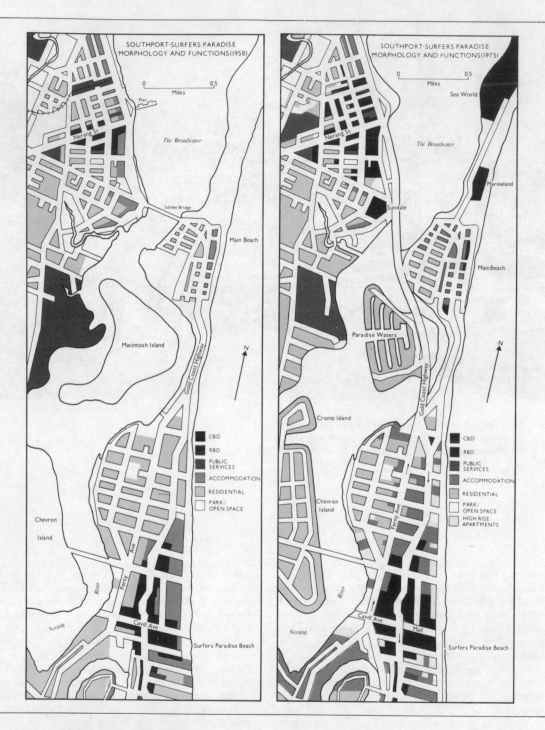

Fig. 10.1 Morphological changes in
Southport–Surfers Paradise (1958–75).

Source: Pigram (1977).

nized historical features of resorts and discussed their evolution in general terms. Few writers, however, have documented in detail the morphological changes which have occurred from one period to another (Lacroix, Roux and Zoido Naranjo 1979; Franz 1983). Where maps of resort form are given, they typically refer to one year only. More emphasis needs to be given now to changes in morphology so that the processes involved can be better understood and the evolution of future forms more readily anticipated.

Some useful work has been done in this field by Pigram (1977) who examined the changing morphology of two pairs of twin towns on the Gold Coast of Australia: Coolongatta–Tweed Heads and Southport–Surfers Paradise. Pigram presents land use maps for each pair of towns for 1958 and 1975 based on published maps and local body records for the earlier period and fieldwork for the latter. Figure 10.1 shows that important changes in both form and function have occurred in Southport–Surfers Paradise over this period. Pigram (p. 539) suggests 'their urban morphology has become effectively fused, with shared attractions and facilities and little duplication of services'. Southport's more traditional resort function has declined (the pier is now gone) with the closing of the railway and improved access to the beaches, but its administrative, commercial and residential roles have expanded. Surfers Paradise, whose coastal bar site is reminiscent of others discussed earlier, has emerged as the dominant tourist centre. Pigram describes the major structural elements and changes in Surfers Paradise thus (pp. 538–9):

> Morphologically, land-use zones are, once again, aligned north–south parallel to the beachfront. The highest density tourist accommodation is found adjacent to the front, where high-rise apartment blocks are progressively replacing lower-density units. A second zone of high-rise development is beginning to emerge further inland overlooking the Nerang River estuary reflecting both the attraction of water-based site and the growing shortage of beachfront land . . .
>
> In general, the zone of permanent residence in Surfers Paradise has migrated from its original location near the beachfront and is now confined to the area west of the highway and well removed from the resort core. The relatively highly valued land flanking the RBD and the front strip has been taken up by medium and lower-density tourist accommodation to form a useful buffer separating two functional zones . . . At the same time, Surfers Paradise remains highly regarded as a residential environment for second homes and retirement . . . Chevron

Island and Paradise Waters are only part of an extensive canal estate development program designed to provide high status and expensive home sites.

Some of these changes, however, have not been without environmental problems. Figure 10.1 also shows changes in the RBD, the development of a one-way street system and the emergence of new attractions to the north in the form of Marineland and Sea World.

Calella, a Spanish resort located 40 km northeast of Barcelona, provides a second example of resort development. Figure 10.2, which is based on vertical aerial photographs taken in August 1966 and January 1980, shows the morphological changes which have occurred over this period, particularly those which have taken place on the margins of the resort, a zone frequently neglected in resort studies. Figure 10.2 shows that in 1966, Calella consisted essentially of a contiguous built-up area, aligned with the coast and lying between the railway and a steeply rising hill to the north. Some more scattered hotels and apartments are found to the west and in the adjoining commune of Pineda to the east where farmhouses can also be seen. Much of the development after 1966 has consisted of infilling on the margins and some inland expansion up the valley in the west. The new apartments and hotels are generally several stories taller than the buildings in the core. Both the infilling and expansion on the margins has involved the encroachment of the urban area on to the surrounding market gardens. Plate 11 provides a good example of the rural/tourism fringe to the west of Calella in 1982 and shows the market gardens separated from apartment buildings by several private houses. If demand for tourist accommodation continues, further encroachment can be expected here and on the horticultural land lying along the Calella/Pineda boundary as market gardening can no longer support the increased land rent.

Earlier research by Ferras (1975) enables these developments to be put into the context of the wider region, the Maresme. Ferras' analysis of building permits for 1969, for example, distinguishes Calella from the other communes in terms of the virtual absence of individual dwellings and the height and size of the new buildings. Much of the Maresme is frequented by second home owners and holiday-makers from Barcelona, but Calella stands out as a resort favoured by foreigners, particularly Germans.

Aerial photograph interpretation involving time-series photography, as this example shows, constitutes a valuable means of analysing

Pl. 11 The rural/tourism fringe of Calella: apartment buildings encroach on former horticultural land.

morphological changes. So far it has rarely been used in tourism studies (Menanteau and Martin Vincente 1979; Fourneau 1983). Ideally, the information obtained in this way should be complemented by other data giving details on function, ownership, land rent and so on in order to build up not only a picture of changing form but also the processes involved.

Urban areas

Research on the structure of tourism in urban areas is relatively recent and less developed than that dealing with coastal resorts. Compared to the extensive literature on outdoor recreation and tourism in rural areas, there are very few studies of urban tourism. This is especially the case in North America where the urban–nonurban imbalance noted by Stansfield (1964) over two decades ago still persists although aspects of tourism have been treated indirectly, e.g. in connection with preservation (Ford 1979). Some Canadian studies have recently appeared (Murphy 1980; Wall and Sinnott 1980) but, in line with the traditional resource-based emphasis, only one paper in a recent volume on tourism in Canada deals primarily with an urban area (Liu 1983). Given the impact which North American geographers have had on urban geography in general, their neglect of tourism in cities is rather surprising. The majority of the work on urban tourism has been ideographic in nature and has come from Europe and the United Kingdom. Comparatively early studies dealt with Paris (Burnet and Valeix 1967; Cadart 1975) and Berlin

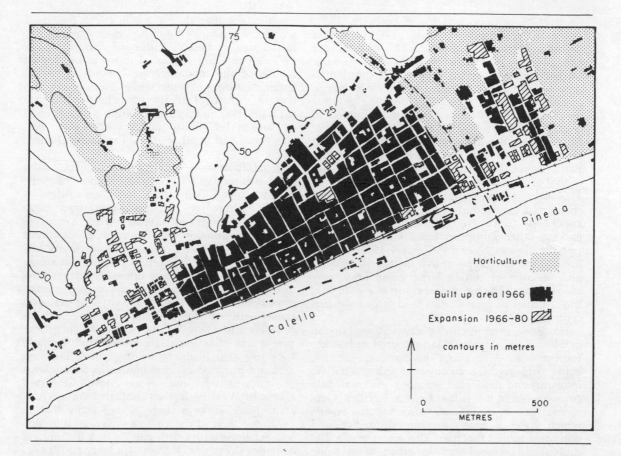

Fig. 10.2 Morphological changes in Calella (1966–80).

(Vetter 1974, 1975, 1976) while London has attracted continuing interest (Hall 1970; Young 1973; Eversley 1977; Murphy 1982).

Tentative theoretical contributions to the problem were made by Yokeno (1968) but his work, published in a French series, was not picked up and developed in the English language literature. More comparative and systematic studies appear a few years later. Chenery (1979) considered planning for tourism in six European cities and, in a significant departure for an urban geography text, Burtenshaw, Bateman and Ashworth (1981) devoted a chapter of their book on the West European city to 'The Tourist City' and a second to 'Urban Recreation Planning'. Pearce (1981a) adopted a more conceptual approach and illustrated theoretical patterns with the example of Christchurch.

The comparative neglect of tourism in urban areas can be attributed in large part to differences in the role of such areas in national tourist industries and to the relative importance of tourism within cities. Earlier chapters have highlighted the importance of major urban areas within countries, both as gateways and as destinations in their own right (see, for example, Figs 1.7, 4.1, 4.4, 9.3). Their importance, of course, varies from country to country, depending on the nature of the demand, the attributes of the cities and the range of other available tourist resources (Ch. 8). London alone, for example, accounted for a quarter of all hotel beds in England in 1980, with 'large' and 'small' towns each having 11%, seaside towns 39% and the countryside 14% (ETB 1981a). Furthermore, in 1978, London attracted 40% of all nights spent by overseas visitors in Britain, two-thirds of their 'staying visits' and 60% of their expenditure (BTA 1981c). London is

179

relatively less important for domestic tourism, however, accounting for only 17% of tourist nights in England in 1980 and 11% of estimated spending by domestic tourists (ETB 1981c). Madrid province, on the other hand, contributed only 5% of Spain's recorded bedspace in hotels, guest-houses, apartments and camping grounds in 1975 but this nevertheless still amounted to over 70,000 beds (Pearce and Grimmeau 1985). Burtenshaw, Bateman and Ashworth (1981: 162) go so far as to state categorically that 'London, Paris, Rome, Copenhagen and Amsterdam are, in that order, the world's top five tourist resorts'. This claim, which is not documented, might be challenged for not only being Euro-centric (what about New York or Hong Kong?) but also for over-looking other European cities such as Munich (see the figures given by Chenery 1979). Never-theless, the general point that the tourist capacity and function of certain large urban areas may exceed that of the traditional resort is a valid one, though truer of capital cities than large industrial centres.

However, even in cities such as Paris, London or New York with their large tourist industries, tourism is far from being the dominant activity, being surpassed by commercial, administrative, industrial and residential functions. An immediate consequence of this is that tourism in cities is less visible than in coastal, alpine or thermal resorts which have a more explicit, distinctive and dominant tourist function. This lower profile has undoubtedly contributed to urban areas being overlooked in a field of research which is still comparatively young. The more cynical might also stress the greater appeal to urban-based academics of fieldwork on the coast, in the moun-tains or in the countryside.

At the same time, the multi-functional nature of cities and the wide range of visitors they attract makes any analysis of tourism there more com-plicated. Some vacationers will come for the enter-tainment and nightlife, others for the historical and cultural features, or to shop in the large depart-ment stores or boutiques. Many may be attracted to cities by what Matley (1976: 30) refers to as 'the individual character and atmosphere which tran-scend the mere sum of their buildings and other physical attractions. An obvious example is Paris. It is doubtful if the average tourist visits the city with the specific intention of seeing the Eiffel Tower or visiting the Louvre or the Folies Bergère. He does so because he wishes to experience the atmosphere and spirits of the individual city . . .' With the exception of the accommodation sector, few of the facilities and services used by tourists are purpose-built or provided especially

for them. Rather they share in varying degrees with local residents the transport services, shops, restaurants, cathedrals, museums, theatres . . . In 1977, tourists are estimated to have contributed a fifth of the total revenue London Transport obtained through fares while overseas visitors bought a third of all theatre tickets in the city (ETB 1981c). The Pompidou Centre which opened in Paris in 1977 had 6 million visitors in its first year, only half of whom were Parisians (Chenery 1979).

In addition to a variety of vacationers, many cities also receive a considerable volume of traffic generated by their other functions. Adminis-tration, commerce and industry attract large numbers of business travellers while a sizeable resident population will generate a significant VFR traffic. Conference and special events will draw other visitors. Together, these groups may well exceed the pleasure-oriented tourists, the mix in any particular case depending on the attractions and functions of the city. For example, those with an international vocation, such as Brussels and Geneva, will have a much greater proportion of business travellers. Multi-purpose trips are also likely to be important. Deriving accurate purpose of visit figures in urban areas is, unfortunately, not an easy task. Restricted access in West Berlin has facilitated comprehen-sive visitor surveys there. These show that in 1972, over half of the visitors stayed with friends and relations and a fifth participated in congress activities (Vetter 1974, 1976). Chenery (1979) cites statistics from Rome airport which suggest that for every 100 business passengers there were 160 leisure passengers. Furthermore, for each of these groups the city may play a variety of roles as was discussed earlier with reference to Fig. 1.7, notably those of a gateway, staging post, stop-over or destination.

Given the complexities of tourism in urban areas, it is not surprising to find that the studies which discuss the structure of tourism in cities have focused on the distribution of hotels, the most visible and pure manifestation of tourism in the city. The following section will review and extend work on the structure of accommodation, exemplified by a case study of the hotel industry in Paris. Subsequent sections will discuss attrac-tions and other sectors of the industry, then developments beyond the city.

Distribution of accommodation

Yokeno (1968) proposes a concentric model of urban land use, based on land rent curves, in which he locates a hotel zone in the central city, between the innermost administrative centre and the commercial zone. Empirical studies of inland urban areas generally confirm the concentration of hotels in the central city, on the margins of the historic core. These central hotels are not of such density, however, that they constitute a uniform single-use hotel zone similar to those found in the seafront of coastal resorts or to the linear concentrations of financial institutions or specialized shopping streets which may characterize other parts of the city. Rather, one or more clusters are usually found where hotels are interspersed with other commercial, administrative and sometimes residential functions. The number and location of these clusters will depend on several inter-related factors including the size of the city, its functions, pre-existing form, means of access and whether it is mononuclear or polynuclear in character.

A central city hotel responds to the needs of a variety of urban visitors whose stay is generally relatively short, typically in the order of two to four days. Many business travellers value proximity to the CBD so as to transact their affairs promptly and efficiently. Here too the shopping-oriented visitor can descend rapidly on a range of high-order shops. It is also in the centre that the sightseeing tourist will find many of the city's historic buildings, monuments and other cultural attractions. The overlapping of the focus of activity of each of these different markets reinforces the concentration of hotels in the central city. Moreover, the clustering of hotels enables the visitor to 'easily choose one according to his taste or budget' (Yokeno 1968: 16).

Tourism on a large scale, however, is a relatively recent phenomenon and few hotels, especially large modern ones, occupy sites in the very core of the city. When the major period of expansion in hotel construction occurred in Europe's cities in the 1960s and 1970s, there was a scarcity of available inner-city sites sufficiently large enough to accommodate hotels on a scale which would make them viable. Moreover, building restrictions and planning regulations designed to preserve the character of the historic core also effectively limited or discouraged hotel construction in many cities (Chenery 1979; Burtenshaw, Bateman and Ashworth 1981). However, as Chenery points out, in relatively small and compact cities such as Copenhagen and Amsterdam, this is not such a disadvantage since 'nowhere is far from the centre'.

Recency, rent and restrictions thus combine to lead to the central concentration of hotels around rather than within the core itself. Eversley's (1977) map of the location of hotels of 200 rooms or more in London shows none within the City,

but major concentrations in Westminster, Kensington, Chelsea and, to a lesser extent, Camden. The scale and rate of hotel construction in London during the 1960s and early 1970s was so great as to spill over into residential areas such as Mayfair, causing much public and political concern over the loss of housing stock (Hall 1970; Young 1973). Chenery's (1979) comparative study shows this 'creeping conversion' of older housing into hotels was not a feature of the other cities he studied, except Amsterdam. In London it led to a tightening up of permission to build hotels in the most affected areas, particularly Westminster and Kensington. Such regulations coupled with financial complications pose major problems for growth in London's hotels. A study in 1978 (BTA 1979a) found that the most viable hotels would be 5- and 4-star hotels in central locations and 3-star and budget hotels in peripheral locations but noted (p. 7 of Appendix):

– application of planning controls, particularly in central locations, creates a serious impediment to the development of new hotels;
– the building of quality hotels in central locations is unlikely to solve the projected shortfall problems because the bulk of the projected additional demand is for hotels of lower standard and price;
– it is doubtful whether developers will be attracted to build lower standard hotels in peripheral locations which would be the ones most vulnerable to changes in overall demand
. . .

As the central location of hotels reflects demand generated by other central functions, it follows that the changes in the distribution of hotels will result from an expansion of the CBD or the appearance of new centres as well as from the shortage of central sites. This is particularly evident in cities where the tourist industry has expanded rapidly at the same time that major morphological changes have occurred. Gutiérrez Ronco (1977, 1980) has traced in detail the evolution of hotels in Madrid and shows how there has been a progressive shift from the Puerta del Sol to the north and north-east as administrative and commercial activities have developed in that direction, particularly in the last two decades. This has given rise to the current pattern where the smaller, older hotels are found clustered around the Puerta del Sol and Avenida Jose Antonio while the large, modern quality hotels are located along the axis formed by the Paseo del Prado–Paseo de le Castellana-Avendida del Generalisimo, where many office blocks have recently been built and many government minis-

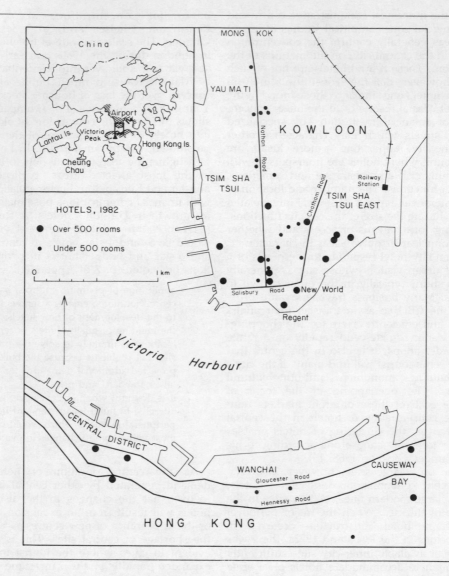

Fig. 10.3 Distribution of hotels in Hong Kong (1982).

Data source: Hong Kong Tourist Association.

tries relocated. A similar pattern occurs in Lisbon, where the Avenida da Libertade links the older smaller hotels of the centre with the more recent, larger and better hotels in the streets surrounding the Parque Eduardo VII, also an area of recent commercial and administrative expansion.

Comparable patterns and processes are to be found in Asian cities such as Hong Kong. Many of the early hotels were located on Hong Kong Island in Central District, Wanchai and Causeway Bay (Fig. 10.3). Much recent hotel expansion has occurred on Kowloon in Tsim Sha Tsui which has developed as a thriving retail centre, specializing in duty-free shopping, perhaps the prime attraction for visitors to Hong Kong. By 1982 the district accounted for almost two-thirds of the colony's registered hotel rooms. From 1975 to 1982 more than 4,000 high tariff rooms were built in Tsim Sha Tsui while no other hotels had been constructed anywhere else in Hong Kong except for one at the airport. Half of these new rooms are in the four hotels built in Tsim Sha Tsui East, on government land zoned commercial in the mid-1970s following the relocation of the railway station. Two further hotels were built on reclaimed land in the New World complex, namely the Regent and the New World. As land becomes increasingly scarce, this pattern is changing, for of the nine hotel/hostel projects in the period 1983–85, only two were in Tsim Sha Tsui, the others being on Hong Kong Island and on Lantau and Cheung Chau Islands.

Changes in the pattern of hotel location have not only resulted from modifications in land use but also from developments in the transport sector. Sometimes these changes have occurred together. Earlier this century when travel by rail was more important, clusters of hotels sprung up around city railway stations, located on the margins of the city centre. These were usually rather small and modest although some major terminus hotels were built. In his study of hotels in Brussels, de Ganseman (1982) notes that in the period 1930–58, the city's three railway stations along with the city centre (Place de Brouckère) constituted the major poles of hotel location. However, little new construction occurred there in the period of hotel expansion which followed in the 1960s and 1970s as Brussels developed its international role (EEC, Nato). Rather there was a *deloculization* towards the *haut de la ville* due to the growth in night-time entertainment there and the attraction of a chic commercial quarter. Burtenshaw, Bateman and Ashworth (1981) observe that in pre-war Berlin there was a distinct clustering of hotels around the city's three main railway stations. By 1976 these had been abandoned in favour of a westwards shift along the Tauentzienstrasse and Kurfurstendam, a process 'strongly reinforced by the political division of the city'.

In the last two decades, other hotels have been located more specifically to meet the needs of the motorists, especially the businessman travelling by car. These are commonly located on the outskirts, on or immediately adjacent to the highways leading into or out of the city. In France, such a pattern is to be found not only in Paris where such hotels are located at the major gateways, e.g. the Porte de Sevres or the Porte Maillot (Cadart 1975), but in smaller cities such as Metz (Spack 1975). Certain French hotel chains, such as Novotel, even tend to specialize in providing such non-central accommodation (Cadart 1975).

Elsewhere, notably in North America and Australasia where rates of car ownership are particularly high, motels (the motor-hotel) have been developed for the motoring public. Many of these simply offer non-serviced accommodation but in New Zealand most provide fully-contained self-catering facilities; that is, they are equipped with a small kitchen and a dining cum living room as well as bedrooms. Motels in New Zealand tend to attract a range of guests, from travelling businessmen to families on holiday, for whom they offer a cheaper alternative to hotels.

In 1980, Christchurch had approximately 1,480 hotel rooms and 700 motel units (given the greater number of beds in the average unit, the actual number of beds in each sector would have been comparable). Figure 10.4 shows that while the city's hotels exhibit the characteristic centralized clustering seen elsewhere, many of the motels, particularly the more recent ones, are distributed in a linear fashion along the major highway axes, a pattern that is repeated in other New Zealand cities (White 1973; Beckett 1978; Longmire 1978). Access, however, is not the only factor here, for the lower densities of motels mean they are unable to support the higher central city rents. Moreover, they are excluded from the centre itself by land use controls. In Tauranga, motels have been restricted to properties fronting major traffic routes but most New Zealand local authorities appear to consider motels as compatible with other uses in residential zones, being comparable to multi-unit dwellings (Grant 1974). Approximately nine out of ten motels in Christchurch in 1979 occupied a former residential site. In Christchurch, and elsewhere, camping grounds, whose densities and rent-paying ability are lower than motels, are found in more peripheral locations, while still being handy to the major access roads.

A similar pattern to that shown in Fig. 10.4 was also observed by Liu (1983) in metropolitan Victoria (B.C.). Three-quarters of the hotels there are located in the Downtown Market area, while the majority of motels occur in a 'corridor-type' development along Highway 1A leading out of the centre. Other North American studies have also stressed the highway orientation of motels (Ohler 1971; White 1969) while Mayo (1974) surveyed 748 American motorists to determine which factors influenced their choice of motel. Mayo's respondents ranked 'being not far from main route' and 'convenient parking' as the second and third most important factors behind moderate prices and ahead of sixteen other variables including a quiet or attractive setting and proximity to tourist attractions. The clustering of

183

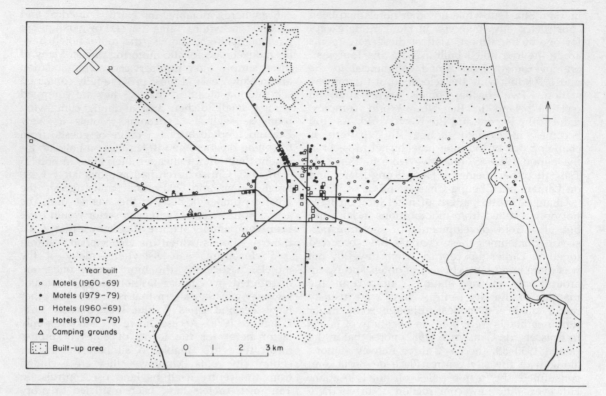

Fig. 10.4 Distribution of accommodation in Christchurch (1979).

motels along a given stretch of highway immediately gives the passing tourist a choice of accommodation as well as ready access.

The development of air travel has, in its turn, given rise to the airport hotel. Some are located within the airport complex itself (as, for example, at Los Angeles), but more often they form a distinct cluster on the margins of the airport, frequently on the road leading into the city (Fig. 10.4; see, also, Cadart 1975; Eversley 1977; Chenery 1979; de Ganseman 1982). Burtenshaw, Bateman and Ashworth (1981: 169) observe that at the city–region scale in south-east England, 'successive rings can be identified including a hotel-rich central city, a hotel-poor suburban ring, and a hotel-rich outer zone including distinct hotel clusters around Heathrow and Gatwick airports'. The number of airport hotels will depend on the volume and nature of the air traffic with, for example, demand for accommodation close to the airport increasing with the proportion of transit passengers and the importance of the gateway and staging post roles of the city.

Other factors have contributed to the growth of sub-centres of hotel accommodation within the city, particularly in larger ones. As de Ganseman (1982) noted with Brussels, evening entertainment may be as significant a location factor for some visitors as day-time interests. Kings Cross in Sydney, for example, famed (or ill-famed) for its restaurants and night-life, has developed a cluster of hotels second only to the CBD (Council of City of Sydney 1980).

Site factors may also break up the central concentration of hotels. This is especially true of cities on the coast, a point which has been largely overlooked due to the concentration in the literature on inland European capitals. The distinction between a coastal resort and a city is not always easy to make although purpose of visit rather than location is a useful starting point. Few primarily sunlust visitors are likely to be attracted to harbour cities such as Hong Kong or even

Sydney, but this group no doubt form a major part of the traffic to San Juan whose beach-oriented hotels form part of Puerto Rico's primate city (Fig. 9.2). Intermediate cases require more detailed analysis. Rio de Janeiro can hardly be considered a coastal resort in a traditional sense, yet two major linear concentrations of hotels overlook the magnificent beaches of Copacabana and Ipanema. A third major cluster is found in the Flamengo district which is on the margins of the downtown area, in close proximity to Santos Dumont airport, and overlooks the Flamengo beach and Guanabana Bay.

In any large city, a number of factors will combine to produce a pattern of hotel distribution which will reflect general tendencies observed elsewhere and factors more specific to the city in question. Paris has been chosen as a case study to be examined to show in more detail spatial variations in the structure of its hotel industry and the inter-relationships of the different factors which contribute to the patterns observed.

Paris

Paris had over 63,000 rooms in 1,300 classified hotels (*hôtels homologués*) in 1982.[1] These recorded more than 7 million arrivals in 1981 but it is unclear just what proportion of all visitors to the city this represents. A 1970 survey of visitors to Paris showed over half of the respondents were staying in hotels, but that sample was biased towards those visiting monuments (Rojo 1970). A boom in hotel construction occurred in the early 1970s, pulling the city's hotel industry out of a dormant post-war period. From 1947 to 1970, 133 hotels representing 7,000 rooms had disappeared while only about ten new hotels had been built. Over 80% of Paris' 2- and 3-star hotels in 1970 had been constructed before the First World War (Anon 1971b). The opening of the Hilton in 1966 and the Sofitel Bourbon in 1970 were the first additions to the upper end of the market since the Georges V in 1935. These hotels marked a resurgence in the hotel industry as Paris sought to meet the growing demand for quality accommodation, particularly from the business sector. Many of the new hotels were to be built by chains, both national and international (Cadart 1975). From 1970 to 1982 the city's hotel capacity expanded by some 7,000 rooms, with the proportion of deluxe and 4-star hotels increasing from 17% to 25% while the share of 1-star hotels dropped from 33% to 24%. In a process opposite to the 'creeping conversion' experienced in London, a number of 1-star hotels were turned into flats (Chenery 1979). Statistics for 1980 show that business travellers accounted for 42% of the demand for deluxe and 4-star hotels, tourists for a third, with the remaining quarter being comprised of those attending conferences and 'other' travellers.

This resurgence in hotel construction has affected the spatial structure of the industry as new locational factors have come into play but, given the age of many of the hotels, the imprint of the past is still very apparent (Fig. 10.5). The distribution of hotels in Paris also reflects both the centralization found elsewhere and the broader east/west structure of the city. While the west, particularly the north-west, is dominated by commercial activity and higher quality residences, the east, especially the north-east, is more industrial and characterized by sprawling lower quality residential areas.

Figure 10.5 shows the hotel industry is still largely concentrated in Central Paris, although not quite to the same extent as at the time of Burnet and Valeix's (1967) study. In 1982, the 1st, 2nd, 8th, 9th and 10th arrondissements accounted for 43% of the city's capacity compared with 49% in 1967. Burnet and Valeix attributed this concentration to 'the co-existence of two functions, work and leisure'. This is not only the commercial heart of the city, drawing many business travellers, but also the prime tourist destination attracting sightseers, shoppers and those seeking entertainment. The Champs-Elysées, for example, bisects the 8th arrondissement while the Tuileries, Louvre and Comédie Française are found in the 1st. The 9th has not only the Opera but also the Folies Bergère. In the 10th, clusters of hotels are found around the Gare du Nord and Gare de l'Est. Older terminus hotels around the Gare de Lyon also account for much of the capacity in the 12th arrondissement. Demand along the Left Bank has been generated by the government ministries in the 6th and the university quarter in the 5th as well as the general atmosphere of the Latin Quarter. Some demand in the outer ring results from an extension of the inner-city activities, notably in the 17th where the scale of analysis conceals the concentration of hotels just off the Place Charles de Gaulle in the sector bounded by the Avenues de la Grande Armée and de Wagram. Hotel development is still limited in the north-east (the 18th, 19th and 20th) but to the south and west in this outer ring are found the only three arrondissements to experience any significant increase in their share of the city's accommodation capacity over the period 1967–82: the 14th (3.5% to 6.6%), the 15th (4.5% to 8.5%) and the 17th (7% to 10%).

Significant spatial variations also occur in the quality of accommodation. One-star hotels are the

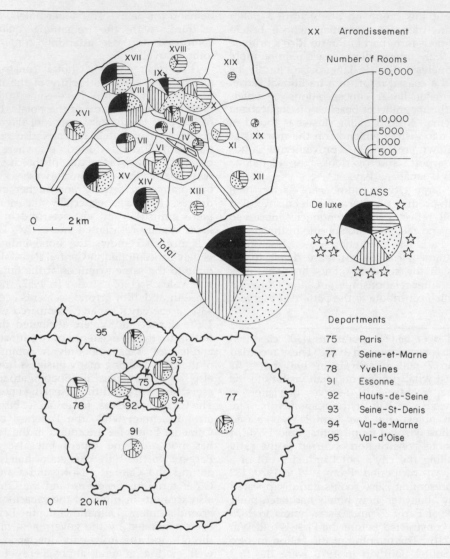

Fig. 10.5 Distribution of hotels in Paris and the Ile de France (1982).

Data source: Office de Tourisme de Paris.

most widely dispersed, being found in every arrondissement, but several lack any 4-star or deluxe hotels. The top five arrondissements in each category account for half of the capacity in 1- and 2-star hotels, two-thirds of the rooms in 3-star hotels, eight out of ten rooms in 4-star and almost 90% of the capacity of deluxe hotels. The 10th arrondissement has the largest share of 1-star hotel rooms (13%), the 9th of 2-star rooms

(16.7%), while the 8th ranks top in terms of the remaining categories, accounting for a fifth of the 3-star and deluxe rooms, and a third of all the 4-star accommodation. The 1st and 8th arrondissements are the only ones with half or more of their capacity in 4-star and deluxe hotels, having the smaller and more established hotels in these classes. Some internal differentiation occurs within these two arrondissements. Virtually all the quality hotels in the 1st are found between the Rue de Rivoli and the Rue St Honoré, while the 1- and 2-star hotels are located to the north of this zone and in the east of the arrondissement. The 4-star and deluxe hotels in the 8th are found in the streets off the Champs-Elysées, with other hotels being concentrated in the area between the Place de la Madeleine and the Gare St Lazare. Of the other major central arrondissements, the 9th is characterized by 2- and 3-star hotels while the terminus hotels in the 10th are mainly 1 and 2 stars. On the Left Bank, the 5th is markedly more down market than the 6th, which attracts a greater share of official business travellers. One-star accommodation predominates in the northern and eastern districts. The 14th, 15th and 17th arrondissements again stand out as a group, this time being characterized by a significant proportion of deluxe hotel rooms but little 4-star accommodation. Together, these three arrondissements now account for over half of the city's deluxe accommodation, and a quarter of its total capacity.

The growth of deluxe hotels in the 14th, 15th and 16th arrondissements represents the major locational change in the distribution of hotels in Paris during the 1970s. Several inter-related factors have contributed to this process, with land rents being the most fundamental (Cadart 1975). Changes and intensification in the central city throughout the 1960s meant new hotels were rarely able to support the new land rents which often would have been equivalent to a third of the cost of a hotel. Not only were larger, deluxe hotels likely to be more viable in these conditions but it was this sector which the authorities were encouraging in order to re-establish the image of Paris and which an expanding market was starting to demand. The city was also seeking to extend its role as a convention centre, notably by the construction of the Palais de Congrès at Porte Maillot. At the same time, Paris was undergoing major urban changes involving the expansion of the office sector and large renewal or redevelopment projects. The planning authorities sought some diversity in these projects and encouraged hotel construction among the office complexes through offering land for hotels at half the rate as for office buildings. Sites in these projects offered not only the advantage of more attractive rents and planning and infrastructural assistance but also the prospect of some new custom generated by the office complexes themselves. As congestion in the inner city grew, more peripheral sites close to ring-roads or motorways began to appeal to many motoring business travellers who could drive there readily, park and use

public transport if necessary to commute to the centre. The lower rents on such sites also meant developers could increase the attractiveness of their hotels by providing swimming pools and other facilities not available in the centre – only one hotel in the 8th and none in the 1st has a pool.

The location of these large luxury hotels reflects these different factors and has had a dramatic effect on the capacity of the arrondissements concerned. The Sheraton (995 rooms) and the PLM St Jacques (797 rooms) now account for 43% of the 14th arrondissement's rooms and all of its capacity above 3 stars. The Sheraton forms part of the Ilot Vandamme renewal project (Plate 12). The PLM St Jacques stands on a site formerly occupied by a warehouse. The Hilton (489 rooms), which is on the northern margins of the 15th arrondissement close to the Eiffel Tower, began the decentralization of luxury hotels into this sector. It was later followed by the Nikko (778 rooms) in the Fronts de Seine redevelopment project and the Sofitel Paris (635 rooms) and the Holiday Inn (90 rooms) at the Porte de Sevres. Both these latter two hotels are very accessible to the motorist, being located respectively on the Boulevard Periphérique and the Boulevard Victor; they are also close to the Palais des Sports. Together, these four hotels account for all the deluxe and 4-star rooms in the 15th and a third of the arrondissement's total capacity. Paris' two largest hotels – the Meridien Paris (1,027 rooms) and the Concorde La Fayette (1,000 rooms) – have been built at the Porte Maillot (17th arrondissement) in association with the Palais de Congrès and the new air terminal with its shuttle service to Charles de Gaulle airport (Plate 13). These two hotels also sit astride the western axis which links the established commercial centre with the new complex at La Defense, all of whose projected hotels did not eventuate. The relative size of these new hotels, and thus the importance of these site factors, can be more readily appreciated when compared to the 50 rooms of the average Paris hotel, or the 292-room Georges V which is the largest hotel in the 8th arrondissement. The scale and appearance of some of these large hotels, e.g. the Meridien, have, however, drawn a certain amount of criticism (Girodin 1981).

Two of the largest clusters of hotels beyond the city limits adjoin the 15th and 17th arrondissements, respectively those in Boulogne and Neuilly in the Hauts-de-Seine department (Fig. 10.5). The hotels in Boulogne are linked to the autoroute and highways arriving from the west while those in Neuilly form part of the north-west extension of the city. Other highway-oriented hotels are

Pl. 12 The Sheraton Hotel in Paris is part of the Ilot Vandamme renewal project.

found throughout the region on the outskirts of the city, notably the majority of the 13 Novotel hotels in the Ile de France. Approximately 1,000 rooms in 3- and 4-star hotels are located around both Orly and Charles de Gaulle airports, accounting for over 40% of all rooms in each department, respectively Val-de-Marne and Val d'Oise. Other major clusters occur in the historic towns of Versailles and Fontainebleau. The city remains dominant, however, for the seven

Pl. 13 New directions for tourism in Paris: the Hotel Concorde La Fayette and the Palais des Congrès at the Porte Maillot.

departments which constitute the *petite* and *grande couronnes* together offer only 17,000 rooms compared with the 63,000 found in Paris itself.

Attractions and other aspects

Attractions and other facilities used by the tourist are more diverse and less well defined in the city than in coastal resorts, with most being shared with local residents. Surveys and other techniques have provided useful insights into where visitors go within particular cities but these rarely provide a complete picture (Ch. 4). Mapping the distribution of urban attractions also has its problems (Ch. 7). Until more detailed information becomes available on the activity patterns of city visitors, perhaps the most useful approach is to consider the different types of attractions and facilities and their distribution, without attempting to assign any relative weighting to them.

The spatial structure of urban tourist attractions and other facilities might be considered in terms of a network of nodes, or clusters of nodes, and routes linking them. While comparatively little is known about the intra-urban movements of tourists in general, it is possible to recognize the more formalized routes and paths. City guides, such as the Guide Michelin and Baedecker, have for long suggested itineraries which the tourist is advised to follow to make the most of his stay. Visitors' maps issued by city tourist offices often include a recommended circuit, with brief notes on the major stops and how to get from one to the other. In some cities, such as Boston, these are reinforced by permanent markers to reassure the visitor he is indeed on the right spot and has not

Pl. 14 Victoria Peak, Hong Kong: 'the look-out may be the highpoint of the city visit, offering tourists magnificient views and perhaps their only opportunity to appreciate the scale and layout of the city as a whole'.

deviated from the set path. Many circuits feature a round trip, beginning and ending in the city square. The circuit becomes even more formalized when it is regularly followed by the bus tour of the city. Examination of current itineraries suggests there has been little change in the formal circuit in Paris since it was mapped by Burnet and Valeix (1967) almost two decades ago. A more flexible variation on the city tour is provided by the Sydney Explorer bus system whereby buses follow a set 17 km route around central Sydney at regular intervals, enabling passengers who have purchased a day ticket to be picked up or set down at any of twenty stops during the day. In cities built along rivers and canals, or around harbours, such as London, Paris, Amsterdam, Bruges, Venice, Bangkok, Sydney and Hong Kong, boat cruises complement these bus tours. Both have their 'city by night' variation, often featuring spectacular illuminations and concluding with a visit to a nightclub. Over half of all visitors to Hong Kong are estimated to take at least one

Pl. 15 A tour coach deposits tourists on the outskirts of Lisbon's Alfama district for a brief visit to one of the city's 'typical' quarters.

organized tour, with more than 10% taking a water tour (Hong Kong Tourist Association 1983). In other cases where the tourist finds his own way around the city, the mode of travel, e.g. London's underground, the gondolas of Venice, and the cable-cars of San Francisco, may be as much an attraction as a means of moving on to the next sight.

A critical node in any of these systems is the look-out point which allows an overall view of the city or network. Some look-outs such as those at Hong Kong's Victoria Peak (Plate 14) or the Sugar Loaf and Corcovada in Rio de Janeiro take advantage of natural viewpoints. In other cases the look-out is man-made, forming part of a tower or building generally built for some other purpose, either historically, such as the towers of Gothic cathedrals and the Leaning Tower of Pisa or, more recently, for example the Eiffel Tower, Empire State Building and the Centrepoint Tower in Sydney. These, of course, may be attractions in their own right or access to them may offer some novelty (e.g. the cable-car up Rio's Sugar Loaf). But the look-out may also be, quite literally, the highpoint of the city visit, offering tourists magnificent views and perhaps their only opportunity to appreciate the scale and layout of the city as a whole. It is here that they may have their first and perhaps only glimpse of well-known sights. The visit to the look-out confirms that a tourist has indeed 'seen' the city, albeit in many cases very briefly and from afar, and for this reason the look-out is almost invariably included in the city tour.

Most cities have a single recognized viewpoint, although in Paris the observation deck on the Tour Montparnasse now complements or competes with the Eiffel Tower and the towers of Notre-Dame Cathedral. Other types of attractions and facilities are usually more numerous and are frequently clustered together in distinct and often overlapping parts of the city. The clustering of like nodes has many advantages for the visitor who may not have a very detailed image of the city and only a short time to spend there. Clustering may occur for a variety of inter-related reasons as Burtenshaw, Bateman and Ashworth (1981: 201) note with reference to the entertainment sector:

> . . . different sorts of entertainment such as theatres, restaurants, nightclubs and bars will tend to cluster near each other, so that together they form the entertainment quarter, or nightlife district, that the customer seeks. Once established this concentration in a particular district will be reinforced both by popular

sentiment that advertises the area to those in search of entertainment in the city, and also by planning decisions. Many such facilities are 'bad neighbours' and will tend to repel other functions. Planners will frequently endeavour to contain the nuisance by opposing its expansion into other areas and encouraging all facilities to locate within the existing entertainment quarter.

The authors distinguish between 'west-end' entertainment, which occupies relatively expensive sites in high-prestige districts, and less reputable redlight districts which may be nearby or spatially quite distinct from them. They identify a relatively localized distribution of nightclubs in Amsterdam and three distinct nightclub areas in Paris – off the Champs-Elysées, in Montmartre and in the Latin Quarter. Dedicated fieldwork has resulted in a detailed map and description of Amsterdam's redlight district (p. 203):

> the Zeedijk district near to, but one street separated from the main commercial thoroughfare, has entertained visiting sailors since the seventeenth century, and today continues the tradition of an international clientele . . . sites used for prostitution, and also shops selling sexual equipment, are strongly concentrated into this one small area. Relatively low rents on the eastern side of the central business district compared with the equivalent area to the west, the availability of suitable premises in what is still largely a working-class residential area of largely privately rented accommodation, and the international reputation of the area which removes the need to advertise, have all tended to maintain the existence of this function in this clearly defined district.

London's Soho district, however, has been less resistant to change as the *Economist* (1 December 1984: 59) notes:

> Soho, for years the sleazy heart of London, is coming clean. The sex shops, cinemas and massage parlours are closing down. There were 156 of them in 1982: now, only 88 are left. Local estate agents report strong demand for properties from advertising agencies, film and television companies. West End businessmen are snapping up pieds à terre.

Relph (1976: 83) has termed the cityscape of such districts 'pornscape', an example of 'other directed architecture' – 'that is, architecture which is deliberately directed towards outsiders, spectators, passers-by, and above all, consumers'.

Passers-by are potential consumers for restaurants which tend to be located in areas with large volumes of pedestrian traffic or attractions such as theatres, cinemas and other forms of entertainment. Bonnain-Moerdyk's (1975) seminal study on the gastronomic geography of Paris shows that restaurant districts there have relocated as changes in commercial activities and the centres of entertainment have occurred. Restaurants are now dispersed throughout the city although distinct clusters can still be observed, e.g. in the Latin Quarter and off the Champs-Elysées. Bonnain-Moerdyk also notes an overrepresentation of restaurants from the high-status western districts in the various restaurant guides published. Studies in Canadian cities, notably Quebec (Gazillo 1981) and Kitchener-Waterloo (Smith 1983b), show a marked linear concentration of restaurants and other eating houses in streets on or leading to the inner-city area. Much restaurant trade is, of course, generated locally. In Vieux-Quebec, where the majority of restaurants are concentrated on two different streets, one (rue Saint-Jean) reflecting a local popular culture and the other (rue Saint-Louis) an elite culture, Gazillo (1981) suggests that 'the presence of tourists serves to mitigate the differences between the two worlds'.

Linearity is also a feature of major commercial thoroughfares or specialized shopping streets. These may have not only an important linking role in the tourist's activity space but also constitute significant attractions in themselves (Table 4.5). Presumably because of the greater difficulty of separating tourist business from that originating locally, retail activities in urban areas have not attracted the same attention from a tourism perspective as coastal resorts (Stansfield and Rickert 1970; Dumas 1982) and little is known about tourist shopping behaviour. In some cases it appears to be not so much the desire to purchase goods but the chance to observe the local colour and participate in the general activity that draws visitors to distinctive shopping or trading centres. These range from the flower stalls of Covent Garden and flea-markets such as El Rastro in Madrid to the bazaars of Middle Eastern cities.

Souvenir shops, however, are directed specifically to the tourist, although local residents may also buy gifts to send abroad. Figure 10.6 shows the concentration of souvenir shops in Christchurch in the CBD around Cathedral Square and along Colombo Street, the city's main commercial axis. Isolated shops or smaller clusters are also found in the main suburban shopping centres, notably at New Brighton. Several of the larger central city souvenir shops are on corner sites, where they are particularly visible to

passing visitors. A few souvenir outlets form part of a long established department store. The concentration of these shops in such a small area also facilitates comparative shopping. In larger cities, clusters of small tourist-oriented shops have sprung up around major attractions.

Figure 10.6 also shows that travel agencies and airline offices in Christchurch seek a very central location. These businesses serve two sets of travellers, visitors to the city making onward travel or local sightseeing arrangements and local residents travelling away from the city (Fig. 1.7). A central, visible location has obvious advantages for the visitor. Although in total they may constitute a major share of the market, individual local residents will only make infrequent trips requiring the services of a travel agent. In other words, travel agencies provide very specialized services and like other high-order functions they seek a central location so as to be accessible to the largest possible market. Again the concentration of travel agencies in an industry which has become increasingly competitive allows the potential traveller to shop around and compare fares and prices. Closer examination of individual agencies reveals that the location of some reflects the pre-existing location of a parent business which has diversified into the travel industry. Two of those in Hereford Street, for example, are associated with banks and three in Cashel Street with the offices or stores of stock and station firms. In larger cities, airline offices tend to be located together in prestige retail streets, for example along parts of the Avenue de l'Opéra and the Champs-Elysées in Paris.

Whereas the central concentration of many retail and entertainment functions reflect contemporary functions, the clustering of many historic buildings and monuments in the inner core is a legacy of earlier times when the city was confined to a much smaller site, often enclosed by defensive walls. Burnet and Valeix (1967), for example note the concentration of historical buildings and monuments along the Left and Right Banks, with the monumental centre of gravity lying close to the Louvre. This is not always the case, however, as in Lisbon where the Jeronimos Abbey, the Tower of Belem and the more recent Discoverers Memorial are clustered together on the outskirts of the city overlooking the Tagus. In other instances it is not so much a cluster of individual features as the overall impression and general atmosphere of a particular district which appeals to the visitor or is promoted as a 'typical' quarter. Two examples of these are the Barrio Gótico in Barcelona and Lisbon's Alfama district, both medieval quarters characterized by narrow,

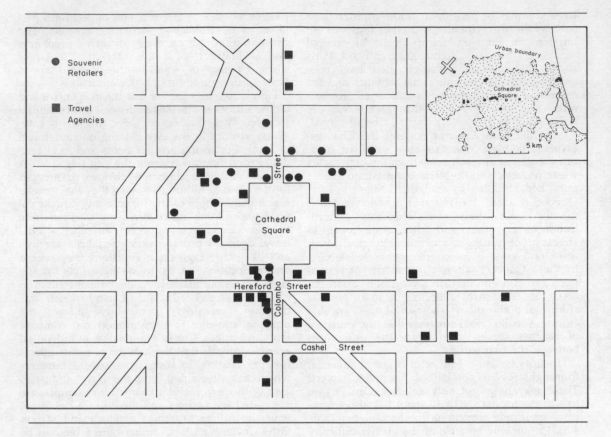

Fig. 10.6 Distribution of souvenir retailers and
travel agencies in Christchurch (1979).

winding cobblestoned streets and the 'pictur-
esque' houses and buildings of an earlier period.
Tour buses are excluded from such confined
spaces, with package tour visitors being depos-
ited on the margins and left an hour or two to
wander through the streets or to purchase
souvenirs and handicrafts (many not of local
origin) from the shops which have sprung up in
the squares or streets leading into the area (Plate
15). Tourists in shorts and sandals may pass the
local residents in the streets, with the older
women in the Alfama still often dressed in black,
but there is little contact between them. Other
tourist districts are identified by their distinctive
cultural features, such as the Chinatowns of San
Francisco and other North American cities.

In more and more cities in Europe, North
America and elsewhere, planning regulations
have been introduced and funds are being made
available to preserve and restore not only individual buildings but also entire quarters (Kain
1978–79; Chenery 1979; Ford 1979; Newcomb
1979; Burtenshaw, Bateman and Ashworth 1981).
In most cases this is not specifically to enhance
the city's tourist attractiveness, although the
increased revenue from tourism may help justify
such policies which tend to be rather costly.
While hotels have often been excluded from such
districts, other tourist facilities have frequently
been encouraged. The English Tourist Board (ETB
1981c: 24) in its review of tourism and inner-city
schemes in England, e.g. St Katherine's Dock in
London and Piece Hall in Halifax, noted: 'The
primary motive in these cases was conservation
rather than the promotion of tourism, tourism
related projects being chosen because they are
adaptable and well suited to providing uses for
old buildings.' Ford (1979) notes that many pres-

ervation projects in North American cities have involved the zone of discard on the margins of the CBD. He also points out (p. 233) that many schemes have been criticized for being elitist, as 'the fancy restaurants, boutiques, architects' offices, and night spots serve primarily a tourist and suburban population rather than locals'. Preservation may also bring other social problems, along with economic benefits, as Ford (p. 216) observes in Charleston where 'residents increasingly complain of noise and fumes from parked tour buses, invasion of privacy by visitors seeking a closer look at "historic residences", and the artificiality of a city full of boutiques and quaint restaurants'.

Others have been concerned with the authenticity of what is being preserved and presented to the tourist, and some interesting discussion in the literature has occurred on the transformation which tourism may hasten or bring about in urban and other areas. The sociologist MacCannell (1976) observes that 'often an entire urban structure is operating behind its tourist front'. He later goes on to present some interesting ideas on the social structure of tourist space which, he suggests, can be seen in terms of front and back regions. Front regions are those which are readily open to the visitor and a place where hosts and guests meet; back regions are the preserve of the residents or workers and are essentially non-tourism oriented in their function. Visitors may stroll through the Barrio Gótico but, except for particular places such as Picasso's Museum or the cathedral, they rarely penetrate inside. MacCannell suggests that there are various ways and degrees to which tourists can penetrate the back regions, to get a glimpse of what goes on 'behind the scene'. He distinguishes between a tourist setting, where provision is made for sightseers to observe an activity not directed towards them, e.g. the visitors' balcony in the New York Stock Exchange, and a stage set which is purposefully designed for the visitor. A good example of the latter is the *son et lumière* display and museum which now takes up most of the visit on the guided tour of Paris' sewers, surely the epitome of Ford's (1979) 'sanitized, idealized past'.

Whereas MacCannell speaks of 'staged authenticity', Relph (1976) sees tourism as one of the major factors developing what he terms 'an inauthentic attitude to place'. He continues (pp. 83–4):

> . . . in tourism individual and authentic judgement about places is nearly always subsumed to expert or socially accepted opinion, or the act and means of tourism become more

important than the places visited. Rasmussen (1964: 16) writes of tourists visiting the church of Santa Maria Maggiore in Rome: '. . . they hardly notice the character of the surroundings, they simply check off the starred numbers in their guide books and hasten on to the next one. They do not experience the place.' This is inauthenticity at its most explicit; the guided tour to see those works of art and architecture that someone else has decided are worth seeing.

Such a view might be considered rather elitist or stereotyped but the concept of the tourist's sense of place warrants further research both in terms of how it affects his activity space and how it relates to travel motivations. Is tourism in historic urban centres founded mainly on ego-enhancement as Relph suggests or does the tourist experience a new sense of place (artificial though that may be) which satisfies his need to escape his usual mundane environment (see Ch. 2)?

Beyond the city

As Fig. 1.7 shows, the city may act as a base for day and half-day trips into the surrounding region. From Paris, for example, trips are made to Versailles, Fontainebleau, Chartres and to the Loire Valley. Tourists visiting Madrid will also use it as a base to visit the surrounding historic centres of Toledo, Segovia and the Escorial. While some visitors do stay overnight in these centres, much of the accommodation demand they generate is captured by the metropolitan centre which acts as a convenient hub, removes the need to change hotels and offers a wide range of complementary attractions, particularly evening entertainment. Consequently, peripheral urban areas tend to have a reduced accommodation sector and the main manifestation of tourism there is often the large number of souvenir shops which line the streets leading from the car parks to the main historic attractions.

Airports, which serve both residents and tourists, may have a considerable impact (Bryant 1973), but by far the greatest changes in land use beyond the city usually result from demand generated by its own inhabitants. Such demand can take several forms, such as open space for tramping, picnicking or fishing, but the biggest impacts have come from second homes. Lundgren (1974) has produced a three-stage model based on the Canadian experience, showing changes in the spatial relationships between the urban centre and a second home or cottage region as the urban area expands (Fig. 10.7). In the first

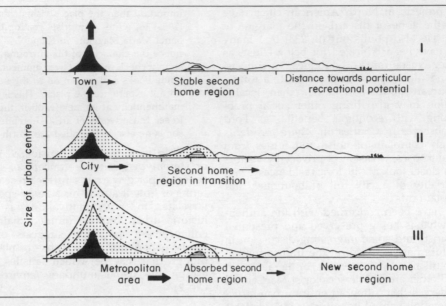

Fig. 10.7 Lundgren's model of urban expansion and second home regions.

Source: Redrawn from Lundgren (1974).

phase, demand from a medium-sized centre has generated a small second home region, typically in an area of broken relief or around a body of water. As the urban area grows, so the demand for second homes increases and the second home region expands, mainly away from the city (Phase II). Lundgren suggests that the 'inside expansion is more urban in character, whereas the outside push still retains the features of the typical vacation home development'. In the third and final stage of the sequence, the original second home region becomes engulfed by the expanding metropolis and now forms a part of the city itself, with the former second homes being transformed into permanent residences. Meanwhile a new, more distinct second home region has developed, for the demand for weekend or vacation accommodation has not abated but rather increased. This outwards expansion and growth in demand is not only a function of the larger population, but development of highways, increased car ownership, greater leisure time, and a desire by many local authorities to increase their tax take through intensification of land use as well as the activities of real estate developers promoting speculative sub-divisions.

A similar three-stage process has also been identified by Boyer (1980) in the Paris basin. In the first stage, existing rural dwellings are acquired by city residents, mainly for use as second homes. This is followed by a period of new construction on land bought from local inhabitants. At the beginning of this phase, second homes co-exist with primary residences but the latter soon become dominant. In a third phase, individual activity by both city and local residents is replaced by larger sub-divisions created either by the local residents, seeking to increase their tax base, or property developers after a profit. Primary residences now become the norm as the peace and isolation sought by the second home owners has now disappeared. The latter group move further outwards and the process is repeated.

Conclusions

Tourism in urban areas has developed largely in response to demand generated directly or indirectly by the city's other functions. As a result, the structure of tourism in the city tends to follow the general form induced by these other functions (as well as by other factors such as site characteristics) rather than shape it. As the CBD has expanded, for example, so the hotel sector has seen its centre of gravity change. Likewise, tourism facilities have formed part of redevelopment schemes but demand for them has rarely initiated those projects which result from more basic urban processes. In these respects the city contrasts with the coastal resort where tourism, characterized by a more homogeneous sunlust market, is a major if not dominant function and where the linear form of the resort reflects this function. Linearity is a feature of the distribution of some tourist facilities in the city, e.g. motels and frequently restaurants, but more often hotels and other facilities are found in distinct and sometimes overlapping clusters concentrated in the central city. Changes in the relative importance of different modes of transport have affected both types of centres, modifying the morphology of coastal resorts and influencing the distribution of hotels and other facilities within the city. Attention in each case has focused on the accommodation sector. More work is now required on other aspects of tourism within the city and on features other than the seafront in the beach resort, with examples being drawn in both cases from a range of examples which is not limited to those found in Western Europe.

Note

1. Paris also has a comparable capacity in lower-quality non-classified hotels (*hôtels non-homologués*). These generally attract a more residential clientele, although one estimate in 1971 suggested some 10% of foreign tourists and 20% of provincial visitors stay in non-classified accommodation (Anon 1971b). Few other statistics are available on these hotels, most of which are located in the more peripheral districts, particularly to the east of Paris.

   The classified hotels are classed in one of five classes, from 1-star to deluxe (*4 étoiles luxe*). The criteria used include number of rooms (a minimum of 7 rooms for 1-star hotels and 10 rooms for 3-stars), services and facilities available in the rooms and staff qualifications (2-star hotels must have staff speaking one foreign language while in 3-star hotels two foreign languages must be spoken). Deluxe hotels are distinguished from 4-star hotels by having a bathroom with all rooms (cf. in 90% of rooms for 4-star hotels), suites containing rooms able to be transformed into drawing rooms and a lift giving access to the first floor.

11

Implications, applications and conclusions

Previous chapters in this book have examined the fundamental geographical dimensions of tourism. Data sources have been outlined, a range of techniques and methods have been examined, patterns of flows and the spatial structure of tourism at different levels have been presented, and the factors and processes giving rise to them discussed. In this concluding chapter, two major and recurring themes – concentration and spatial interaction – are reviewed and their implications for tourist development, planning, marketing and management explored. Particular emphasis is given to the value of a geographical approach to assessing the impact of tourism. Conclusions are then drawn and suggestions for further research made.

Concentration

The preceding chapters have shown that tourism at all levels is generally characterized by a marked degree of concentration. The extent of this, of course, varies from place to place depending on the kind of tourism involved and the type of measure used. The following observations and generalizations are drawn from the examples cited throughout the book and may therefore not be as applicable to certain forms of tourism, notably that in rural and alpine areas, which have not been given as much emphasis here as tourism in coastal regions and urban areas.

In Chapter 3 it was shown that a small number of developed Western countries account for a large share of all international tourist movements, that most countries draw the majority of their visitors from three or fewer markets and that these are likely to be either neighbouring countries or the United States, West Germany, France and Great Britain (Tables 3.3 to 3.8, Figs 3.1 to 3.3). This concentration is compounded by significant regional biases within both generating and destination countries. In the former, there is evidence to suggest that not only does the general propensity for international travel vary from region to region (Tables 2.4 and 2.7) but that different regions will experience a greater or lesser propensity for travel to particular destinations. Certain Pacific or Caribbean countries, for example, may not only depend heavily on the United States market but they may draw the bulk of their visitors from respectively the West Coast or Atlantic Coast states (Fig. 2.3). Chapter 9 showed that within small island states, tourism plant may be very localized, but even in larger mainland countries there is a tendency for the top two or three regions to account for the lion's share of the recorded international bed nights (Fig. 8.1). Different nationalities, however, may exhibit specific spatial preferences (Fig. 8.3). Figure 8.1 also indicates that domestic tourism too is spatially concentrated within countries, although not, in most cases, to the same degree as international tourism. Chapter 6 indicated that much domestic tourism is very localized in nature, with a marked distance decay effect being observed in many studies and a large share of all domestic holidays being spent within the home region itself (Figs 6.1 to 6.6).

Further analysis shows that within regions, tourism may be very localized. In the case of coastal regions, it is often limited to an extremely narrow coastal fringe with relatively little development occurring inland. Ribbon development may give rise to a continuously built-up littoral in the most developed regions but elsewhere development is more nucleated (Figs 8.5 to 8.8). There is also evidence here of more specific concentrations along the coast of different sorts of accommodation, forms of tourism and types of tourists. Hotels may be more important in one locality and camping in another, package tourism may dominate certain resorts while other sectors of the coast are characterized by a less structured form of tourism centred on second homes. Certain resorts or sectors may attract a greater or lesser share of either the international or domestic demand and there is some indication of distinct spatial preferences being exhibited by different groups, both nationals and foreigners, along certain coasts (Figs 8.5 and 8.6). In other regions, tourism may be concentrated in major urban areas as both international visitors and many domestic visitors head for the big city rather than the surrounding hinterland which is the virtual preserve of the city's residents. Further concentration exists at the local level. The densest development in the coastal resorts occurs along a narrow seafront while central city clusters of tourist facilities are found in urban areas (Figs 9.2, 10.1 to 10.5, Plates 2, 5, 6).

The progressive concentration at these different levels gives rise in many cases to a pronounced funnelling effect which results in many tourists, particularly international ones, being concentrated within countries along the seafront of a limited number of resorts or clustered together in the central city of a major metropolitan area. Spain, for example, is one of the major tourist-receiving countries in the world, the Balearic Islands constitute the dominant tourist province in Spain, Majorca is the most important of these islands, most of the accommodation there is found around the Bay of La Palma in a strip adjacent to the seashore. Puerto Rico receives the largest volume of international arrivals in the Caribbean, drawing the vast majority of its tourists from the United States, notably from the Atlantic coast. Three-quarters of the island's hotel capacity is found within metropolitan San Juan, with most of the hotels being concentrated along

beachfront sites in the Condado, Ocean Park and at Punta Las Marias. In other words, a significant share of the international sunlust market in Europe ends up along a few kilometres of beach on the outskirts of Palma de Majorca, and a relatively small number of beachfront hotels in San Juan account for an important portion of the United States traffic to the Caribbean. Such concentration is not limited to sunlust tourism. London dominates international tourism within Britain while Paris is a major destination within France. Tourist activity within both capitals is concentrated in the central city. Both, however, are less important as domestic destinations and domestic tourism in general tends not to be funnelled to quite the same extent as international tourist flows. In other instances, concentration occurs not so much in regions or resorts but along well-defined routes, such as in New Zealand where a distinct tourist circuit can be identified, particularly for overseas visitors (Fig. 4.8).

This concentration results from the interaction of a variety of supply and demand factors which may operate in similar ways at different scales. The resources which attract tourists are numerous and varied but at each level these attractions are generally rather limited in number, distribution, degree of development and the extent to which they are known to the tourist. At the international, national and regional levels, distance plays a major role in influencing which attractions and destinations are accessible to particular markets or tourists, whether in terms of time, money or effort. Accessibility is also determined by other factors such as the nature and extent of the transport network (particularly the number and location of gateways and the modes of transport available), the degree of tour operations, costs within the destination itself and promotion activities. These may modify the broad distance decay effects normally observed and concentrate further or, conversely, disperse the tourist traffic. Accessibility is also a key factor at the local level. Within the resort or city, tourists will seek to be as close as possible to the attractions they desire. This has led to densely developed seafronts within coastal resorts and to the clustering of tourist facilities and activities in the central city. Land rents, planning restrictions, pre-existing activities and site factors may, however, limit the extent to which accommodation, or certain types of accommodation, can locate close to the attractions, whether the beach or historical monuments. Economies of scale in the development of plant and infrastructure are often achieved by concentrating development at a national and regional scale while locally planners may confine certain types of activities to particular zones. A strong regional image can also be promoted in this way while the clustering of particular facilities in certain districts gives them a more readily identifiable image.

Success may reinforce the process of concentration as new hotels are built in areas where others have already proved viable or new resort projects are developed within well-established regions to take advantage of existing infrastructure, services and a well-known 'name'. The number of longitudinal studies undertaken and the quality and quantity of time-series data available are still rather limited but there is evidence of some dispersion in tourist flows over time and signs of a delocalization of tourist plant and facilities. Chapter 3 showed, for example, that the Japanese are not only travelling in greater numbers beyond Asia but within the region they are visiting a wider range of destinations. Tourism within island states is generally very localized but there has been some dispersion as new accommodation has been built away from the gateway cities and movement to the outer islands develops. In both these examples, Japanese travel abroad and tourism on islands, dispersion has occurred within a period of growth so that although there may have been a relative deconcentration of tourist activity, in absolute terms there has rarely been much if any decline in established centres or resorts. The growth of tourism in major metropolitan centres like London and Paris has been responsible for the delocalization of accommodation, if not of most tourist attractions, as suitable central sites have become increasingly scarce, as new economic factors and planning decisions have come into force or as the importance of different modes of transport have changed. The tendency in the design of coastal resorts, however, has generally been to bring accommodation closer and closer to the attractions. This has generally resulted in the intensification of the seafront, the construction of hotels *pieds dans l'eau* and the building of very functional marinas. Development in depth inland has, however, been promoted by some resort developers by building golf courses and encouraged by planners anxious to avoid excessive ribbon development.

The degree of concentration or dispersion at a particular scale is related to the overall stage of development of the country, region, resort or city. The basic pattern might be established at an early stage as the infant tourist traffic quickly identifies the most appealing attractions or the early entrepreneurs acquire and develop the most desirable sites. Or a settling-down period may occur wherein a small number of travellers visit several different regions until, for a variety of reasons, some assume a greater degree of popularity than others. At the same time, developers and entrepreneurs may experiment with a range of different sites and localities, types of attractions and so on, with the success or failure of these early ventures influencing the pattern of location for subsequent development. In either event a process of circular cumulative growth may occur as access to the more popular or successful destinations is improved, as land values rise encouraging further speculative development, as the area becomes more widely known with a feedback system of information developing, as increasing volumes lower travel costs enabling the market to be broadened and so on. During this phase, the pattern may be one of increasing concentration, in both relative and absolute terms, as growth is channelled into a limited number of regions and resorts or cities within those regions and to selected sites and districts within those resorts or cities. At a later stage, other factors may come into play and bring about some deconcentration or dispersion, at least in relative terms. The scarcity of room for further expansion or development is one obvious reason for this, as there are limits to intensification. Moreover, as development occurs, there may be a change in the clientele, with those seeking more novel, exclusive or just less crowded destinations moving on to other areas. New markets may also develop, e.g. that for winter sports, or other areas may seek a share of the growing tourist cake by developing new resources or facilities, upgrading their communications and so on. Policy-makers may encourage this dispersion as a means of spreading the benefits of tourism or reducing its negative impacts.

The possibilities of manipulating tourist flows and influencing the spatial structure of the tourist industry are not, however, unbounded. In many cases, it seems conditions are such that existing patterns may well be perpetuated. Attempts at managing and planning the growth of tourism will be enhanced though if a broader spatial perspective is adopted and greater attention is paid to patterns of spatial interaction.

Spatial interaction

This book has systematically explored and analysed the inherent geographic dimensions of tourism, emphasizing the different types and levels of spatial interaction which underlie, indeed constitute, this phenomenon. It is clearly insufficient to ask simply where visitors come from and leave the 'geographical breakdown' at that as most visitor surveys and marketing studies do. We must also know how visitors have come to that destination, their movements within it and their subsequent travel patterns. Likewise, studies of flows generated by a given market should not be restricted just to where they go, but to how they get there and back and where they go once at a destination. Moreover, the role of any given area in a larger tourist system can be appreciated more fully by undertaking both types of studies, that is, examining both its generating and receiving functions. The study area should be placed in a broader geographical framework and considered in terms of how it is linked to other markets and destinations. These patterns of interaction can be analysed at different scales, e.g. country to country or city to resort flows, as well as between different levels, for instance the intra-national travel patterns of international visitors.

Analysis of patterns of spatial interaction has often been limited by the paucity of relevant data and the need to develop or adapt appropriate techniques to investigate what can be rather complex problems. Nevertheless it has been possible throughout earlier chapters to identify a wide variety of data sources and to provide examples of how these can be analysed with respect to different types of interaction. In this section, selected patterns of interaction will be reviewed in terms of their significance to the tourist industry. Other examples will also be used to show how a spatial perspective can be and has been used for planning, marketing, development and impact assessment.

By establishing how one destination relates to another in terms of particular markets, a geographical perspective can be especially useful in the field of international circuit tourism. To promote a destination effectively it is essential to know whether or not a country is a main destination in itself or a stopover on a circuit and, if part of a circuit, what is the nature and composition of that circuit. How might that circuit be exploited further and how might new markets be developed? Writing on the need for co-operation among South Pacific destinations, for instance, Brault (1980: 45) notes:

> Unfortunately many of the South Pacific islands, especially the small ones, do not have enough attractions to justify . . . lengthy visits. Consequently potential visitors end up choosing

alternative travel destinations. If through co-operation, several South Pacific islands jointly promote and market their destinations so that a tourist can visit several, rather than just a single destination, then together there might be enough attractions to justify the high cost of getting there.

But such joint promotion and marketing requires knowledge of existing and potential circuits and the identification of the 'prime magnets' around which strategies might be developed. Figure 3.4 and Table 3.9 provide examples of how this can be done.

Developing tourism, however, is not just a case of increasing total arrivals: the impact of different sorts of visitors, e.g. destination visitors and circuit travellers, must also be considered. This is where an integrated approach to tourist flow analysis involving different scales of development and levels of flows becomes important. In the case of French Polynesia, discussed in Chapter 5, it was possible to relate the amount of movement within the territory to the extent to which French Polynesia was being visited as a destination in itself or as part of a circuit. Figure 5.1 shows that destination visitors had a greater propensity to make multiple-island visits with the majority of the circuit travellers limiting their stay to one island, notably Tahiti. Differences were also found in the extent to which tourists from particular countries travelled within the territory and visited it as part of a circuit (Fig. 5.2, Table 5.1). Furthermore, the level of satisfaction of visitors to French Polynesia appeared to be much higher among those tourists visiting more than one island. Such information has important implications in terms of distributing the impact of tourism and of promoting the territory. Encouragement of a destination traffic with its greater tendency towards travel away from Tahiti might, for example, lead not only to more satisfied tourists and subsequently an increase in the overall traffic but result in a greater dispersal of tourism throughout the territory and in its impacts being more widely spread. Encouragement in this case might involve not only specially directed promotion but such action as increasing direct international flights to Tahiti, improving inter-island transport, increasing the accommodation on the outer islands and developing new holiday packages. In recent years there has been evidence of a growing appreciation among hoteliers of the significance of the inter-island traffic. In 1983, for example, the French chain Climats de France built or acquired hotels on Tahiti, Moorea and Bora Bora, and other hotels in Tahiti are strengthening their links with those on other islands.

Other examples have also been given of how trends in international arrivals can be translated into changes in demand and impact in particular parts of a country. Reference was made in Chapter 8 to the work by Pearce and Grimmeau (1985) who attempted a general synthesis of the spatial structure of tourism in Spain based essentially on an analysis by principal components of hotel bed nights. They showed that not only did different markets exhibit distinct spatial preferences but that these preferences remained remarkably constant over the period 1965/66–80 (Figs 8.2 to 8.4). However, as growth rates differed significantly from market to market during this time, marked regional differences in demand occurred, with the number of bed nights increasing much more rapidly in the coastal and insular provinces favoured by the Europeans than in the regions more heavily dependent on the slower growing domestic market or the declining 'Rest of the World' market. Overall, the picture was one where the prominence of the 'sun-sand-sea' provinces contrasted with the much less dynamic urban and historical centres. In other words, changes in total demand at the national level can have specific geographical consequences and identifying these at an early stage may enable appropriate measures to be taken in each area.

Similarly in Chapter 4, it was shown how certain groups of international visitors to New Zealand limit their visits to the main urban areas and major resorts while others include smaller centres and resorts (Figs 4.4 and 4.5). This information might be used by local managers and developers to identify the possible effects for them of changes in international demand and for selective promotion campaigns if regional development and not merely an overall increase in tourist arrivals were deemed to be a worthwhile goal. For example, other things being equal, an increase in Australian holiday-makers would increase visits to Westland National Park more than a comparable expansion of the United States or Japanese tourist traffic. However, as it is these latter two markets which have shown the largest relative increases in recent years, no significant upsurge in Westland can be expected. Considerable interest, on the other hand, is being shown in building hotels in Christchurch, the gateway to the South Island, and in Queenstown, a major resort, both centres favoured by the shorter-stay visitors.

Patterns of spatial interaction can also be viewed from a local perspective. Use of the Trip Index showed that Christchurch acts as a gateway for most international and many North Island visitors but constitutes a major destination in itself for the majority of South Island visitors (Table 4.4). Other research showed that the overseas tourists visited inner-city attractions much more frequently than outer-city ones and that the frequency of day trips from the city increased with length of stay, number of visits made and purpose of visit. Different strategies might therefore be used to develop specific segments of the market identified in this way, with promotional efforts being directed, for example, at the regional visitor, the specific purpose traveller or, more ambitiously, the overseas visitor who might be encouraged to spend more time in the city on a subsequent visit to the country (Pearce and Elliott 1983). Given its gateway function, however, the volume of international visitors to Christchurch will continue to be influenced by the health of the tourist industry in the South Island in general, with co-operative regional campaigns being essential here. Table 4.4 also suggests that the volume of visitors to Westland National Park is even more dependent on the tourist traffic 'doing the South Island' and that attempts to stimulate business in the area might be carried out at the broader regional level and not independently. One exception to this might be a market for short, second holidays for South Islanders in the off-season. It has also been possible to determine patterns of visits within the park (Fig. 4.11). Such information is particularly useful for park management, for example, in determining the range of interpretative material displayed at each visitor centre or for allocating resources for developing access within the park.

Recognition of the different types and functions of gateways is important for planning for tourism at all levels. Two basic sorts of gateways might be identified, those which act simply as points of entry which visitors pass through en route to a destination elsewhere in the region or country and those, chiefly capital cities, which also constitute major destinations in themselves. In the first instance, local interest may be directed at generating more business by increasing the visitors' length of stay in the area. In the second, attempts may be made to disperse the traffic away from the gateway in order to ease pressures there and to benefit other parts of the region or country. Where a city draws on several different markets, as in the case of Christchurch, a variety of interests and potential strategies might exist.

In the case of gateways which act basically as entry points which are passed through on a larger circuit, the potential for retaining visitors may be limited, as in the cases of Cherbourg (Soumagne

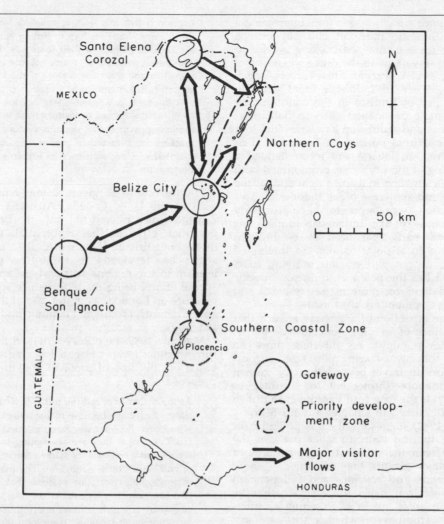

Fig. 11.1 Spatial aspects of Belize's tourist development plan.

Source: Pearce (1984b).

1974; Clary 1978) and the Aosta Valley (Janin 1982) discussed in Chapter 4. In the latter case, Janin suggests that the number of stays in the area might be increased by improving the distribution of information and systems of hotel reservation for passing motorists. He also stresses that local interests should not lose sight of two different types of clientele: the touring visitor who might be attracted by more modern but competitively priced hotels built along the major axes, and the longer-stay visitor who might be tempted by some form of alternative accommodation, such as *gîtes ruraux*.

Recommendations for improved distribution of information at its gateways was also a feature of Belize's recent ten-year development plan (Pearce 1984b). Here the aim was not so much to retain passing visitors in the gateways themselves, but to lengthen the stay in the country of overland visitors, many of whom appear to have flexible schedules, by directing them out to the cays, the most attractive part of Belize, and to selected areas along the coast (Fig. 11.1). The success of this strategy will also depend on improving access to these areas from the gateways. In the case of air arrivals to Belize City, attention was directed at improving transfers from international flights to domestic transport and suggestions were made for a centralized booking service to handle all reservations to the cays and coast.

A recent PATA (Pacific Area Travel Association) Task Force to Indonesia identified two different types of tourism in the country: that involving single destination visits to Bali direct from overseas and multi-stop itineraries 'that can be fanned out from Jakarta' (PATA n.d.). Their report centred on Jakarta and recommended a strengthening of the city's role, promoting it both as a travel destination in its own right and 'as the gateway to and showcase of, all Indonesia'. This latter function was seen to be particularly important since (p. 61): 'Indonesian tourism has many varied parts that need to be brought together at a focal point to form an integrated whole. Bali cannot perform this unifying function. Jakarta has the potential to do so.' Specific recommendations for more market research and product development are then made.

Where the attraction of a gateway is such that it absorbs much of a region's or country's tourist traffic, efforts might be directed more to enhancing the city's staging post role, encouraging visitors to travel beyond the city to visit other destinations throughout the country or region. Such is the case with Vancouver in British Columbia discussed in Chapter 4, with Murphy and Brett (1982) suggesting there is potential for developing touring visits to other parts of the province. Given the different travel patterns of the two major groups they identified – those visiting friends and relations and independent vacationers – it is arguable, however, whether the metropolitan areas are in effect acting as intervening opportunities or whether they are just magnets for a particular sector which is not greatly interested in touring in any case. Murphy and Brett suggest other areas could be developed if repeat visits were encouraged, noting (p. 160): 'The United Kingdom experience indicates London has become less of an interceptor to overseas visitors as their number of visits increases.' Elsewhere, Murphy (1980) notes only limited success in redirecting visitors within Victoria.

Given the problems which London was experiencing in the early 1970s, (see Ch. 10), much attention has been given to the question of not only dispersing international visitors beyond London but managing their activities within the city. Strategies at various scales have been developed. At a national level, the BTA (1979b: 9) noted in its report, *International Tourism and Strategic Planning*:

London is Britain's leading gateway for traffic to the regions. Most visitors to Britain still want to see London as part of their total stay. London could accommodate a greater volume of traffic in transit to and from the regions if the length of stay in London continued to fall.

A desirable and feasible strategy for BTA is to continue the spread of visitors from established markets provided that enough visitors from new markets are attracted to ensure that London maintains its pre-eminence as Britain's greatest destination.

Priority was to be given to long-haul markets such as the USA, Canada, Australia and New Zealand which offered not only the best growth potential but the best potential for travel throughout Britain. Regional tourism plans have also been developed to foster the growth of tourism in the regions with, where appropriate, special efforts being made to reduce some of the pressure on London, as in the case of the Thames and Chilterns (Tourism Planning and Research Ltd 1977).

Murphy (1982: 19) observes that within London three distinct levels of spatial management exist based on the type of problem and the solutions proposed:

At the micro-level are the individual amenity sites which have become major tourist attractions. Few are purpose designed tourist facilities, rather they are attempting to accommodate the visitor while fulfilling their original and primary function. The major concern is developing circulation systems that permit the two functions to co-exist. At the meso-scale are city districts which contain many tourist attractions and facilities. Here local government attempts to balance the industry's landuse demands with local needs and desires, so as to maintain a viable community. At the macro-level is the metropolitan region administered by the Greater London Council. Spatial management issues at this level concern the uneven development of the city's tourism resources which leads to an inefficient, and sometimes self destructive operation. Hence the emphasis shifts from immediate and reactive planning to long term resource management.

Examples of micro-level management include ways of controlling the flow of visitors through Westminster Abbey and the Tower of London, meso-level planning may involve zoning accommodation so as to reduce conflict with other forms of land use, while macro-level policies include those designed to direct tourists to outlying attractions. Murphy then describes attempts to redress the seasonal imbalance in London's tourist traffic but concludes in both cases that it is not particularly easy to manipulate visitor demand. Eversley (1977) also doubts whether the basic pattern of demand in London can be greatly altered, noting that the majority of attractions are fixed in space and the timing of some, such as the Changing of the Guard, may also be fixed.

In other instances, routes rather than nodes will provide the framework for promotion, planning and development. Theme itineraries promoting visits to a series of like attractions have proved a useful way of generating traffic to sites which may not, individually, warrant a trip. One of the most popular types of such circuits are the *routes du vin* which link up different vineyards. Historical sites, buildings and monuments can also be promoted in this way such as the Route Lafayette in the upper Loire Valley and the Route Jacques-Coeur in the Haut Berry region of France. In Andalucia it is the Route of the 'White Towns' which links up a series of hilltop villages with their white-washed walls and tiled roofs.

Elsewhere, planning and development has been based on tourist 'corridors'. Such is the case in the Yukon where Wolman Associates (1978: 23) suggest that 'in view of the distances between existing and potential attractions and services, the corridor system is the key to the tourist experience in Yukon, and is the foundation for the proposed development strategy for Yukon's tourism industry'. Various corridors are then identified, along with the segments of the market they are likely to attract, proposals for product development and constraints on the expansion of tourism. Gunn (1972) also emphasizes the role of the 'circulation corridor' – 'the entire visual sweep along all the travel ways' – in the design of regional tourist plans. He notes (p. 92): 'In a broad sense the design is heavily dependent upon two basic functions, sometimes overlapping: (1) a means to an end (to get there and back) and (2) an end in itself (a part of an attraction experience). In both cases the emphasis is upon the people being moved, the means is incidental.'

Gunn (1972, 1979) also deals with other spatial components of physical planning, as do Lawson and Baud-Bovy (1977). Other aspects of spatial planning for tourism at the national, regional and local levels have been reviewed by this author elsewhere (Pearce 1981c).

The impact of tourism

Over the last decade, a considerable body of literature has been developed on the impact of tourism. Initially seen mainly in economic terms and in a favourable light, the assessment of the impact of tourism has been broadened to include environmental and socio-cultural considerations and costs as well as benefits are now attributed to its development (Smith 1977; Cohen 1978; de Kadt 1979; Travis 1982). Geographers have been to the fore in advocating a more balanced approach (Pearce 1981c; Mathieson and Wall 1982) but much debate still occurs over the nature and extent of these impacts and the ways in which they might be assessed. A geographical perspective can undoubtedly contribute to clarifying many of the issues and formulating solutions to the problems identified.

There seems little doubt that many of the negative impacts attributed to tourism have been accentuated by the process of concentration outlined, whether in terms of the degradation of beaches through the discharge of inadequately treated effluent, the congestion of inner-city streets by tour buses, the disruption of local lifestyles or the over-dependence on one or two major markets. At the same time the benefits of tourism, such as increased job opportunities and higher revenues, may be limited to only a few areas. In some cases where the concentration of tourist activities drains investment capital, services and population away from other areas, tourism may lead to a dual economy or heighten regional imbalances. Conversely, where this concentration occurs in areas away from established industrial or agricultural centres, it may help redress regional inequalities. Likewise, concentration may be deemed beneficial if by grouping tourist facilities in selected areas or concentrating on specific regional markets, a more viable and competitive industry can be established and economies of scale achieved so that adequate infrastructure can be provided, thus eliminating or reducing such problems as water pollution. Concentration may also reduce the social impacts of tourism to a few areas, but if not done carefully the tourists may also overwhelm the local residents in the areas concerned.

Concentration too cannot be divorced from the types of operation and forms of development from which it results. In particular, spatial concentration in the form of tourist enclaves, both in developing and developed countries, is frequently symptomatic of large-scale integrated operations, organized by the state or controlled by a limited number of powerful external operators and developers. Policy-makers in some areas, especially multiple-island states, have attempted to counter this trend by encouraging smaller-scale indigenously owned projects, but these have often been unsuccessful. In Paris, on the other hand, large chain-owned hotels have led the delocalization of the hotel industry in the city.

Analysis of tourist flow patterns at different scales can also contribute to an understanding of why particular impacts are experienced in some areas and not others, and suggest measures which might be taken to spread the benefits of tourist development or alleviate its negative impacts. Useful contributions have also been made in this area by geographers using similar techniques but studying different types of flows. Studies of migration induced by tourist development, for example, have been undertaken in Spain (Dumas 1975) and Yugoslavia (Poulsen 1977). Lundgren (1975) has analysed food supply flows to Jamaican resort hotels while others have considered flows or leakages of profits from particular regions or areas (Knafou 1978; Pearce 1982b).

Geographical analyses of the type discussed in this book can shed light on where the different impacts generated by tourism are occurring and who is being affected. These are important issues and ones which have often been neglected. Economic research, for example, has traditionally focused either on aspatial national studies which have stressed costs and benefits in overall terms or on more detailed local case studies with little or no attempt to bridge the gap between the two. Likewise, social impact studies rarely examine the geographical context of the processes or impacts they are describing, and environmental research often does not consider the extent of the impacts identified. Analysis of spatial variations in the nature and extent of tourist development can thus provide essential inputs into the assessment process. Until more specific economic, social and environmental geodata become available, maps of tourist bed nights or accommodation capacity will continue to be useful indicators of the geographical distribution and intensity of tourism. As such, they may signal the success or failure of regional development strategies or indicate the need for these, alert authorities and researchers to likely problem areas and suggest solutions that might be adopted. Moreover, when integrated with similar analyses of other activities, geographical studies of tourism may lead to a fuller understanding of the role of the tourist industry in the general structure of the country, region or community in question.

Ironically, two of the most explicit spatial models of tourism impact assessment have not been developed by geographers, but by an inter-disciplinary Swiss team (Federal Dept. of Forestry 1981) and a French sociologist (Thurot 1980). Both emphasize processes of spatial interaction and use an origin–linkage–destination framework to identify different causes of impact and types of problems in different but inter-related places.

The Swiss team were concerned with assessing environmental stress arising out of the growth of ski tourism in Switzerland. A central feature of their study was a model of ski tourism and the natural landscape, comprised of three sub-systems (Fig. 11.2). The first sub-system involves the outward and return trip; the second, accommodation and the stay in the resort; the third, skiing and associated facilities. Each of these sub-systems was then examined in more detail in terms of the specific problems which arose and possible solutions which might be implemented. Problems in sub-system A, for instance, essentially result from the traffic generated by skiers and give rise to such impacts as an overloading of arterial routes, congestion in villages en route to the ski fields, bottlenecks in passes, increased vehicle emissions and so forth. Solutions to these problems include extending existing roads or building new ones, creating a more efficient public transport system or developing alternative ski fields and redirecting the traffic to them. Each of these choices may ease the pressure in one area but generate new stress elsewhere. Bypasses, for instance, may relieve congestion caused by transit traffic in the villages but at the same time directly result in the loss of cultivated land and, by improving access, attract additional traffic which may cause greater emissions and increase demand on the other two sub-systems.

Activities within the skiing sub-system are seen in terms of a cycle of events: 'the individual's skiing activity begins at a specific point of departure, progresses via intermediary stages and terminates with the unbuckling of the skis after the return.' The processes at work in the development and expansion of the ski field are then analysed in terms of this 'run-cycle'. Ecological impacts associated with the development of a ski field may include soil compaction, disappearance of plant species and the transformation of the existing drainage system. Such impacts can generally be reduced by careful planning at the outset while the unnecessary expansion of the ski slopes may be avoided by improving the efficiency and capacity of existing facilities and promoting other types of skiing with different requirements, notably cross-country skiing.

The use of a spatial interaction model such as

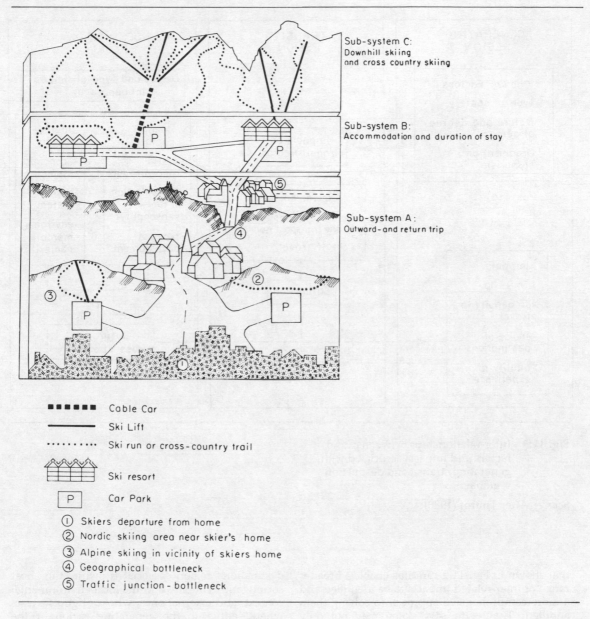

Sub-system C:
Downhill skiing
and cross country skiing

Sub-system B:
Accommodation and duration of stay

Sub-system A:
Outward- and return trip

▪▪▪▪▪▪ Cable Car

──────── Ski Lift

············ Ski run or cross-country trail

Ski resort

P Car Park

① Skiers departure from home
② Nordic skiing area near skier's home
③ Alpine skiing in vicinity of skiers home
④ Geographical bottleneck
⑤ Traffic junction - bottleneck

Fig. 11.2 A framework for assessing the impact
of tourism on the natural landscape.

Source: After Federal Dept. of Forestry
(1981).

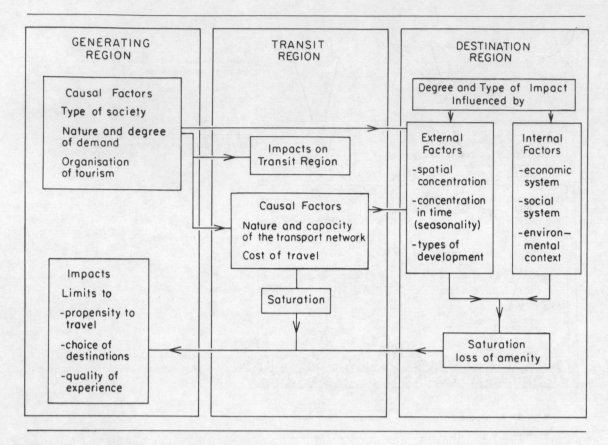

Fig. 11.3 Inter-relationships between causal factors and impacts associated with generating, transit and destination regions.

Source: After Thurot (1980).

that shown in Fig. 11.2 can thus enable a broader range of inter-related impacts to be identified and a more comprehensive approach to solving them adopted. That is to say, skiing may not only generate stress outside the resort itself, the traditional focus for impact studies, but solutions to the pressures in the resort may also lie elsewhere, for instance, in the manipulation of traffic along feeder routes.

Thurot (1980) too adopts a more comprehensive approach in his review of carrying capacity, arguing that most studies to date have been too limited as they have only focused on conditions and impacts in the destination region. He distinguishes between internal factors in the destination region associated with the host society and economy and the local environmental context, and external ones, whose origins lie elsewhere, either in the generating region or the transit region (Fig. 11.3). In particular, conditions in the generating region will not only affect total demand, but factors such as institutionalized holiday-making and traditional habits may give rise to a marked seasonality in demand and to distinct preferences for certain types of holidays and destinations. These conditions can accentuate the impacts felt in the destination region by concentrating demand spatially and at certain times of the year, week or day. How the tourist industry is organized may also reinforce or reduce these patterns, with much domestic tourism being unstructured and more dispersed and international tourism being more organized and directed. The nature, capacity and organization of the transport network in the transit region may accentuate further this spatial and temporal concentration. Chapter 9, for instance, outlined the significance of air transport for the spatial organization of tourism on islands. Conditions in the transit region, notably those which influence the cost of travel, may also significantly affect the volume of traffic generated and thus the pressure which develops at the destination. This region will also be affected by demand emanating from the generating region in the same way that sub-system A was affected in Fig. 11.2. Severe bottlenecks may be experienced at the interfaces of the different regions; that is, the outskirts of cities and the approaches to resorts, at the beginning and end of the main holiday season and at the start and finish to the weekend. Moreover, feedback loops might be built into the system. If the destination region becomes saturated, this will limit the propensity to travel from the generating region, reduce the amount of choice available to potential holiday-makers or lower the quality of their experience such that the original need to escape may not be fulfilled. Overloading of the transport system in the transit region will aggravate these problems.

A spatial perspective then can add greatly to the assessment of the impact of tourism; firstly by indicating the nature and extent of tourist activity and likely problem areas, secondly by highlighting the sorts of problems which may occur in different places and arise from different sources. Adopting a framework such as that shown in Figs. 11.2 and 11.3 may at first sight seem only to complicate the issue by extending the traditional focus of activity but, ultimately, the broader perspective it gives will enhance the likelihood of finding and implementing more effective solutions.

Conclusions

A substantial if disparate body of literature now exists dealing with the geographical dimensions of tourism. An attempt has been made in this book to structure this material and to present the results of new research in this field. Various models of tourist flows, spatial interaction and development were reviewed in Chapter 1. These generally provide a useful point of entry into particular areas of analysis and interpretation, but the geography of tourism is not yet underpinned by a strong theoretical base. Chapter 2 examined the questions of demand and motivation which underlie and give rise to the phenomenon under study. Much interesting work has been done in this field but the whole area of tourist demand is still far from being understood. Chapters 3 to 6 dealt with the analysis of tourist flows at different scales, with many studies here being limited by the lack of appropriate data. Nevertheless it was possible to provide examples of different types of analysis at different levels and to show that data difficulties are not insuperable. A variety of techniques for analysing spatial variations in tourism were reviewed in Chapter 7. This diversity suggested a general lack of direction in the literature, both in terms of questions addressed and approaches adopted. Despite this, it was possible in Chapters 8 to 10 to identify certain general patterns in the spatial structure of tourism at the national and regional level, on islands, and in coastal resorts and urban areas. Finally, the earlier sections of this chapter have been concerned with the implications of the major recurring themes of concentration and spatial interaction and with the application of a geographical perspective and geographical techniques in planning, development, marketing and, in particular, the assessment of the impact of tourism.

Significant contributions have been made by geographers in a wide range of areas but much scope exists for further research. In the first instance, much more work needs to be done in each of the areas outlined, whether this been intra-national flows or tourism in urban areas. Several different avenues might be followed here. Firstly, the geographical coverage of topics needs to be greatly enlarged. While the material reviewed here has admittedly been filtered by the author's experience and contacts, there is clearly a need to extend the types of studies undertaken primarily in Europe to other parts of the globe – to Asia, Africa, Latin America and, even in many instances, North America. Secondly, there is a need to move away from the isolated, ideographic case study to more systematic and comparative research and to replicate studies from place to place and time to time so that the general might be distinguished from the specific. This would involve the identification of appropriate themes, the adoption of common approaches, the standardization of terminology and the collection of comparable data. Clearly these are dangers if a bland uniformity in tourism research were to develop and initiative and originality were to be lost, but little progress in our understanding of the geography of tourism will be achieved if the fragmentation and diversity such as that outlined in Chapter 7 continues. Thirdly, more longitudinal studies are required, showing how patterns and processes have evolved or developed through time. Emphasis also needs to be given to the future as well as the past, with the development of forecasting techniques being essential to tourism planning. Undertaking such studies will involve not only the availability of time-series data but also a sustained commitment to tourism research. While useful research was done in early years by those having a temporary flirtation with tourism and while new ideas will continue to be injected by outsiders with a transient interest in the subject, without a core of committed researchers no coherent body of knowledge is likely to develop.

At the same time, the links between the various topics discussed in the preceding chapters need to be developed further. Firstly, the links between the various geographical levels of research need strengthening. How does the resort fit into the region, what is the region's role in the nation and the nation's place in the world? Or, reversing the focus, how do international trends affect a given country and particular places within that country? Examples of an integrated approach to these problems were given in Chapter 5 while the value of adopting such an approach was discussed earlier in this chapter. Secondly, more attention needs to be given to how one type of research relates to another and how different research topics are interconnected. Those developing models, for instance, have not widely tested their creations by empirical research and most case studies have not been based on any particular theory. Studies stressing methodology are frequently weak on interpretation while others offering plenty of comment are often thin on technique. Work on motivation needs to be related to studies of tourist flows so that patterns cannot only be identified but explained more soundly. Likewise research on distribution needs to take fuller account of development processes. Our understanding of the impact of tourism could benefit from work in all these areas.

Many of these features are of course characteristic of any relatively new field of research. With tourism, however, the phenomenon under study continues to develop at a rapid pace and there is little doubt its significance throughout the world can only increase in coming decades. Already a tourism research gap exists; if it is not to become a veritable chasm, tourism research must quickly come of age.

References

Abbey, J. R. (1979), Does life-style profiling work?, *J. of Travel Research*, **18**(1), 8–14.

Aldskogius, H. (1977), A conceptual framework and a Swedish case study of recreational behaviour and environmental cognition, *Economic Geography*, **53**(2), 163–83.

Andrieux, D. and **Soulier, A.** (1980), Physionomie du tourisme en Languedoc-Roussillon: une enquête sur les résidences secondaires, *Etudes et Statistiques Languedoc Roussillon*, Repères No. 2, Août, INSEE, Montpellier.

An Foras Forbatha (1973), *Brittas Bay: a planning and conservation study*, An Foras Forbatha, Dublin.

Anon (1971a), Package tours – where are they heading? Part 1, *International Tourism Quarterly*, 1, 59–74; Part 2, *International Tourism Quarterly*, 2, 50–63.

Anon (1971b), La situation du tourisme parisien, *Paris Projet*, **6**, 66–75.

Anon (1973), Air holidays: two years of progress?, *International Tourism Quarterly*, 2, 25–52.

Archer, B. and **Shea, S.** (1973), *Gravity Models and Tourist Research*, Tourist Research Paper TUR2, Economics Research Unit, Bangor.

Armstrong, C. W. G. 1972), International tourism: coming or going: the methodological problems of forecasting, *Futures*, **4**(2), 115–25.

Ashworth, G. J. (1976), *Distribution of Foreign Tourists in the Netherlands*, Occasional Papers No. 2, Department of Geography, Portsmouth Polytechnic , Portsmouth.

ATC (1980), *Survey of International Visitors 1979–80*, Australian Tourist Commission, Melbourne.

Baker, R. J. (1983), *An Analysis of Urban Morphology and Precincts Within Selected Coastal Resorts of the Port Stephens-Great Lakes Area, New South Wales*, M.A. thesis (unpublished), University of New England, Armidale.

Banco Central de la República Dominicana (1977), La experiencia del Fondo para el Desarrollo de la Infraestructura Turistica (Infratur), pp. 169–82 in *El Turismo y su Financiamiento en España, Caribe y Centro America*, Instituto de Credito Oficial, Madrid.

Baptistide, J.-C. (1979), *Tourisme et Développement de la Guadeloupe*, Thèse de Troisième Cycle (unpublished), Institut de Géographie, Faculté des Lettres et Sciences Humaines de Rouen, Rouen.

Barbaza, Y. (1970), Trois types d'intervention du tourisme dans l'organisation de l'espace littoral, *Annales de Géographie*, **434**, 446–69.

Barbier, B. (ed.) (1975), *Atlas de Provence Côte d'Azur*, ACTES, Le Paradou.

Barbier, B. (1978), Ski et stations de sports d'hiver dans le monde, *Weiner Geographische Schriften*, **51/52**, 130–46.

Barbier, B. and **Pearce, D. G.** (1984), The geography of tourism in France: definition, scope and themes, *GeoJournal*, **9**(1), 47–53.

Bardolet, E. (1980), Tourism in the Balearic Islands, *Tourist Review*, **35**(4), 18–21.

Baretje, R. and **Defert, P.** (1972), *Aspects Economiques du Tourisme*, Berger-Levrault, Paris.

Barrett, J. A. (1958), *The Seaside Resort Towns of England and Wales*, PhD thesis (unpublished), University of London, London.

Beckett, R. N. (1978), *Motel Accommodation and Summer Tourism in Auckland*, M.A. thesis (unpublished), University of Auckland, Auckland.

Bell, M. (1977), The spatial distribution of second homes: a modified gravity model, *J. Leisure Research*, 9(3), 225–32.

Benthien, B. (1984), Recreational geography in the German Democratic Republic, *GeoJournal*, 9(1), 59–63.

Berriane, M. (1978), Un type d'espace touristique marocain: le littoral méditerranéen, *Revue de Géographie du Maroc*, 29(2), 5–28.

Bielckus, C. L. (1977), Second homes in Scandinavia, pp. 35–46 in J. T. Coppock (ed.), *Second Homes: Curse or Blessing?*, Pergamon, Oxford.

Blanchet, G. (1981), *Les petites et moyennes entreprises polynésiennes: le cas de la petite hôtellerie*, Travaux et Documents de l'ORSTOM, 136, ORSTOM, Paris.

Bonnain-Moerdyk, R. (1975), L'espace gastronomique, *L'Espace Géographique*, 4(2), 113–26.

Bonnieux, F. and **Rainelli, P.** (1979), Une typologie des cantons littoraux de Bretagne, *Etudes et Statistiques Bretagne*, Octant No. 4, Nov.

Bounds, J. H. (1978), The Bahamas tourism industry: past, present and future, *Revista Geográfica*, 88, 167–219.

Boyer, J.-C. (1980), Residences secondaires et 'rurbanisation' en région parisienne, *Tijdschrift voor Economische en Sociale Geografie*, 71(2), 78–87.

Boyer, M. (1972), *Le Tourisme*, Editions du Seuil, Paris.

Brault, S. (1980), The use of research for developing tourism in New Caledonia, pp. 41–9 in D. G. Pearce (ed.), *Tourism in the South Pacific: the contribution of research to development and planning*, N.Z. MAB Report No. 6. N.Z. National Commission for Unesco/Department of Geography, University of Canterbury, Christchurch.

Britton, J. N. H. (1971), Methodology in flow analysis, *East Lakes Geographer*, 7, 22–36.

Britton, S. G. (1980a), A conceptual model of tourism in a peripheral economy, pp. 1–12 in D. G. Pearce (ed.), *Tourism in the South Pacific: the contribution of research to development and planning*, N.Z. MAB Report No. 6, N.Z. National Commission for Unesco/Department of Geography, University of Canterbury, Christchurch.

Britton, S. G. (1980b), The spatial organisation of tourism in a neo-colonial economy: a Fiji case study, *Pacific Viewpoint*, 21(2), 144–65.

Britton, S. G. (1982), The political economy of tourism in the Third World, *Annals of Tourism Research*, 9(3), 331–58.

Brumbaugh, M. (1983), Research on the new consumer, pp. 195–202 in *1983 PATA Travel Research Conference Proceedings*, Pacific Area Travel Association, San Francisco.

Bryant, C. R. (1973), L'agriculture face à la croissance métropolitaine: le cas des exploitations de grande culture expropriées par l'emprise de l'aéroport Paris Nord, *Economie Rurale*, 95, 23–35.

Bryden, J. (1973), *Tourism and Development: a case study of the Commonwealth Caribbean*, Cambridge University Press, New York.

BTA (1976), *Touring patterns of overseas motorists in Great Britain, summer, 1975*, British Tourist Authority, London.

BTA (1979a), *Tourism Growth and London Accommodation*, British Tourist Authority, London.

BTA (1979b), *International Tourism and Strategic Planning*, British Tourist Authority, London.

BTA (1981a), *Digest of Tourist Statistics No. 9*, British Tourist Authority, London.

BTA (1981b), *A Survey of Overseas Visitors to London, Summer 1981*, British Tourist Authority, London.

BTA (1981c), *Regional Spread and Accommodation and Transport Usage of Overseas Visitors to the UK 1978*, British Tourist Authority, London.

Burfitt, A. (1983), Research in Australian Tourism Commission Marketing, pp. 65–72 in *1983 PATA Travel Research Conference Proceedings*, Pacific Area Travel Association, San Francisco.

Burkart, A. J. (1971), Package holidays by air, *Tourist Review* 1971, 26(2), 54–64.

Burkart, A. J. and **Medlik, S.** (1974), *Tourism: past, present and future*, Heinemann, London.

Burnet, L. (1963), *Villégiature et Tourisme sur les Côtes de France*, Hachette, Paris.

Burnet, L. and **Valeix, M.-A.** (1967), Equipement hôtelier et tourisme, pp. 833–43 in *Atlas de Paris et de la Région Parisienne*, Berger-Levrault, Paris.

Burtenshaw, D. (1981), Austria, pp. 335–46 in Clout H. (ed.), *Regional Development in Western Europe* (2nd edn), Wiley, Chichester.

Burtenshaw, D., Bateman, M. and **Ashworth, G. J.** (1981), *The City in West Europe*, Wiley, Chichester.

Bush, R. I. and **Lipp, G.** (1983), The Pacific experience in implementing national and regional tourism plans – using Hawaii as an example, pp. 48–51 in *Proc. First Tourism Plan-*

ning Workshop: planning for tourism development, Pacific Area Travel Association, San Francisco.

Butler, R. W. (1980), The concept of a tourist area cycle of evolution: implications for management of resources, *Canadian Geographer*, **24**(1), 5–12.

Cadart, C. (1975). *Les Nouvelles Implantations Hôtelières à Paris et dans la Région Parisienne*, Mémoire de Maitrise (unpublished), Centre d'Etudes Supérieures de Tourisme, Paris.

Cals, J., Esteban, J. and **Teixidor, C.** (1977), Les processus d'urbanisation touristique sur la Costa Brava, *Revue Géographique des Pyrénées et du Sud-Ouest*, **48**, 199–208.

Cambau, D. and **Lefevre, G.** (1981), *Panorama of World Non-Scheduled Passenger Transport, Part Two: major origin–destination flows*, ITA Study No. 4, Institute de Transports Aériens, Paris.

Campbell, C. K. (1967), An approach to research in recreational geography, pp. 85–90 in *B.C. Occasional Papers No. 7*, Dept of Geography, University of British Columbia, Vancouver.

Carlson, A. S. (1938), Recreation industry of New Hampshire, *Economic Geography*, **14**, 255–70.

Carlson, A. W. (1978), The spatial behaviour involved in honeymoons: the case of two areas in Wisconsin and North Dakota, 1971–76, *J. of Population Culture*, **11**, 977–88.

Carter, M. R. (1971), A method of analysing patterns of tourist activity in a large rural area: the Highlands and Islands of Scotland, *Regional Studies*, **5**(1), 29–37.

Cazes, G. (1980), Les avances pionnières du tourisme international dans le Tiers-Monde: réflexions sur un système décisionnel multinational en cours de constitution, *Travaux de l'Institut de Géographie de Reims*, **43–44**, 15–26.

CECOD (1983), *Le Tourisme en France: Edition 1983 Réactualisé*, Centre d'Etude du Commerce et de la Distribution, Paris.

Central Planning Office (1980), *Fiji's Eighth Development Plan, 1981–1985. Vol. 2: Policies and Programmes for Regional Development*, Government Printer, Suva.

C.G.O.T. (1981), *Vacation Travel by Canadians in 1980*, Canadian Government Office of Tourism, Ottawa.

Chadefaud, M. (1981), *Lourdes: un pèlerinage, une ville*, Edisud, Aix-en-Provence.

Chenery, R. (1979), *A Comparative Study of Planning Considerations and Constraints Affecting Tourism Projects in the Principal European Capitals*, British Travel Educational Trust, London.

Christ, Y. (1971), *Les Metamorphoses de la Côte d'Azur*, Balland, Paris.

Christaller, W. (1964), Some considerations of tourism location in Europe, *Papers, Regional Science Association*, 95–105.

Ciaccio Campagnoli, C. (1975), Développement touristique et groupes de pression en Sicile, *Travaux de l'Institut de Géographie de Reims*, **23–24**, 81–7.

Ciaccio Campagnoli, C. (1979), The organisation of tourism in Sicily, *Weiner Geographische Schriften*, **53/54**, 132–42.

Clary, D. (1977), *La Façade Littorale de Paris: le tourisme sur la côte normande, étude géographique*, Editions Ophrys, Paris.

Clary, D. (1978), La frontière maritime de la Normandie et l'impact régional du tourisme internationale, *Etudes Normandes*, **2**, 39–54.

Cleverdon, R. and **Edwards, E.** (1982), *International Tourism to 1990*, Abt Books, Cambridge.

Cohen, E. (1978), Impact of tourism on the physical environment, *Annals of Tourism Research*, **5**(2), 215–37.

Conseil Supérieur du Tourisme (1978), *Développement Touristique et Protection du Patrimoine*, Conseil Superieur du Tourisme, Paris.

Cooper, C. P. (1981), Spatial and temporal patterns of tourist behaviour, *Regional Studies*, **15**, 359–71.

Cooper, M. (1980), The regional importance of tourism in Australia, *Australian Geographical Studies*, 1980, **18**(2), 146–54.

Coppock, J. T. (ed.) (1977), *Second Homes: curse or blessing?*, Pergamon, London.

Corsi, T. M. and **Harvey, M. E.** (1979), Changes in vacation travel in response to motor fuel shortages and higher prices, *J. Travel Research*, **17**(4), 6–11.

Council of City of Sydney (1980), *City of Sydney Strategic Plan*, Council of City of Sydney, Sydney.

Cribier, F. (1969), *La Grande Migration d'Eté des Citadins en France*, C.N.R.S., Paris.

Cribier, F. and **Kych, A.** (1977), *L'hébergement touristique dans les 318 stations du littoral français au coeur de l'été*, Laboratoire de Géographie Humaine, Paris.

Crompton, J. L. (1979), Motivations for pleasure vacation, *Annals of Tourism Research*, **6**(4), 408–24.

Cross, M. (1979), *Urbanization and Urban Growth in the Caribbean*, Cambridge University Press, Cambridge.

Cullinan, T. *et al*, *Central American Panama Circuit Tourism Study*, SRI International, Menlo Park.

Dann, G. M. S. (1977), Anomie, ego-enhancement and tourism, *Annals of Tourism Research*, **4**(4), 184–94.

Dann, G. M. S. (1981), Tourist motivation: an appraisal, *Annals of Tourism Research*, **8**(2), 187–219.

Deasy, G. F. and **Griess, P. R.** (1966), Impact of a tourist facility on its hinterland, *Annals Assn. American Geographers*, **55**(2), 290–306.

Defert, P. (1960), Introduction à une géographie touristique et thermale de l'Europe, *Acta Geographica*, **36**, 4–11.

Defert, P. (1966), *La Localisation Touristique: problèmes théoriques et pratiques.* Editions Gurten, Berne.

Defert, P. (1967), *Le Taux de Fonction Touristique: mise au point et critique*, Cahiers du Tourisme, C–13, C.H.E.T., Aix-en-Provence.

de Ganseman, P. (1982), *Hôtels de Bruxelles*, Projet de Licence (unpublished), Université Libre de Bruxelles, Brussels.

de Kadt, E. (1979), *Tourism: passport to development?*, Oxford University Press, Oxford.

Dewailly, J.-M. (1978), Un révélateur de contrastes régionaux: l'indice de confort des logements touristiques, *Travel Research Journal*, **1**, 23–9.

Dewailly, J.-M. (1979), Fascination et pesanteur d'une frontière pour le tourisme et la récréation: l'exemple franco-belge, *Frankfurter Wirtschafts – und Sozialgeographische Schriften*, Heft 31, 309–17.

Direccao Geral do Turismo (1980), *O Turismo Estrangeiro em Portugal: inquérito 1979*, Direccao Geral do Turismo, Lisbon.

Doering, T. R. (1976), A re-examination of the relative importance of tourism to state economies, *J. Travel Research*, **15**(1), 13–17.

Donehower, E. J. (1969), *The Impact of Dispersed Tourism in French Polynesia*, M.A. thesis (unpublished), University of Hawaii, Honolulu.

Duffield, B. S. (1984), The study of tourism in Britain–a geographical perspective, *GeoJournal*, **9**(1), 27–35.

Dumas, D. (1975), Un type d'urbanisation touristique littorale: la Manga del Mar Menor (Espagne), *Travaux de l'Institut de Géographie de Reims*, **23–24**, 89–96.

Dumas, D. (1976), L'urbanisation touristique du littoral de la Costa Blanca (Espagne), *Cahiers Nantais*, **13**, 43–50.

Dumas, D. (1982), Le commerce de détail dans une grande station touristique balnéaire espagnole: Benidorm, *Annales de Géographie*, **506**, 480–9.

Elliott, J. M. C. (1981), *Tourism in Christchurch*, M.A. thesis (unpublished), University of Canterbury, Christchurch.

Ellis, J. A. (1976), *Industrial Concentration*, Research Paper No. 20, N.Z. Institute of Economic Research, Wellington.

Elson, M. J. (1976), Activity spaces and recreational spatial behaviour, *Town Planning Review*, **47**(5), 241–55.

Equipo Investigador del IET y CIS (1980), Comportamiento vacacional y turístico de los Españoles (Enero–Septiembre 1979), *Estudios Turísticos*, **66**, 17–110.

Equipo Investigador del IET (1981), Comportamiento vacacional y turístico de los extranjeros: encuesta a extranjeros que visitaron algunas zonas de España, diciembre de 1980 y enero de 1981, *Estudios Turísticos*, **70/71**, 41–107.

Eriksson, G. A. (1981), Finnish charter tourism to the Mediterranean region in the 70s and 80s, Mimeo, Abo.

Estrada, A. (1973), Los vuelos charter: su nacimiento y evolución en España, *Estudios Turísticos*, **40**, 115–28.

ETB (n.d.a.), *A Study of Tourism in York*, English Tourist Board, London.

ETB (n.d.b.), *Towards a National Tourism Marketing and Development Strategy*, English Tourist Board, London.

ETB (1981a), *English Hotel Occupancy Survey*, English Tourist Board, London.

ETB (1981b), *England's Tourism*, English Tourist Board, London.

ETB (1981c), *Tourism and the Inner City*, English Tourist Board, London.

Etzel, M. J. and **Woodside, A. G.** (1982), Segmenting vacation markets: the case of distant and near-home travellers, *J. Travel Research*, **20**(4), 1982, 10–14.

Eversley, D. (1977), The ganglion of tourism: an unresolvable problem for London?, *London Journal*, **3**(2), 186–211.

Farrell, B. H. (1982), *Hawaii, the Legend that Sells*, University Press of Hawaii, Honolulu.

Federal Department of Forestry (1981), A case study of the growth of ski tourism and environmental stress in Switzerland, pp. 261–318 in *Case Studies on the Impact of Tourism on the Environment*, O.E.C.D., Paris.

Fernandez Fuster, L. (1974), *Teoría y Técnica del Turismo*, 4th edition, Editora Nacional, Madrid.

Ferras, R. (1975), Tourisme et urbanisation dans le Maresme Catalan, pp. 135–42 in *Tourisme et Vie Régionale dans les Pays Méditerranéens*, Actes du Colloque du Taormina, Centre Géographique d'Etudes et de Recherches Méditerranéens and Scuola di Studi Turistici in Rimini dell Universita di Bologna, Rimini.

Flament, E. (1973), *Capacité d'Accueil et Fréquentation Touristique du Littoral Belge*, Les Cahiers du Tourisme, Série B, No. 19, Centre d'Etudes du Tourisme, Aix-en-Provence.

Ford, L. R. (1979), Urban preservation and the geography of the city in the USA, *Progress in Human Geography*, **3**(2), 211–38.

Forer, P. C. and **Pearce, D. G.** (1984), Spatial

patterns of package tourism in New Zealand, *New Zealand Geographer*, **40**(1), 34–42.

Fornairon, J. D. (1978), Note sur l'origine des touristes fréquentant le littoral languedocien, *Economie Méridionale*, **25**(100), 67–73.

Fourneau, F. (1983), Loisirs de proximité et résidences secondaires autour d'une métropole régionale: le cas de Seville, *Norois*, **120**, 619–24.

Franz, J. C. (1983), Development and growth of seaside resorts in Southeast Asia, Paper presented at the 15th Pacific Science Congress, Dunedin.

Funnell, C. (1975), *By the Beautiful Sea: the rise and high times of that great American resort, Atlantic City*, Knopf, New York.

Garcia, M. V. (1976), Social production and consumption of tourist space: outline of methods applied to the study of the Bay of Palma, Majorca, pp. 83–94 in ECE, *Planning and Development of the Tourist Industry in the ECE Region*, United Nations, New York.

Gardavsky, V. (1977), Second homes in Czechoslovakia, pp. 63–74 in Coppock J. T. (ed.), *Second Homes: curse or blessing?*, Pergamon, London.

Garrett, W. (1980a), Review of the difference between the Quebec French market and selected English markets, pp. 160–93 in Wilson C. (ed.), *Caribbean Tourism Markets: Structures and Strategies*, Caribbean Tourism Research and Development Centre, Christ Church.

Garrett, W. (1980b), The Canadian travel market to sun destinations and outlook for potential growth, pp. 135–59 in Wilson C. (ed.), *Caribbean Tourism Markets: structures and strategies*, Caribbean Tourism Research and Development Centre, Christ Church.

Gaviría, M. *et al* (1974), *España a Go-Go. Turismo charter y neocolonialismo del espacio*, Ediciones Turner, Madrid.

Gaviría, M. (1975), *Turismo de Playa en España*, Ediciones Turner, Madrid.

Gazillo, S. (1981), The evolution of restaurants and bars in Vieux-Quebec since 1900, *Cahiers de Géographie du Quebec*, **25**(64), 101–18.

Gibson, L. J. and **Reeves, R. W.** (1972), The spatial behaviour of camping America: observations from the Arizona Strip, *Rocky Mountain Social Science Journal*, **9**(2), 19–30.

Gilbert, E. W. (1939), The growth of inland and seaside health resorts in England, *Scottish Geographical Magazine*, **55**, 16–35.

Gilbert, E. W. (1949), The growth of Brighton, *Geographical Journal*, **114**, 30–52.

Gillmor, D. A. (1973), Irish holidays abroad: the growth and destinations of chartered inclusive tours, *Irish Geography*, **6**(5), 618–25.

Ginier, J. (1974), *Géographie Touristique de la France*, SEDES, Paris.

Girard, P. S. T. (1968), Geographical aspects of tourism in Guernsey, *La Société Guernesiaise Reports and Transactions*, **18**(2), 185–205.

Girault, C. (1978), Tourisme et dépendance en Haiti, *Cahiers des Amériques Latines Série Sciences de l'Homme*, **17**, 23–56.

Girault, C. (1980), Gulf + Western en République Dominicaine. De l'enclave sucrière au controle d'une partie de l'économie nationale, *L'Espace Géographique*, **9**(3), 223–9.

Girodin, P. (1981), L'Hôtellerie française consomme mais préserve aussi l'espace, pp. 138–49 in *La Consommation d'Espace par le Tourisme et sa Préservation*, C.H.E.T., Aix-en-Provence.

Goldsmith, O. F. R. and **Forrest, J.** (1982), Spatial context of holiday travel, pp. 214–18 in *Proc. 11th N.Z. Geog. Conf.*, N.Z. Geog. Soc., Wellington.

Goonatilake, S. (1978), *Tourism in Sri Lanka: the mapping of international inequalities and their internal structural effects*, Working Paper No. 19, Centre for Developing-Area Studies, McGill University, Montreal.

Gormsen, E. (1981), The spatio-temporal development of international tourism: attempt at a centre-periphery model, pp. 150–70 in *La Consommation d'Espace par le Tourisme et sa Préservation*, C.H.E.T., Aix-en-Provence.

Gormsen, E. (1982), Tourism as a development factor in tropical countries – a case study of Cancun, Mexico, *Applied Geography and Development*, **19**, 46–63.

Grant, R. H. (1974), *Planning controls for motels*, Diploma of Town Planning Dissertation (unpublished), University of Auckland, Auckland.

Gray, H. P. (1970), *International Travel–International Trade*, Heath Lexington, Lexington.

Greer, T. and **Wall, G.** (1979), Recreational hinterlands: a theoretical and empirical analysis, pp. 227–45 in Wall G. (ed.), *Recreational Land Use in Southern Ontario*, Department of Geography Publication Series, No. 14, University of Waterloo.

Grimmeau, J. P. (1980), Petite géographie du tourisme étranger en Belgique, *Revue Belge de Géographie*, **104**(5), 99–110.

Gueorguiev, A. and **Andonov, M.** (1974), *Développement et Perspectives du Tourisme International sur le Littoral Bulgare de la Mer Noire*, Cahiers du Tourisme, Series B, No. 11, Centre d'Etudes du Tourisme, Aix-en-Provence.

Gunn, C. A. (1972), *Vacationscape: designing*

tourist regions, University of Texas, Austin.

Gunn, C. A. (1979), *Tourism Planning,* Crane Rusak, New York.

Guthrie, H. W. (1961), Demand for tourists goods and services in a world market, *Papers, Regional Science Assn,* **7**, 159–75.

Gutiérrez Ronco, S. (1977), Localización actual de la hostelería madrileña, *Boletin de la Real Sociedad Geografica 1976,* part 2, 347–57.

Gutiérrez Ronco, S. (1980), Evolución en la localización de la hostelería madrileña, pp. 283–8 in *Jornadas de Estudios sobre la Provincia de Madrid,* Diputación Provincial de Madrid, Madrid.

Hall, P. (1970), A horizon of hotels, *New Society,* 12 March 1970, 445.

Herbin, J. (1982), Le tourisme hivernal dans les Alpes Autro-Allemandes: présentation d'une étude cartographique, pp. 201–10 in *Montagne et Aménagement,* Institut de Géographie Alpine, Grenoble.

Hills, T. L. and **Lundgren, J.** (1977), The impact of tourism in the Caribbean: a methodological study, *Annals of Tourism Research,* **4**(5), 248–67.

Hoivik, T. and **Heiberg, T.** (1980), Centreperiphery tourism and self-reliance, *Int. Soc. Sci. J.,* **32**(1), 69–98.

Holm-Petersen, E. (1978), *Consequences of mass tourism in developing countries. Case studies of the Seychelles and the Gambia,* The author, Copenhagen.

Hong Kong Tourist Association (1983), *A Statistical Review of Tourism, Hong Kong 1982,* Hong Kong Tourist Assn., Hong Kong.

Horwath and Horwath (1981), *L'Hôtellerie Parisienne,* Horwath and Horwath, France, Paris.

Hudman, L. E. (1979), Origin regions of international tourism, *Weiner Geographische Schriften,* **53/54**, 43–9.

Hudman, L. E. (1980), *Tourism: a shrinking world,* Grid Inc., Columbus.

Huetz de Lemps, A. (1976), *L'Espagne,* Masson, Paris.

Hugill, P. J. (1975), Social conduct on the Golden Mile, *Annals of Assn. of American Geographers,* **62**(2), 214–28.

Ilbery, B. W. (1981), *Western Europe: a systematic human geography,* O.U.P., Oxford.

Institut National de Statistiques (1980), *Enquête Vacances 1978–1979,* Institut National de Statistiques, Brussels.

Instituto Centrale di Statistica (1977), *Indagine speciale sulle vacanze degli italiani nel 1975,* Note et Relazioni No. 55, Instituto Centrale di Statistica, Rome.

Ishii, H. (1982), Distribution of major recreational regions in Japan, *Frankfurter Wirtschafts – und Sozialgeographische Schriften,* **41**, 187–203.

Iso-Ahola, S. E. (1982), Toward a social psychological theory of tourism motivation: a rejoinder, *Annals of Tourism Research,* **9**(2), 256–61.

IUOTO (International Union of Official Travel Organisations) (1975), *The Impact of International Tourism on the Economic Development of the Developing Countries,* IUOTO/WTO, Geneva.

Jackowski, A. (1980), Methodological problems of functional typology of tourist localities, *Folia Geographica, Series Geographica-Oeconomica,* **13**, 85–91.

Jackson, E. L. and **Schinkel, D. R.** (1981), Recreational activity preferences of resident and tourist campers in the Yellowknife region, *Canadian Geographer,* **25**(4), 350–63.

Jackson, R. T. (1973), Problems of tourist industry development on the Kenyan coast, *Geography,* **58**(1), 62–5.

Janin, B. (1982), Circulation touristique internationale et tourisme étranger en Val d'Aoste, *Revue de Géographie Alpine,* **70**(4), 415–30.

Japanese National Travel Organisation (1976), *Now and the Future of Japanese Domestic Tourism,* J.N.T.O., Tokyo.

Johnston, D. C., Pearce, D. G. and **Cant, R. G.** (1976), Canterbury holidaymakers: a preliminary study of internal tourism, pp. 5–19 in Cant R. G. (ed.), *Canterbury at Leisure,* Publication No. 4, Canterbury Branch, N.Z. Geog. Soc., Christchurch.

Kain, R. (1978–79), Conservation planning in France: policy and practise in the Marais, Paris, *Urbanism Past and Present,* **7**, 22–34.

Kamp, B. D., Crompton, D. M. and **Hensarling, D. M.** (1979), The reactions of travellers to gasoline rationing and to increases in gasoline prices, *J. Travel Research,* **18**(1), 37–41.

Keogh, B. (1980), Motivations and the choice decisions of skiers, *Tourist Review,* **35**(1), 18–22.

Keogh, B. (1984), The measurement of spatial variations in tourist activity, *Annals of Tourism Research,* **11**(2), 267–82.

Kikue, T. (1975), Japan and Korea: Kisaeng tourism, pp. 31–7 in O'Grady R. (ed.), *Tourism, the Asian Dilemma,* Christian Conference of Asia, Singapore.

Knafou, R. (1978), *Les Stations Intégrées de Sports d'Hiver des Alpes Françaises,* Masson, Paris.

Knox, A. D. (1967), Some economic problems of small countries, pp. 35–44 in Benedict B. (ed.), *Problems of Smaller Territories,* The Athlone Press, London.

Lacroix, J., Roux, B. and **Zoido Naranjo, F.** (1979), La 'Costa de la Luz' de Cadix: le cas de

Chipiona, pp. 117–239 in Bernal A. M. *et al.*, *Tourisme et Développement Régional en Andalousie*, Editions de Boccard, Paris.

Langenbuch, J. R. (1977), Os municipios turisticos do estado de Sao Paulo: determinaçao e caracterizaçao geral, *Geografia*, **2**(3), 1–49.

Lavery, P. (1974), The demand for recreation, pp. 22–48 in P. Lavery (ed.), *Recreational Geography*, David and Charles, Newton Abbot.

Lawson, F. and **Baud-Bovy, M.** (1977), *Tourism and Recreation Development*, The Architectural Press, London.

Leiper, N. (1984a), Tourism and leisure: the significance of tourism in the leisure spectrum, pp. 249–53 in *Proc. 12th N.Z. Geography Conference*, N.Z. Geog. Soc., Christchurch.

Leiper, N. (1984b), International travel by Australians, 1946 to 1983: travel propensities and travel frequencies, pp. 67–83 in B. O'Rourke (ed.), *Contemporary Issues in Australian Tourism*, Department of Geography, University of Sydney, Sydney.

Levantis, G. (1981), *Analyse Factorielle du Phenomène Touristique: l'espace touristique grec*, Centre des Hautes Etudes Touristiques, Aix-en-Provence.

Lichtenberger, E. R. (1984), Geography of tourism and leisure society in Austria, *GeoJournal*, **9**(1), 41–6.

Liu, J. C. (1983), Hotel industry performance and planning at the regional level, pp. 211–33 in P. E. Murphy (ed.), *Tourism in Canada: selected issues and options*, Western Geographical Series Vol. 21, University of Victoria, Victoria.

Lockheed-California (1980), *Gateway Fragmentation Analysis: the transatlantic market*, EATF No. 2975, Lockheed-California Coy, Burbank.

Longmire, I. M. (1978), *Summer Tourism in Tauranga and Mt Maunganui*, M.A. thesis (unpublished), University of Auckland, Auckland.

Lowe, J. C. and **Moryadas, S.** (1975), *The Geography of Movement*, Houghton Mifflin, Boston.

Lundgren, J. O. J. (1966), Tourism in Quebec, *Revue de Géographie de Montreal*, **20**(le2), 59–73.

Lundgren, J. O. J. (1972), The development of tourist travel systems – a metropolitan economic hegemony par excellence, *Jahrbuch für Fremdenverkehr*, 20 Jahrgang, 86–120.

Lundgren, J. O. J. (1974), On access to recreational lands in dynamic metropolitan hinterlands, *Tourist Review*, **29**(4), 124–31.

Lundgren, J. O. J. (1975), Tourist penetration/the tourist product/entrepreneurial response, pp. 60–70 in *Tourism as a Factor in National and Regional Development*, Occasional Paper 4, Department of Geography, Trent University, Peterborough.

Lundgren, J. O. J. (1982), The tourist frontier of Nouveau Quebec: functions and regional linkages, *Tourist Review*, **37**(2), 10–16.

Lundgren, J. O. J. (1984), Geographic concepts and the development of tourism research in Canada, *GeoJournal*, **9**(1), 17–25.

McAllister, D. M. and **Klett, F. R.** (1976), A modified gravity model of regional recreation activity with an application to ski trips, *J. Leisure Research*, **8**(1), 22–34.

MacCannell, D. (1976), *The Tourist: a new theory of the leisure class*, Macmillan, London.

McCool, S. F. (1980), Vacation travel and fuel shortages: a critical comment, *J. Travel Research*, **19**(2), 18–19.

McDonnell Douglas (1981), *Route Dispersion: a growing trend in air transport*, McDonnell Douglas, Longbeach.

McEachern, J. and **Towle, E. L.** (1974), *Ecological Guidelines for Island Development*, International Union for the Conservation of Nature, Morges.

McIntyre, A. (1983), Statistics never lie, *Talanoa*, Jan, 15–16.

Malamud, B. (1973), Gravity model calibration of tourist travel to Las Vegas, *J. Leisure Research*, **5**(1), 23–33.

Mankour, N. (1980), Localisation et function des équipements touristiques étatiques algériens, *Cahiers Géographiques de l'Ouest*, **4**, 46–57.

Marenne, J. and **Puissant, D.** (1979), Transport régulier et transport charter: concurrence ou complementarité, *Revue Belge de Géographie*, **103**(2), 69–88.

Marsden, B. S. (1969), Holiday homescapes of Queensland, *Aust. Geog. Studies*, **7**(1), 57–72.

Mathieson, Alister and **Wall, Geoffrey** (1982), *Tourism: economic, physical and social impacts*, Longman, Harlow.

Matley, I. M. (1976), *The Geography of International Tourism*, Resource Paper No. 76–1, Assn. of American Geographers, Washington.

Mayo, E. J. (1974), A model of motel-choice, *Cornell Hotel and Restaurant Administration Quarterly*, **15**(3), 55–64.

Menanteau, L. and **Martin Vincente, A.** (1979), Environement et Tourisme, pp. 241–304 in A. M. Bernal *et al*, *Tourisme et Développement Régional en Andalousie*, Editions de Boccard, Paris.

Mercer, D. C. (1970), The geography of leisure: a contemporary growth-point, *Geography*, **55**(3), 261–73.

Mercer, D. C. (1971), Discretionary travel behaviour and the urban mental map, *Aust. Geog. Studies*, **9**, 133–43.

Mignon, C. and **Heran, F.** (1979), La Costa del Sol et son arrière-pays, pp. 53–133 in A.M.

Bernal et al., *Tourisme et Développement Régional en Andalousie*, Editions de Boccard, Paris.

Mings, R. C. (1982), Classroom use of the National Travel Survey: a recreation travel exercise, *Journal of Geography*, **81**(2), 215–23.

Miossec, J. M. (1976), *Eléments pour une Théorie de l'Espace Touristique*, Les Cahiers du Tourisme, C–36, C.H.E.T., Aix-en-Provence.

Miossec, J. M. (1977), Un modèle de l'espace touristique, *L'Espace Géographique*, **6**(1), 41–8.

Mirloup, J. (1974), Eléments méthodologiques pour une étude de l'équipment hôtelier: l'exemple des départements de la Loire moyenne, *Norois*, **83**, 443–52 and **84**, 563–83.

Mitchell, L. S. (1984), Tourism research in the United States: a geographic perspective, *GeoJournal*, **9**(1), 5–15.

Molnar, E., Mihail, M. and **Maier, A.** (1976), Types de localités touristiques dans la République Socialiste de Roumanie, *Revue Roumaine de Géologie, Géophysique et Géographie, Série de Géographie*, **20**, 189–95.

Moran, W. (1979), Processes and policies for land use diversification, *Proc. 10th N.Z. Geog. Conf. and 49th ANZAAS Congress*, N.Z. Geog. Society, Auckland, pp. 240–5.

Morgan Research Centre (1982), *Domestic Tourism Monitor, 1981–82* (unpublished), Morgan Research Centre, Sydney.

Murphy, P. E. (1980), Tourism management using land use planning and landscape design: the Victoria experience, *Canadian Geographer*, **24**(1), 60–71.

Murphy, P. E. (1982), Tourism planning in London: an exercise in spatial and seasonal management, *Tourist Review*, **37**(1), 19–22.

Murphy, P. E. and **Brett, A. C.** (1982), Regional tourism patterns in British Columbia: a discriminatory analysis, pp. 151–61 in T. V. Singh, J. Kaur and D. P. Singh (eds), *Studies in Tourism Wildlife Parks Conservation*, Metropolitan Book Co., New Delhi.

Murphy, P. E. and **Rosenblood, L.** (1974), Tourism: an exercise in spatial search, *Canadian Geographer*, **18**(3), 201–10.

Myrdal, G. (1957), *Economic Theory and Under-Developed Regions*, Duckworth, London.

National Planning Office (1983), *Republic of Vanuatu: First National Development Plan, 1982–1986*, National Planning Office, Port Vila.

Newcomb, R. M. (1979), *Planning the Past*, Dawson, Folkestone and Archon, Hamden.

Nishiyama, K. (1973), *Japanese Tourists Abroad*, The author, Honolulu.

NZ TPD (1983), *New Zealand International Visitors Travel Survey 1982, Vol. 1*, N.Z. Tourist and Publicity Department, Wellington.

ODT (1980), *Etude de Satisfaction*, Office de Développement du Tourisme, Tahiti.

Odouard, A. (1973), Le tourisme et les Iles Canaries, *Les Cahiers d'Outre-Mer*, **102**, 150–71.

O'Hagan, J. W. (1979), *The dispersal pattern of United States tourists in Europe, 1967–1977*, European Travel Commission, Dublin.

Ohler, K. E. (1971), *The Distribution of Inns, Hotels and Motels in Somerset County, Pennsylvania: a geographical sequential analysis*, M.A. thesis (unpublished), University of Pennsylvania, Indiana.

Opinion Research Corporation (1980), *A Study of Potential U.S. Vacation Visitors to the Pacific Area: executive summary*, PATA, San Francisco.

O. T. T. N.–C. (1983), *Le Tourisme en Nouvelle-Calédonie*, Office Territorial du Tourisme de Nouvelle-Calédonie, Noumea.

Owen, M. L. and **Duffield, B. S.** (1971), *The Touring Caravan in Scotland*, Scottish Tourist Board, Edinburgh.

P. A. Management Consultants (1975), *The Role of Tourism and Recreation in the Albury–Wodonga Growth Centre*, Australian Department of Tourism and Recreation, Canberra.

PATA (n.d.), *The Role of Jakarta and West Java in Indonesian Tourism*, Pacific Area Travel Association, San Francisco.

Pearce, D. G. (1978a), Demographic variations in international travel, *Tourist Review*, **33**(1), 4–9.

Pearce, D. G. (1978b), *Tourism in France: regional perspectives*, Canterbury Monographs for Teachers of French, No. 3 (Fifth Series), Department of French, University of Canterbury.

Pearce, D. G. (1978c), Form and function in French resorts, *Annals of Tourism Research*, **5**(1), 142–56.

Pearce, D. G. (1979a), Towards a geography of tourism, *Annals of Tourism Research*, **6**(3), 245–72.

Pearce, D. G. (1979b), Geographical aspects of tourism in New Zealand, pp. 327–31 in *Proc. 10th N.Z. Geog. Conf. and 49th ANZAAS Congress (Geographical Sciences)*, N.Z. Geog. Soc., Auckland.

Pearce, D. G. (1981a), L'espace touristique de la grande ville: éléments de synthèse et application à Christchurch (Nouvelle-Zélande), *L'Espace Géographique*, **10**(3), 207–13.

Pearce, D. G. (1981b), Estimating visitor expenditure, a review and a New Zealand case study, *Int. J. Tourism Management*, **2**(4), 240–52.

Pearce, D. G. (1981c), *Tourist Development*, Longman, London.

Pearce, D. G. (1982a), Preparing a national tourist geography: the New Zealand example, pp. 136–49 in T. V. Singh, J. Kaur and D. P. Singh (eds), *Studies in Tourism, Wildlife Parks, Conservation*, Metropolitan Book Co., New Delhi.

Pearce, D. G. (1982b), *Westland National Park Economic Impact Study*, Department of Lands and Survey/Department of Geography, University of Canterbury, Christchurch.

Pearce, D. G. (1983a), Intra-regional traffic in the South Pacific, pp. 22–33 in *1983 PATA Travel Research Conference Proceedings*, Pacific Area Travel Association, San Francisco.

Pearce, D. G. (1983b), The development and impact of large-scale tourism projects: Languedoc-Roussillon (France) and Cancun (Mexico) compared, pp. 59–71 in C. C. Kissling et al. (eds), *Papers, 7th Australian/N.Z. Regional Science Assn*, Canberra.

Pearce, D. G. (1984a), International tourist flows: an integrated approach with examples from French Polynesia, pp. 254–8 in *Proc. 12th N.Z. Geography Conference*, N.Z. Geog. Soc., Christchurch.

Pearce, D. G. (1984b), Planning for tourism in Belize, *Geographical Review*, 74(3), 291–303.

Pearce, D. G. and Elliott, J. M. C. (1983), The Trip Index, *J. Travel Research*, 22(1), 6–9.

Pearce, D. G. and Grimmeau, J.–P. (1985), The spatial structure of tourist accommodation and hotel demand in Spain, *Geoforum*, 16(1), 37–50.

Pearce, D. G. and Mings, R. C. (1984), Geography, tourism and recreation in the Antipodes, *GeoJournal*, 9(1), 91–5.

Péré, M. (1975), Le développement touristique de la côte méditerranéene du Maroc, pp. 303 8 in *Tourisme et Vie Régionale and les Pays Méditerranéens*, Actes du Colloque du Taormina, Centre Géographique d'Etudes et de Recherches Méditerranéens and Scuola di Studi Turistici in Rimini dell 'Universita di Bologna, Rimini.

Piatier, A. (1956), *Sondages et Enquêtes au Service du Tourisme*, Geneva.

Piavaux, C.–M. (1977), *Valorisation de l'Environnement par le Tourisme dans le Luxembourg Belge. Propositions de specialisation par compartiments touristiques*, Fondation Universitaire Luxembourgeoise, Arlon, 1977.

Pigram, J. J. (1977), Beach resort morphology, *Habitat International*, 2(5–6), 525–41.

Plettner, H. J. (1979), *Geographical Aspects of Tourism in the Republic of Ireland*, Research Paper No. 9, Social Sciences Research Centre, University College, Galway.

Plog, S. C. (1973), Why destination areas rise and fall in popularity, *Cornell H. R. A. Quarterly*, November, 13–16.

Pollock, A. M., Tunner, A. and Crawford, G. S. (1975), *Visitors 74: a study of visitors to British Columbia in the summer of 1974*, B.C. Research, Vancouver.

Poncet, J. (1976), Le développement du tourisme en Bulgarie, *Annales de Géographie*, 468, 155–77.

Porteous, J. D. (1981), *The Modernization of Easter Island*, Western Geographical Series Vol. 19, University of Victoria, Victoria.

Potter, R. B. (1981), Tourism and development: the case of Barbados, West Indies, *Geography*, 68, 46–50.

Poulsen, T. M. (1977), Migration on the Adriatic Coast: some processes associated with the development of tourism, pp. 197–215 in H. L. Kostanick (ed.), *Population and Migration Trends in Eastern Europe*, Westview Press, Boulder.

Pred, A. (1965), Industrialization, initial advantage, and American metropolitan growth, *Geographical Review*, 55(2), 158–85.

Price, R. L. (1981), Tourist landscapes and tourist regions, a preliminary framework, Paper presented at the annual meeting of the AAAG, Los Angeles.

Rajotte, F. (1975), The different travel patterns and spatial framework of recreation and tourism, pp. 43–52 in *Tourism as a Factor in National and Regional Development*, Department of Geography, Trent University, Occasional Paper 4, Peterborough.

Rajotte, F. (1977), Evaluating the cultural and environmental impact of Pacific tourism, *Pacific Perspective*, 6(1), 41–8.

Relph, E. (1976), *Place and Placelessness*, Pion, London.

Richez, G. and Richez-Battesti, J. (1982), Tourisme et mutations socio-économiques en Corse et à Mallorca, *Etudes Corses*, 10, 18–19, 329–61.

Ritter, W. (1975), Recreation and tourism in the Islamic countries, *Ekistics*, 236, 56–9.

Robinson, G. W. S. (1953), The geographical region: form and function, *Scottish Geographical Magazine*, 69(2), 51–7.

Robinson, G. W. S. (1972), The recreation geography of South Asia, *Geographical Review*, 62(4), 561–72.

Robinson, H. (1976), *A Geography of Tourism*, Macdonald and Evans, London.

Rogers, A. W. (1977), Second homes in England and Wales: a spatial view, pp. 85–102 in J. T. Coppock (ed.), *Second Homes: curse or blessing?*, Pergamon, Oxford.

Rojo, J. (1970), *Les Touristes de Paris*, Atelier Parisien d'Urbanisme, Paris.

Royer, L. E., McCool, S. F. and Hunt, J. D. (1974), The relative importance of tourism to state economies, *J. Travel Research*, 24(1), 13–16.

Ruppert, K. (1978), Mise au point sur une géographie générale des loisirs, *L'Espace Géographique*, **7**(3), 187–93.

Ryan, B. (1965), The dynamics of recreational development on the South Coast of New South Wales, *Australian Geographer*, **9**(6), 331–48.

Sarramea, J. (1978), L'origine géographique des touristes au cours d'une année, méthodes de recherches et exemple de Fréjus-Saint Raphael, *Méditerranée*, **33**(3), 67–73.

Sarramea, J. (1979), Origine géographique des touristes estivaux à Méribel, *Revue de Géographie Alpine*, **67**(1), 105–11.

Schewe, C. D. and **Calantone, R. J.** (1978), Psychographic segmentation of tourists, *J. of Travel Research*, **16**(3), 14–20.

Schmidhauser, H. P. (1975), Travel propensity and travel frequency, pp. 53–60 in A. J. Burkart and S. Medlik (eds), *The Management of Tourism*, Heinemann, London.

Schmidhauser, H. P. (1976), The Swiss travel market and its role within the main tourist generating countries of Europe, *Tourist Review* **31**(4), 15–18.

Schmidhauser, H. P. (1977), *Le Marché Touristique Suisse*, Institut du Tourisme de l'Ecole des Hautes Etudes Economiques et Sociales de Saint Gall, Saint Gall.

Secrétariat d'Etat au Tourisme (1977), Les flux interrégionaux de départ en vacances, *Statistiques du Tourisme*, 16.

Service de la Recherche Socio-Economique (1977), *Le Touriste Non-Résident au Quebec 1975*, Vol. III, Données de Base II, Ministere du Tourisme, de la Chasse et de la Pêche, Quebec.

Shand, R. T. (1980), Island smallness: some definitions and implications, pp. 3–20 in R. T. Shand (ed.), *The Island States of the Pacific and Indian Oceans: anatomy of development*, Development Studies Monograph no. 23, Australian National University, Canberra.

Shirasaka, S. (1982), Foreign visitors flow in Japan, *Frankfurter Wirtschafts – und Sozial geographische Schriften*, Heft 41, 205–18.

Singapore Tourist Promotion Board (1980), *Survey of Overseas Visitors to Singapore, 1979*, Singapore Tourist Promotion Board, Singapore.

Smith, R. H. T. (1970), Concepts and methods in commodity flow analysis, *Economic Geography*, **46**(2), 404–16.

Smith, S. L. J. (1983a), *Recreation Geography*, Longman, London.

Smith, S. L. J. (1983b), Restaurants and dining out: geography of a tourism business, *Annals of Tourism Research*, **10**(4), 515–49.

Smith, V. L. (ed.) (1977), *Hosts and Guests: the anthropology of tourism*, Pennsylvania Press, Philadelphia.

Solomon, P. J. and **George, W. R.** (1977), The bicentennial traveler: a life-style analysis of the historian segment, *J. of Travel Research*, **15**(3), 14–17.

Soumagne, J. (1974), Cherbourg: la fonction d'escale maritime des touristes brittaniques, *Norois*, **82**, 223–39.

Spack, A. (1975), Aspects et problèmes touristiques en milieux urbains et periurbains: l'exemple de la ville de Metz et du pays messin, *Mosella*, **4**(1/2), 1–238.

Spill, J.–M. (1976), Les charters en Méditerranée, *Annales de Géographie*, **468**, 206–24.

Sprincova, S. (1968), Tourism as a regionalizing factor, pp. 197–210 in Koloman, I. (ed.), *Function and Forming of Regions*, Slovak Pedagogical Publishers, Bratislava.

Stang, F. (1979), Internationaler Tourismus in Indien, *Erdkunde*, **33**(1), 52–60.

Stansfield, C. A. (1964), A note on the urban–nonurban imbalance in American recreational research, *Tourist Review*, **19**(4), 196–200 and **20**(1), 21–3.

Stansfield, C. A. (1969), Recreational land use patterns within an American seaside resort, *Tourist Review*, **24**(4), 128–36.

Stansfield, C. A. (1978), Atlantic City and the resort cycle: background to the legalization of gambling, *Annals of Tourism Research*, **5**(2), 238–51.

Stansfield, C. A. and **Rickert, J. E.** (1970), The Recreational Business District, *J. Leisure Research*, **2**(4), 213–25.

Steinecke, A. (1979), An analysis of differences between the travel attitudes and demand patterns of diverse visitor groups and their reaction to political–military conflicts: the Republic of Ireland as a case study, *Weiner Geographische Schriften*, **53/54**, Part II, 114–31.

Swizewski, C. and **Oancea, D. I.** (1978), La carte des types de tourisme de Roumanie, *Revue Roumaine de Géologie Géophysique et Géographie, Série Géographie*, **23**(2), 291–4.

Symanski, R. and **Burley, N.** (1973), *Tourist development in the Dominican Republic: an overview and an example*, Paper presented at the Conference of Latin American Geographers, Calgary (mimeo).

Takeuchi, K. (1984), Some remarks on the geography of tourism in Japan, *GeoJournal*, **9**(1), 85–90.

Thompson, P. T. (1971), *The Use of Mountain Recreational Resources: a comparison of recreation and tourism in the Colorado Rockies and the Swiss Alps*, University of Colorado, Boulder.

Thurot, J. M. (1973), *Le Tourisme Tropical Balnéaire: le modele caraibe et ses extensions*, Thesis, Centre d'Etudes du Tourisme, Aix-en-Provence.

Thurot, J. M. (1980), *Capacité de Charge et Production Touristique*, Etudes et Mémoires No. 43, Centre des Hautes Etudes Touristiques, Aix-en-Provence.

Tokuhisa, T. (1980), Tourism within, from and to Japan, *Int. Soc. Sci. J.*, **32**(1), 128–50.

Tourism Planning and Research Ltd (1977), *Thames and Chilterns Tourism Study*, English Tourist Board, London.

Travis, A. S. (1982), Managing the environmental and cultural impacts of tourism and leisure development, *Tourism Management*, **3**(4), 256–62.

Turner, L. and **Ash, J.** (1975), *The Golden Hordes: international tourism and the pleasure periphery*, Constable, London.

Turnock, D. (1977), Rumania and the geography of tourism, *Geoforum*, **8**(1), 51–6.

United Nations (1970), *Report of the Interregional Seminar on Physical Planning for Tourist Development*, Dubrovnik, Yugoslavia, 19 October–3 November 1970, ST/TAO/Ser. C/131, United Nations, New York.

Valenzuela Rubio, M. (1981), La incidencia de los grandes equipamientos recreativos en la configuración del espacio turístico litoral: la Costa de Málaga, Paper presented at the Coloquio Hispano-Francés Sobre Espacios Litorales, Madrid (mimeo).

van Doren, C. S. and **Gustke, L. D.** (1982), Spatial analysis of the U.S. lodging industry, 1963–1977, *Annals of Tourism Research*, **9**(4), 543–63.

van Wagtendonk, J. W. (1980), Visitor use patterns in Yosemite National Park, *J. Travel Research*, **19**(2), 12–17.

Vanderheyden, A. (1979), L'offre touristique de quelques tours operators belges, *Travaux Géographiques de Liège*, **167**, 63–78.

Vanhove, N. (1980), Le littoral belge, *Hommes et Terres du Nord*, 4, 52–62.

Vetter, F. (1974), Le tourisme dans les grandes villes: Berlin, *Espaces*, **5–6–7**, 30–41.

Vetter, F. (1975), Present changes in West German big city tourism, pp. 53–9 in *Tourism as a Factor in National and Regional Development*, Occasional Paper 4, Department of Geography, Trent University, Peterborough.

Vetter, F. (1976), The economic impact of tourism upon big cities, pp. 114–18 in *Geography of Tourism and Recreation, Proc. 13th International Congress*, Moscow.

Vila Fradera (1966), Trois cas d'actions de l'Etat pour la localisation touristique dans la nouvelle legislation espagnole, *Tourist Review*, **21**(4), 161–3.

Villegas Molina, F. (1975), Areas turísticas andaluzas, *Boletin de la Real Sociedad Geografica*, **1**, 309–22.

Vuoristo, K.–V. (1969), On the geographical features of tourism in Finland, *Fennia*, **99**(3), 1–48.

Vuoristo, K.–V. (1981), Tourism in Eastern Europe: development and regional patterns, *Fennia*, **159**(1), 237–47.

Wall, G. (1971), Car-owners and holiday activities, pp. 106–7 in Lavery, P. (ed.), *Recreational Geography*, David and Charles, London.

Wall, G. (1982), Cycles and capacity: incipient theory or conceptual contradiction, *Tourism Management*, **3**(3), 188–92.

Wall, G. and **Sinnott, J.** (1980), Urban recreational and cultural facilities as tourist attractions, *Canadian Geographer*, **24**(1), 50–9.

Ward, M. (1975), Dependent development – problems of economic planning in small developing countries, pp. 115–33 in P. Selwyn (ed.), *Development Policy in Small Countries*, Croom Helm, London.

Washer, R. M. (1977), *Holiday Homes on Banks Peninsula: an Impact Assessment*, M.A. thesis (unpublished), University of Canterbury, Christchurch.

Weiss, C. R. (1971), *An exploratory cross-national study of older foreign tourists*, Ed.D. thesis, Columbia University, University Microfilms, Ann Arbor.

White, A. (1973), *Summer Tourism in the Rotorua Basin*, M.A. thesis (unpublished), University of Auckland, Auckland.

White, P. and **Woods, R.** (1980), *The Geographical Impact of Migration*, Longman, London.

White, W. R. (1969), *Location of Motels in a Resort Area: an analysis of motel location in Barnstable County, Massachusetts*, M.A. thesis (unpublished), Clark University, Worcester.

Williams, A. V. and **Zelinsky, W.** (1970), On some patterns of international tourist flows, *Economic Geography*, **46**(4), 549–67.

Williams, P. W., Burke, J. F. and **Dalton, M. J.** (1979), The potential impact of gasoline futures on 1979 vacation travel strategies, *J. Travel Research*, **18**(1), 3–7.

Wolfe, R. I. (1951), Summer cottagers in Ontario, *Economic Geography*, **27**(1), 10–32.

Wolfe, R. I. (1966), *Parameters of Recreational Travel in Ontario*, Downsview, Ontario.

Wolfe, R. I. (1970), Discussion of vacation homes, environmental preferences and spatial behaviour, *J. Leisure Research*, **2**(1), 85–7.

Wolman Associates (1978), *Yukon Tourism Development Strategy*, Department of Tourism and

Information, Yukon.

Woodside, A. G. and **Etzel, M. J.** (1980), Impact of physical and mental handicaps on vacation travel behaviour, *Journal of Travel Research*, **18**(3), 9–11.

WTO (1978), *Methodological supplement to World Tourism Statistics*, World Tourism Organisation, Madrid.

WTO (1981), *Technical handbook on the collection and presentation of domestic and international tourism statistics*, WTO, Madrid.

WTO (1983a), *Prospects for Restructuring Tourist Flows, Destinations and Markets*, WTO, Madrid.

WTO (1983b), *Domestic Tourism Statistics 1981–82*, WTO, Madrid.

Yamamura, J. (1982), The course of development of tourism and recreation in Japan, *Frankfurter Wirtschafts – und Sozialgeographische Schriften*, **41**, 175–85.

Yokeno, N. (1968), La localisation de l'industrie touristique: application de l'analyse de Thunen-Weber, *Cahiers du Tourisme*, C–9, C.H.E.T., Aix-en-Provence.

Yokeno, N. (1974), The general equilibrium system of 'space-economics' for tourism, *Reports for the Japan Academic Society of Tourism*, **8**, 38–44.

Young, B. (1983), Touristization of traditional Maltese fishing-farming villages: a general model, *Tourism Management*, **4**(1), 35–41.

Young, G. (1973), *Tourism: blessing or blight?*, Penguin, Harmondsworth.

Zipf, G. K. (1946), The P_1P_2/D hypothesis: on inter-city movement of persons, *American Sociological Review*, **11**, 677–86.

Author index

Subject index

Place index